The Future of Revolutions

Rethinking Radical Change in the Age of Globalization

Edited by John Foran

ZED BOOKS

The Future of Revolutions was first published in 2003 by
Zed Books Ltd, 7 Cynthia Street, London N1 9JF, UK,
and Room 400, 175 Fifth Avenue, New York, NY 10010, USA

www.zedbooks.demon.co.uk

Designed and typeset in Monotype Bembo by Illuminati, Grosmont
Cover designed by Lee Robinson/Ad Lib Designs
Printed and bound in Malaysia

Distributed in the USA exclusively by Palgrave, a division of
St Martin's Press, LLC, 175 Fifth Avenue, New York, NY 10010

A catalogue record for this book is available from the British Library
Library of Congress Cataloging-in-Publication Data available

ISBN 1 84277 032 2 (Hb)
ISBN 1 84277 033 0 (Pb)

Contents

Acknowledgements

My first thanks go to Jeff Goodwin for originally encouraging me to work on this project, and for suggesting that I approach the American Sociological Association for a Fund for the Advancement of the Discipline grant, which we received. This opened the door to other generous funders, most notably the Wenner–Gren Foundation for Anthropological Research and the Institute on Global Conflict and Cooperation of the University of California. Their support made possible the convening of the group for three days in late January 2001, which has made this a unique and rich collective work. In addition, my home institution, the University of California at Santa Barbara (UCSB), was characteristically generous, and I wish to thank the departments and programs of sociology, Latin American and Iberian studies, anthropology and political science, and the division of the social sciences for financial support. People at two other units at UCSB provided enormous logistical support: Tim Schmidt and Nicole Du Bois, and all the staff of the Institute for Social, Behavioral Economic Research (ISBER) did the hard work of organizing the workshop, and the Interdisciplinary Humanities Center (IHC) provided the room and other facilities for our meeting. Linda Klouzal and Dave Fearon taped the proceedings flawlessly; Mary Jo Poole transcribed our conversations; Lucero Quiroga and J.-P. Reed provided translations of texts – I am grateful to you all.

Robert Molteno and Zed Books have been a pleasure to work with and I am delighted that this book appears with Zed, a press whose readership is the intended one for its ideas.

My greatest thanks are reserved for all the contributors, who bore with my length constraints, pushing them to write less social scientifically, and with endless editorial comments and requests. Noel Parker, who couldn't attend the workshop, helped me get the book's subtitle right. Huge thank-yous to the UCSB faculty and graduate student discussants – Rich Appelbaum, Ralph Armbruster-Sandoval, Kate Bruhn, Douglas Carranza, Light Carruyo, Dick Flacks, Tim Harding, Mark Juergensmeyer, Linda Klouzal, Becky Overmyer-Velazquez, Tony Samara, Darcie Vandegrift, Tiffany Willoughby-Herrard, Vanessa Ziegler and Kara Zugman – who improved the individual chapters by their commentaries and created a lovely and lively workshop atmosphere when we all got together. Working so closely with this group was a pleasure as well as a privilege, and never a chore.

This book is dedicated with love and affection to Kum-Kum, constant revolutionary, and to the next generation, already practicing their revolutions on both of us – Cerina and Amal.

I

Introduction to the
Future of Revolutions

John Foran

The twentieth century we depart appears in many ways the classic age of revolutions, in Theda Skocpol's sense of 'rapid, basic transformations of a society's state and class structures ... accompanied and in part carried through by class-based revolts from below' (1979: 4). As we now enter headlong the era of globalization, the future of revolutions is beginning to receive sustained scholarly attention. This is, to be sure, an intrinsically creative and speculative sort of work, attempting to answer such questions as: Is the age of revolutions over? If so, why? If not, what might the revolutions of the future look like? This book, based on a very active collaboration among a group of scholars of revolution, attempts to debate and explore these and other crucial questions about the future of revolutions under conditions of globalization.

The conservative position is that the age of revolutions is – of course – over (Nodia 2000: 167–71; see also Snyder 1999). And even as they refused to accept the celebratory end-of-history thesis, by the mid-1990s many activists and citizens in both First and Third Worlds implicitly seemed resigned to the view summed up by the dispirited acronym TINA – 'There is no alternative' – originally uttered by a jubilant Margaret Thatcher.[1] In a vein more sympathetic to those who would still like to transform the world, Jeff Goodwin and Eric Selbin have debated these propositions, with somewhat different (though not diametrically opposite) conclusions. Focusing on the type of state that has been historically vulnerable to revolution, Jeff Goodwin sees a diminished stage in the future for sharp revolutionary conflict – though not other progressive social movements – with the passing of colonialism and indiscriminately repressive dictatorships: 'The ballot box is the coffin of revolutionaries' (Goodwin 1998: 8). Eric Selbin, well known for his advocacy of agency-centered explanations of revolutions, has countered, a bit surprisingly, with an economic argument: 'as global gaps between the haves and have-nots increase and neoliberalism fails to deliver on its promise, revolution will be more likely' (1998: 2). To this he has added his characteristic emphasis on cultures of resistance, noting that revolutions have always promised new beginnings, tapped into timeless myths and inspired magical possibilities; thus he wagers confidently that people will continue to articulate compelling stories about change to enable them.

My own views (Foran 1997) coincide with Selbin in this far from settled debate, feeling as I do that North–South inequality will only continue to deepen on many levels with the 'triumph' of neoliberalism, and that the Third World left has not suffered a fatal or permanent blow in its political creativity with the collapse of what has till now passed for socialism. Moreover, both Goodwin (Goodwin 1997: 18, though see his 2001a discussion of Eastern Europe) and Selbin, as well as Mark Katz (1999: ch. 5), who has commented on this discussion, have not taken seriously enough the possibility that revolutionaries may take non-violent and/or democratic routes to power, and in fact have done so, in Guatemala in the 1950s, May 1968 in France, Allende's Chile, Jamaica under Michael Manley, Iran (both in the Mussadeq era and in 1978), Eastern Europe and China in 1989, and Chiapas, to name the most notable cases (it is of course true that none of these found lasting success, with the ironic exception of the restoration of capitalism in the socialist bloc).

I will elaborate throughout this introduction on the reasons I think revolutions will continue to be with us, just as the contributors to this volume will debate this open-ended question throughout its pages. The issues addressed by us here will include: What is the impact of globalization, for ill or good, on the prospects of revolution? Should we reconsider the forms revolutions may take in changing circumstances? How are political cultures – especially notions about radically democratic revolutions – evolving, and what role will the new technologies, particularly those associated with cyberculture, play in them? What relationship – if any – exists or might come to exist between the emergent global justice movement[2] and national revolutionary actors? Finally, what is the import of the world-shattering events of 11 September 2001? Addressing these matters necessarily raises the question of how we might think about and analyze the future, to which I will first turn.

How to Study the Future

It is of course true that we cannot know the future. Social scientists have nevertheless spent much time and effort making predictions of all kinds (see Hechter et al. 1995 for a sample of views). As Carlos Vilas puts it in his essay, it is risky to assess the probability of a revolution in any given situation, and the question can only be settled when and if the anticipated revolution occurs (see also Irish-Bramble 2000; and the essays by Nikki Keddie, Timur Kuran and Jack Goldstone in Keddie 1995 on this question). Vilas quotes Eric Hobsbawm to the effect that revolutionary situations are 'about possibilities, and their analysis is not predictive' (Hobsbawm 1986: 19). *Thinking about* the future, I submit, is different from predicting it, and seems both less presumptuous and potentially more liberating in freeing the thinker from the problems of prediction and in opening up insights that might provide clues as to how to achieve a better future. It was in this spirit that I convened this project.

It was therefore surprising to see how resistant the group initially was to speculating boldly beyond the present. To encourage this, I offered three ideas about the methods that might be useful in doing so. One is to base one's analysis on the past, as a number of us do in the chapters that follow. This means talking about past revolutions and trying to 'filter' them through what might be different about the present in order to make some conjectures about what the future might look like. This seems a well-grounded, clearly social scientific, way to proceed. A second, not unrelated approach, is to look at the future in terms of theories. We hold among us a variety of theories about revolutions — their causes, processes and outcomes. These are of course generated mainly through comparison of past cases. Here, one takes the elements of those theories and again filters what we take to be the characteristics of how the present may be changing, measuring these against the factors identified by our theories and projecting them into the future (I do this in Foran 1997). A third, rather wide open angle is achieved by simply applying our imaginations, sociological and otherwise, to the future and speculating with playful seriousness about what might come. Each will do this with different measures of theory, casework and imagination, into which, as Carlos Vilas notes, enter also our personal ideological biases, hunches, fears or wishes. It was my brief to the group to push beyond any reluctance they felt about engaging in this kind of thinking, because this is what is specifically different about this project. And I purposely made the length of the chapters shorter rather than longer so we could have many voices, more than one often finds in an edited volume, to get more perspectives about this.

Globalization: The Highest Stage of Capitalism?

In his classic 1916 account of imperialism, Lenin conceived it as the highest stage of capitalism, and dated its rise in words that echo eerily a century later: 'the beginning of the twentieth century marks the turning point from the old capitalism to the new, from the domination of capital in general to the domination of finance capital' (Lenin 1997: 46; Eric Selbin notes this echo in his essay too). Just as the years around 1800 gave us the dawn of industrial capitalism, and those around 1900 the dawn of imperialism (and eventually neo-colonialism), in the early years of the new millennium the dawn of globalization seems to be breaking. As imperialism represented for Lenin a special stage in capitalism (1997: 90), globalization may well represent a special stage in imperialism and neo-colonialism. It is, less controversially perhaps, the latest stage in the development of capitalism.

But what *is* globalization? There is no space here to enter into a long discussion of the vast and growing literature on this multi-sided phenomenon. It would be hard to do better than the list of features identified by David Harvey in *Spaces of Hope* (here paraphrased by myself):

1. Financial deregulation and the breakdown of the Bretton Woods trade system, begun by the US in the early 1970s as a response to stagflation and then generalized elsewhere from 1979 to 1985. Bretton Woods was a hierarchical global system largely controlled by the US; today's system is more decentralized (with other poles in Japan and Europe), coordinated through a market, and with a volatile financial sector.
2. A 'galloping' wave of technological innovation, akin to past advances but accelerated by the arms trade and international science. Many popular analyses see this as driving or constituting globalization.
3. The 'information revolution' is similarly viewed by many as *the* essence of globalization: new forms of media and communication are changing workplaces and allowing financial transactions to take place instantaneously, as well as generating entirely new needs and wants.

Other features include: (4) reduced costs of moving commodities and people; (5) the development of transnational corporate export processing zones (EPZs), new forms of flexible production and elaborate global commodity chains; (6) a constantly growing wage labor force, more exploited, diverse and divided than in the past; (7) migrations that have changed the face of the working class; (8) hyper-urbanization; (9) the loss by many states over control of fiscal policy to IMF structural adjustment programs (SAPs); (10) the rise of global ecological issues and problems; and (11) culture coming to the forefront in unpredictable ways as processes of both homogenization and resistance speed up (Harvey 2000: 61–7).

To this admirable working list must be added an equally momentous political development: the collapse of socialism in the USSR, Eastern Europe and elsewhere in the 1990s, bringing with it the end of the bipolar antagonisms of the cold war and the opening of a new period of US military and (would-be) geopolitical hegemony. Several of the essays in this collection, including those of Doug Kellner, Noel Parker and John Walton, address various dimensions of this process directly, and all use it as the backdrop for their reflections on the future.

Moreover, in the first of three thematic conversations included in this book, the group debates the validity of Perry Anderson's characterization of the present state of the world economy, based on the propositions that (1) America leads the world's economy and that it dictates the terms for the rest; (2) European social democracy in power has paradoxically de-regulated and privatized in ways that conservative governments had feared to do; (3) Japanese capitalism has fallen into a deep slump and along with South Korea is being gradually pressured to submit to deregulatory stand-ards with increasing unemployment; (4) China is eager to enter the World Trade Organization (WTO) at virtually any price (accomplished in November 2001) and is itself, of course, inviting in foreign capital and weeding out state industry; (5) India is for the first time now willingly dependent on the IMF; and (6) the new Russian economy is the weakest link in the global market system but, in spite of catastrophic regression in production and life expectancy, there has been no popular backlash (Anderson 2000).

Two themes in the globalization literature deserve special mention in this introduction since they bear on the future of revolutions quite di-rectly: the debate on the extent of world poverty, and the thesis on the declining significance of the nation-state. The first hinges on the degree to which globalization has reduced or exacerbated inequality and poverty worldwide in the last decade or so. It seems clear enough that North–South relations remain highly hierarchical and unequal, and several of the essays in this volume defend this proposition directly. Misagh Parsa, for example, claims that economic disparities are on the rise virtually every-where in the world, noting that the assets of the three richest people in the world in 1998 exceeded the combined GNP of the twenty-five least developed countries, with a population of over 500 million; while the assets of the 200 richest people in the world in the same year exceeded the combined income of 41 percent of the world's people (data based on UNDP 1999: 38; see also Hawken 2000: 15; Singer 1999: 153; Galeano

1998: 28).[3] Valentine Moghadam also draws on the UNDP's *Human Development Report* to document increasing inequality, globally and within societies. World Bank studies suggest, at least by one estimate, that '*world income inequality in the 1980s and early 1990s grew much more rapidly than domestic income inequality in the U.S. and the U.K. ... global inequality has grown [in the past twenty years] as much as it did in the 200 years [previous]*' (Murphy 2001: 350, his emphasis, citing Milanovic 1999). Inequality has grown both within and between nations, in North and South, as 'The gap in per capita income between the industrial and developing worlds tripled from 1960 to 1993' (S. Anderson et al. 2000: 53, citing UNDP 1996: 2; on inequality in the US and elsewhere in the First World, see Hahnel 1999: 8–9). And poverty has grown in absolute as well as relative terms: 200 million more people entered absolute poverty between 1995 and 1999 (Brecher et al. 1999). As Robin Hahnel puts it:

> As best as I can tell, for every NIC (Newly Industrializing Country) there were 10 FEBs (countries Falling Ever-more Behind) during the neoliberal 'boom'. And for every wealthy beneficiary of rising stock process, rising profit shares, and rising high-end salaries, there were 10 victims of declining real wages, decreased job security, and lost benefits. The recent experiment in deregulation and globalization was indeed both 'the best of times and the worst of times'. But unfortunately it was the best of times for only a few, and the worst of times for most. At least that is what had been happening *before* the bubble burst in July 1997. (1999: 12, emphasis in the original)

Contributor Noel Parker makes an important connnection between the trend and its mediation by new technologies: 'there is plenty of evidence that inequalities of wealth and of power become both more marked and, through the effects of global communication, more *visible* under conditions of globalization.' While there remain important questions about the degree to which processes of globalization are the key causes, the general trend seems established: Chossudovsky (1998) and Murphy (2001) discuss the complexity of the data and confirm my conclusion here, with the former opening his survey thus: 'The late 20th century will go down in world history as a period of global impoverishment' (Chossudovsky 1998: 293). It is true that the link between poverty and inequality and globalization is complex and indeed disputed (compare Hahnel 1999: 111–5 with Ghose 2000), but if we consider the devastating consequences of Third World debt and structural adjustment for development, as John Walton does in this volume, the impact of globalization seems clear enough and should be borne in mind in the discussions that follow.

There is also a widespread assumption in the literature that globalization has weakened the power of nation-states. Though this is a complex issue as well and even further from being settled, here I am more skeptical, and for reasons that bear on the future of revolutions. The world economy is changing, to be sure, as transnational companies develop ever greater capacities to escape the regulation of states, control the distribution of profits along commodity chains, and depress the wages of workers. This line of reasoning is then sometimes extended by scholars of revolution to the corollary that state power is no longer a worthwhile goal, undermining the logic and viability of revolutionary activity. This debate can be addressed on several levels, of which at least two are salient in these pages: whether state power is in fact waning irreversibly, and whether revolutionaries have shifted or therefore should shift the focus of their struggles.

The declining significance of the state is most often attributed to the loss by Third World states of control over fiscal policy to IMF structural adjustment programs, and the vulnerability of all states to the volatility of huge unregulated financial markets and the passing of sovereignty in trade matters to transnational bodies like the WTO that favor multinational corporations in economic disputes with nation-states. These new facts are indisputable, but some see in this situation of crisis a *renewed* role for states to play in trying to buffer their citizens against such forces, making the state a key potential locus of resistance to globalization – defending jobs, ethnic and cultural identities, the environment, welfare benefits and much more (Harvey 2000: 65; Evans 1995). As Farideh Farhi puts it in her essay:

> The state may no longer be perceived as the body to be 'taken over' and turned into an instrument of drastic social change. But the way it inserts itself into social, economic and cultural life and the way its institutional arrangements inhibit 'meaningful' as opposed to superficial or procedural democratic participation have become more and more crystallized as the focal point of political struggle in countries as varied as Iran, Indonesia, Peru, Mexico and so on.

Another approach is that of George and Jane Collier in this volume, who present the interesting thesis that there has been a shift from economic weakening of states through SAPs and trade agreements to strengthening a formally democratic law-and-order state with military and legal guarantees for foreign investors. This shift – or, perhaps better put, the addition of a second emphasis – in globalization strategies appears to be a response to the unrest unleashed by SAPs.

We should perhaps therefore not rush too quickly to conclude that the classic revolutionary goal of seizing state power is no longer relevant or viable. For Jeff Goodwin,

Rather than uniformly diminishing states, in fact, globalization has been just as likely to spur attempts to employ and, if necessary, expand state power for the purposes of enhancing global competitiveness.... There is no reason to believe, in any event, that in the future people will accept the depredations of authoritarian states and shun revolutionaries on the grounds that state power 'ain't what it used to be'.

At the same time, new revolutionary movements like the Zapatistas *have* questioned this goal, reflecting their subtle understandings of the workings of political power in conditions of globalization: that creating democratic spaces for the free discussion of political, economic and cultural alternatives to globalization is a more suitable goal for revolutionaries than direct seizure of state power, and that linking the national liberation struggle to both local needs and global concerns might be the most effective – if even more daunting – coalition-building project for deep social transformation. I will say more about the Zapatistas below.

The Revolutions of the Future

Hopefully, these brief remarks suffice to indicate the timeliness of a call for reflecting on the future of revolutions in the era of globalization. It is time now to highlight some of the themes that this book addresses more specifically about how revolution may be changing in these emerging new circumstances.

Redefinitions

Jeff Goodwin rightly notes that the answer to the question of whether there will be more revolutions in the future depends on how we define the term. He sees in the future fewer 'movements seeking to radically recast national societies by seizing state power through extraparliamentary, though not necessarily violent, means' but more 'mass movements for social justice'. Jeffery Paige, after an extensive survey of definitions of revolutions, proposes a new one:

> A revolution is a rapid and fundamental transformation in the categories of social life and consciousness, the metaphysical assumptions on which these categories are based, and the power relations in which they are expressed as a result of widespread popular acceptance of a utopian alternative to the current social order.

He goes on:

Does revolution have a future? The answer to this question depends on the definition chosen. If revolution means the violent seizure of state power though class-based revolts from below the answer is almost certainly no.... Prospects look very different, however, from the perspective of an alternative definition stressing changes in social categories and metaphysical assumptions.

He concludes:

The line of argument presented here does not suggest that such a revolutionary transformation need necessarily be violent, based on worldwide class struggle, or involve seizures of sovereign power at the national or international level, although any or all of these things could occur. It could well be, on the other hand, that a deepening of the currents of human rights, the increasing assertiveness of the formally suppressed gender, ethnic, age and class groups and the rise of the global South may bring the world to a kind of revolutionary transformation in consciousness, lived social experience and power relations seen previously only in particular national societies.

Democracy and revolution

Redefining revolutions in this way opens up interesting debates about the relationship of democracy to radical social transformation. Jeff Goodwin and Misagh Parsa see formal democratization as decreasing the chances for revolutions by channeling discontent into legal arenas. In addition, both Farideh Farhi and Abdollah Dashti note the embrace of 'democracy' by the forces of globalization from above, and the rhetorical limits and demobilizing effects of this, the practical devaluation and diminishing of its liberatory content. But Farhi, Dashti and I engage in a common search for the democratic, non-violent roots of past and future revolutions, and Goodwin himself and Jeffery Paige are also interested in this for the future. There are differences: Farhi is focused on mass civil disobedience (Iran 1979; Eastern Europe 1989; Indonesia, Serbia and South Africa in the 1990s); Dashti on post-revolutionary participatory democracy; and I on electoral paths, among others, as in Chile under Allende, Guatemala in the Arbenz/Arévalo era, post-1994 Chiapas, El Salvador since the 1992 peace accords, Uruguay and Iran at present. Christopher McAuley, following Samir Amin and like Dashti, points hopefully to the prospects for a participatory democracy with special emphasis on protecting and extending the political participation and social well-being of rural populations; he sees the original Zapatismo of the first Mexican revolution as the best historical model of this practice, and parts of Asia and Africa as the most likely future sites for such revolutions. For him, autocentric development requires autonomous communities directly engaged in setting their own agendas. The contributors to this volume express a common interest in the education of civil society through a Gramscian war of position. All of us are pushing away from the violent models of the past, even as some – most compellingly Adolfo Gilly – see violence as endemic to conflict in today's world.

New cultures, new technologies

These debates open onto the broader issues of culture and technologies in the revolutions of the future. As in other matters, Jeff Goodwin advances a healthy skepticism: 'mass support for revolution typically derives less from attractive visions of the future – although such visions have been important for intellectuals – than from a widely shared conviction that the status quo is simply unendurable.' In this he follows Jorge Castañeda:

> The most powerful argument in the hands of the left in Latin America – or anywhere else – has never been, and in all likelihood will never be, exclusively the intrinsic merit or viability of the alternative it proposes. Its strong suit is the morally unacceptable character of life as the overwhelming majority of the region's inhabitants live it. (1993: 254)

Adolfo Gilly's reading of the subaltern studies approach at first appears to confirm this view of the motivating imagery of resistance as backward looking, but ultimately concludes 'Such is the way an original discourse is forged in every revolution or rebellious movement, at once old and new and shared by all: not the preservation of the past, but the redemption of its hopes in the novelty, discourse and actions of the revolution.' The apparent contradiction is perhaps resolved by noting Gilly's emphasis on everyday life and experience, at once the stuff of a moral defense of past rights encroached upon and future-oriented imaginaries. Gilly reminds us of Walter Benjamin's rereading: 'For Marx, revolutions are the locomotive of world history. But perhaps things are different. Perhaps revolutions are the way that humanity, riding on this train, reaches for the emergency brake' (1990: 1232). Jeff Goodwin also invokes Marx to counterpose future and past practices in respect of culture: 'To paraphrase Marx, the socialist movements of the twenty-first century cannot draw their poetry from the past, but only from the future.' Farideh Farhi, Jeffery Paige, Abdollah Dashti and Christopher McAuley have all advanced visions of a more participatory culture based on their readings of the past. For Valentine Moghadam, this culture is becoming more feminist in the current conjuncture. In my own view, the most revolutionary cultures of the future will repose on a magical mixture of realism and utopianism, guaranteed by radically democratic forms of decision-making. John Walton puts it thus: 'The broader lesson is the emergence of a new global political consciousness ... which attempts to define a coherent code of global justice embracing indigenous people, peasants, the urban poor, labor, democrats and dolphins.'

Eric Selbin is perhaps the most focused contributor to this debate:

> There is a global or transnational role played by the ideas, myths and conceptions which people share with one another.... Thus memories of oppression, sagas of occupation and struggle, tales of opposition, myths of once and future glory, words of mystery and symbolism are appropriated from the pantheon of history of resistance and rebellion common to almost every culture and borrowed from others and fashioned into some sort of usable past which confronts the present and reaches out to the future.

Among these symbols are to be found Zapata's white horse, Che's beret, Sandino's hat, Ho's pith helmet, bamboo walking stick and wispy beard, Cabral's knit cap. Selbin asks of the future: 'Will they wear Che T-shirts in Algiers as they did in Tehran in 1979? "See" Zapata's horse in Havana as some did in Nicaragua? Sing the "Internationale" or perhaps even air the "Marseillaise" in Jakarta?' The answers to such questions will suggest the ways in which the old and new might jointly make the revolutionary cultures of the future.

Noting that the new technologies of web and e-mail are a contested terrain, Douglas Kellner urges that

> Radical democratic activists should look to its possibilities for resistance and the advancement of political education, action and organization, while engaging in struggles over the digital divide.... If forces struggling for democratization and social justice want to become players in the cultural and political battles of the future, they must devise ways to use new technologies to advance a radical democratic and ecological agenda and the interests of the oppressed.

Cyberculture, then, also presents itself as one of the tools of the revolutionary political cultures of the future, at once a form of organization and a venue for exercising agency and subjectivity.

The (declining?) significance of the Zapatistas

One key marker of many of the issues raised so far is the Zapatista rebellion in Chiapas, the focus of an enormous amount of writing and central to the essays here of Jane and George Collier, Karen Kampwirth and myself. Several of those who have done extensive ethnographic work in Chiapas – the Colliers, plus Jan Rus – are generally cautious about elevating the lessons of the rebellion into principles for future revolutions, but others, such as Kampwirth and I, find in this a legitimate project. Certainly many First (and Third) World academics romanticize this case, but the richness of Zapatista discourse, the élan of their projects and actions on the Mexican political scene, their direct and indirect impact on the emerging global justice movement, and the gender and ethnic composition of their ranks suggest the significance of this experiment for future attempts at change. The essays and conversations in this volume draw out many of the implications of these several positions.

From anti-globalization movements to a global revolution

The dimensions of the anti-globalization/global justice movement, visible since the historic shutdown of the WTO in Seattle, November–December 1999, also deserve careful consideration. Jeff Goodwin is perceptive on the movement's tasks; Valentine Moghadam assesses the networks it has so far spun, Douglas Kellner its use of cyber-tactics. John Walton's essay addresses the matter centrally: 'Something new is afoot in the globalizing world and in the notions people have of the situation they are in…. It is, in brief, an era of neoliberal policies and global counter-movements.' Arguably, the 'anti-globalization' movement may also herald a new kind of revolution – a global revolution. This term is found in Kevin Danaher and Roger Burbach, who write in terms consonant with much of our own analysis:

> If we look closely we can see the pieces of the first global revolution being put together. Every revolution up until now has been a national revolution, aimed at seizing control of a national government. But the blatant corporate bias of global rule-making institutions such as the IMF, World Bank and WTO have forced the grassroots democracy movement to start planning a global revolution. It is a revolution in values as well as institutions. It seeks to replace the money values of the current system with the life values of a truly democratic system. (2000: 9)

The new conditions of globalization call forth new versions of the broad alliances that have made revolutions in the past, a matter whose tasks and problems are taken up in my concluding essay, and which underlies much of what is said in the final thematic conversation.

11 September: The Crisis Everyone/No One Was Waiting For…[4]

We live in a new era, now doubly marked by the processes of globalization and the events of 11 September 2001. As Jeff Goodwin puts it presciently in the third thematic discussion, 'There is always the possibility, indeed the likelihood, of contingent, unpredictable, unforeseen events that will completely alter our sense of what's going to happen next and what possibilities there are.' Or, as Eduardo Galeano asked, *in 1998*:

> In mid-1998, the White House put another villain up on the global marquee. He uses the stage name Osama bin Laden; he's an Islamic fundamentalist, sports a beard, wears a turban, and caresses the rifle in his lap. Will this new star's career take off? Will he be a box-office hit? Will he manage to undermine the foundations of Western civilization or will he only play a supporting role? In horror movies, you never know. (1998: 121)

The essays in this volume were all virtually completed by the summer of 2001 and the conversations herein took place in January 2001, but some of us − Karen Kampwirth in her essay and Valentine Moghadam in the second thematic conversation − were already debating whether the Taliban are to be considered a revolutionary movement. Kampwirth's location of the Taliban in the context of the cold war is aptly juxtaposed with their fall as a consequence of global geopolitics. Others, such as Eric Selbin and Farideh Farhi, foreshadow the heavy use of the American 'fist' as a ready counter-blow to threats to the global order, and Adolfo Gilly concludes his essay with a strong emphasis on 'the violence of capitalist modernity', setting in motion a certain dialectic:

> New relations among domination, resistance and violence are being forged within globalization. If this is the case, globalization brings with it the seed of new wars and revolutions in which violence, as ultimate reason, will redefine these relations. Any other assumption, given the current state of human affairs, lies within the realm of utter fantasy.

Noel Parker takes up 11 September directly in his conclusion: as perceptions grow of the US as 'the universal, intrusive state across the seas ... revolutionary opposition to the latest version of modernization can define itself in resistance to, or as attacks upon the US state or upon US society.' This is true in Parker's sense of a 'revolutionary narrative' available to many forces; some among us, Valentine Moghadam in the lead,[5] deny *any* revolutionary credentials to al-Qaeda or the Taliban. But the logic of the argument suggests that globalization will face threats from other quarters, in addition to revolutionary ones.

The eleventh of September was therefore *not* the crisis that democratic revolutionaries wanted; it was more the confrontation that their rivals (al-Qaeda and Osama bin Laden) and adversaries (the US) were seeking. As Mary Ann Tétreault suggested, a full eight months before the events of September:

I think we should be getting ready because I do think there will be a crisis.... Maybe we'll be lucky and we won't have a world war. Maybe we'll just have a phenomenal environmental catastrophe which at least won't polarize us in the same way and won't affect things in quite the same way although it would have a similar capacity to kill. I think we need to be prepared to move in the case of a crisis, to make it work for us, and anticipate that crisis, as ugly as any kind of crisis is to think about, by planning ahead.

The repercussions of the US war on the Taliban throughout the Middle East and Central Asia *are* consequential for both the conservative regimes of these regions and their rivals. Thus Karen Kampwirth's question of whether future revolutionaries will dance like Zapatistas or march like the Taliban assumes heightened significance, as do the questions of whether US foreign policy is forcing more of the latter type of movement upon us, and seeking to use the crisis to curtail the activities of the global justice movement – Susan George warns of the 'faulty but sometimes effective logic' of 'You're antiglobalization, therefore you're anti-American, therefore you're on the side of the terrorists' (2002: 12).

If we cannot know the future, it becomes all the more incumbent to speculate as fully as we can about its possibilities. Roberto Unger notes 'We are torn ... "between dreams that seem unrealizable" (the fantasy worlds given to us by the media) "and prospects that hardly seem to matter" (daily life on the street)' (quoted in Harvey 2000: 258). If we refuse to dream because the odds of waking up to 'reality' are so great, we abdicate any role in shaping the future for the better. As Carlos Vilas puts it, 'Political success, for both insurgencies and governments, is a contingency, and contingency, as Commander Ruiz's *magia*, has to be tirelessly worked out. Then it may, or may not, show up.' Our own answers are found, at least in part, in the final conversation of this volume, addressing the question of how the revolutions of the future might have better outcomes. For, as Eduardo Galeano has concluded, 'If we can't guess what's coming, at least we have the right to imagine the future we want' (1998: 334). Where we are today, and where we may be going, is not the same place. At least, it need not be, and will not be, if enough people refuse to accept it.

Notes

I received valuable feedback on a draft of this essay from Jeff Goodwin and Mary Ann Tétreault, among others.

1. Thatcher is identified as the source of this famous declaration in Harvey (2000: 63). Daniel Singer traces its genealogy further, noting 'Tina is now the

unwritten premise of virtually the whole political debate' (1999: 2). For Perry Anderson, 'the only starting-point for a realistic Left today is a lucid registration of historical defeat' (Anderson 2000: 16). Of course, it was Rosa Luxemburg who noted in *Die Rote Fahne* on 14 January 1919: 'Revolution is the only form of "war" in which ultimate victory can only be prepared by a series of "defeats"' (quoted in Singer 1999: 278).

2. Susan George makes the telling point that the term 'anti-globalization movement' is a negative label applied by the media, whereas 'to its thousands of participants and millions of sympathizers [it is known as] the movement for global justice' (2002: 11). Though the former is not fatally flawed in my view, I am starting to adopt the latter term in my writing.

3. Galeano reports the following from an earlier UNDP report: 'Ten people, the ten richest men on the planet, own wealth equivalent to the value of the total production of fifty countries, and 447 multimillionaires own a greater fortune than the annual income of half of humanity' (UNDP 1997, as quoted by Galeano 1998: 28). By 1999, there were reported to be 475 billionaires in the world (S. Anderson et al. 2000: 53, citing UNDP 1999 and *Forbes*, 5 July 1999).

4. This section has benefited from an e-mail exchange with the contributors. Douglas Kellner offers a very detailed analysis of the domestic consequences of 11 September at www.gseis.ucla.edu/faculty/kellner/kellner.html. The US-based Social Science Research Council has constructed a large archive of valuable analyses at its website: www.ssrc.org.

5. 'It is important to define revolutions as mass-based emancipatory movements that bring about economic, political and cultural development. Such a definition – which situates revolution in the Enlightenment and Marxian traditions – excludes reactionary or terrorist movements. The Taliban are/were not revolutionaries; they were counterrevolutionaries, as were the Mujahidin before them. The revolutionaries were the "communists" of the period 1978–92.... By no means can Osama bin Laden and al-Qaeda be called revolutionaries. Nor can the Khmer Rouge, Sendero Luminoso, UNITA, Renamo, the Lord's Resistance Army, GIA, or any other fascistic or terrorist organization or movement devoid of an emancipatory or egalitarian social and political program': e-mail communication from Valentine Moghadam to the editor, 23 November 2001. Jeff Goodwin replies: 'Do we really want to define away bad revolutionaries, instead of asking how some revolutions have gone horribly bad?': e-mail communication with the editor, 11 December 2001. Thus, the debate continues.

PART I

Defining the Terms of Revolution and Globalization

2

Finding the Revolutionary in the Revolution: Social Science Concepts and the Future of Revolution

Jeffery M. Paige

Redefining Revolution

An increasing body of recent literature (Fukuyama 1992; Goodwin 1998; Goodwin and Green 1999; Snyder 1999; Nodia 2000) has argued that the age of revolution is over or even that the concept of revolution is obsolete. Current concepts of revolution may well be obsolete, but this does not necessarily imply that revolution properly understood has no future. This chapter will argue that the concept of revolution as it is conventionally defined in both the social sciences and revolutionary Marxism-Leninism does not capture the social and cultural transformations that make revolutions revolutionary. Nor does it capture the utopian visions and popular enthusiasms that underlie the mass levies of revolutions and provide much of their transforming power. These definitions actually describe anti-revolutionary or even counterrevolutionary processes and fail to fit many of the classic cases – the French, the American, the Chinese or more recent Third World revolutions. Properly understood, it will be argued here, revolution has a future even if many theoretical definitions of revolution do not.

Virtually all contemporary social science definitions of revolution emphasize a violent transformation of the 'state' and 'class' structure. The following are typical:

- Theda Skocpol: 'rapid, basic transformation of a society's state and class structure, accompanied, and in part carried through by class based revolts from below' (1979: 4).

- Samuel P. Huntington: 'a rapid, fundamental and violent domestic change in the dominant values and myths of a society, in its political institutions, social structure, leadership and government activities and policies' (1968: 264).
- Anthony Giddens: 'the seizure of state power through violent means by the leaders of a mass movement, where that power is subsequently used to initiate major processes of social reform' (1989: 605).
- Charles Tilly: 'A forcible transfer of power over a state in the course of which at least two distinct blocs of contenders make incompatible claims to control the state, and some significant portion of the population subject to the state's jurisdiction acquiesce in the claims of each bloc' (1993: 8).
- The author: 'Any event in which the participants are associated with a revolutionary socialist party and demand either unconstitutional political change, radical transformation of the rural class structure or both.... Usually such demands [are] associated with demands for the violent overthrow of the existing political system' (Paige 1975: 94).

Given that Tilly includes classes as one of his principal 'distinct blocs of contenders', and that classes are the putative mass base of most twentieth-century mass movements, the definitions actually overlap more than might at first appear, although most emphasize political process over class struggle. In this they resemble the Lenin of *What Is To Be Done?* more than the Trotsky of *Results and Prospects* or Marx and Engels in the *Communist Manifesto*. In both social science and orthodox Leninist Marxism, however, political power and the state are the object of revolutionary struggle, organized political violence the means, and state-led social transformation the end. Class-based social groups directed by a self-conscious revolutionary leadership are either the exclusive or a principal actor. Although Skocpol rejects self-conscious revolutionary leadership she makes interstate violence, state breakdowns, state transformations and class-based revolts central to her theory.

If we look at the way in which actual revolutions play themselves out we find striking deviations from the class-based and state-centric model of instrumental political violence so emphasized by theorists of revolution. The following accounts are taken from three of the foremost authorities on the French, American and Cuban revolutions, respectively, and summarize extensive recent scholarship.

French revolution, 1789

The night of August 4th [1789] was the crucial turning point of the revolution.... Thanks to a combination of astute planning on the part of the patriot faction and a wave of magnanimous radicalism that swept over the deputies, the Assembly abolished the entire privileged corporate order. The way in which this happened is significant: privileges were renounced amid joyous weeping by those who had been their beneficiaries, great seigneurial land owners proposed abolition of seigneurial dues, representatives of the clergy offered up their tithes, representatives of the provinces and cities renounced provincial and municipal privileges, and so on. The result was a holocaust of privilege. (Sewell 1985: 69)

American revolution, 1776

In a monarchical world of numerous patron–client relations and multiple degrees of dependency, nothing could be more radical than the attempt to make every man independent. What was an ideal in the English-speaking world now became for Americans an ideological imperative. Suddenly, in the eyes of the revolutionaries, all the fine calibrations of rank and degrees of unfreedom of the traditional monarchical society became absurd and degrading. The Revolution became a full-fledged assault on dependency. (Wood 1993: 179)

Cuban revolution, 1959

The dominant paradigm of 'civilization' was in transition. The power of the revolution was in its capacity to rearrange in usable form the standards by which to measure civilization and in the process summon a vision of an alternative moral order. The proposition of *patria* took on new meaning as an all-inclusive community through which to find a sense of purpose and a source of identity. The notion of *patria*, free and sovereign, was reinvented around instrumental functions in which an egalitarian project served as the necessary condition of civilization. (Peréz 1999: 482)

What is striking about these three attempts to define the heart of the revolutionary process in three paradigmatic revolutions by three of their most distinguished interpreters is that there is no mention of the state, class, class struggle, political violence, seizures of state power, state-directed efforts at reform, mass social movements or any other of the categories which Marxist-Leninist and social scientific definitions of revolution find to be defining characteristics of revolution. Indeed the American revolution is not a revolution at all according to the traditional definitions. There was no class-based revolt from below by peasants or proletarians, no transformation of the 'class structure', no reign of terror, no seizure of state power (only a rejection of foreign control), no state-directed reform project. Yet Gordon S. Wood argues that 'it was as radical and social as any revolution in history' (1993: 5).

The Cuban revolution did not depend on a class-based revolt from below (the April 1958 general strike was a failure) and the military forces arrayed against the Batista regime were laughable (Castro had fewer than 300 men under his command when he began his final offensive). In the end there were no contending social groups, nor did Batista suffer either an internal or external military defeat – the regime dissolved and its army lost the will to fight after losing fewer than 300 killed. There was no seizure of state power by a disciplined political party or mass movement. Fidel Castro's July 26 Movement was a loose coalition of moderate and radical forces – Communist support came only later. Castro marched into Havana to general and universal acclamation propelled by the powerful and widespread vision of *patria* described by Pérez, not by his meager military resources. Only later when Cuba began to embrace the Soviet model did it begin to resemble the categories of traditional revolutionary theorists – a class-based social reform project imposed from above with the aid of a revolutionary Communist Party and centralized state.

Nor does the French revolution correspond to the categories of the theorists. As an increasing body of revisionist historical work has argued, the class categories posited by the Lefebvre/Soboul, Republican/Marxist social interpretation hardly fit the order of aristocratic privilege of pre-revolutionary France. The 'class' differences between the contending factions were not pronounced and the transformation of the 'class' structure much less than had been thought. The revolution was initiated by the calling of the Estates-General, not by a mass party. Feudalism was abolished, the rights of man declared and a new regime established with a relative absence of violence against persons – the violence of the terror occurred only after the 'second revolution' of 1792. There was no seizure of state power since there was no state in the modern sense to seize – indeed the revolution itself was one of the most important forces in the creation of the idea of the modern state distinct from society.

Nor do the processes by which the revolutionary transformations occurred resemble those postulated by conventional theories. For Sewell the night of 4 August was a 'holocaust of privilege', a 'wave of magnanimous radicalism', not a violent seizure of power by a mass party. For Wood the revolution resembled the 'breaking of a dam'; people and their energies were set loose 'in an unprecedented outburst'. What Wood calls the 'most radical and powerful ideological force', the idea of equality, 'tore through American society with awesome power' (1993: 232). For Pérez the revolution was 'spontaneous joy and prolonged jubilation, exuberance and exhilaration'. What he calls the 'metaphysics of *pueblo* [people] and *patria* [Cuban national identity]' assumed 'power and promise' that they had not achieved since the independence struggles in the nineteenth century. The revolution raised these concepts to 'exalted heights', and endowed them with a 'widespread capacity for popular mobilization' (1999: 477).

The awesome power of the revolution, according to Sewell, Wood and Pérez lies in these waves of energy and enthusiasm and the utopian visions that inspired them, not in vanguard parties, guerrilla bands or peasant revolts. In their concepts this revolutionary power tears through the social and conceptual categories of the pre-revolutionary society with remarkable speed and energy. Sewell's 'holocaust of privilege' eliminated the ideology of the corporate, monarchical and aristocratic order of the *ancien régime* along with its institutional and legal arrangements and, equally important, destroyed the 'metaphysical assumptions' on which this order was based. In their place the Declaration of the Rights of Man and of the Citizen set forth the metaphysical basis for the new order – the inalienable rights of man. The rights of man had a similar effect in the American revolution. Sewell's 'holocaust of privilege' finds its parallel in Wood's 'full scale assault on dependency'. The world of monarchy and aristocratic privilege, paternal dependency and deference was swept away just as it was in France. Indeed Wood argues that the revolutionary transformation might have been more profound in America.

The same is true in Pérez's account of Cuba where, he asserts, the dominant paradigm of 'civilization itself' was in transition (1999: 482). The pre-revolutionary paradigm was shaped by American models and influenced by the presence of America in Cuba and the presence of Cubans in America. It emphasized the politically independent and sovereign people of the American revolution and the material abundance of American commercial life. 'People', 'sovereignty' and 'abundance' were all redefined in the inclusive notion of *patria* (literally, fatherland) – Cuban national identity was now to be based on an egalitarian vision of abundance shared by all Cubans. The terms of 'civilization' were reversed, with the Cadillac becoming a perverse symbol of the barbarism of elite consumption and the material welfare of the Cuban people becoming the new standard. One metaphysical order (that born in the American revolt against the metaphysics of monarchy) was swept away, just as in France and America, and a new order based on Cuban nationality was created.

These fundamental transformations in metaphysics, ideology and deference swept through each society leaving few aspects of social life unchanged. Sewell, Wood and Pérez describe the process in strikingly similar ways. The French revolution invented new terms of address (citizen), renamed the months of the year, restructured the calendar, rationally recalibrated weights and measures, redefined marriage as a civil contract, made birth and death civic rather than religious events, made decapitation the universal form of capital punishment rather than the privilege of the nobility, reorganized provincial administration along 'natural' lines, attempted to reform the selection of priests; as Sewell (1985: 79) says, 'The list goes on and on.' The American revolution, according to Wood, did not simply eliminate monarchy and establish republican government; it made over 'art, architecture and iconography', and 'even altered their understanding of history, knowledge and truth'. As in France forms of address changed to reflect the new reality with the aristocratic Esquire disappearing to be replaced with the democratic Mr (1993: 8).

Similarly in Cuba. A passion for Cuban products swept the island. Cuban fashion replaced American, cotton replaced dacron, architects called for a national building style, national film, ballet and record companies were established, private schools were abolished (Pérez 1999: 483), American suits and ties were replaced with the *guayabera*, Spanish words were invented to replace Americanisms (*jardinero* for *jonron* – home run). Holidays were transformed – Santa Claus and the Christmas tree were eliminated, to be replaced with the suitably Cuban Don Feliciano – and anti-Americanism replaced Americanism as the accepted discourse of the political class (Pérez 1999: 485). The reforms in culture and social life accompanied and reinforced the profound material and institutional changes of the revolution (more than 1,500 laws were enacted in 1959 alone) organized around the idea of *patria* as a shared material and cultural community defined now in opposition to the United States.

These transformations are at the heart of the idea of revolution itself – indeed this is why we call the French, American and Cuban revolutions, revolutions, but they are largely ignored in traditional definitions of revolution. What is needed is a new definition that captures what these three revolutions (and others) have in common and puts the revolution back in revolutionary theory. Jack Goldstone's most recent definition – 'an effort to transform political institutions and the justifications for authority in society, accompanied by formal or informal mass mobilization and non-institutional actions that undermine existing authorities' (2001: 142) – shifts the focus away from instrumental violence and class-based seizures of state power. Its focus on politics, however, leaves out the profound cultural and metaphysical changes and utopian visions described by Sewell, Wood and Pérez. As an alternative definition I propose the following:

> A revolution is a rapid and fundamental transformation in the categories of social life and consciousness, the metaphysical assumptions on which these categories are based, and the power relations in which they are expressed as a result of widespread popular acceptance of a utopian alternative to the current social order.

This definition is not simply cultural or ideological. Rapid and fundamental transformations in religion or ideology can occur without necessarily altering the lived experience of social life or the distribution of power; in such cases revolutions are not said to have occurred. Similarly revolution can occur without violence, class conflict, seizures of state power or other of the traditional elements of revolution (as in the American, and possibly Cuban, cases), although given the profound transformation in power relations implied by the definition, violence and conflict are not surprising. These aspects of the traditional view of revolution are not, however, definitive and at least in theory revolutions could proceed without them if the transformations in basic categories were widespread enough and opposition sufficiently weak or acquiescent. Finally, and importantly, violent seizures of power through class-based revolts from below and transformations in the class structure could occur *in the absence of revolution*. This last observation requires more consideration.

Counterrevolution as Revolution: State Socialism from 1921 to 1989

Given the inability of traditional definitions of revolution to describe adequately the summaries of recent scholarship on the French, American and Cuban revolutions by Sewell, Wood and Peréz, it might well be wondered to what phenomenon the traditional definitions actually refer. There is at least one revolution that resembles in some important respects these definitions of revolution – the Bolshevik. The similarity between social science theories and Leninist notions of the seizure of state power and orthodox Marxist conceptions of class conflict has already been noted. The Bolshevik seizure of power in the midst of widespread peasant upheavals and worker revolts in Moscow and St Petersburg fits the definitions perfectly. Power was taken through force and consolidated through an intense terror and a devastating civil war. A radical project of reform was undertaken from above by a massive bureaucratic state created in the revolutionary process itself.

Could the Bolshevik revolution also satisfy the requirements of the alternative definition of revolution presented above and thus be a revolution according to both definitions? Or, in other words, in addition to the class-based revolts and violent seizure of power was there a fundamental transformation in the basic categories of social life and their metaphysical assumptions? Although sociological obituaries of the failed Bolshevik experiment are still being written, a preliminary assessment based on the work of Scott (1998), Kornai (1992), Verdery (1996), Konrad and Szelenyi (1979) and others is that such fundamental transformations did not long survive the consolidation of the state socialist regime. The strongest argument in favor of this position is provided by Scott. He argues that the Bolshevik revolution did not break with the categories of capitalist modernity or even with the categories of the pre-revolutionary imperial order. Instead it reflected an authoritarian ideology he terms 'high modernism', 'a strong, one might even say muscle-bound, version of the self-confidence about scientific and technical progress, the expansion of production ... the mastery of nature (including human nature), and, above all, the rational design of a social order' (1998: 4) of industrial capitalism.

The 'high modernism' of Lenin's *The State and Revolution* enunciates a view of revolution remarkably similar to that of the social scientific theories quoted above. 'The proletariat needs state power, the centralized organization of force, the organization of violence ... for the purposes of guiding the great mass of the population – the peasantry, the petite bourgeoisie, the semi-proletarians – in the work of organizing Socialist economy' (1931: 23). Skocpol and the other social scientific theorists have the Soviet experience right. The building of an authoritarian state was indispensable to Lenin's high modernist project. But this unfortunately has little to do with how revolutions, including the Russian revolution, actually occurred. The Bolsheviks were on the sidelines in February 1917 when the popular revolution began. Their seizure of power represented not only a negation of that revolution but also a discursive reversal of the meaning of revolution itself.

For François Furet (1999: 90) the popular revolution was over by March 1921 with the crushing of the Kronstadt rebellion, the defeat of the workers' opposition and the ban on factions at the Tenth Party Congress. Although Furet ignores the cultural and social ferment of NEP Russia (1921–28), 1921 consolidated the Bolshevik dictatorship and, as Robin Blackburn (1991: 189) argues, set the stage for Stalin's (counter) revolution of 1929–33. Similarly the utopian elements in revolts in favor of national or reformed Communism in Hungary (1956), Czechoslovakia (1968) and Poland (1980) were so thoroughly obliterated by Soviet counterrevolution that the pragmatic 'velvet revolutions' of 1989 lacked the utopian vision that is a defining feature of revolution. The collapse of the Soviet Union itself, as Furet again notes, was not so much a revolution as 'the collapse of a social system', and left behind 'no real parties, no new society, no new economy ... only an atomized and uniform population' (1999: viii). The extinction of utopia could not have been more complete.

Although the Chinese revolution also involved a peasant revolt from below and a violent seizure of state power, the utopian ideology of Maoism clearly differentiates this revolution from the Bolshevik counterrevolution and explains much of the Chinese revolution's mobilizing power both before and after 1949. As Mao himself explained in the foundational text of Maoism, his 1927 *Report on an Investigation of the Peasant Movement in Hunan* (1967: 1–2), in words that closely resemble the images of revolution of Sewell, Wood and Pérez:

> In a very short time, several hundred million peasants in China's central, southern and northern provinces will rise like a fierce wind or tempest, a force so swift and violent that no power however great will be able to suppress it. They will break though all the trammels that bind them and rush forward along the road to liberation.

Mao's observations on revolution also represent a statement of the Maoist faith in the spontaneous voluntarism of the Chinese people to break through the traditional social categories of Confucian deference and the modern hierarchies of office, skill, education, urbanization, science and material wealth to create an egalitarian, disciplined communal society striving collectively for the good of all. Maoism challenged the metaphysical principles and social categories of both the traditional and the liberal capitalist social order and offered a utopian vision of an alternative sufficiently compelling to mobilize both extraordinary political triumphs and catastrophic acts of political and economic folly. Thus the Chinese revolution in the Maoist period was a revolution according to the definition proposed here in a way that the Bolshevik revolution never was. The end of Maoism in China has left a metaphysical and ideological vacuum that threatens the revolutionary credentials and legitimacy of Mao's successors.

The Future of Revolution

Does revolution have a future? The answer to this question depends on the definition chosen. If revolution means the violent seizure of state power though class-based revolts from below the answer is almost certainly no. The Leninist model has been so thoroughly discredited that it is difficult to see how anyone could revive it now or ever. Certainly other variants of authoritarian high modernism may emerge in Russia and elsewhere to attempt to solve the perpetual paradoxes of underdevelopment. But it is unlikely they will have or claim to have the kind of utopian vision that the Soviet-style regimes once relied upon, however falsely, for their legitimacy. The collapse of the Soviet Union also marked the end of Marxist-Leninist revolution as a historical form.

Prospects look very different, however, from the perspective of an alternative definition stressing changes in social categories and metaphysical assumptions. As Arrighi, Hopkins and Wallerstein have argued, the world-wide uprisings of 1968 profoundly challenged the fundamental categories of social life, particularly in the 'hidden abodes of everyday life' (1989: 23). Although 1968 failed politically the ascriptive hierarchies of race, ethnicity, sex, age, physical condition were fundamentally challenged. In this sense the heritage of 1968 endures. Furthermore, relations between 'civilization' and 'barbarism' or, in developmentalist categories, 'developed' and 'underdeveloped' have been similarly deconstructed. The global relations of states and citizens were fundamentally altered by 1968 – everywhere authoritarian governments are on the run in the face of an emerging discourse of 'human rights'. Although Arrighi et al. argued that the antinomy of labor and capital was also under attack, at present it might be more accurate to say that these categories are being fundamentally transformed by corporate globalization.

These transformations in the fundamental categories of social life made possible a transformation in the metaphysical basis of society, toward what William Greider (1997: 469) calls 'global humanism', in which the human subject is no longer conceived as the abstract juridical individual of liberal capitalism but rather as a bundle of human creative potentialities close to Marx's early conceptions of species being. As Greider notes, this new ideology represents a merging of the currents of traditional socialism, human rights, feminism, environmentalism and respect for cultural diversity which would never have been possible without 1968. The 'spirit of '68' lives on in these manifold movements, increasingly global rather than national in scope. At the moment this global humanism coexists uneasily with a global resurgence of the liberal capitalist doctrines of 'neoliberalism' and 'democracy'.

Paradoxically, as David Harvey (2000: 91–2) has suggested, globalization itself is intensifying the contradictions between global neoliberalism and the spirit of '68. According to Harvey the discourse of globalization presents images of self-realization and human potential which its structural inequalities and commodification of social and personal life increasingly deny; its rhetoric of democratic rights provides a weapon against the denial of rights necessary to maintain these inequalities and indignities. It is not surprising therefore that some of the fiercest resistance to corporate globalization has come from indigenous peoples defending their own distinct cultural potential as human beings with the universal language of democratic participation and civil rights. But structural inequality and the commodification of personal and social life are not limited to the indigenous world; increasingly they affect the North as well as the South, the new professional and managerial class as much as the old working class, men as well as women – Seattle as well as San Cristóbal.

If the contradiction between globalizing neoliberalism and the spirit of '68 continues to deepen, it is possible that it will be resolved by revolutionary transformation. The line of argument presented here does not suggest that such a revolutionary transformation need necessarily be violent, based on worldwide class struggle, or involve seizures of sovereign power at the national or international level, although any or all of these things could occur. It could well be, on the other hand, that a deepening of the currents of human rights, the increasing assertiveness of the formally suppressed gender, ethnic, age and class groups and the rise of the global South may bring the world to a kind of revolutionary transformation in consciousness, lived social experience and power relations seen previously only in particular national societies. If this is so, the institutional arrangements will change to reflect the changes in lived experience just as they did in France, America and Cuba. Is there a future for revolution? If we mean by revolution the global deepening of the spirit of '68 the future may already be upon us.

3

The Democratic Turn: New Ways of Understanding Revolution

Farideh Farhi

'It is perhaps an irony that revolutions led by intellectuals should produce no new ideas – only new realities', was the assessment of Timothy Garton Ash (1999) on the tenth anniversary of the Eastern European revolutions. Inspired by this comment I would like to explore changes in the way revolutions are perceived in the light of new realities. I leave it to others to assess Garton Ash's point about lack of novelty.[1] But I would like to suggest that irrespective of the argument about the end of revolutions as 'great' and time-bound historical phenomena, the events and processes of the past twenty years – including at a minimum the stunning and sudden meltdown of states previously seen as invincible, the increasing importance of formal and informal international networks and the attendant meteoric globalization of electronic media – have influenced the way revolutions and revolutionary change will be perceived in the future.

Of course, there are some keen students of revolutions who suggest that the idea of revolution both as 'motivating ideal and as modular repertoire of contention ... has lost much of its popular appeal and influence' (Goodwin 1998). There are also those who more specifically argue that revolutions are no longer perceived as progressive and hence must be deemed as obsolete products of a bypassed era of 'state-led industrialization and national integration and a product of international war and imperialism' (Snyder 1999: 23–4). From another corner there are those who see future revolutions more as world rather than national events, punctuated by the rise of global social movements and the blur-ring of the distinction between revolutions and social movements (see for instance Boswell and Chase-Dunn 2000). But here I would like to suggest

that while a particular understanding of state-centered revolution seems
to have lost much of its utility, the idea of revolution, broadly conceived
as a relatively abrupt and popularly inspired change in a country's rulers,
cannot be expunged from popular imagination that easily. In fact, the
least that can be said about it is that, in its new variation so meticulously
captured visually on global television, it continues to issue threats to
national states, which despite arguments to the contrary remain among
the most powerful domestic and international agents.[2] As such, rather
than declaring its death as an idea, we would be better advised to take
note of the metamorphosis it is going through in the light of new
realities.

For Garton Ash, the most important implication of the events that
unfolded in Eastern and Central Europe in the late 1980s as well as in
South Africa, and perhaps more recently in countries such as Indonesia
and Serbia/Yugoslavia, has been the increasing blurring of the line between
reform and revolution. This has created the potential for the popularity of
what Garton Ash calls 'a non-revolutionary revolution' in one place, or
'refolution' or 'revelection' in other places. These largely urban events
combine an insistence on non-violence, or 'the well-considered use of
violence',[3] with the creative use of civil disobedience guided by an
opposition elite, calculated pleas to world public opinion through the use
of electronic media, attention and pressure from the outside world, and
'a readiness to negotiate with power holders while refusing to be co-
opted'.[4] The ideological engine of these revolutions is fueled by a means-
or method- rather than ends-oriented critical reflection. As such it is
more consciously aware of the steps taken and the steps not to be taken
given the perceived disastrous trajectory of previous revolutions. It is also
fed by a re-awakened[5] or now much more broadly and deeply internalized
consciousness by an increasing number of middle classes, students, urban
popular classes and rural and indigenous actors of universal democratic
values, which aspires to be translated into practical agendas for local
political reform. It is my contention that this democratic *turn* in consciousness must be better taken into account in the eventual study of
future revolutions. This is particularly needed in an era in which we are
literally bombarded, in an Orwellian fashion, with terms like 'democracy'
and 'freedom' (of interaction among individuals or states) to characterize
processes that effectively translate into increased social inequalities and loss
of local control over the means of daily life. It seems to me that a
combination of reflection on past revolutionary experiences and dissatisfaction with the state of affairs is fueling dynamics that create the potential
for the appropriation of these key concepts and then turning them into

calls for the radical reshaping of political power as a new entry point into the more long-term and gradual project of socioeconomic change.

The first question to be answered, of course, has to do with categorization. Indeed if the Eastern European revolutions obfuscate the lines presumably so clearly drawn in relation to the more 'classic' revolutions, why the insistence on lumping together seemingly non-kindred categories?[6] The hesitance to let go of the idea of revolution within contexts that presumably are amenable to more non-revolutionary concepts or explanations, such as reform or change of regime through non-revolutionary means, seems to have to do with the presence of elements of revolutionary mobilization. Although these events lack what Charles Tilly calls the 'charismatic vision', or faith in politics as a cure-all and of course vindictive violence, they exhibit other characteristics present in revolutions. They are in fact not lacking in 'combining popular uprisings with ineffectual centralized efforts at reform, in featuring intellectuals and in arriving at times of general breakdown in social order' (Tilly 1993: 233–4). In short, they can be considered revolutions because they sought to rearrange the state and its relationship to society through the insertion of popular will. In the latest version of a 'non-revolutionary revolution', centered in Belgrade, demonstrations, a general strike, storming of the parliament and planned takeover of what was perceived to be the nerve center of political power (the headquarters of state television!) were used to push a dictator to accept elections results. To add more confusion to the idea of revolution, when he seemed to have run out of options, this dictator calmly conceded power on television and even tried to resurrect himself as the opposition leader in the new regime before he was arrested as a means to allay external pressure. Of course, no one can claim that this type of 'new-style peaceful' or 'one-night' revolution will be imitated in its entirety in every revolutionary situation. It is also conceivable that such events will be identified as examples of failed attempts, their true character revealed in time with the increasing immiseration caused by uneven development (globalization's shadow, as Nederveen Pieterse (2000) puts it) or heightened criminalization (à la Russia) of societies already suffering from massive lawlessness. But the fact remains that even present and future failures cannot undermine the perception that something 'revolutionary' was involved in these events, which is now part of a repertoire of more 'palatable' paths available to others interested in bringing about an 'alternative country and not [merely] an alternative in power' (Subcomandante Marcos, quoted in Johnston 2000: 479). New realities have indeed made for some shifts in thinking.

In understanding these shifts, definitions count, and Skocpol's now classic definition of revolution as a rapid, basic transformation of a society's state and class structure (and ideology), accompanied and in part carried through by class-based revolts from below, is a good place to begin (Skocpol 1979, and 1982 for the afterthought on ideology). This definition does not include violence but other similar definitions do. This is also what can be called a rather 'tight' or 'narrow' definition, referring to a particular set of events that is sudden, volcanic and convulses or consumes a nation and a state for a particular period of time. It also has an emphasis on the 'social' insofar as it sees the revolutionary state as a mechanism that intervenes heavily and brings about fundamental changes in everyday life. Forrest Colburn is even more explicit about this in his definition of revolution. He sees revolution as the 'sudden, violent, and drastic substitution of one group governing a territorial political entity for another group formerly excluded from the government, and an ensuing assault on state and society for the purpose of radically transforming society' (1994: 6). As mentioned above, understanding revolutions in this way, decidedly influenced by the French and Russian patterns, has allowed some students of revolutions to declare an end to the era or century of revolutions. Simply stated, the diminishing presence of important prerequisites – namely a personalist authoritarian or neopatrimonial state, and ideological dispositions and the confidence that justifies the liberal use of violence by revolutionaries – they argue, is making such revolutions obsolete. On the one hand, the perceived failure of the model of violent revolution have undercut the appeal of social revolutions and made reformist liberal politics more of a global trend. The rise of a limited form of competitive electoral politics and the ideological and economic weight of globalized 'neoliberalism', it is argued, have robbed revolutionaries of one of the most basic and necessary preconditions for revolution, namely state authoritarianism. Much more effectively than authoritarianism, 'low intensity democracies' serve to legitimize existing inequalities and expunge revolutionary politics (Gills and Rocamora 1992; Gills, Rocamora and Wilson 1993; Robinson 1996). They become marked by their institutional flexibility to allow for a limited degree of change, rather than their transformative capacity. The new elected regimes also imply a shift of power within the local ruling elite and a delinking of the middle classes from the alliance with popular forces, hence undermining the possibility of grand style and violent social revolution.[7]

The question here is whether the continued reliance on such a narrow definition is useful given the transformations in the nature of states and state systems as well as the changed underlying understanding of revolutions themselves. As Tilly (1993: 234) points out, social conditions, states and the international system have changed far too much to allow for the repetition of the old scenarios. From this line of thinking changed states and state systems may be as much the source of changed revolutions as no revolutions. That may be so but my concern here is more with the changing understanding of revolutions as opposed to changing states.

According to Hannah Arendt, four elements have been crucial in our post-French revolution understanding of revolution, a quintessentially modern concept. They are novelty, beginning, violence and irresistibility. The interesting part of Arendt's complex argument is the juxtaposition of seemingly contradictory concepts in the idea of revolution. Arendt argues that as soon as revolutionary men and women began to conceptualize revolutionary political phenomena as a new beginning and a novelty (as reflected in Robespierre's famous words about the French revolution producing 'in a few days greater events than the whole previous history of mankind'), they also began to decouple the idea from political choice and action. Revolution, although staged by people, turned out to be not the work of men and women but of irresistible processes. From the French revolution onwards, revolutionary actors seemed not in control of the course of events. As such, this course took a direction that had little if anything to do with the willful aims of human beings. Instead the revolutionaries had to subject their will and purpose to the anonymous force of revolution going through its Terror, Thermidor and Bonapartist stages if they wanted to survive at all. Later on, and even more emphatically, the Russian revolutionaries 'learned history and not action' from their French counterparts. In Arendt's apt words, they 'acquired the skill to play whatever part the great drama of history was going to assign them, and if no other role was available but that of the villain, they were more than willing to accept their part rather to remain outside the play' (1965: 51). If indeed historical necessity called for the devouring of the children of revolution, then the agents of revolution had no other choice but to oblige.

There is no doubt that 'new realities' have unsettled this understanding of revolution. There has been an ideological collapse of the teleology of class formation, universalist consciousness and political method, and a complementary weakening of the teleology of modernization theory (or any large-scale project of social engineering whether organized by states, international agencies or other technocratic elites). The grip of history does not seem that ironclad. As the different trajectories of various Eastern European revolutions attest, retrogression, genocidal chaos and progress all seem possible under similar historical circumstances, highlighting the significance of varying political choices even under similar international circumstances. At the same time, the possibility of peaceful transition of power in bureaucratic states has also brought into question the centrality of violence in revolutions.

To be sure, the rejection of historical determinism cannot be considered hegemonic. To the contrary there seems to be a strong ideological effort to posit neoliberal economic globalization as either historically necessary or inevitable. But as Barry Gills (2000) points out there are enough counter-trends and resistance to suggest that such a globalization is not 'received theory' but a contested concept. It is not external to society, the state or political processes. It elicits resistance precisely because it attacks the right of people to claim and deploy state power in their own self-defense, at all levels from the local, national and regional to the global, whether through radical, revolutionary or reformist politics.

As such, despite the influence of the globalization project, which has presumably turned the state's focus outward away from national accountability to its citizens, the state continues to remain at the center of the struggle to bring about fundamental change. The state may no longer be perceived as the body to be 'taken over' and turned into an instrument of drastic social change. But the way it inserts itself into social, economic and cultural life and the way its institutional arrangements inhibit 'meaningful' as opposed to superficial or procedural democratic participation have become more and more crystallized as the focal point of political struggle in countries as varied as Iran, Indonesia, Peru, Mexico and so on. And this has occurred at both local and global levels. The immediate actors (middle classes, students, urban popular groups and in some places like Chiapas even rural and indigenous actors) most interested in the deepening of democratic participation continue to be internal and their actions are aimed at local authorities. Civic organizations that have taken a leading role have also developed in symbiosis with the nation-state. However, there is no doubt that formal and informal international networks of non-governmental organizations focused on women, minorities and human rights in general as well as the environment are also having an impact, at least in terms of the normative valuation of democratic action at the global level. Also influential are the exiled or émigré communities that, given the power of global electronic mediation, are now able to cross borders much more easily in terms of influence and ideas. Common to all these groups and organizations, both local and international, is a consciousness of universal democratic values that must nevertheless translate into practical and local political agendas.

There is, of course, no doubt that at least a good part of this agenda can be and has been usurped and put to use for different purposes by upholders of the core tenets of structural liberalism, including procedural democracy, the market and transnationalism. Even more complicating is the fact that the rhetoric of developmental modernization (economic growth, high technology, agribusiness, schooling, militarization and now globalization), as some astute anthropologists – for example, Arjun Appadurai (1996) – are pointing out, has become more experiential and less disciplinary (as was done in the 1950s and 1960s through the propaganda apparatuses of the newly independent nation-states and their 'great' leaders). It has become subtly and not so subtly integrated in the everyday life of consumerism and cultural appropriations. At the same time it would be foolish to think of this as a mere narrative of success for the global neoliberal agenda. On the more overt political level, the flip side of the same neoliberal triumphalism can be found in the failure to deliver both politically and economically. This in turn furthers the desire and urge on the part of a multitude of classes, increasingly but not exclusively urban, to bring about more accountability and deepen the democratic values continuously and so disingenuously touted on an everyday basis by the state and its international network. The more experiential appropriation of whatever the global market of goods, ideas and culture can disseminate is also often punctuated, interrogated and domesticated by the micronarratives of local expressive forms (literature, music, film, even spontaneous street celebrations, etc.). These allow 'modernity' to be rewritten more as vernacular or appropriated forms of globalization and less as a concession to large-scale national and international policies. These subversive micro-narratives also fuel oppositional movements ranging from the Taliban to the Zapatistas to Habitat for Humanity and Human Rights Watch to Tamil nationalists in Sri Lanka or even different variants of Islamic reformism/fundamentalism in Egypt and Iran and breakaway nationalist guerrillas in Chechnya. Of course, not all these movements are revolutionary, non-violent or democratic. They suggest the range of ideological and political dispositions available to anti-systemic forces. But the democratic turn in the idea of revolution has had an impact on at least some of them.

A good place to examine this impact is Iran, a country where the struggle over the meaning and shape of power emerging from the country's volcanic revolution of more than twenty years ago is still in process. The democratic aspirations that were reflected in the multi-class coalition against a dictatorship *and* monarchy were, of course, immediately stunted in the name of Islam and war (for more detail, see Farhi 2000). Monarchy and dictatorship were decoupled and the latter reinstated, this time in the name of an odd creation called Islamic republicanism. In short, a republican form of government was installed to declare the end of monarchy but in effect one dictatorial and arbitrary form of power was exchanged for another. Furthermore, a formidable ideological apparatus was erected to justify the blatant contradictions, within the new constitution and in daily life, between popular sovereignty and what was reputed to be a divinely ordained sovereignty. However, these contradictions, given the disastrous trajectory of the Iranian revolution itself and the unfolding of events in Eastern Europe, also carried within them the making of a reform movement with clear determination to reshape political power radically.

This movement, heavily influenced by the productions and activities of intellectuals and students, identifies itself as 'reformist' because it declares its objectives to be the promotion of the 'true' Islamic *and* democratic message or meaning of the revolution. It also acknowledges its intent to work within the Islamic discourse to bring about change. More importantly, as a movement spearheaded by challengers from within the state, with widespread support among the moderate forces within society, it sees its role mostly as one of establishing a framework within which the preconditions for a more equitable political game can be laid. Four consecutive elections have confirmed the popularity of the reform project among the population, but the opposition has so far proved unyielding. There is no doubt that those identified as the 'opponents of reform' or 'power mafia' inside Iran, because of their entrenched economic interests, do not see anything 'reformist' about the movement. Accordingly they have used the many institutions at their disposal and all the tricks they can muster, including imprisonment of and physical attacks against the key proponents of reform, to prevent further erosion of their own political and economic power. Meanwhile the reformists, confident of the popular support for the reform project, remain wedded to their 'bargaining at the top, pressure from below' strategy to bring about a peaceful and non-violent transition to a more democratic game. Intransigence at the top of course makes outright confrontation increasingly more likely. Whether there will be a political blowup or a negotiated settlement to steer Iran out of the political stalemate in which it is currently stranded is yet to be seen. Meanwhile, it is of no small consequence that the elaborate and extremely rich conversation that has taken shape in Iran in the past few years concerning the requirements of a democratic and transparent political system and the relationship between faith and freedom has already changed perceptions about how 'legitimate' politics should be conducted. In the words of the astute observer of Iranian politics Morad Saghafi (1999) it has replaced the 'authoritarian temptation' with the 'democratic temptation',[8] and this confidence in the ultimate ascendancy of democratic means and methods keeps the reformist movement in the political scene despite sustained, fierce and very dangerous opposition.

Iran's democratic discourse is only one example. Other examples can be reflected upon in settings as varied as Indonesia and Mexico. The point is that this democratic turn has implications not only for the methods used but also for what revolutions are expected to be about. To be sure the socialist imaginary, for a good many years centered solely on the reorganization of labor and redistribution of wealth through the instrumental use of the all-powerful state, has gradually ceased to supply the terms of political contestation. As the prospects for heavy-handed and centrally commanded redistribution have waned, the world, in the words of political theorist Nancy Fraser, has begun to see a rise in 'postsocialist' demands, centered on claims of the 'recognition' of difference aimed at remedying cultural and political injustice (Fraser 1997; see also Taylor 1992). But as Fraser rightly points out, in a world of increased commercialization of social relations and rampant economic inequality, heavily marked by cultural hybridization propelled by migration and global media flows, struggles for redistribution and recognition can only be conceived as separate for analytical purposes. In the real world remedies for each of these claims presuppose the other. More importantly, remedies can no longer be conceived as wholesale impositions from above. They come about through the struggle to deepen the meaning of democratic participation and through material and discursive struggles among groups competing for leadership in the public sphere. In other words, these struggles are intended to create an arena for interest recognition and identity formation made possible by democratic politics.[9] However, they are also intended to bring new issues to the forefront of democratic discussion and state regulation through interaction with public officials in the hope of providing input into decision-making at various levels of government, and of contributing to legally binding decisions on important matters.

But this can only be done if some fundamental issues about the democratic process and rules of the game are worked out. The struggle here is not conceived as one of turning the state into an instrument of social change but as a political struggle of redefining the state and pulling it back from its traditional role of imposing its will on society in an arbitrary fashion. It is at the interstices of this democratic struggle for societal and cultural autonomy by the popular classes that possibilities for the enlargement of civil society are being generated. But is also here that the ideological underpinnings of what can be considered the potentially and at least initially political (rather than social) revolutions of the future are being generated.

Understanding the nature of revolutions in this way of course has implications. Implicit in it is an understanding that revolutionary forms of politics cannot succeed overnight with a change in the reins of power, even if an abrupt change at the top may indeed be a necessary step. Long-term change at the level of individual consciousness, state institutions, material structures and civil society is needed. And such an engagement with various entrenched forms of domination works slowly and perhaps can even better be done indirectly. This type of struggle engenders and requires human agency through a multilayered and diffused process, through a gradual transformation of societal values. And, of course, this process has no end since revolutionary forms of dissent are never complete. But nevertheless the demand on the state to acknowledge and act upon the kind of changes society is ready for remains, and as such the potential for a confrontation with recalcitrant states will continue to be a powerful weapon that non-revolutionary revolutionists must envision among their possessions.

Patience is the key word here in making a shift from reformist politics into revolutionary politics. To be sure, there should be concern about a politics of patience in an era in which globalization is shrinking the distance between elites, shifting key relations between producers and consumers, breaking many links between labor and family life, and obscuring the lines between temporary locales and imaginary national attachments. But the point is that there is no emancipatory peak to be climbed. Revolutionary or progressive politics is the very act of climbing, daily, tenaciously and incessantly. It is not an event that happens once, a spectacular outburst of energy that overcomes the dark forces of oppression and lifts liberation into a superior state of perpetual triumph. Does this mean, as Garton Ash (1999: 18) points out, a resurrection of Lenin's most ardent critic, the reformist Eduard Bernstein, and his oft-quoted dictum 'the goal is nothing, the movement is everything?' Perhaps, but obviously the deeper message is generated out of a long process of reflection, both in Europe and in the Third World, and through the twin lessons learned about the flaws of separating ends from means and the loss of legitimacy and sense of direction experienced during all twentieth-century volcanic revolutions in particular, and imposed modernization in general. As Norman Geras eloquently points out, it is based on an understanding of human progress not as some linear advance to a utopian endpoint but as an ongoing struggle:

> Opposing the idea of perfectibility or intrinsic goodness, accepting the threat of evil as a permanent human possibility, we cannot entertain any confidence in some would-be universal benevolence and harmony, or in the prospect of an end to the rule of law. On the contrary, in the light of what human beings can do and have done to one another, we have every reason to want to continue setting limits around the more harmful and menacing types of human potentiality. (Geras 1998: 117)

Notes

I would like to thank John Foran for very helpful comments on an earlier version of this essay.

1. 'In spite of all the agitation and noise, no new idea has arisen in 1989 in Eastern Europe' was the harsh judgement of François Furet, the eminent historian of the French revolution (quoted in Plesu 1997: 53). Needless to say, for Furet no new ideas also meant no revolution. For Garton Ash, on the other hand, the great new idea of Eastern European revolutions was the form of the revolutions themselves: the fact that people deliberately set out to do something different from the classic revolutionary model. This idea of doing something deliberately different finds echo in other places as well. For instance, the recent Iranian reform movement explicitly draws on the idea of doing something different within the context of Iranian history by consciously trying to break from the recurring cycle of violent revolutions and absolutism that has gripped Iran for more than a century.

2. For instance, the events leading to the abdication of Slobodan Milošević were duly noted and reported as a warning to the anti-reform leaders in Tehran in case their opposition continues.

3. In the discussion of the criteria for a 'well-considered theory of violence', borrowed from Bikhu Parekh, Josee Johnston (2000) argues that the Zapatistas in Chiapas fulfill the criteria: 'By keeping their military actions minimal, and developing a close relationship with Mexican civil society, the Zapatistas were able to maintain the moral high-ground in their conflict with the state, and legitimize their overarching demand for greater democracy in Mexico.'

4. For the latest version of the argument, see Garton Ash 2000. It is interesting to note the similar dynamics of urban revolutionary mobilization that were already evident in the Iranian revolution of 1979. Obviously the unwillingness of the revolutionary coalition to negotiate when the regime finally became willing and the ensuing violence were critical differences in terms of outcomes.

5. I bring up the possibility of re-awakening because of the argument made by some students of the French revolution about that revolution's universal democratic aspirations. According to Patrice Higonnet (1998: 332), 'the ebbing of Leninist and communist assumptions enables us to realize anew the strengths of the Jacobin and Republican idea, which we can again envisage not as a stepping stone to an elusive socialist nirvana but as a free-standing, real life principle of social fairness.'

6. The wisdom of mixing the idea of reform with revolution has not only been debated in relation to the Eastern European events but elsewhere as well. In Chiapas, for instance, Jorge Castañeda (1995: 86) has argued that, despite the strategic use of violence and their self-understanding as revolutionaries, the Zapatistas would be better considered as 'armed reformists' because of the unconventional combination of tactics they use.

7. It is important to note that for Gills and Rocamora, the new formal democracies are weak regimes controlled by outside powers through international financial institutions. Interestingly they see the new democracies in the Third World as the result of a global strategy by the United States as the hegemonic power, together with local ruling classes, to preempt the revolutionary potential of the 1989 rising. But they also see their social reform prospects as bleak, with the future holding economic chaos, deepening social conflict and neo-authoritarianism. As such they

do not foreclose the possibility of abrupt change in the future. Robinson, who uses the term 'polyarchy' to refer to a carefully managed system in which democracy is limited to electing competing elites designed to be responsive to the exigencies of globalization, also suggests that formal democracy combined with a socioeconomic system of vast inequality is bound to engender political upheavals and possibly revolutions. Others, however, such as Goodwin (1998) and Snyder (1999) see the institutionalization of limited competition for state power as a hindrance to future revolutions.

8. The idea of democratic temptation can be posed against the notion of authoritarian temptation, most aptly discussed by Adam Przeworski (1991: 93–4). For Przeworski the authoritarian temptation is generated out of the messiness of democracy. The democratic temptation, on the other hand, is generated from the failures of authoritarian regimes, unable to resolve internal conflicts and faced with an educated population able to seize on the internal conflicts within the regime.

9. The importance of a politics of recognition is reflected, for instance, in Zapatista slogans such as 'Nevermore a Mexico without us'. And this is what Marcos told the crowd in the Zapatista march to Mexico City: 'Don't let there be another dawn without the flag having a place for us' (as reported in the *Washington Post*, 12 March 2001).

4

Parallaxes: Revolutions and 'Revolution' in a Globalized Imaginary

Noel Parker

Globalization, Revolution and the State

Along with other contributors to this volume, I am a sceptic about globalization. That is not to say that I believe there is *nothing* going on out there behind the expression. Rather, I find that to an unusual degree the term overlays reality with political rhetoric (cf. Hirst and Thompson 2000; Rosenberg 2001; Wallerstein 2000). Given the evidence that the concept can apply equally well to tendencies at various periods of history (e.g. Denemark et al. 2000; Held et al. 1999; Holsti 1992), there are good grounds for regarding 'globalization' as a new expression for something that has been going on at various times in the past but is now happening faster, with renewed meaning and rhetorical force for this particular historical moment in world-level relations (Holm and Sørensen 1995). Nonetheless, since 1990 certain new realities have given a powerful new surge and new meaningfulness to globalization, and this impinges on the 'meaning' of revolutions.

The meaning of revolution matters for two sets of persons: those who seek to understand revolutions as a site of human action; and those who are, or might be, involved (as advocates or opponents) in revolutionary challenges. For those involved act partly out of the idea they have of earlier revolutions and of 'revolution' itself. So I take as my task to consider what revolutions can mean where this globalizing context is newly meaning*ful*. What, then, does globalization *mean*? It strengthens greatly the world-level/global/universal as an arena to discover, explain and interpret what happens in our world, and as a basis for our values. This is what

Martin Albrow (1996) and others refer to by the expressions 'globality' and 'globalism'. And the evident quid pro quo of all that is to bring renewed prominence to what has actually always been the case: that the power concentrated in national statehood may not be inevitable and may not possess the highest authority – though statehood is more viable for some power structures in some times and places than it is for others.[1]

If that observation is brought to attention, however, it has implications for the meaning of revolution. For revolution and the state have always existed in tension with each other. For participants, revolution has, for some centuries, had a specially favored position amongst the wider set of power conflicts in human societies. Revolutions have been aimed at the seizure of the power ostensibly concentrated in the state, and the modification of the social and power relations which the state has convincingly claimed were subject to it. Given a newly resurgent 'globality' and a newly challenged state power, it is far less obvious that a revolutionary attack upon the state is the high road to a reorganization of power. In short, the retreat of the national state that is implicit in globalization must entail a loss of faith in revolution as the *ne plus ultra* of what Tilly calls 'contention' over power.[2]

The consequence for established commentary on revolutions is complex. Classic theorizations (Tilly et al. 1975; Tilly 1990, 1993; Skocpol 1979, 1994) have successfully incorporated revolutions into the European/world history of statehood. Revolutions challenged states in their rise to dominance and impacted on their formation (Kimmel 1988). My own account of the career of revolution (Parker 1999) extrapolates from that line of thought, and from a Braudelian picture of the growth and spread of statehood (Braudel 1984; Wallerstein 1979, 1984). Keeping in step with statehood, I contend, revolution has spread out as resistance/confirmation of the waves[3] of modernization emanating over the last three centuries from Europe and then the Western world. It is in this way that 'parallax' enters into the history of revolutions: how the thing is perceived varies according to the location you are looking from. I conclude (Parker 1999: ch. 4) that the area of firmly rooted modern statehood unlikely to be successfully challenged by a revolution has greatly extended over the course of time, driving revolutions increasingly to the margins where, *on their own*, they can impact less and less upon the area dominated by the society of states.

There was a pessimism and an irony (strongly informed by Tocqueville) in Skocpol's classic view of revolution and statehood: revolutions ostensibly conducted *against* the state have been more or less *productive* of statehood. In a world of rising statehood, revolutionary agents believing (or at any rate asserting) that they were confronting the state have in fact served the fuller realization of statehood. Whilst they may have *modified* the state's growth, statehood continued to develop and any subsequent state re-inforced its power the better to ward off future insurgency. Now, to the degree that the idea of globalization has force, it undermines this logic in the incidence of revolutions. Where statehood itself is in decline, revolu-tionary resistance to the state can no longer be the middle term between contention and social change. Whereas revolutionaries have in the past been guided by an (often frustrated) ambition to impede, modify or adopt modern statehood, if statehood appears less crucial, future contending groups must focus their attention elsewhere than the state. Likewise their successes and their failures will serve to challenge and/or confirm powers other than those of the state.

One could point to a number of already visible non-state-focused forms of contention: the cosmopolitan, such as transnational globalization-from-below movements (Evans 2000; Brecher and Costello 1998; Falk 1999; and see Kellner in this volume); the religious and/or ethnic, prominent in the Iranian and Afghan revolutions; secessionism from existing states in southeastern Europe and the Middle East (Bartkus 1999; Katz 1999: 75–99); and the 'subaltern' insurrections visible in the Third World (Rabasa 1997). These are modes of contention where statehood as such is not primary or where nationhood, if it is present, is ambivalently related to statehood.[4] I will return to the aspirations of newer contending groups after an exploration of the nature of revolutionary agency, of identity for contending groups (and others), and of the parallaxes that suggests for the future.

The Globalization Narrative and 'the Revolutionary Narrative'

Even though the globalization narrative cuts across the inherited models of revolution, a sufficiently globalized account of earlier history would skirt round the limitations of highly state-centric accounts of revolution and history such as Skocpol's. For world-system theory, for example, the dissemination of the Western model of statehood has always been a function of something greater than the states themselves: that is, the demands of the globalizing market. World-system theory thus offers resources to con-ceptualize the new situation where the state is no longer a plausible center of power in any specific 'national' society.[5] Accordingly, for world-system theory, oppositional movements have long been able to act 'counter-systemically': that is to say, upon the world system *as a whole*, over and above the individual state. Under globalizing conditions, this possibility takes on new force. Two already canvassed instances would be the movements of 1968 (Wallerstein 1991) and the Zapatista uprising in Chiapas in 1994 (Burbach 2001; Castells 1997: 72–84). The timing and location of each gave it an impact well beyond its immediate force: 1968 to delegitimize the whole post-World War II pattern of development in the West; and 1994 to destabilize the international money markets just at their moment of triumph with the arrival of NAFTA. In short, insofar as states were not in any case the highest instance organizing the worldwide distribution of power, revolutions may not need to reshape *states* in order to have an impact at world level.

This conception focuses attention upon action destabilizing the totality beyond the agents' immediate focus. An important qualification here, though, is that any impact beyond that intended by the contending group may not square with the politics of opposition. This possibility is amply illustrated by the 1970s' turn to the political right in the West, when responsibility for the dysfunctionality put forward by the 1968 resistance was turned inwards, into a critique of Western societies for not living up to the requirements of the market. Clearly, revolutionary politics has always been met by *counter*revolutionary politics, including the strategy of diverting the demands made in pursuit of revolution. Outside the frame of the given state and its transformation, on the other hand, counter-systemic actions may more easily be turned towards global narratives with results quite at odds with the expectations framed for the narrower national-state setting.

This is the point to introduce the central terms of my own work about the movement of revolution across history and global space. They offer a way, regardless of the impact of revolutions 'on their own', of conceptualizing the autonomous dynamic in world history of what John Foran and others call 'cultures of resistance'. As I have already suggested, actors in revolutionary situations have operated, at least since the American revolution of the late eighteenth century, with a conception of 'revolution' and its possibilities partly conveyed in an appreciation of earlier revolutionary episodes. Thus, for over two centuries, there has been an 'imaginary',[6] locating the idea of revolution, which circulates between sites and actors in revolutionary episodes. This imaginary has also contained conceptions of statehood, modernity, progress, and so on, as things to be developed, directed, challenged or what have you. Within this imaginary, there is, I contend, a 'revolutionary narrative': a schema for the revolutionary intervention of the human group in the otherwise alien imposition of modernization from outside/above. The revolutionary narrative, conveyed by example from one contending group (and its opponents) to another and reinforced by its special capacity to repossess an otherwise alien process of change, postulates that the human group may reshape society by an act of collective will, the revolution itself. The question of the future of revolutions in the context of globalization can usefully be posed, then, as the question of the future of the revolutionary *narrative* under globalization. There are various components of action under this revolutionary narrative (Parker 1999: ch. 5): the prospect/threat of irreversible change; the supposition of power on the part of some or other agents to advance, prevent or divert that change; and some end-state to which the change is directed. Revolution and revolutionary narrative are separate, albeit interrelated, phenomena with distinct logics and different spatio-historical existences.[7]

Up to now, the key conduit of change and space for challenge envisaged by the revolutionary narrative has been the state itself, with its plausible claim to legislate for all the power relations in a society. No longer, apparently. It might perhaps be more correct to speak of the state today as a 'self-negating' conduit of modernizing change, since under the dominant neoliberal discourse there is a pressure on states to modernize 'governance' by scaling down *themselves* (see Walton and Udayagiri 2000). But the state as such, however described, is less able to be a fundamental component of the revolutionary narrative. Yet, if the revolutionary narrative loses the state as the supreme arbiter of power to be contended with, it does not by the same token lose its capacity to convey across space and time a schema for contention. Moreover, under conditions of globalization, it must certainly retain all its former capacity to speak to the condition of human beings whose way of life is impinged upon by the pressures of an alien modernization. Thus the revolutionary narrative can be expected to frame, in its concept of group action for social change, new ways of engaging in 'revolution'.[8]

And clearly nothing has brought to an end the exploitation, oppression, inequality and other sociopolitical ills found with the pressures of modernization. It is common to all those in this volume that what Gilly refers to as 'relations of domination/subordination' (RDS) will continue to exist, to change and to be challenged. Indeed, there is plenty of evidence that inequalities of wealth and of power become both more marked and, through the effects of global communication, more *visible* under conditions of globalization. I contend, then, that in spite of the decline of the state as an object of revolutionary challenge, within the newly globalized imaginary, revolutionary movements will continue to articulate the revolutionary narrative in acts of contention against the RDS. But, naturally, the refigured version will be subject to a new set of parallaxes: these depend upon the site envisaged for the existence of the contending group; and upon the feasibility of an older statehood in the given group's geographical location.

Parallaxes: New Sites for Contending Groups

I suggest that three elements in the earlier revolutionary narrative can be expected to survive the new globalization: the prospect/threat of change; the belief that a challenge can be mounted against *some* arbiter of power or other; and a corresponding expectation of capacity on the part of *some human group or other* to reconstruct society for the better. It is the last two that require close attention. The target for challenge, and the correspond-ing agent to make any challenge, are now problematic. The first – that is, up to now, the state – has long been the easier of these two to identify. Indeed, it is not too much to say that the second has often been a derivative of the first: that is to say, the people of the *nation* could be identified as the agents of a challenge because they had first been the subject of the unifying power of a given state's institutions. The inter-nationalist idea that it was the given class that was the agent of challenge and change was always far less firmly grounded in sociopolitical organiza-tion than the idea that the nation governed by the given state was that agent – though the two ideas have been successfully combined. The key issue, then, is the future formation of contending groups. We need to look afresh at the processes that identify the group and speculate about how that identification may happen under conditions of globalization.

As a matter of fact, thinking on the political left had been addressing this problem for some time before the recent globalization, from the period when the New Left reconsidered the basis of revolutionary politics as the USSR-centered Communist Party progressively lost authority. Easy formulas correlating economic class, revolutionary potential and loyalty to the USSR-centered revolutionary movement were extensively reconsidered by ex-Party members and by dissidents within. This produced, on the one hand, much discussion on the meaning of class, exploitation, and so on (e.g. Althusser 1969; Poulantzas 1978; Thompson 1966; Wright 1997) and, on the other, a turn towards debates on what *politics* belongs with what class membership.[9] These tendencies were pursued most starkly by Ernesto Laclau and Chantal Mouffe, whose 'post-Marxist' *Hegemony and Socialist Strategy* (1985) sought to rebuild left politics without presuppositions about classes.

Conscious of new types of revolution in South Africa, the Middle East and South America, Laclau has gone on to assert that all present-day politics can be explored via the discourse that *constructs* oppositional alliances (Laclau 1994, 2002). As globalization makes states *everywhere* look weaker, the oppositional rhetoric of populism, characteristically found in weak Third World states, thus defines the present possibilities of political contention. Acts of naming, and of rehearsing either membership of, loyalty to or hostility towards the group are indeed now more than ever visibly essential to collective identity, intention and capacity for action. This is rightly highlighted in the 'fourth generation' of studies of revolution,[10] where reiterated narrations of past or mythic acts of resistance are adopted as expressions of the shared identity of those who struggle. A similar mythification of more recent acts holds together part of the globalization-from-below movement (McKay 1996). And as one might suspect from its implicit logic, insofar as naming asserts identity in order for identity to come about, naming the resistant group can step over into the absurd. Thus accounts of the Zapatista movement note both the astuteness of their politics and the persuasive 'absurdity' of demands made by anony-mized, educated representatives on behalf of an ethnie timelessly engaged in struggle (see Selbin's chapter in this volume).

Yet procedures for naming are, as Per Aage Brandt reminds us,[11] distinct from the causal systems used to interpret the world. It follows that while linguistic acts may be fundamental in constituting the group, they cannot function alone. What causal categories permit the acts of naming that relate contending identities to a real world? Whatever structure can be assigned to the real world within which the self is to be located is central. For, as Brandt argues persuasively, though 'sameness and difference' with some others are 'absolute and unconditional', there is also 'a continuously ongoing battle of competing models' for which instances belong to which generic descriptions (Brandt 1995: 194, 196). In sum, the naming/identifying of a group, revolutionary or otherwise, needs a determinate model of the world where the difference between any 'them' and any 'us' can be plotted.

Yet in a globalized imaginary the mental plotting of difference has a sharpened complexity, because globalized communication and the manifest effectiveness of global influences mean that, as Roland Robertson put it, 'the world as a whole has been increasingly "organized" around sets of shifting definitions of the global circumstance' (1991: 89). The direct and often oppressive effects of neoliberal globalization, which I referred to earlier, impinge, for example, upon identities.[12] Identities are marketed to the ostensible bearers of those identities themselves (Mathews 2000). And nostalgia for a homeland they never knew is conveyed to modern city-dwellers (Appiah 1992). Alongside economic globalization, then, we can observe models of the self and of the other intruding more rapidly, more widely and more deeply than before.[13] Whilst it is by no means a new phenomenon in itself (von Laue 1987; Said 1993),[14] there is, then, a heightened possibility for contending groups to identify themselves either by self-*assimilation* or by self-*juxtaposition* with distant, more or less imagined others.

This is not necessarily a passive, one-way process, because the mutual penetration of ideas of the local and the global defines *both* – a fact captured by Robertson's concept of 'glocalization' (1995). But it would follow that the 'identity space' which the putative contending group can hollow out in its 'definition of the global circumstance', and how it then relates itself to one or more 'others', are complex dimensions. Can we then categorize the scope for the contending group's self-identification where, as under globalizing conditions, national-territorial sites are put in question? I suggest that we can indeed extrapolate the categories for self-identification from the non-state-focused forms of contention referred to earlier. These categories, which are are not mutually exclusive,[15] provide strategies for the construction of the global and of the identity of the contending group in relation to it.

- Cosmopolitan contention locates itself in the universal of the human race, its values and interests, or the biological integrity of the globe. In an Enlightenment fashion, the contending group may choose to identify itself with these universal values. As John Walton shows in his chapter in this volume, what he calls 'anti-globalization' contention is distributed across a wide range of losers from globalization. Where the state itself is weakened, the cosmopolitan group proposes to bypass it, or pressure it, to pursue action against global forces (primarily global capitalism) in the name of the universal. Evidently, this particular identity space finds it hardest to place the 'other' against whom the group directs its efforts, since they too are by definition members of the human race – though perhaps unworthy members.
- Contention grounded in religious and/or ethnic identity constructs cultural identities which disregard national statehood, or at least established national states (Castells 1997). This identity space therefore covers the category of non-state-focused secessionism. It naturally tends to treat the other as profoundly different, or even worthy of contempt – though less so in the case of religious fundamentalism, where conversion of opponents is conceivable (Eisenstadt 1999: 105ff.). Religion and/or ethnically grounded contention has a more complex definition of global circumstances than cosmopolitanism, leaving a range of possibilities for

defining the other.[16] It validates challenges for the sake of two alternative transcendentals: the culture/ethnie, thought of as existing *in* history past, present and future; and the supernatural intruding *into* history. The two are analytically distinct strategies: but the two transcendentals are not incompatible, and indeed often occur together, in the sense that 'ethnic' identity is often centered upon loyalty to a god-given direction. The latter is a survivor of the earlier 'axial' reference point by which to challenge the given condition of the real world.[17]

- The strength of the everyday sense of 'national' belonging *regardless of statehood* indicates that national identity can also appear alongside ethnic identities, in a non-*state*-focused identity space where contending groups can define their own identities, even without an especially 'nationalist' political agenda (Motyl 1991: 69–82; Smith 1995).

- Finally, subaltern identity and contention cut across all the above, exhibiting a unique strategy with regard to the other. What is peculiar, and peculiarly fruitful about it for the globalized imaginary, is its capacity for defining the contending group as both ineluctably subordinate and representative of universal, even transcendent values. By holding to its subordinate status, the subaltern group may root itself in a history of struggle and/or oppression. Subaltern narratives include the continued coexistence of various others. The Zapatista movement made its mark as a 'post-modern' revolution precisely by responding to long-standing grounds for revolutionary resistance whilst distancing itself from the grander expectations of earlier hegemonic narratives (Burbach 2001). As Subcomandante Marcos has expressed it:

> You cannot reconstruct the world or society, nor rebuild national states now in ruins, on the basis of a quarrel over who will impose their hegemony on society. The world in general, and Mexican society in particular, is composed of different kinds of people, and the relations between them have to be founded on respect and tolerance, things that appear in none of the discourses of the politico-military organizations of the sixties and seventies. (Marcos 2001: 71)

Subaltern narratives 'are tragic, because they mark not an end of history, but rather a continuation in struggle' (Rabasa 1997: 409). The subaltern group may also pursue revolutionary opposition not directed at the takeover of the state with its universal claims, which leaves it peculiarly well placed to achieve 'metonymic' identification (where part represents the whole but remains part) with other oppositional groupings, both locally and globally (Rabasa 1997: 404). Up to now, the Zapatista revolutionaries have been markedly strengthened by the subaltern strategy.

Parallaxes: The Differing Possibilities of Statehood

Globalization, too, is subject to a parallax: it, too, looks different in different places. Finally, we have then to reimport the variable intensity of globalization into the above account of the identity spaces for contention. Hence a further dimension of parallax: the extent to which contending groups *need* to follow alternatives to state-based identity depends on the survival of the older type of statehood in their geographically differentiated imaginary. We have, in short, to differentiate between the new versions of contention we can expect in differentially globalized parts of the world.

Very schematically, we could categorize the different experiences and expectations of statehood between: weak-state areas, roughly in the Third World, where statehood has appeared as a modern ideal never properly realized; declining-state areas in the First and Second Worlds, where modern statehood appears to have been realized in the past but is now in decline under globalization pressures; and strong-state areas where the state is so big or so powerful that fully functioning state power does not seem challenged at all. A closer look at cases naturally indicates that this three-part categorization is really a *scale* along which post-globalization contention may vary. The last category has a peculiar membership: the US, whose manifold concentration of power and status in the interstate system permits it to continue with the full dignity of statehood identifiable with universal right itself; and China, whose size and strategic hesitation over getting involved in the global stand like a volcanic stump resisting the glacier of globalization wearing others down. In particular, the position of the US, as we shall see in due course, produces a peculiarly paradoxical setting for global revolutionary contention.

The current weakness of former 'hyperactive' states, particularly in Latin America, is well covered elsewhere in this volume (see the chapters by Parsa and Vilas, for example). Even clearer cases within my first category are to be found in Africa, where political orders distant from the European model of statehood were disrupted long and late, and where a particularly impracticable Western model of modern, state-led development was then adopted and overturned (Chaliand 1977, 1990; Waites 1999; Wolf 1997).[18] Late-twentieth-century revolutions here have neither a state to possess nor its associated narratives to redirect (Mmembe and Roitman 1996), with the result that contention has a strong tendency to take on a defensive, backward-looking ethnic-to-ethnic character (Scherrer 1997).

That said, the degree to which statehood seems out of reach in 'weak-state areas' varies, and so therefore does the manner of recourse to non-state-focused identity spaces. Latin America has a long, if incomplete, history of state development (Castañeda 1993: 273ff.), together with solidly established peasant societies, capable of uniting around ethnicities that can straddle national identities (Churchill 1995; Cleaver 1994). Latin American states are also under heavy 'globalizing' pressure from the US to the north. Other things being equal, then, you would expect that both ethnic and nation-state identity spaces could survive in that zone of globalization. In general, I would argue, identities in contending groups here will often be the net effect of globalizing pressure to run down statehood meeting non-state-focused societal identities of one kind or another. One accordingly finds evidence, in countries such as Cuba or Mexico, of resilient national *and* ethnic identity regardless of state weakness (McCaughan 1997). In both Peru and Mexico, ethnic rural revolutionary movements have sustained their existence in a balance with the state that may presage long-term subalternity. In another part of the globe, the post-revolutionary Vietnamese state was forced to accept scaling down (Abuza 1996), but was able as it did so to draw on societal cohesion from below for ways of managing things compatible with the reduced size of the state (Liljeström et al. 1998).

The Middle East contains a number of states on the boundary between weak and declining. The Turkish state, reinforced by the distinguished history of its own governmental order, and solidified around a military that has pursued the nearby European republican ideal of statehood and been buoyed up by US support during the cold war, has (up to the time of writing in late 2001) resisted pressures to scale down; but it meets, in Kurdish rebellion, an ethnic identity with pretensions to launch an alternative boundary-transcending nationalism (White 2000). The Middle East, Turkey included, also exhibits the strongest contending religious identity in the contemporary world: Muslim fundamentalism. Whilst analytically detachable from statehood, however, it too seems to be at its strongest where it can be linked to a given nationalism – notably in Iran, another 'strong weak' state – or where, as in Afghanistan, it was assisted in seizing power by big players in the international system of states (Ahmed 1999; Cooley 1999).

The original core states of Europe are those most clearly in my 'declining' category. European state structures are now heavily dependent upon mutual cooperation to maintain dignity in spite of weakness (Milward 1992), while contending groups, such as they are, are uncertain whether to oppose the national state or to align with 'Eurosceptic' opposition to the projected 'superstate' beyond (Anderson and Camiller 1994; Elliott and Atkinson 1998: 158–88). Over and above this fractured opposition to state and to state-like structures, the European declining-state area exhibits, in ecologism and in human rights, the greatest tendency to elevate cosmopolitan values, adapted from Europe's Enlightenment past. In terms of my account, the logic of this is clear: these principles for resistance can be detached from opposition to states under pressure from globalization. Indeed, there can be a considerable affinity between these values as they are embraced by contending groups and as they are adopted by European states themselves and by the Europe-wide bodies created to pursue them.[19]

Concluding Remarks: State-focused versus Non-state-focused Contention and the Case of the US

Finally, the US is a most paradoxical, and revealing, case. For it is the area where statehood is *least* challenged by globalization. In a world setting where states as such make progressively poorer targets of 'revolutionary' contention, the US state has the greatest potential to fulfill the role formerly accorded to states in the revolutionary narrative. In domestic US politics, a 'traditional' state-focused revolutionary narrative is thus possible: some heirs of the native revolution pursue national autonomy – in opposition to the US's involvement in institutions, such as the UN, which embody transnational global values. The Patriot movements, for example, construct their self-identity in a struggle to recapture the US state and/or return it to its original, sovereign national purpose (Castells 1997: 84–97). Conversely, the US state remains the inheritor of the European cosmopolitan tradition, and continues as a state with an undisputed capacity to carry through at world level the 'universal' values it adopts (Møller 1997; Kagan 2000; Lipset 1996).[20]

In the global environment as I have described it over the length of this chapter, the revolutionary narrative of the past is, as it were, adrift in the globalized imaginary: short of *states* worthy of revolutionary contention. I have argued that, consequently, the force of the revolutionary narrative is transposed into newer formats where the contending group is identified in *non*-state-focused contention: cosmopolitan, religious, ethnic, secessionist, subaltern. But the US is the state at one and the same time least diminished by globalization and most forcefully advocating it.[21] 'Globalization', including the consequent *diminution* of statehood, can itself be pursued as American national interest (Brennan 1997). In global politics, therefore, the US has a unique position as a *state* identifiable with the transnational imposition of modernization in its current, globalizing form. Thus, in *global* politics, revolutionary opposition to the latest version of modernization can define itself in resistance to, or in attacks upon, the US state or US society.

This appears, indeed, to be the rationale behind the devastating terrorist attack upon New York on 11 September 2001, carried out by the Islamic fundamentalists of the al-Qaeda movement. Radical, Muslim opponents of the current version of modernization define their identity as a group which can stop worldwide US or US-sponsored modernization in defense of an alternative religious/ethnically grounded direction of change. Like earlier revolutionary movements, their resistance confronts an extending, modernizing power. But now its opponents, skeptical of 'their own' state's autonomy as a conduit of the incoming modernization, latch on to the most tangible next best target: the US – the universal, intrusive state across the seas. The future course of this development is anybody's guess. But one strong possibility is that US/Western pressure for globalization will reinforce the trend. By visibly weakening further the autonomy of states across the globe, it may further reduce their suitability as terms in the revolutionary narrative, and so encourage more *non*-state-focused contention. And, since the contending group's identity is harder to define without the state, revolutionary contention may turn instead on the US state-as-globalization as a target. The revolutionary narrative of the reappropriation of the social order may thus be played out in global terms, either against globalizing modernization as such, or against the US.

Notes

1. See Spruyt 1994 for a fine account of how the state's earlier success in monopolizing power was no foregone conclusion.

2. For many, revolution never was the highest order of contention. Other schemata of social change and of how to establish new power relations could always have plausibly claimed to be feasible and more surefire, if less complete and dramatic than revolution: Therborn 2000: 149. But they had always to be measured and defended alongside this *ne plus ultra* of social change.

3. Though the geometry of these waves is complex and should not be likened to a straightforward concentric spreading – see Parker 1999: 69ff.

4. The fact that at one and the same time they were driven by an aspiration to nation-statehood and by admiration of the latest Western model of heavily reduced statehood has rendered the Central European revolutions of the late 1980s/early 1990s particularly difficult to evaluate in terms of the previous history of state and revolution – see, for example, the awkward assessment in the final chapter of Tilly 1993.

5. Arrighi (1994) takes up this possibility within world-system theory. Following his logic, one could hypothesize that, at the point where statehood has been established *extensively* enough for the purposes of the market, pressure against

governments being too *intensive* is to be expected. An earlier global trend to *establish* states would accordingly be replaced by one to *diminish* their role; and that is globalization. Cf. Wallerstein 2000: 262ff.

6. By which I refer to a totality of symbolic resources available to a society to represent a real world, the entities within it and their mutual relationships.

7. Which I sketched out summarily for the nineteenth and twentieth centuries (Parker 1999: chs 6 and 7). Already, before the arrival of the present globalization, the revolutionary narrative could appear in Europe or the US as a complex mirror of nations' own revolutionary past, their present adversary, and, hence, an unattainable renewal of themselves via the other. This return happened very strikingly in France and in the US confronted with national liberation revolutions in Algeria and in Vietnam respectively.

8. Cf. Katz (1999: 117), who observes that in a world where the probability of democracy is changing, 'a relatively static conception of revolution' continues to hold sway' amongst theorists. My claim is broader than Katz's: that the fundamental elements of what we have called revolutions can be carried over into a range of forms of contention.

9. A move symbolized by interest in Gramsci, whose concept of 'hegemony', fashioned to deal with mass support for Italian Fascism, led the way into the question of how political posture might be variously related to class membership.

10. In which, according to Goldstone (2001), the search for structural factors has progressively broadened out to incorporate leadership, ideology and processes of identification – though Goldstone himself seems inclined to have his structural cake and eat it, by directing his account to action to be avoided *by the state* in order that contending groups should not build identities.

11. In a short article from 1995 about European identities and European integration, the Danish semiotician sums up much of the psychology underpinning the way human beings relate meanings and identities to a real world. Group identities, he affirms, are formed and sustained through human linguistic acts of referring (Brandt 1995). Such acts attribute to the identity named the sustained intentionality without which no political organization is possible – and, I would add, no revolutionary narration complete.

12. In impoverished Third World countries, for example, there occurs a restructuring of options for personal identity which were originally conveyed in post-colonial modernization (Mmembe and Roitman 1996).

13. Jonathan Friedman's account of the contemporary 'construction of identity space' as 'the dynamic operator linking economic and cultural processes' (1994: 171) accordingly incorporates into globalization the modeling of a reality where 'us' and 'them' can be named, and contended over. 'The vitality of certain indigenous movements', he writes, 'is measurable by the degree to which indigenous peoples manage to capture or replace' their carpet-bagging 'representatives' on the global scene (Friedman 1998: 15).

14. Taylor (1996, 1999) has developed a model that incorporates in the centuries-long history of modernization processes that disseminate images, identities and rewards and have repeatedly reshaped modernization and won over elites everywhere to new identifications of themselves as modernizers.

15. Any more than identity has to be singular – Handler 1994; Hall 1992.

16. One may, as Stuart Hall (1991) has pointed out with regard to ethnic identities

in Western societies, make the ethnic 'local' a site for challenging a universal imposed from above.

17. Though it would be blinkered to conclude (as Eisenstadt's 1999 analysis tends to suggest) that modern 'Jacobin' and the more recent 'fundamentalist' versions of religiously grounded identity are in any sense *mis*appropriations.

18. As Tiruneh, commenting on Ethiopia, puts it: 'the end of the cold war ... has meant that poor states can no longer hide behind the skirts of such principles as the sovereign equality of states and non-interference' and there has been a 'loss of [poor states'] economic self-determination ... since the West's assertion of structural adjustment' (1993: 374). South Africa, which was twice colonized and deeply restructured by the British and as an Afrikaner nation-state, is a partial exception.

19. The Council of Europe, for example, or the EU, whose so-called 'Copenhagen' principles portray it as an agent for the spread of the recognition of human rights to new members in Central and Eastern Europe.

20. Oren (1996) provides, in the case of the US's treatment of Germany over the length of the twentieth century, a fine example of the historical capacity of hegemonic states to adjust their description of others so that the latter fit the dominant, universal values.

21. As Rosenberg (1994) points out, this ambiguity regarding 'sovereign, national' independence is, like so many other aspects of globalization, not new. The principal states in the international system (i.e. Britain and later the US) were never parties to the sovereign independence of the Treaty of Westphalia and always encouraged statehood instead as a demarcation of responsibility for the maintenance of the private sphere where transnational market relations could proceed.

PART II

Rethinking Revolutions in Light of Globalization

5

The Renewal of Socialism and the Decline of Revolution

Jeff Goodwin

The socialist critique of capitalism remains as relevant as ever. In an age of corporate globalization, in fact, this critique has become especially urgent. Capitalism, moreover, has always been characterized and indeed driven by social conflict, based as it is on an inherently contentious opposition between owners and workers. Globalization in no way removes this opposition, and in some ways exacerbates it. However, globalization and other characteristics of the present age have certainly shifted the *strategic* terrain on which opponents of capitalism and other forms of social domination now find themselves. As a result, socialist or 'socialist-oriented' revolutions are less likely than they were during the cold war era. Even less likely is a revolutionary overthrow of global capitalism as such. A prolonged 'war of position', in Gramsci's sense, would seem to lie ahead of us, a period in which socialist and other radical movements continue to battle capitalism's worst manifestations, experiment with local and national forms of resistance, and begin perhaps to strategize a transition to a post-capitalist order that lies largely beyond the horizons of the present conjuncture.

A Renewal of Socialism?

The contemporary era would not seem to bode well for socialists of any stripe. The Soviet bloc has collapsed, and many erstwhile socialists and social democrats have embraced neoliberalism, in some cases with unbridled enthusiasm. The triumph of capitalism seems complete. And indeed markets and corporations are today more powerful, intrusive and extensive in their reach than ever before. In the words of Perry Anderson, 'Whatever limitations persist to its practice, neoliberalism as a set of principles rules undivided across the globe: the most successful ideology in world history' (2000: 17). And yet, I wish to argue, this too shall pass and, indeed, is already passing.

Why? On what basis, given current conditions, might we reasonably expect a renewal of socialism? 'Current conditions' are precisely that basis. For the triumph of unfettered markets, history shows, cannot long endure; it is self-negating. This insight was well expressed more than fifty years ago by Karl Polanyi in his 1944 masterwork, *The Great Transformation*. It is worth quoting Polanyi at some length on the disastrous consequences of the 'crude fictions' of market societies:

> To allow the market mechanism to be the sole director of the fate of human beings and their natural environment ... would result in the demolition of society. For the alleged commodity 'labor power' cannot be shoved about, used indiscriminately, or even left unused, without affecting also the human individual who happens to be the bearer of this particular commodity.... Robbed of the protective covering of cultural institutions, human beings would perish from the effects of social exposure; they would die as victims of acute social dislocation.... Nature would be reduced to its elements, neighborhoods and landscapes defiled, rivers polluted ... the power to produce food and raw materials destroyed.... Undoubtedly, labor, land, and money markets *are* essential to a market economy. But no society could stand the effects of such a system of crude fictions even for the shortest stretch of time unless its human and natural substance ... was protected against this satanic mill. (Polanyi 1957 [1944]: 73)

Of course, as Polanyi himself documented, notwithstanding their need for 'protective covering' from the market, many people *did* die of 'social exposure', neighborhoods and landscapes *were* defiled, and rivers *were* polluted. And yet Polanyi also noted that 'simultaneously a countermovement was afoot. This was more than the usual defensive behavior of a society faced with change; it was a reaction against a dislocation which attacked the fabric of society, and which would have destroyed the very organization of production that the market had called into being' (Polanyi 1957: 130).

The central component of this transnational countermovement, which saved capitalism from itself in Polanyi's view, was undoubtedly the socialist movement of the nineteenth and early twentieth centuries. Today, we are witnessing, I believe, the incipient stages of a similar transnational countermovement against an apparently triumphant market capitalism. And, as before, the central thrust of this countermovement is socialist, in practice if not in name, albeit a socialism with environmentalist and feminist inflections. Whether this new movement will bury or save global capitalism from itself remains to be seen.

The signs of this emergent countermovement are hardly obscure. They include the rebellion in Caracas, Venezuela – the so-called *Caracazo*[1] – and its still unfolding aftermath; widespread protests against the 'structural adjustment' policies of the International Monetary Fund; the indigenous rebellions in Chiapas, Mexico, and in Bolivia and Ecuador; the massive movement of the landless in Brazil; and of course the mass protests against corporate globalization in Seattle, Washington, Prague, Quebec City, Genoa and beyond (Cockburn and St. Clair 2000). And these are only some of the most visible signs of popular protest motivated and indeed organized by and against corporate globalization and its aftershocks, from South Korea to South Africa, from the sweatshops of El Salvador to those of Los Angeles and New York.

Clearly, not all the reactions against globalization – in fact, comparatively few – are explicitly or primarily socialist in ideological orientation (let alone revolutionary in their strategic orientation). Some assume the mantle of nationalism, others of ethnicity and still others do not have much ideological coloration at all. The remarkable protests against corporate globalization in the United States and Western Europe, for their part, have not been altogether clear about what, if anything, they are actually *for*. 'The time has come', suggests Boris Kagarlitsky, 'for left activists not just to denounce globalisation, but to formulate their own demands' (2000: 51). The call for 'fair trade', for its part, has potentially radical implications, although it is also fully compatible with corporate globalization.

Much of the emergent countermovement against global capitalism, however, is at least *implicitly* or practically socialist (with a small 's') insofar as it seeks to seek to publicize (literally, to make public) and ultimately to socialize the processes by which authoritative decisions about global economic as well as political affairs are now privately – that is, secretively – made. 'The sin of capitalism', wrote W.E.B. Du Bois, 'is secrecy: the deliberate concealing of the character, methods, and results of efforts to satisfy human wants.... Not mass production but mass concealment is the sin of the capitalistic system' (1965 [1946]: 257). By publicizing the (mis)uses of 'private' capital, as well as public and natural resources, the anti-globalization movement also seeks, through mechanisms that have not yet been clearly articulated, to 'de-commodify' labor, natural resources and capital itself: to replace the logic of the market, in other words – somehow, and as quickly as possible – with a logic of public transparency and democratic accountability.

This implicitly socialist reaction to globalization is a social fact. The key questions are not whether or when it will happen, for it has been under-way for more than a decade, at least. Rather, the key questions pertain to the goals that this new anti-corporate movement or, more accurately, *movements* will set for themselves, the strategies and tactics they will adopt, and the likelihood of their success.

In terms of goals, a whole range of crucial questions remain unanswered and even unasked. What mix of local, national and transnational institu-tions should make, or at least regulate, the major economic decisions that are now determined, more or less unilaterally, by multinational corpora-tions and unaccountable transnational agencies? Will national states be the ultimate arbiter of such decisions or will it be necessary (and possible) to create effective international institutions for this purpose? And how will local communities and subnational regions participate, if at all, in such national or transnational institutions? What mix of markets and politics will new socialist movements demand, assuming that forms of socialism based on nationalized property and national economic planning are un-viable? Is a transnational version of even limited, Scandinavian-style social democracy possible? Will more radical or participatory forms of socialism prove attractive? To whom? Sooner or later, new socialist movements will have to answer these questions, which include the same big questions that were addressed by socialists of the Second International during the first global reaction to corporate liberalism, prior to the Russian revolution: What type of socialism is desirable, and possible? And how do we get there?

The Decline of Revolution in the Contemporary Period

This last question brings us to the topic of this volume, namely, the future of revolutions in an age of globalization. In my own view, many new socialist movements will of necessity be militant and even violent, but very few of them will be practically (as opposed to rhetorically) revolu-tionary, in the sense of seeking to recast radically whole societies by seizing state power through extraparliamentary, though not necessarily violent, means. As a result, there will be fewer social revolutions in the foreseeable future than occurred in the recent past. (Regime transitions and demo-cratic revolutions, on the other hand, are more likely, albeit precisely to the extent that they eschew radical change, as I argue below.)

The decline of great Revolutions (with a capital 'R') is already evident in the post-cold war era. We have witnessed considerable ethnic conflict and several regime changes in recent years, including popular revolts in Indonesia and Serbia which unseated dictators but did not bring about substantial socioeconomic change. The rebellion in Chiapas contributed significantly to the democratization of Mexico and inspired millions of people in Mexico and beyond, but the Zapatista movement failed to spread beyond a few rather isolated regions of that state. In fact, not a single social revolution has occurred in the dozen or so years since 1989, nor does one seem likely in the immediate future. Of course, this period may be too short to draw firm conclusions about broad historical tendencies, but I believe that the absence of social revolutions in the post-cold war period is far from coincidental. The conclusion to be drawn from this fact, however, is not that history has somehow ended; mass movements for social justice obviously continue and, I have suggested, are likely to become even more prominent in the medium term. For good political and strategic reasons, however, most of these movements are not and will probably not become revolutionary, and those that do will find it more difficult than ever to seize power.

Before examining these political and strategic realities, however, I should note that this reading of contemporary global politics is in no sense a conservative position, as it might appear. It is, I think, a realistic position. Lenin and Trotsky were famously pessimistic about the prospects for revolution on the very eve of the Russian revolution, but that hardly made them conservatives. And cold warriors were hardly radicals because they accepted the 'domino theory', according to which revolutions were a real and even likely possibility from India to Japan. My pessimistic assessment of the likelihood of future revolutions is simply orthogonal to any particular political or moral stance. With Gramsci, moreover, one may be an optimist of the will and a pessimist of the intellect.

The decline of revolution, furthermore, is not something that should immobilize socialists or other people concerned with social justice. After all, it is not as if social revolutions have an unblemished record in terms of bringing about peace, justice, democracy and equality. It is no longer possible, if it ever was, to believe in the inherent progressivity of revolutions. Not after Stalin, Mao, Kim Il Sung, Pol Pot, Khomeini and Abimael Guzmán's 'Shining Path'. The burden of proof in this respect falls clearly upon those who would claim that 'the social injustices of this world can be erased only by revolutionary means' (Harris 2000 [1970]: 20). I personally do not accept this view, which seems to me a truly pessimistic position, but neither ought one subscribe to the notion that social revolutions – whatever the intentions of revolutionaries – are *inherently* disastrous in their consequences. According to this view, the breakdown of state power, which is a defining feature of social revolutions, invariably touches off a bloody struggle among rival domestic actors and foreign powers to reconsolidate power. According to Jack Goldstone,

> The exigencies of this struggle generally lead to terror, disorder, and the growing dominance of military men. The rebuilt armies of the revolution embody its energy and ideals but have little patience with national democracy or individual freedom.... In short, revolution is not part of the solution to authoritarianism and tyranny; instead it is part – indeed, a recurrent part – of the problem. (1991: 479–80)

This view seems overdrawn to me, failing to describe accurately the course and consequences of a good many revolutions. Still, there is more than a kernel of truth to this perspective. Socialists and other progressives certainly cannot assume that revolution will get them where they want to go. We must at least ask – and here I agree completely with John Foran's reflections in this volume – how future revolutions might have better endings. To paraphrase Marx, the socialist movements of the twenty-first century cannot draw their poetry from the past, but only from the future. And of course socialists and other radicals must continually strive to redress or mitigate social injustices in ways that fall short – perhaps well short – of revolution.

In thinking about the likelihood of future revolutions, we should also remember that great revolutions have *always* been relatively rare and unexpected. Those who have planned (or simply predicted) revolutions – including revolutions that would have better endings than those that came before – have failed much more often than they have succeeded. Eric Hobsbawm (1962) wrote a book about a putative 'age of revolutions', stretching from 1789 to 1848, during which precisely one successful revolution occurred. During the two centuries prior to the Second World War, in fact, there occurred exactly three social revolutions: the French, Russian and Mexican. Many more revolutions occurred during the cold war era, but, as I have argued elsewhere (Goodwin 2001a), almost all of these were incubated by, and overthrew, three rather peculiar types of political order that have now almost completely passed from the scene: the rigidly exclusionary colonies of relatively weak imperial powers (Vietnam, Algeria, Angola, Mozambique); personalistic, 'above class' dictatorships (Cuba, Iran, Nicaragua); and dependent, Soviet-imposed Communist regimes (Eastern Europe). Broad, multiclass coalitions overthrew these unusually narrow political orders, which even economic elites and foreign patrons eventually abandoned. Very few political orders, it must be stressed, facilitate the formation of such broad revolutionary coalitions.

In fact, much of my pessimism – or is it optimism? – about the future prospects for great revolutions stems precisely from the character of the *political contexts* in which new movements currently find themselves. With few exceptions, these political contexts are simply not conducive to successful revolutionary struggles. (This is not to say, of course, that popular or revolutionary movements that have little chance of seizing power may not be morally justified or politically important. This is another matter altogether.) How exactly have current political conditions, considered on a global level, made great revolutions more difficult? And is 'globalization' to blame?

Some have suggested, certainly, that globalization has destroyed the very rationale for revolutions. According to this perspective, state power – that great prize of revolutionaries – has been dramatically eroded by the growing power of multinational corporations and transnational financial institutions and by the increasingly rapid and uncontrollable movements of capital, commodities and people. These realities, according to Charles Tilly, 'undermine the autonomy and circumscription of individual states, make it extremely difficult for any state to carry on a separate fiscal, welfare or military policy, and thus reduce the relative advantage of controlling the apparatus of a national state' (1993: 247). In other words, the more globalization diminishes and hollows out state power, the less rational becomes *any* political project aimed at capturing state power, including revolution.

I believe that globalization has helped make revolutions less likely, but not for this rather dubious reason. Rather than uniformly diminishing states, in fact, globalization has been just as likely to spur attempts to employ and, if necessary, expand state power for the purposes of enhancing global competitiveness. Historically, in fact, there has been a strong *positive* correlation between a country's exposure to external economic competition and the size of its public sector (Evans 1997). Some have argued that globalization is itself a *project* of strong states (Weiss 1997). Popular support for revolutionaries, in any event, is usually not based on estimations of their likely success in enhancing the autonomy of a country's fiscal policy or even its longterm global competitiveness. Rather, ordinary folk have typically supported revolutionaries when the latter have spoken up for them where no one else would (or could), provided for their subsistence, defended their traditional rights and, not least, protected them from state violence. As Jorge Castañeda has argued, mass support for revolution typically derives less from attractive visions of the future – although such visions have been important for intellectuals – than from a widely shared conviction that the status quo is simply unendurable:

> The rationale for revolution, from seventeenth-century England to Romania at the close of the second millennium, has always lain as much in the moral indignation aroused by an unacceptable status quo as in the attraction exercised by an existing blueprint for the future. The most powerful argument in the hands of the left in Latin America – or anywhere else – has never been, and in all likelihood will never be, exclusively the intrinsic merit or viability of the alternative it proposes. Its strong suit is the morally unacceptable character of life as the overwhelming majority of the region's inhabitants live it. (Castañeda 1993: 254)

There is no reason to believe, in any event, that in the future people will accept the depredations of authoritarian states and shun revolutionaries on the grounds that state power 'ain't what it used to be'.

Democracy as a Barrier to Revolution

In my view, the current period is unlikely to exhibit the same *scale* of revolutionary conflict as the cold war era primarily because of the wide diffusion of formally democratic and quasi-democratic electoral regimes throughout much of Latin America, Eastern Europe and parts of Asia and Africa during the past two decades. This is a development for which revolutionaries themselves can take considerable credit. And yet, be this as it may, these types of regimes are powerfully counterrevolutionary. It is not coincidental, in fact, that no popular revolutionary movement has ever overthrown a consolidated democratic regime. Certainly, no consolidated democracy is today even remotely threatened by a revolutionary movement – not in Western or Eastern Europe, Japan, North America, Costa Rica, Australia or New Zealand. As one noted sociologist has written,

> There is now no substantial reason to believe that marxist revolutions will come about in the foreseeable future in any major advanced capitalist society. In fact, the revolutionary potential – whatever the phrase may reasonably mean – of wageworkers, labor unions and political parties, is feeble. This is true of the generally prosperous post-World War II period; it was also true of the thirties when we witnessed the most grievous slump so far known by world capitalism. Such facts should not *determine* our view of the future, but they cannot be explained away by references to the corrupt and corrupting 'misleaders of labor', to the success of capitalist propaganda, to economic prosperity due to war economy, etc. Assume all this to be true; still the evidence points to the fact that, without serious qualification, wageworkers under mature capitalism do accept the system. Wherever a labor party exists in an advanced capitalist society, it tends either to become weak or, in actual policy and result, to become incorporated within the welfare state apparatus. (Mills 1962: 468–9)

These words were written four decades ago – although they require not the slightest revision – not by a conservative, but by the radical sociologist C. Wright Mills.

Why is democracy so inhospitable to revolutionaries? First and foremost, democracy pacifies and institutionalizes – but does not eliminate – many forms of social conflict. Seymour Martin Lipset (1960: ch. 7) has aptly referred to elections as a 'democratic translation of the class struggle'. Indeed, democracy 'translates' and channels a variety of social conflicts – including, but not limited to, class conflicts – into party competition for votes and the lobbying of representatives by 'interest groups'. Of course, this 'translation' involves distortions and sometimes provokes violence, especially when and where the procedural fairness of electoral contests has been widely questioned. But the temptation to rebel against the state – which is rarely acted upon without trepidation, given its typically life-or-death consequences – is partly quelled under democratic regimes by the knowledge that new elections are but a few years off and with them the chance to punish incumbent rulers.

Even more importantly, democracies have generally provided a context in which ordinary people, through popular protest, can win important concessions from economic and political elites, although this often requires a good deal of disruption, if not violence (Gamson 1975; Piven and Cloward 1977). But armed struggles that are aimed at *overthrowing* elected governments rarely win extensive popular support unless such governments (or the armies that they putatively command) effectively push people into the armed opposition by indiscriminately repressing suspected rebel sympathizers. As Che Guevara wrote,

> It must always be kept in mind that there is a necessary minimum without which the establishment and consolidation of the first [guerrilla] center [*foco*] is not practicable. People must see clearly the futility of maintaining the fight for social goals within the framework of civil debate.... Where a government has come into power through some form of popular vote, fraudulent or not, and maintains at least an appearance of constitutional legality, the guerrilla outbreak cannot be promoted, since the possibilities of peaceful struggle have not yet been exhausted. (1985 [1960]: 50–51)[2]

With very few exceptions, to paraphrase Alan Dawley (1976: 70), the ballot box has been the coffin of revolutionaries.

Does the foregoing mean that political radicalism and militancy go unrewarded in democratic societies? Hardly. Democracy, to repeat, does not eliminate social conflict; in fact, in many ways democracy encourages social conflict by providing the institutionalized 'political space' or 'political opportunities' with which those groups outside elite circles can make claims on political authorities and economic elites (Tarrow 1994). Not just political parties, then, but a whole range of interest groups, trade unions, professional associations, social movements and even transnational networks become the main organizational vehicles, or 'mobilizing structures', of political life in democratic polities. But these institutions of 'civil society' are generally just that – civil. Their repertoires of collective action include electoral campaigns, lobbying, petitions, strikes, boycotts, peaceful demonstrations and civil disobedience – forms of collective action that may be undertaken with great passion and militancy (and sometimes for quite radical ends), and which sometimes involve or provoke violence, but which are *not* aimed at bringing down the state. (Nor are riots, from which democracies are hardly immune, revolutionary in this sense.) So, whereas radicals and militants (socialist or otherwise) may survive and even thrive under democracy, or at least some democracies, revolutionaries seldom do.

Democracy, then, dramatically reduces the likelihood of revolutionary change, but *not* because it brings about social justice (although justice *is* sometimes served under democracies). Formal democracy, as we all know from practical experience, is fully compatible with widespread poverty, inequality, racism and social ills of all sorts, which is why Karl Marx criticized 'political emancipation' and so-called bourgeois democracy in the name of 'human emancipation'. The prevalence of poverty and other social problems is precisely why extraparliamentary movements for social justice so often arise in democratic contexts. These movements, however, almost always view the state as an instrument to be pressured and influenced, not as something to be seized or smashed. To be pessimistic, then, about the likelihood of revolutions during the current period is not at all to be pessimistic about the likelihood of mass struggles for social justice or socialism.

It might be objected that many of the new democracies in the 'Third World' are not 'real' democracies at all. But even imperfect and poorly consolidated democracies tend to defuse revolutionary pressures. The neglected case of Honduras illustrates this point well (Booth and Walker 1993: ch. 8; Goodwin 2001a: ch. 5). During the 1980s, violent revolutionary conflicts raged in neighbouring countries, but Honduras remained relatively quiescent. No significant revolutionary movement challenged the Honduran state, despite levels of poverty, landlessness, dependence and inequality which rivaled or surpassed those of its neighbours, and despite the existence of several small revolutionary groups that attempted to recruit supporters. Although several elections took place in Honduras during the 1980s, the democratic regime in that country was (and remains) deeply flawed. The two dominant political parties were (and remain) virtually indistinguishable. A special battalion in the armed forces, moreover, 'disappeared' more than a hundred actual or suspected radicals. Still, the government generally tolerated and occasionally granted concessions to trade unions and peasant organizations. Dissident intellectuals and human rights activists spoke out against the government. Most importantly, the armed forces in Honduras never indiscriminately attacked peasant villages or popular organizations in the manner of their Salvadoran or Guatemalan counterparts. As a result, Hondurans never felt the need to join or support revolutionaries in order to defend themselves or to improve their welfare. So, although Honduras's quasi-democracy did few things well, it was very effective at preventing the emergence of a revolutionary movement.

History shows, in fact, that people do not turn to revolution easily. I think Leon Trotsky put it best: 'People do not make revolution eagerly any more than they do war. There is this difference, however, in that in war compulsion plays the decisive role, in revolution there is no compulsion except that of circumstances. A revolution takes place only when there is no other way out' (Trotsky 1961 [1932]: 167). Actually, compulsion may play a *very* important role in revolutions, but this only reinforces Trotsky's point about the lack of eagerness with which most people embrace revolutionary politics. Revolution is usually a last, desperate resort.

A new era of widespread revolutionary conflict will surely dawn, if my analysis is right, if the most recent wave of democratization dramatically recedes – if, that is, the democracies and quasi-democracies in Latin America, Eastern Europe, Asia and Africa are replaced by violent authoritarian regimes. (Revolutionaries are unlikely to overthrow such regimes, however, unless they are unusually weak or suddenly weakened; even powerful revolutionary movements, we need to remember, do not always succeed.) A widespread reversion to violent authoritarianism seems unlikely, however, if only because economic and political elites, including even army officers, seem increasingly aware of the growing costs of political violence in a globalized economy and of the unique vulnerabilities of narrow dictatorships in particular. The United States government has become increasingly astute at 'sacrificing dictators to save the state' (Petras and Morley 1990: ch. 4) – that is, pre-empting revolution by abandoning or replacing dictators (Marcos, Duvalier, Noriega, Mobutu, Suharto and Milošević) in favor of more broadly based and even formally democratic regimes. Since the 1980s, in fact, the United States government has proactively sponsored a number of formally democratic or 'polyarchal' regimes in the Third World, where it previously supported authoritarian regimes as the best guarantors of its geopolitical and economic interests

(Robinson 1996). This does not mean that US foreign policymakers or Third World elites have suddenly become humanitarians; they have learned, rather, that formal democracy may be a powerful barrier to revolution.

Globalization and Democracy

Democracy may be an especially powerful barrier to revolution in an age of corporate globalization. And globalization, in turn, may help underpin democracy. Certainly, the unprecedented speed and mobility of capital in the current era hang like the sword of Damocles over those on both the left and right who would disrupt predictable business climates and 'investor confidence'. In the new world order, the fear of capital flight or boycott may stay the hand of would-be Pinochets as well as that of would-be Lenins. Globalization, in other words, notwithstanding its often disastrous socioeconomic effects on working people, may actually help undermine authoritarianism and preserve democratic and quasi-democratic regimes. This may explain the striking coincidence of globalization and democratization, which many analysts view as contradictory, during the past two decades. Elisabeth Wood, for example, has shown how globalization facilitated democratization – and defused revolutionary challenges – in El Salvador and South Africa: the integration of domestic markets into the global economy and 'the growing hegemony of neoliberal economic policies made it unlikely that postconflict states would have the capacity to implement confiscatory redistributive policies that would threaten elite interests. Deviation from the neoliberal model would be punished by capital movements' (Wood 2000: 15). Globalization thus provided an incentive for previously authoritarian economic elites finally to accept the full political inclusion of subordinate classes, since the latter would have limited means to threaten elite interests. In effect, elites accepted democracy, while their opponents accepted capitalism. Today, the former revolutionaries of El Salvador's Farabundo Martí National Liberation Front (FMLN) and South Africa's African National Congress (ANC) seek at most to reform capitalism, not to overthrow it.

Capital mobility also haunts the 'parliamentary road' to revolutionary change. For the reasons previously discussed, this is not a well-trodden path. (And the best example of it, the Popular Unity government in Chile, suggests how truly treacherous it can be.) Those tempted to take this path to revolution will face the same threats as erstwhile revolutionaries in El Salvador and South Africa: capital flight, capital boycott and the economic nightmare that would predictably follow. In fact, the more tightly a national economy (to the extent that this concept still makes sense) is integrated into global circuits of capital, the greater the economic costs of any anti-capitalist political program. Some of these costs might be avoided if a whole bloc of countries simultaneously enacted such a program, but this scenario – so ardently hoped for by Trotsky, Lenin and the old Bolsheviks after the Russian revolution – seems no more probable than in the past. On the other hand, it would presumably be the 'parliamentary road' to revolution which would be taken if and when masses of people in a democracy – ideally, a substantial majority – became convinced that radical socioeconomic change was the only solution to their most urgent, everyday problems. In the midst of a very severe economic crisis, such a possibility certainly cannot be ruled out. Yet revolutionaries would no doubt have to compete for popular support in this context with reformists and populists of various types, including proponents of authoritarian 'solutions'. Even severe capitalist crises, history teaches us, do not guarantee radical, let alone revolutionary, change.

Finally, as a political project of the most advanced capitalist countries, especially the United States, corporate globalization seeks to undermine all forms of economic nationalism and clientelism, whether of the left or right, and to foster the type of free trade that powerful multinational banks and corporations will inevitably dominate. Globalization thus abhors the autocratic and oligarchic forms of 'crony capitalism' that nurtured so many revolutionary movements during the past century. In short, Lenin was undoubtedly right to argue that formal democracy provides the ideal 'political shell' for capitalism.

Revolutions, in sum, will undoubtedly continue to occur in those societies characterized by a combination of gross economic injustices and extreme political exclusion and repression by weak or suddenly weakened states. However, due partly to globalization and partly to revolutions themselves, the latter factor is rather less prevalent today than in the past, and it may become rarer still. The *political* and *geopolitical* contexts, especially, that the new movements against global capitalism currently confront, and are likely to confront for the foreseeable future, are not nearly as conducive to the strategy of revolution as during the cold war era. Yet this hardly implies that history has ended or that socialism is dead. Mass movements against globalization, among other continuing conflicts, are an ineradicable feature of the current period. Most of these movements will attempt to enact reforms through militant extra-parliamentary struggles or by winning a share of power through electoral means. They are no less important than revolutionary movements, and no less worthy of critical intellectual support, for having chosen this path.

Notes

1. The *Caracazo* of February 1989, which was sparked by a rise in gasoline prices (and, accordingly, bus fares), and which was part of President Carlos Andrés · Pérez's IMF-backed neoliberal economic program, resulted in hundreds and perhaps thousands of deaths. It marked the beginning of the end of Venezuela's two-party system and the concomitant rise to power of the military populist Hugo Chávez. Pérez himself was impeached and removed from office in 1993 on charges of corruption (see Gott 2000).

2. Unwisely, Guevara later abandoned this view, claiming that even democracies could be toppled by revolutionaries.

6

Will Democratization and Globalization Make Revolutions Obsolete?

Misagh Parsa

Revolutions are very complex phenomena and, consequently, very difficult to predict. They often involve the breakdown of the social, political and economic structures of societies. Theories of revolution must take into account a large number of variables that contribute to societal breakdown and large-scale social conflict, among them international conditions and forces, which affect the likelihood and even the nature of revolutions. Although several generations of scholarly works have emerged in the past few decades, no single theory or model can explain the entire process that results in revolution.

A fruitful analysis of revolutions may emerge by linking structural and process approaches. This perspective is rooted in an examination of state structures, process approaches that predict the eruption of social conflicts, and those variables that facilitate coalition formation and the disruption of the social structure. Each perspective contributes to an understanding of the very complex processes that culminate in large-scale social conflicts and revolutions in developing countries. Structural theories analyze the nature of the state and the economy within the context of the larger world system, the structure of the state and the polity, and the state's relation to various social classes. In structural theories, an analysis of the nature of the state and economy is central to the study of revolutions. These variables help illuminate the extent of state vulnerabilities and the likelihood that the state will become the target of attack. They also enhance an understanding of the extent of possible opposition to the state in times of social conflict and crisis. Process approaches help explain the timing and nature of social conflict and collective action as well as the

73

likelihood of coalition formation and the disruption of the social structure. Of course, any analysis of social revolution must also explain the
causes of the rise of radical challengers to positions of leadership. In combination, these perspectives can help explain a great deal about the causes
and processes of revolutions. A complete analysis of revolution must also
examine the structure of the armed forces and their relationship to the
civilian population, as well as external forces and international conditions.
In the following, however, I will primarily focus on structural changes
that affect the likelihood of revolutions. The analysis will draw heavily
from my recent work on revolutions in Iran, Nicaragua and the Philippines
(Parsa 2000).

In broad outline, democratization and the emergence of a global market
economy seem to set in motion complex and contradictory forces in the
political systems of developing countries. While some changes point in the
direction of the reduced likelihood of revolutions and social revolutions in
particular, others point to the continuation of intense conflicts. On the
one hand, democratization, reduced state intervention, and the expansion
of markets may remove the state as the principal target of attack for
challengers. At the same time, democratic institutions may strengthen the
position of moderate challengers and diminish the likelihood of coalition
formation between moderate and revolutionary challengers. This, in turn,
may isolate and render ineffective radical revolutionary challengers. These
structural transformations should tend to reduce the likelihood of revolutionary conflicts and revolutions.

On the other hand, expanding market forces and the growing integration of developing economies into the global capitalist system tend to
increase social and economic inequalities and expose national economies
to the vagaries of the world market, adversely affecting various segments
of the population. Rising social and economic inequalities have the
potential to generate two kinds of conflict. The expansion of market
forces may intensify class and regional conflict and generate movements
for social change. Alternatively, integration into the global economy may
produce broad nationalist movements against external forces that adversely
affect the population. In either case, the intensification of these conflicts
may result in large-scale social violence and possibly revolutionary challenges or the reimposition of authoritarian rule and the elimination of
democratic institutions.

States that are characterized by exclusive rule tend to become vulnerable to challenge and attack in times of crisis. Such states contract the
scope of the polity and block access to the state and the centers of political
power. They often tend to eliminate or render irrelevant formal demo-

cratic institutions. In extreme cases, highly exclusive states may develop an exceedingly personalistic rule, which virtually excludes the entire population, even the economic elite, from decision-making and government resources. Such regimes also tend to minimize or eliminate accountability to the public and rule independently of the underlying population (McDaniel 1991: 6; Midlarsky and Roberts 1986: 24–7). Centralized, dynastic regimes are especially vulnerable because they restrict elite access to the polity and remain exclusive for prolonged periods without providing any option for change (Foran 1997a: 229; Goodwin 1994: 758; Snyder 1998: 56). To remain in power, such regimes may have to resort to continuous violence and repression to demobilize or eliminate their opponents. The continuous use of repression may reduce social support for the regime and force it to become dependent on both the military and external support to maintain power.

Many twentieth-century revolutions occurred in Third World countries with highly centralized and exclusive states. The Pahlavis and Somozas had established regimes that lasted for decades and excluded the vast majority of the population from the polity. Power was transferred from father to son with no option for others to gain control over state power. As a result, these rulers denied access to the polity not only to the moderate opposition but also to large segments of the upper class. Both regimes also became highly dependent on coercion and the power of the military and the United States for survival.

Exclusion and repression affected the nature of the conflicts and mobilization options available in the conflicts. Repression generally led to the radicalization of segments of the population, particularly students, who were in the forefront of revolutionary struggles. Repression also weakened or eliminated the moderate, reformist political challengers in favor of radical revolutionaries. The regimes in both Iran and Nicaragua either severely repressed the moderate opposition, as in Iran, or rendered them ineffective, as in the case of Nicaragua. As a result, moderate, reformist challengers were obliged to form coalitions with radical challengers and even accept their leadership. Exclusion and repression also encouraged radical challengers to wage armed struggle against such regimes. In combination, these factors provided the ground for the hegemony of radical challengers who pressed for social revolutions once in power.

To the extent that the new political structures in developing countries are marked by lower levels of centralization and exclusive rule, they will reduce the likelihood of large-scale political conflicts and revolutions. The development of formal democratic institutions, which expand the polity and permit moderate political organizations and challengers access to the state, tends to reduce the radicalization of segments of the population, particularly the middle class. Democratic institutions may also strengthen the position of moderate challengers and isolate and render ineffective revolutionary and radical challengers. These processes, in turn, diminish the likelihood of coalition formation among reformist and revolutionary challengers and thus reduce the likelihood of social revolutions. The elimination of repressive measures and the development of formal democratic institutions also tend to reduce the likelihood of support for armed struggle that often favored the hegemony of radical challengers. The end result of democratization may be both the decline of large-scale social conflicts and the decline of the fortunes of radical political challengers.

State intervention in the economy also affects the nature of development and revolutionary conflicts. High levels of state intervention expand the extent of political conflicts because of the convergence of economic and political conflicts in the political arena. In addition to ordinary political conflicts, states also become the center for economic conflicts. High state intervention replaces the abstract, decentralized and depoliticized market mechanism with a visible, concrete, social entity, which can be attacked during conflict or crisis (Parsa 1989; Rueschemeyer and Evans 1985: 69). The level of state intervention also affects the nature and the outcome of social and political conflicts. While low state intervention encourages disadvantaged collectivities to demand state intervention on their behalf, higher levels of intervention tend to encourage such collectivities to target the state for attack. Where state intervention is low and market forces predominate, disadvantaged collectivities mobilize to demand that the government intervene in the social structure and the economy on their behalf. Most of the social movements in the twentieth-century United States mobilized to alter certain aspects of the social system. Much of the labor struggle during the Great Depression and the civil rights movement of the 1960s remained within this reformist framework (Parsa 1985).

Conversely, where state intervention is high, it reduces the range and operation of the market, politicizes economic processes and conflicts, and renders the state vulnerable to challenge and attack. In periods of economic decline or crisis, highly interventionist governments are directly blamed for economic mismanagement; disadvantaged and excluded collectivities target the state and act collectively to change the situation. States in tsarist Russia and Iran were highly interventionist prior to their revolutions in 1917 and 1979. When the crisis precipitated, both regimes became easy targets to attack and were overthrown in revolutions. In addition, the level of state intervention affects the nature of class conflict and consequently the likelihood for coalition formation. A low level of state intervention insulates the state from economic conflicts. Consequently, social conflicts tend to be confined among contending social classes. This, in turn, reduces the likelihood of coalitions among various social classes. In contrast, a high level of state intervention reduces the intensity of class conflicts and contributes to the formation of broader class coalitions. Workers and capitalists may set aside their own conflicts and join together to topple the state.

Many of the states that experienced revolutions in the twentieth century became hyperactive and intervened highly in the economy, which, in the long run, rendered them vulnerable to revolutionary challenges. In contrast to states in developed countries that remained regulative, states in developing countries intervened extensively in the economy to promote capital accumulation and development. These hyperactive states often became major economic actors and controlled a great deal of economic resources. Some of them became the loci of accumulation, directly producing goods and allocating capital. In extreme cases, the hyperactive states even became the single largest entrepreneur, industrialist, banker and landowner in the country.

Despite impressive growth, increased state intervention in many countries was also accompanied by development strategies that exacerbated social and economic inequalities and adversely affected certain social classes, setting the stage for social conflicts and, once again, rendering the state the principal target of attack. Government intervention often served the interests of large capital at the expense of medium and small capital. Interventionist states typically repressed working-class organizations and radicalized segments of labor. Such government policies served a narrow set of interests, inevitably politicized economic conflicts, and rendered the state vulnerable to challenge and attack. Conflicts against the state often reduced the intensity of class conflict and encouraged broad coalitions of workers and capitalists against the government. The formation of broad coalitions among major social groups and classes was important in Third World revolutions, particularly where states had remained intact or where insurgents had not succeeded in overthrowing the government through armed struggle. These coalitions, in turn, increased the likelihood of the overthrow of the interventionist states and revolutions. Such a coalition formed in both Iran and Nicaragua in the 1979 revolutions (Parsa 2000).

To the extent that governments become less hyperactive, less interventionist, and allow market forces to determine capital allocation and accumulation, the state will be insulated from the type of challenges that occurred during large-scale social conflicts in developing countries in the twentieth century. Thus, the state is unlikely to become the principal focus of attack where abstract, impersonal market forces determine economic processes. Although adversely affected collectivities and classes may organize and demand state intervention on their behalf, they may be less likely to organize to overthrow the state. In such conditions, the target of social conflict tends to be other social groups and classes, rather than the state. As a result, social conflicts become more segmented and fail to generate broad coalitions. The absence of such coalitions increases the likelihood of social reforms where adversely affected social groups and classes organize to pressure the government for moderate changes within the existing structures.

On the other hand, the current trend in reduced state intervention and the expansion of market forces may generate contradictions and crises that prepare the ground for conflicts. With increased globalization, economic decline or crisis in advanced industrial economies will affect developing countries more than ever before. As developing countries become increasingly integrated into the world economy, they remain vulnerable to the vagaries of the world market and decisions made by transnational corporations and financial institutions, as demonstrated in Brazil, Mexico, Thailand and South Korea. Market forces tend to generate economic swings that cannot be easily controlled, a trend that is likely to be intensified under conditions of greater integration into the world economy. Regional integration will also have broader implications in times of economic downturn, as occurred in 1998 with the decline in Asian markets.

In addition, the current trend toward greater economic integration may create new winners and losers across class lines and different economic sectors. With increased globalization, capital has gained an advantage over labor and is able to move across national boundaries on a very large scale. No other social group or class enjoys such a privilege. Although proponents of free markets and globalization defend the institution of private enterprise and private ownership of the means of production, in actuality competitive capitalism tends to eliminate smaller and weaker competitors, giving rise to greater concentration of capital and resources. The elimination of national capital by transnational corporations in such competitive markets can potentially adversely affect broad segments of the population in developing countries. These conditions may result in the formation of broad coalitions against adverse external forces. They may generate nationalist movements by the losing sectors and classes that may oppose powerful international actors, such as transnational corporations, the IMF and the World Bank. These movements and coalitions may demand greater state intervention and protection from unfavorable global trends.

Furthermore, the expansion of free markets may continue to exacerbate class, ethnic and regional inequalities. Although reduced state intervention may cut down on crony capitalism and state-sponsored accumulations of wealth, expanding market forces may also intensify inequalities among classes and regions in developing countries. Currently, with the expansion of market forces, economic disparities are on the rise virtually everywhere in the world. The gap between the rich and the poor of the world is widening at an alarming rate. The assets of the three richest people in the world in 1998 exceeded the combined GNP of the twenty-five least developed countries, with a population of over 500 million. Similarly, the assets of the 200 richest people in the world in the same year exceeded the combined income of 41 percent of the world's people (UNDP 1999: 38). The combined net worth of the 400 richest people in the United States amounted to $1.2 trillion in 1999, or slightly less than the GDP of the United Kingdom. William Gates's $63 billion in the fall of 2000 was larger than the GDP of Peru, which has a population of over 25 million (*Forbes*, 9 October 2000).

In the short run, these social and economic inequalities may not result in political conflicts. In the first place, social and economic inequalities that are generated through market mechanisms cannot be as easily politicized (Parsa 1989: 13–20). Adversely affected collectivities may blame themselves, fate or other causes for their misfortune and refrain from mobilization and collective action. Furthermore, rising income inequalities may not generate social conflicts if the earnings of the lower- and middle-income population continue to rise in absolute terms.

In the long run, however, rising social and economic inequalities that polarize the stratification system may generate causes for social conflict in at least parts of the developing world. Rising inequalities in the past tended to mobilize segments of the population, including the working and middle classes, for social change and greater equality. Rising inequalities also played a role in radicalizing students and segments of the working classes to mobilize for fundamental transformations of the social structure. Radical students and workers played crucial roles in the struggles against regimes in Iran, Nicaragua and the Philippines (Parsa 2000). In the future, these two collectivities may constitute the principal forces that favor radical transformations. Finally, rising inequalities may also intensify regional as well as ethnic conflicts, paving the way for separatist social movements. The struggles of the Kurds in Iran, Iraq and Turkey, and of the Muslim separatists in the Philippines are clear examples of the consequences of such unequal distribution and the mistreatment of ethnic minorities.

With the removal of authoritarian regimes, adversely affected social groups and classes will have greater capacities for mobilization and collective action in countries where formal democratic political institutions have been established. Those adversely affected by globalization now have greater access to international media and new means for communicating among themselves. Victims of globalization in various countries, particularly those located in the same geographic regions, will have enhanced capacities to develop solidarity beyond their national boundaries and struggle for common goals and interests. Unlike global capital that has the option of moving beyond national boundaries, most ordinary people do not enjoy such ease of movement. As capital becomes increasingly global, so does the struggle of those who are adversely affected by the large-scale movement of capital. The elimination or decline of repression will have a positive impact on the struggle of excluded populations to demand social justice, inclusion and greater social equality. Interest in maintaining democracy and a stable climate to attract foreign investment may restrain governments from repressing their people. States that are democratic will have to respond to the demands of the population.

Large-scale mobilization and collective actions will threaten the established rights and interests of privileged social groups and classes. Under such conditions, privileged groups and classes may favor limiting democratic rights and even the reimposition of authoritarian rule. Although the end of the cold war has eroded American support for such regimes, intensification of social conflicts in some countries may result in the reimposition of repression in order to maintain the existing order. Of course, such a move could backfire, increasing the chances for further radicalization of broader segments of the population, including the middle class, and formation of broad coalitions.

The imposition of authoritarian rule along with rising social and economic inequalities may, in time, provide opportunities for revolutionary challengers to mobilize and even gain the leadership of such movements. For social revolutions to occur, radical, revolutionary challengers must gain the leadership of movements for social change and social justice. The leadership of these challengers was essential in the social revolutions of the twentieth century. Revolutionary challengers were often in the forefront of political and ideological struggles in developing countries. These challengers were successful in ideologically converting and radicalizing students and youth for political struggles throughout much of the developing world. Radical, revolutionary challengers in Iran, Nicaragua and Philippines were able to launch their armed struggle with the support of university students. In both Nicaragua and the Philippines, revolutionary challengers were also able to gain the political and ideological support of segments of the working class. The support of these groups played a significant role in the political ascendancy of revolutionary challengers.

Recent scholarship seems to have overemphasized the role of revolutionary ideology of radical challengers (Skocpol 1982; Moaddel 1993; Farhi 1990; Colburn 1994). Some analyses of revolutions have portrayed ideology as an independent actor with its own powers and dynamic. Any analysis of ideology must examine its relationship to the existing social structure. Analyses that attribute sweeping powers to ideology tend to mystify it and isolate it from its social context and origin. Revolutionary ideology appeals differently to different groups in the social structure. Individual collectivities have different propensities towards different political ideologies, depending on their position in the social structure, regardless of the country or the culture. This is because the collectivities that carry out the revolutionary processes are located in different positions in the social structure and represent disparate interests and articulate different demands.

Furthermore, the states and social structures of the countries that experience social revolutions are not based on broad ideological consensus. Indeed, political repression and external support rather than ideological consensus played an important role in the formation and continuity of states in many of the countries that underwent revolutionary transformations. While revolutionary ideologies and challengers were popular among certain segments of the population, particularly students, analyses of social revolutions should not exaggerate the role of revolutionary ideologies in revolutions. Revolutionary challengers could not and did not always present all aspects of their ideologies to the public, either because of government repression or out of concern for broad political support and formation of coalitions. Radical challengers succeeded in seizing power through armed struggle or the formation of broad coalitions with moderate challengers often through compromise and modification of their ideology. In this connection it is crucial to note that in his messages during the revolutionary struggle Ayatollah Khomeini never told the Iranian people about his plans for a theocratic state in Iran (Parsa 1989 and 2000).

Of course, the weakening or virtual absence of revolutionary challengers in the past decade in the international arena has certainly reduced the likelihood of social revolutions. Although democratization has expanded the capacity of social groups to mobilize for collective action, the virtual absence or weakening of revolutionary challengers in many parts of the developing world has resulted in the elimination of the revolutionary agenda among major segments of the intelligentsia in the developing countries. Perhaps only major changes in the world economy, along with a polarization in the distribution of resources, may prepare the context for a shift in favor of revolutionary challengers.

In sum, economic vulnerability of developing countries in the context of greater integration in the world market, and rising social and economic inequalities, along with the expansion of higher education, may lead to continued threats of large-scale social conflicts and revolutions. Failure of genuine democratization will contribute to the continued involvement of students and youth in political struggles in developing countries, always in the vanguard of struggles for democracy and social justice in the Third World in the latter part of the twentieth century. Concentrated in colleges and universities, students possess a readily available communication network that can be activated for collective action. The expansion of new means of communication such as the Internet and e-mail throughout the developing world will only strengthen the capacity of students for mobilization and collective action. In addition, students enjoy immense prestige among the population in developing countries, and their insurgency often has some impact on society at large. Students also benefit from academic freedom and enjoy a measure of immunity from government repression. In combination, these factors have placed college and university students in the forefront of ideological and political struggles in developing countries. As long as rising social inequality and adverse global trends negatively affect developing countries, students will continue to struggle for social justice and democracy. Under such conditions, students and institutions of higher education will continue to produce dissident intellectuals and possibly radical challengers. Whatever the future direction, it appears that many of the factors that produce large-scale social conflicts and violence persist, at least in parts of the developing world.

7

Zapata's White Horse and Che's Beret: Theses on the Future of Revolution

Eric Selbin

Given recent pronouncements of the demise of revolution, perhaps a more apt title would be 'Fourteen Theses in Search of an Audience'. Over 150 years after Tocqueville announced that 'Great' revolutions would become more rare (1990: 251), a declaration which has reappeared with some regularity, a number of people assure us again that such phenomena are a thing of the past.[1] If revolutions which closely resemble our most common reference points – France, Russia, China, Cuba or Iran – may be scarce, it seems premature to dispense with a very basic assumption: people will struggle for liberty, equality, democracy, opportunity and freedom in a world where the material and ideological conditions of their daily lives reflect none of these and will do so using the array of tools at their disposal. Profoundly human creations rather than inevitable natural processes, revolutions do not come, they are made – to turn around Skocpol's (1979: 17) invocation of Phillips's memorable phrase.

There is no small irony that the declaration of the end of revolution has coincided with a renewed interest in revolution. After a relative lull, the study of revolution is increasing in popularity and there has been a veritable explosion of quality work on the topic; some have even detected the emergence of what may be the 'fourth generation of theorists of revolution' (Foran 1993; Emirbayer and Goodwin 1996: 374; Selbin 1997: 124; Goldstone 2001). And there are cases to consider: Chiapas in Mexico, Algeria, Colombia, Indonesia, Palestine and Nepal; there are even murmurs, however faint, about Russia.

Our propensity for subjecting puzzling moments of social disorder to the calming order of 'scientific' analysis has not provided the sensitive instruments necessary for exploring and explicating the puzzling enter-prise of revolution. Approaches overly reliant on the political, the psycho-logical, or the economic are ill equipped, for example, to capture the ways in which Zapata's white horse, Che's beret, Sandino's hat, Ho's pith helmet, bamboo walking stick and wispy beard, or Cabral's knit cap have become symbols freighted with significance and import, consequential in their invocation and deployment, their story – and the part they are made to play in other stories – contested by people from all sides in the struggle to articulate the case for or against revolution.

I contend that, along with the material or structural conditions which commonly guide our investigations, it is imperative to recognize the role played by stories, narratives of popular resistance, rebellion and revolution which have animated and emboldened generations of revolutionaries across time and cultures. To deepen our understandings of revolution, not least the future of such a concept in an increasingly globalized world, we need new approaches which serve not only to marry the 'traditional' tools of modern scholars but include the traditional tools of scholars and revolu-tionaries, powerful and purposive stories. Perhaps something like Marx's *Eighteenth Brumaire*, a wonderful and rich example of the sociological imagination at work, may be a guide. This far more modest contribution is meant to stimulate your imaginations. Rather than persuade you by argument, I hope what follows will prompt questions, open a discussion and get us to consider possibilities all too often shunted aside.

To this end, the ideas and pieces presented here represent what might be best construed as pre-theory, offering 'raw materials [that] may serve as the basis for all kinds of theories' (Rosenau 1980: 127). I have deliberately bitten off more than I can chew here and appropriate 'tests' of the utility of what follows are beyond the scope of this paper. It is my hope that eventually these will be a platform from which to address the intriguing issues of why revolutions are made here and not there, now and not then, among these people and not those, and whether people are likely to continue to do so.[2]

Theses on the Future of Revolution
I

Despite the propensity many of us share for discerning a single unbroken string of revolutions going back to 1789, there is no single tradition of revolutionary processes. A variety of people – revolutionaries, counter-revolutionaries, government bureaucrats and academics – have, for an array of reasons, created one. While this allows for useful and compelling comparisons to be drawn and suggests that there may be some 'deep rules' at play, most cases of revolution are more notable for their differences than their similarities. It is imperative that we explore and understand these differences even as we search for the common themes, the narrative, which connect, if at times tangentially, many of these processes. Thus at least part of the discussion over the future of revolution is profoundly intertwined with our conceptualization of revolution's past(s).

II

Any discussion of the past(s) should be approached with great caution. Beyond the problems of history in its many manifestations as well as the variety of extant memories – collective, collected, folkloric, mythic and so on – there is the trap of nostalgia. Nostalgia is a particular form of memory, often encountered in the context of the powerful who use it to legitimate their privileges and those who would read it as proof that the present is what is meant to be. But nostalgia also influences and impinges upon would-be revolutionaries and intellectuals, each group prone to relishing a heroic–mythic time which legitimates their struggles. Our effort must be to uncover and explore and illuminate our past(s) from a multiplicity of voices and an array of sources. This plurality of realities conspires to shape who and what we are, what we think is possible and why, how those things might be achieved, and what it will mean, or we hope it will mean, if and when we do. Thus the past(s) are remembered in the present[3] and our present desires envision our future. Despite our best efforts and the images of calendars, clocks and the like, none of these – past, present, future – is neatly demarcated from the others. As the nineteenth-century French historian Michelet said of France in 1789, 'On that day everything was possible ... the future was present ... that is to say time was no more, all a lightening flash of eternity' (quoted in Kimmel 1990: 186).[4] Even those who proclaim the demise of revolutions recognize that 'revolutions are like migrations to the future ... [where] the promised lands exist ... in the minds of those who believe in them' (Nodia 2000: 164). In either formulation, people forge what seems like the incredible opportunity to reshape their world and themselves.

III

Recognizing that revolution is inherently local and is fundamentally about the material and ideological conditions of people's everyday lives does not mean that global teleologies are irrelevant: they remain useful heuristics and certainly help explain international reactions to and behaviors toward revolutionary processes, even if they undervalue the profound role of human agency in bringing about such processes and sustaining their possibility. Connections between and among revolutionaries and revolutionary processes are deep and strong, whether the link is to France (liberté, égalité, fraternité) or Russia ('Bread, Peace and Land') or Mexico ('land and liberty'). But everywhere such 'universal' claims have been adopted, they have been adapted to exigencies of the local, wedded to stories specific to the case at hand. It is misleading to focus on *a* teleological dimension which has hypothetically linked two hundred years of revolutions. There is something a bit peculiar, unfortunately male, linear and rationalistic, about the notion that any one revolution – or, perhaps, the writings of Karl Marx – somehow provided *a* teleological dimension to revolution or revolutionary processes. Thus, if there was *a* teleological dimension to revolution, can we discern who created it, for whom, and why? We might even ask who exactly knew it was there?

IV

There is a global or transnational role played by the ideas, myths and conceptions which people share with one another. Hence an argument for the local is not to ignore that some sort of international revolutionary *bricolage* has emerged – a vocabulary of words and concepts from a variety of sources forged by people into some sort of practical ideology with which they confront the inequities and exigencies of their time and place, crafting new stories, new visions, out of old, while retaining important contextual links to the past. Thus memories of oppression, sagas of occupation and struggle, tales of opposition, myths of once and future glory, words of mystery and symbolism are appropriated from the pantheon of history of resistance and rebellion common to almost every culture and borrowed from others and fashioned into some sort of usable past which confronts the present and reaches out to the future. Stories establish obligations between past, present and future generations in which each generation is called to defend the struggles of previous ancestors and to fulfill a historic duty to the future (see for example Martin 1992: 178, who cites Benjamin 1969 [1940]: 254).

V

Long before the current fascination with globalization, revolutionaries constructed a global community, a web of myths, symbols and connections which served to support and nurture the irruption of revolutionary processes in a surprising number of places under a surprising array of circumstances. While this may be handily traced back to the 'subterranean revolutionary eschatology' of millennial Christianity (Cohn 1990) or the story of Exodus (Walzer 1985), I am inclined to think it is far more complicated, reflecting both roots that are far deeper and older as well as rhizomes spread very broad and shallow. The 'globalizing' efforts of the French revolutionaries, the Comintern, Che Guevara, Iran's mullahs, or Subcomandante Marcos suggest that whatever inhibitions the globalizing sweep of liberal democracy/late capitalism might present are unlikely to forestall the continued invocation and evocation of revolutionary calls and claims. Che Guevara, for example, now weaves in and out of history with incredible sinuosity, meandering and looping around not unlike old rivers, cutting through landscapes, leaving behind 'lost rivers', bends which become lakes, or even areas which become high and dry.[5] Will they wear Che T-shirts in Algiers as they did in Tehran in 1979? 'See' Zapata's horse in Havana as some did in Nicaragua? Sing the 'Internationale' or perhaps even air the 'Marseillaise' in Jakarta (the former happened in Namibia, the latter in El Salvador)? Or will they draw on other less 'globalized' figures, symbols and myths imbued with meanings we have yet to decipher, discern or define? How and why these will be written and constructed, by whom and for whom, and how they will be deployed, merits far more of our attention than they have received to date.

VI

'Globalization' – eerily reminiscent of what used to be called imperialism[6] – has clearly had enormous consequences. With apologies for some gross generalization on a heated debate, the primary causes of revolution in almost every conceptualization of the term remain profoundly present: it is a time of great global change, people are hungry and resent the widening gap between the rich and the poor, people are confronted by the failed promises of neoliberalism and/or liberal democracy, and people have a model – themselves, overflowing with historical narratives of rebellion and revolution and the possibilities inherent in creating a new world – and opportunity, as everyone struggles to define and decipher the (not-so) New World (dis)Order. Hence revolution is arguably as likely, perhaps even more likely than ever before; rather than a shrinking space for revolutionary and related processes, we may well witness more space for such activities not really the worse for having lost some vague imprimatur – usually conferred on them by others – of moribund revolutions elsewhere.

VII

Thus while we can reasonably construe ours as an age of globalization, there is much about that claim which remains unclear – the issues, the dynamics, the limits, the possibilities – in short, what globalization means, what the implications and ramifications are. Nowhere, it seems to me, is this truer than with regard to the relationship between this thing we call globalization and the material and ideological conditions of people's everyday lives. Despite the talk of globalization and its attendant glories, the immense majority of humanity remains profoundly immiserated, by any reasonable measure. Whether revolution will be an option they choose remains to be seen.

VIII

An approach is needed that collates and convenes political, social, economic, psychological and cultural perspectives, with apologies for the obvious overlap in some of these categories. That overlap may be the strength of such an approach. What they share, in part, is a recognition that people have long bonded together in groups for a variety of reasons and that those assemblages, however loose or (un)structured, however far flung, are fundamentally bound together by the stories they tell and the tales they weave. While there is a propensity, especially in the West and among academics, to render these tales with a familiar 'beginning–middle–end structure that describes some sort of change or development, as well as a cast of dramatis personae' (Steinmetz 1992: 490), there are many stories which are not nineteenth-century narrative novels replete with logical plot progressions and amazing closures. More often one encounters odd tales that pop up almost out of nowhere and disappear, leaving behind only traces.[7] Such tales may be ensconced within the dream worlds/times of myths, or may converge around popular 'trickster' tales (e.g. the 'Gueguense' in Nicaragua). They may appear in the guise of claims that Che was here, or there, able to cover enormous distances in moments; so too Cabral, apparently able to visit people in Mozambique in their dreams. Perhaps even in an implausible tale of Ho engaging President Roosevelt in a discussion of the US Declaration of Independence in Paris. Explicating and exploring stories of both types may well be our best bet for answering why revolutions are made here and not there, now and not then, by these folks and not those.

IX

People do not fight, do not risk their lives and those of their families, do not put their hopes and dreams on the line lightly; certainly they do not

do so for dry, distant, theoretical concepts. Revolutions are about passionate commitment and, as such, 'more cultural than social or economic in
their origins and unfolding, even if social and economic forms [are] both
critical cause and effect of cultural belief' (Higonnet 1998: 13, citing Furet
1999 [1995]). Thus, along with various social science measures, we must
search for something, perhaps a mythopoetic element, which moves
people's hearts as much as their heads. This thing we call globalization has
brought us to a time and place redolent of a magical realist novella replete
with forking paths, mystical markets, and things, not least liberal democracy, not what they seem. The fantastic, the mythic and the magical seem
commonplace.[8] While we may have seen the last revolutionary conflict of
the cold war era and arguably marked the end of a cycle of at least
nominally Marxist-Leninist (and later, Maoist) revolutions that began in
October 1917, does anyone really believe that the assorted events and
processes identified by at least three generations of scholars of revolution
and innumerable generations of revolutionaries will disappear? Túpac
Amaru in various guises will reappear from the dead, from the mists of
the jungle and time, a different person or persons occupying the same
space, echoing Marcos's contention that behind the ski masks are different
Marcoses (Marcoses creating neuroses for the Mexican government?) and
animating people to struggle.

X

A part of that reality is a timeless story told and retold, a story of brave,
valiant, committed people, often youth, who realizing the gross inequities
of their situation or those of their parents/people rise up to demand
freedom, to demand equality, to demand justice. It is a tale as old as we
are, seeming to stretch as far back and almost certainly as far forward as
we can imagine and beyond. It is a tale told by neither idiots nor by
savants, though both may tell it. What seems key is that people want to
hear a story that they already know, with familiar characters, and action
they anticipate with fear or delight (a similar point is made by Bates 1996:
72). And there seems little question that there is a desire for heroes, quasi-
mythic but also human. Hence it is a story inscribed and reinscribed from
generation to generation, across myriad cultures in an astounding array of
places strewn across staggering reaches of time and an even more compelling panoply of peoples. Written within and outside of time, within and
against history determined by no one, structured only insofar as we im-
pute such structures (and the concomitant strictures) to it. As one scholar
of myths notes, 'myths survive for centuries, in a succession of incarnations,
both because they are available and because they are intrinsically

charismatic' (Doniger 2000: 26). These myths come to form a 'reality' defended, extended and maintained by people in song, in plays, in stories; their compelling articulation may be what moves people into, if more rarely through, a revolutionary process. In Chiapas, for example, it is possible to discern key pieces of the narrative: an endless struggle against occupation and oppression, for justice and dignity (and bread); stories/ tales/sagas/myths of the 'stranger from the north/south/east/west' as well as a tale of the return of the prodigal son, who will lead the people to the promised land. It is, in most of the ways that matter, the same story found in so many cultures across so many times.

XI

If there is a mythopoetic vision surprisingly basic and enduring, featuring stock characters and familiar situations, in structure enshrining many, perhaps most or even all of our most basic dreams and desires, there is mystery aplenty about where and when and how the tale comes into play, when it ceases to be stories whispered around campfires, tales told from grandmother to mother to daughter, skits or songs performed among friends and family or only those most trusted confidants. At what point – when and where and why and how – does it become the story of the struggle of the day? Faced with an array of political, economic or social inequities and injustices, what makes today the day that someone awakens and decides to pick up a gun, if they have one, and head for the hills (or desert or swamps) to join the revolutionaries? Whose voice and what tale turn the disenfranchised and dispossessed into the makers of their world? Ultimately, such an event, such processes, such confluences, if they are such, of structures and agency, can only be adequately explored by recourse to narrative, to story – specifically to the stories that those self-same people themselves tell, told and retold over generations and across cultures, tales that may be best understood for their rhizomic quality, appearing and reappearing like crabgrass that cannot be defeated, bamboo that cannot be tamed, the dry riverbed that distant rains can suddenly renew into a roaring river. Stories keep the past alive and assert one's own place – and version – of critical historical processes. Told and retold, polished to a high sheen and in the service of an array of masters, these tales offer us a wealth of information.

XII

The role these stories or myths might play raises another prospect, that of exercising, rather than exorcizing, one's ghosts. The bold act of necromancy, the conjuring[9] of the spirits of the dead for the purposes of influencing the course of events and revealing the future, carries with it considerable risk, as revolutionaries seek to move between the past and the present, the real and the fictional, 'fact' and 'fantasy'. Idolatry becomes necromancy, as revolutionaries seem to attempt to communicate with the dead – Che or Cabral or others – through their writings or even talking to them, often in public speeches in public places. Who controls these spectral figures? Whom they speak through and who is allowed to speak for them are complex issues. Those who are able to invoke and evoke the dead – 'the true guardians of the words of our dead' in the estimation of Mexico's EZLN (Marcos et al. 1995: 150) – speak with a special resonance to the living and help forge links in a timeless struggle.

Thus there seems little question that the ability to invoke revolutionary heroes and martyrs is a powerful and persuasive tool, much sought after by those who would make revolution *as well as* those who would oppose it. For those who oppose not only seek to coopt, but more commonly seek to exorcize; thus the Bolivians, the US and others sought to exorcize Che while Cubans and millions elsewhere sought to bring him into play, to exercise him. The Mexican government in its idiosyncratic fashion sought if not exactly to exorcize Zapata, to mediate him; many others have exercised Zapata's ghost (perhaps, if some are to be believed, even with him).[10] Here, we are back in the realm of myth and story, a realm in which the telling, the narrative, is key.

XIII

The perspective implied above, reflecting culture as a 'multifaceted and a contested concept – intersecting with mentalities, strategic framing, and political ideologies' is open to charges that 'without a solid rational base and a relationship to structural constraints, culturalism risks broadening conflict until, in Hegelian fashion, all politics becomes enmeshed in meaning' (McAdam, Tarrow and Tilly 1997: 144).[11] Moreover, as noted above, an analysis of stories and narrative alone is unlikely to explain adequately the origins and process and outcomes of revolutions; food shortages, recessions, the vagaries of the international system and the resultant domestic implications (to take a few examples) are not in and of themselves cultural constructions. Yet the ability of revolutionaries, specifically revolutionary leaders, to conjure up cultural artifacts and connections and, once summoned, to manipulate and rewrite them, is critical. Such stories must be compelling, speaking to people's hearts as well their heads, to their emotions – with none of the normal academic derisiveness usually reserved for that term implied – as well as to whatever 'calculations', rational or otherwise, people may make. Thus these leaders of revolutionary processes consciously set out to (re)construct narratives predicated upon timeless aspects of the story/ies. But the population is not passive, waiting to be acted upon. While the revolutionaries may provide an impetus and present the population with a vocabulary or intellectual framework that helps organize and channel their visions, revolutionary leaders can go no farther than the population is prepared for them to go. People have their context, their culture, independent of the revolutionaries, and respond to these stories or not; they have their own narrative (Peru, Mexico and Indonesia might all be examples here). Perhaps more often, people have their stories, their narrative, built on timeless conceptions, and revolutionaries either find a way to accord with these or not; when they do, it is more likely that a revolutionary situation will emerge.[12]

XIV

In 1845, Marx penned what may be the single most succinct revolutionary credo, concluding his provocative and compelling 'Theses on Feuerbach' by pronouncing that 'the philosophers have only interpreted the world, in various ways; the point is to change it' (1978: 145). Recently, the Zapatistas updated this maxim for the twenty-first century: 'It is not necessary to conquer the world. It is sufficient with making it new. Us. Today' (EZLN 1996). If it is no longer some putative ideology or teleological concept that we seek, what links these groups and their visions? Rather than a common ideology, the link is the daily needs and practical necessities within the advanced/late capitalist world economy and the increasing demand for social justice and equality by peoples whose daily lives reflect neither. While the heuristic provided by the French revolution may no longer serve us well – and may never have served us as well as we thought! – who among us is really prepared to claim that people will no longer seek to transform themselves and their world? In seeking to resist, rework and reform their lives, there is every reason to think that revolutions will persist, perhaps in forms we have yet to consider, as people struggle at various levels and in a variety of ways – traditional, new and not yet imagined – to protect, defend and improve their lives in accordance with their visions and aspirations. Until those dreams and desires are met, regardless of how we define them, resistance, rebellion and revolution will persist.

Notes

1. Claims for the end of revolution as we have known it abound. Among these, the most deft is Goodwin (2001), the most blunt Snyder (1999), and the most casual Garton Ash (2000); the last two accord somewhat with Wright (2000) and Nodia (2000). These claims were presaged to some extent by Colburn's (1994) admonition that the 'vogue' of revolution among developing countries had come to an end. For a different perspective, see Radu 2000.

2. My appreciation to Laura Hobgood-Oster, Phil Hopkins and Shannon Winnubst for sharing their understandings of the term 'theses' with me as I wrestled with it.

3. 'All times', in the estimation of Fuentes (1996: 16), 'are living, all pasts are present'. To Mexico's modern-day Zapatista leader Subcomandante Marcos, Fuentes argued, 'can there be a living future with a dead past?' (1996: 124).

4. The 'possible' which Michelet invokes is the font of Darnton's (1989: 10) compelling contention that the incredible staying power of the French Revolution resides in its enshrinement of 'possibilism'. A fascinating twist on this is the contention that Mexico's modern Zapatista manifest the impossibility of their reality and that it is in this very impossibility that hope resides; see Rabasa 1997.

5. The mythos that has become 'Che' is a phenomenon worthy of (even) greater study. Che has not only been ascribed to the future – showing up in an array of locations at a variety of times and places and inscribed on material and ideological goods; one could also argue that Che has been transcribed/reinscribed almost Zelig/Gump-like into critical areas of Latin American and revolutionary myth: the voiceover in the fictionalized account of the life of Argentine heroine Evita; the determined leader of a band of foreign radicals standing against the US overthrow of the democratic government of Guatemala in 1954; an interloper with some nascent Mexican guerrillas in the 1950s, who may never have even existed, and who passed him on to Fidel; and various sightings throughout Africa and Asia long after he was, at least in theory, dead – the most recent that the guerrilla, now well into his seventies, is leading a unit in Nepal. The stories go on and on and on, making prescient Martin Guevara's remark, while his brother was still very much alive that he was 'like the white horse of Zapata. He is everywhere' (made in a slightly different context, Guevara's remark is quoted in Ryan 1998: 36). Such stories and sightings seem likely to continue. Their veracity matters less than how and why these claims are true for those who believe them to be, and why they are passed on as talismans and torches to enable and ennoble people's resistance and struggles.

6. 'The need of a constantly expanding market for its products chases the bourgeoisie over the whole surface of the globe. It must nestle everywhere, settle everywhere, establish connexions everywhere' (Marx and Engels 1978a: 476).

7. My thanks to Shannon Winnubst for this point.

8. Elsewhere (Selbin 1999: 145) I have argued for the notion of 'magical revolutions', meant, however inelegantly, to invoke 'magical realism', the literary style denoted by blending fact and fiction. A much more sophisticated and nuanced take on this is available in this volume; see the chapter by John Foran.

9. The concept of conjuring is a fascinating and, not surprisingly, complicated one. I am guided here by Tucker, who notes that 'When faced with the task of

defining conjure, scholars often create divisions which, while useful, tend to over-simplify the subject and almost always reflect an ethnocentric bias. To associate conjure with sorcery, witchcraft, or necromancy is to further align it with occult practices which in Western traditions have been perceived to be opposed to Christianity and are, therefore, the work of the devil' (Tucker 1994: 177).

10. 'Because of these connections with the past, Buena Vistans view themselves as the custodians of the memory of Zapata and the Zapatista fighters. They are particularly concerned with the authenticity of images of Zapata and the revolutionary fighters that the government tries to use to gain legitimacy. The issue of authenticity became important in the state of Morelos almost immediately after the assassination of Emiliano Zapata. In 1926, six years after Zapata's death, Robert Redfield recorded a corrido in Morelos that raised the question of whether the government troops killed the "real Zapata". The corrido ends, "It is certain and cannot be doubted, but they were deceived about Zapata, they cannot put Zapata down"' (Martin 1992: 181–2). Como Che, Zapata vive.

11. McAdam, Tarrow and Tilly (2001) are sensitive to the importance of culture in their formulation and address it in their volume on contentious politics.

12. One of the most fruitful places for exploring such matters may well be Chiapas. What are we to make of this putative postmodern uprising featuring Mexico's modern-day Zapatistas, the EZLN? This grants the EZLN a revolutionary status which is not uncontested both by academics (revolution? rebellion? armed social movement? social movement with a propensity for street/jungle theater which just happens to include the display of weapons? 'coup de théâtre'?) and even other revolutionaries. See, for example, the disdainful assessment of their fellow Mexican revolutionaries the EPR (an excellent introduction to the People's Revolutionary Army (EPR) is Bruhn 1999; Gatsiopoulos 1997 offers a brief overview). Chary of 'the outdated vocabulary of Che Guevara', Fuentes (1996: 93) suggests that 'the Chiapas revolution, among its other virtues, speaks a language that is fresh, direct, post-Communist. I would say that Subcommander Marcos, the Zapatista leader, has read more Carlos Monsiváis than he has Carlos Marx.' (Carlos Monsiváis is an important Mexican writer and public intellectual, a contemporary of Fuentes.) Elsewhere, (Selbin 1999: 147) I have argued similarly that 'Marcos ... owes as much to Groucho as Karl, to John as Vladimir'; see also Gómez-Peña's (1995: 90–91) compelling portraiture of Marcos as the 'consummate *performancero*', his 'persona was a carefully crafted collage of twentieth-century revolutionary symbols, costumes, and props borrowed from Zapata, Sandino, Che, and Arafat as well as from celluloid heroes such as Zorro, and Mexico's movie wrestler, *El Santo*'. And their actions (and look) are at best decidedly modern(ista?) and perhaps even pre- (but not PRI-) modern.

8

Between Market Democracies and Capitalist Globalization: Is There Any Prospect for Social Revolution in Latin America?

Carlos M. Vilas

Social revolutions are massive progressive processes confronting from below the whole arrangement of power structures. If successful, they involve profound changes in class relations on social, economic and political terrains, as well in the material and symbolic dimensions of individual and collective life. Social revolutions are the contingent outcome of political, ideological, social and economic factors at both national and international levels, put together by political agency. Revolutionary settings tend to develop when (1) political oppression and illegitimate rule (e.g. dictatorships, autocratic rule, systematic electoral fraud) compound with (2) regressive social and economic changes fostering new social inequalities or deepening ongoing ones, (3) political organizations waving the banners of social revolution win over the active support of large segments of the population, and (4) internal conflicts in the ruling elites together with specific international conjunctures (or a combination of both) improve chances to seize state power in order to build a better society. It is this conjunction which sets up what is usually called a revolutionary situation, and it can readily be seen therefore why social revolutions are such infrequent events in history.

Interrogating the prospects for social revolutions in Latin America involves asking questions about the ability of Latin America's current democracies and progressive political forces to cope with the most socially perverse dimensions of economic backwardness, capitalist rule and globalization. In the following pages I will focus on the quality of ongoing democratic regimes and their recent evolution towards what have been called 'market democracies'. Then I will proceed to a very brief assessment of the impact of recent capitalist globalization in reshaping power relations at both national and international levels, and on the living conditions of large segments of the Latin American population as well as fostering new strategies of social mobilization and protest. Finally, some preliminary conclusions will be advanced as to what can be expected for revolutionary prospects out of these institutional and structural settings.

Democratic Settings

In sharp contrast to most of the twentieth century, the current Latin American landscape is one of representative democracies, with left-of-center parties as active participants in institutional politics. Democratic polities have never been conducive to revolutions and have often proven ineffective at advancing progressive reforms. Yet democracy provides, at least in theory, institutional resources to change things peacefully, which tends to convince many that if they devise the proper means – a progressive political party, the buildup of a broad enough political coalition, a talented leader, a social security system – things can be improved. Even if, from a Marxist perspective, the democratic capitalist state is nothing more than the veil for bourgeois dictatorship, revolutions have been attempted when state power took on the appearance – let alone the reality – of dictatorship. Social unrest motivated by harsh living conditions and government policies – such as cost of living, environmental pollution, police brutality or downsizing social services – is widespread in today's Latin America, not infrequently involving violent actions and subsequent state repression. Yet these are mostly defensive struggles usually coupled by issue-targeted negotiations with government agencies. Revolution is not seen either as a necessity or a possibility by even the most powerful confrontational social movements.[1]

From neither a theoretical nor a historical standpoint is democracy an obstacle to advance structural changes. As a matter of fact, the relationship between political regimes and structural change is rather loose. Structural change can be implemented or attempted by government agencies and bureaucratic actors not supported by or resulting from revolutionary struggle against state power, as in post-1948 Costa Rica, the 1968–75 Peruvian military regime, Chile's Unidad Popular in 1970–73 or even populist or social-democratic experiences such as Argentina's early Peronismo or Michael Manley's government in Jamaica in the 1970s.[2] Whereas some of these attempts could not withstand fierce opposition from coalitions of domestic and foreign actors, others proved extremely effective in bringing about long-lasting restructuring. In turn, there is no direct correlation between political revolutionary efforts and social or economic outcomes. Despite their commitment to far-reaching restructuring and the tremendous social mobilization and violence they usually involve in order to seize power and consolidate their own rule, revolutionary performance in terms of structural change frequently relies on a different set of alliances, resources, capabilities and power arrangements than those that propelled the confrontation with the old regime.

All through the 1990s a disjunction deepened between the way a great many Latin Americans approached democratic regimes, and the way really existing democracies performed in most countries. People's criteria for assessing whether a particular government is legitimate or democratic appeal not just to legal or institutional issues but also to daily ones. Democracy is seen as the combined product of institutional tools and policy outcomes, pointing as much to a particular institutional system for decision-making as to the content of the decisions made. Grassroots and middle-class concepts of democracy articulate and suggest institutional procedures for the ability of political rule to implement progressive socio-economic and political changes (Alarcón Glasimovich 1992; Franco 1993; Lagos 1997). On the contrary, what we have today is a number of polities subordinating democratic procedures and institutions to market goals: what former US president Bill Clinton branded 'market democracies' – that is, democracies whose legitimating principle and main goal is the advancement of capitalism.[3] Thus, 'market democracies' go back to crass eighteenth- and nineteenth-century definitions of state/capital articulation as they put emphasis on such specific outcomes as securing property rights, fostering the conditions for capital accumulation, and widening the involvement of market forces in the allocation of public goods (World Bank 1997).

Power shifts from the late 1970s onward prompted this reinterpretation of democracy. Capital reinforced its rule over labor as financial valorization of capital and articulation to new global markets substituted for productive valorization and domestic or regional markets. World Bank- and IMF-sponsored state reforms facilitated the dismantling of incipient populist/social-democratic welfare states and afforded institutional imprint to the symbiotic relationship between economic and political power (Rodriguez Reina 1993; Vilas 1995; Concheiro Bórquez 1996; Fazio 1997; Basualdo 2000). In little more than a decade privatization of state-owned firms, public utilities, health and educational services and pension and retirement systems; across-the-board deregulation of finance; downsizing of unions' bargaining power; and dismantling of institutional solidarity networks, pushed for drastic changes in power resources and quality of life for a great many Latin Americans, damaging not just social but also individual physical security.

For the first time since the 1920s the Latin American ruling classes have been able to match capitalist rule and bourgeois democracy. Under the aegis of the 'Washington Consensus' representative democracy turned out to be the institutional tool to advance increasing concentration of wealth, power and well-being, risking confirmation of the most vulgar depictions of the state as the 'steering committee' of the ruling classes. Capitalist restructuring was conducted through systematic by-passing of parliaments or downgrading their institutional capabilities as far as strategic decision-making was concerned – for instance, privatizations, economic policies, foreign-debt management, state reform and the like. Most market-oriented reforms were implemented through executive order. The traditional democratic principle of majority rule is thus confined to periodic elections of governments, while effective governance is run in accordance with economic power holders (Vilas 1997; Diniz 2000).

Political Agency

Increasing inequality and economic hardships are insufficient conditions for social revolutions. Revolutions involve consciousness, organization and leadership, which do not develop spontaneously, although there are always ingredients of spontaneity in every revolutionary process. Revolutionary consciousness has to be developed and confrontational will has to be strengthened through organization. Revolutionary political activists teach the common people to link their individual experiences of oppression or exploitation to general impersonal processes and actors; they praise the advantages of organizing; they provide leadership. They bring about a political explanation of people's grievances and convince them that victory is only attainable through their own direct involvement, and that the only meaningful and successful involvement is revolutionary struggle. The outcome of this process was summed by an FSLN Comandante: 'Peasants ... responded as if by magic, yet there was really no more magic than the years we spent in the mountains' (Ruiz 1980).

The project of an overall restructuring of social, political, economic and cultural relations has receded in most of Latin America's countries, inasmuch as participation in state and government institutions has substituted for confronting or replacing them. In both El Salvador and Guatemala guerrilla warfare ended up in rounds of political negotiation which eventually led to constitutional reforms and the insertion of the former insurgents into civil life and mainstream politics; this looks also to be the inevitable future of the Chiapas conundrum. In Colombia, guerrillas seem to approach war as a means to strengthen their positions until the moment arrives when political negotiation will be the only feasible option for the government. Across the continent several dozens of city, municipal and provincial governments are held by modernizing democratic forces – including capitals or megacities such as Buenos Aires, Montevideo, São Paulo, Porto Alegre and Mexico City. They have also been able to build electoral coalitions running national governments in Chile. Prospects for broad political and economic restructuring have stepped back in favor of pragmatic programs to attack the most apparent social effects of economic restructuring. These are not the times for assaulting the Winter Palace, but to remodel it and book some of its new accommodations.

Mass rebellions took place in several countries during the last decade: Guatemala (1993), Ecuador (1997 and 1999), Peru (2000). Governments were ousted as a reaction to economic crisis, corruption and authoritarian manipulation of democratic institutions. Yet the absence or fragility of revolutionary actors prevented the inorganic masses taking advantage of their own efforts to fill the power vacuum they had engendered. Lacking organization, leadership and something more than anti-government rage, what might have evolved towards a revolutionary situation ended up in new rounds of electoral participation or backroom dealings among traditional political parties. However, revolutionary power building and accumulation of forces are protracted processes that claim for long-term approaches much more than short-term observations. Conjunctural failures can afford lessons and contribute later to more successful tries. Revolutions, like drama, may have rehearsals, as Lenin referred to the 1905 revolution in Russia.

Capitalist Globalization

Twentieth-century Latin American revolutions developed in a variety of regional and international settings, interacting in a number of ways with external actors and processes. Mexico's revolution made its way at a time when the US was still building its hegemony within the Western hemisphere; Guatemala's and Bolivia's revolutions belong to the beginning and early years of the cold war, whereas revolutions in Cuba, Grenada and Nicaragua triumphed during the peak of the cold war system in areas of uncontested US regional supremacy. Free trade and free cross-border investment were central traits of the world economy at the time of the Mexican revolution; capitalism was looking for a new transnational architecture when the Guatemalan revolutionaries seized power in 1944; Bolivia's and Cuba's revolutions belong to the golden years of the Bretton Woods-regulated world economy – a system that was crumbling under the initial blows of the current stage of globalization when the New Jewel and the FSLN began to implement their revolutionary programs in Grenada and Nicaragua.

As modern social revolutions have taken place in a world of nation-states, the end of the cold war plus ongoing global restructuring and increasing trade and financial integration pose questions about the impact of new international settings and actors on the prospects for revolutionary change. Statements on the emergence of a 'borderless world' (Ohmae 1990) or 'the end of geography' (O'Brien 1991) have paved the way to heaping scorn on revolutions as something belonging to past times. As long as revolutions aim to seize state power in order to advance progressive changes, the impact of economic globalization and new informational technologies on state capabilities might make of them a misguided, backward-looking fantasy. While traditional conservative politics opposed revolutions from a class perspective, updated conservative rhetoric blames them on the grounds of being passé. Yesterday they were dangerous; today they are outmoded.

In a number of ways revolutionary situations in Latin America have been an outcome of an increasing tributary articulation to global capitalism, mediated by domestic power arrangements. New or renewed modes of capitalist penetration and their impact – shifting land uses, evictions of peasant or Indian villages, migration to cities, commercial chains pushing small shops or traders to marginality or bankruptcy, growing urban poverty, downsized employment levels because of new technical biases, increasing labor exploitation, augmented dependence on food imports and thus on international prices, the heavy burden of foreign debt – are all associated with changes in subaltern articulation to the global capitalist economy. In turn these changes owe as much to market forces as to state promotion through legal reforms enforced by courts and actual or threatened police or military coercion, not infrequently with foreign support or advice from the US Marines to USAID, the World Bank or the IMF. The market's invisible hand wears the iron glove of polices and armies as well as the more sophisticated one of government officers and technocrats.

The reciprocal articulation of anti-imperialism and democracy has been a persistent ingredient in all Latin American revolutions. It points to the efficacy of revolutionary appeals in recruiting supporters beyond class boundaries. The *political* divide between actors benefiting from, or supporting, political oppression or foreign domination versus the revolution, substituted for the *class* divide of capital versus labor. At one moment or another, all Latin American revolutions have been able to collect activists and allies from almost every corner of society. This explains the increasing and eventually overwhelming strength of the revolutionary coalition in its confrontation with state power, as well its internal conflicts with regard to economic, social or any other reforms once it becomes the government. Yet it is the massive involvement of the laboring poor with their own demands for social and economic justice and their own symbolic constructions of democracy and social equality that pushes for further radicalization. In Mexico, what was initially an expression of liberal democratic anti-reelection demands turned into a social revolution when Morelos's peasants, headed by Emiliano Zapata, joined the revolution with demands for 'Land and Liberty'. Or, as Che Guevara put it in Cuba: 'Agrarian reform was not our invention: it was a formal denunciation from the peasantry, it was their imposition upon the revolution' (Guevara 1970: 18).

Hypotheses assessing some sort of neoliberal withering away of the state or the development of a global ruling capitalist class are highly contested and have scant empirical support. True, the above-mentioned power shifts as well as overwhelming government acceptance of neoclassical economic recipes have downgraded traditional Keynesian policy tools for state intervention. However, there is also a development of new state policies and capabilities (e.g. institutional safety nets for financial investment, regional trade agreements, export-promotion agencies or subsidizing of private foreign debt) in addition to furthering more traditional ones, such as police and military capabilities, electronic surveillance of the population, and severe border control of migrant labor. States are not just the victims of globalization; they are also their partners and even their midwives. Moreover, competition for markets among transnational corporations or investment funds has not receded; nor has their push for control over labor relations or imposition of favorable environmental policies (Doremus et al. 1998; Weiss 1998; Macedo Cintra 1999; Guedes 2000).

Capitalist globalization owes as much to market forces as to armies, navies and government decision-making. Washington's current proposal of a hemispheric free trade agreement is an appropriate illustration of the strategic role of state agencies in furthering market forces to the ultimate benefit of US multinational corporations (Estay 2001). The characteristic icons of global capitalism such as the WTO or OECD are multi-state organizations. Business firms hurt by an individual state's policies have to resort to their own government in order to have their complaints processed by those multilateral organizations, not to mention the IMF and the World Bank, in whose policy recommendations to developing countries the US government holds strategic control (Green 1998; Wade and Veneroso 1998; Cox and Skidmore-Hess 1999; Vilas 2000; Wade 2001).

As in the early and mid-twentieth century, current global processes and actors contribute to the buildup of the new regional and domestic settings. World Bank, IDB or IMF technocrats accomplish the roles once performed by US Marines or USAID in reforming state institutions and advancing market economies, tightening relations between increasingly 'globalized' domestic elites and increasingly 'internalized' foreign actors. 'Globalization' of domestic elites clearly updates the traditional outward biases of Latin American ruling classes. Income and welfare concentration in the upper levels of society grows at the expense not only of the laboring poor or the unemployed, as 'new poverty' chases increasing segments of the middle classes and deregulation and global finance drive not a few business sectors into bankruptcy.[4] Far from reducing social inequalities, capitalist globalization reproduces at the domestic level its contribution to uneven development and to deepening cleavages in the quality of life on a world scale. From this perspective, kinship ties between late-twentieth-century globalization and early and mid-century imperialism are worthy of exploration. From a Latin American stance ongoing globalization reinforces a hierarchy of states which has more to do with the persistent transnational power structure of capitalism – which has not experienced relevant changes for almost a century – than with recent global shifts (Dunning and Hamdani 1997; González-Casanova 1998; Panitch 2000).

As the hegemonic power in twentieth-century Latin America, the US government approached revolutions as dimensions of its own confrontations with third, non-hemispheric parties, be they Germany or Great Britain during the Mexican revolution, or the USSR with regard to the post-Second World War revolutions. Policy actions with regard to revolutions were extremely dependent on US government perceptions of the challenges effectively or supposedly posed by revolutions to national security, perceptions which in turn were decisively influenced by the third parties' policies towards revolutionary processes and regimes. The traditional support afforded by most US governments to oligarchic or dictatorial rule in Latin America convinced policymakers that challenges to their Latin American allies could only be the product of some kind of overseas intrusion in Washington's national affairs. Against this backdrop, US reactions were also shaped by the particular traits of each revolutionary process, as well as by the ability of specific actors to influence Washington's foreign policymaking – either US actors or those belonging to the country in revolution.

Real or supposed threats to US political and military hegemony in the hemisphere vanished with the end of cold war. However, new global foes have been added to Washington's repertoire of foreign-policy concerns. International terrorism, money laundering or drug production substitute for communism or Soviet intrusions: as in the 1989 invasion of Panama, in security operations in strategic areas such as the Brazil/Argentina/Paraguay border, in current involvement in the Andes through 'Plan Colombia', or even economic nationalism as long as it affects US policies on strategic resources such as oil – as seen in Washington's unfriendly relations with Venezuela under Chávez. In turn, a growing flood of both European and Japanese investments, plus a new breed of Latin American transnational capitalists, are challenging traditional strongholds of US transnational corporations in a number of economic branches such as banking, insurance, automobiles, infrastructure investment, communications, wholesale trade and foodstuffs. Monopoly capital on both the financial and productive terrains looks much more diversified today than thirty years ago, which could enhance the opportunities of governments and social actors to advance reform-oriented policy negotiations.

Certainly, the Soviet bankruptcy together with ongoing economic reforms in both China and Cuba have made socialism no longer a promising alternative for structural rearrangement. Yet socialism was not a central ingredient in Mexico's, Bolivia's or Guatemala's revolutions. To a great extent Cuba's socialist transition was a by-product of its defensive articulation with the Soviet bloc in the face of increasing US diplomatic and military confrontation – a dimension of cold war power politics much more than an ingredient of the original nationalist democratic revolutionary design. Whether there was a transition to some variety of socialism in either Grenada or Nicaragua remains an open question. The hypothesis of a 'non-capitalist path to development' pointed to the many specificities and divergences of these processes with regard to standard Soviet or even classical socialist/Marxist approaches. Central to those discussions was the 'moral obligation' of advanced socialist countries to support more backward ones, as Che Guevara spelled out in the 1963 Algiers meeting of non-aligned countries. Or, as Engels put it in 1894, 'to teach them how to do it' (Engels 1980 [1894]: 89–90). Doubtless, today's international settings no longer supply a great number of teachers.

Social unrest is growing everywhere as market-friendly democracies prove unable or unwilling to set limits on the most perverse dimensions of capital accumulation. In recent years government-sponsored policies to enhance the scope of global capitalism have triggered massive protests across the continent with a variety of connections to similar phenomena in Europe and the Pacific. Access to new communication and information technologies has been conducive to this increased outreach of social, political, economic and even symbolic demands. While in not a few cases traditional organizations of 'pre'-global times such as labor unions, student organizations or progressive parties have been strategic backbones for this new breed of social mobilization, a great deal of the most active involvement comes from a variegated array of social movements and NGOs dealing with environmental issues, identity politics, human rights and cultural concerns. Nevertheless there is no meaningful correlation between access to new information or communications technologies, or mobilization at the global level, and effective policy outcomes. A comparative look at Ecuador's indigenous organizations and Mexico's EZLN provides an interesting perspective on this score. The ability of CONAIE (Confederación de Nacionalidades Indígenas de Ecuador) to enhance its stance in Ecuadorian politics, or its success in fighting neoliberal reforms, in spite of international isolation and disregard from the most committed actors of global progressive activism, is in sharp contrast to the inability of the EZLN to attain basic legal reforms on communal and cultural rights, notwithstanding privileged access to global solidarity.

Whither Latin American Revolutions?

Whether a revolutionary situation exists is always a disputable question that can only be settled when and if the revolution occurs. Consequently it is extremely risky to assess in advance the probability of a revolution occurring or the chances for rulers to prevent it. In Hobsbawm's words, revolutionary situations 'are ... about possibilities, and their analysis is not predictive' (Hobsbawm 1986: 19).

Revolution is a particular strategy to which actors resort when conventional institutional ways for progressive change are closed. As in other epochs of capitalism, globalization affords opportunities as much as it enacts obstacles either to revolution or to any other type of progressive politics. International or global actors and processes play an indirect role through the mediating operation of domestic settings and actors. Consequently, the relationship between social revolutions and global environments, as well as the chances for revolutions to develop in the current articulation of domestic/global settings, involve a number of complex issues which have to do not just with social or historical analysis but also with the author's concept of revolution and of globalization, as well as with the role state agencies and political power are expected to play in globalized settings.

Social revolutions are infrequent events in history; or, in Tocqueville's words, they are *rare* events. Whether they will become more or less rare in global times is a contentious matter which appeals to each author's interpretation of historical trends and would-be developments, as well as personal ideological biases, hunches, fears or wishes. Social revolutions are specific power strategies to reach democracy and structural change, both associated in the revolutionary discourse with the idea of a *better society*, their specificity having to do with the scope and depth of the latter, but also with the violence and suffering they involve, particularly for the people pushing for them. This is perhaps the very reason for their being last-resort strategies, when no other strategy for democracy and socio-economic change is available or meaningful.

While structural change from a progressive perspective is still an un-realized project, the basic institutions of democracy, even in its mild market-friendly version, are the dominant political arrangement across Latin America. Even if the hypothesis of new revolutions cannot be re-jected as a subject of academic discussions, it does not look (any longer? yet?) a relevant source of concern for political or social actors. Fostering representative democracy and endowing it with the ability to carry out social reforms and to confront the negative sides of capitalist globalization and its domestic expressions are the most that can be expected from today's progressive political or social activism.

Every historical period has its own kinds of social injustice, political oppression, collective actions, emancipatory aspirations. The challenge to political analysts, then, is to acknowledge the permanent features of social revolutions beneath their shifting phenomenologies, as well the alternatives to them that may be available at particular moments of political life. Revolutions are as much a product of will as of necessity – and necessity, as political will, is a collective construct. Whether the socioeconomic and political scenarios set forth by globalization and market democracies help to foster or to prevent them is a question that can only elicit discrete, case-oriented responses. Even within these bounds, the social sciences can only provide hypothetical assessments of whether a specific combination of those ingredients, in a given setting, may or may not lead to a revolutionary situation. Political success, for both insurgencies and govern-ments, is a contingency, and contingency, like Commander Ruiz's *magia*, has to be tirelessly worked out. Then it may, or may not, show up.

Notes

1. This is clearly the case with Brazil's Landless Movement (the MST). It has been able to combine land seizures and open confrontation with landowners and provincial governments with a dynamic relation to the Workers Party – while keeping strategic autonomy from it – and a tense bargaining relation to the federal government in order to achieve legal enactment of peasant demands. In turn, this does not preclude the federal government from launching harsh police repression whenever its own alliance with northeastern landowners and their parliamentary representatives are threatened by the MST's claims.

2. According to some observers, Venezuela's current developments fit into this type of reformist democratic regime: López-Maya and Lander 2000; Vilas 2001.

3. 'Our leading purpose must be expanding and strengthening the world community of market democracies' stated Clinton in his speech at the UN's General Assembly on 27 September 1993. See also Lake 1993.

4. According to CEPAL (1998), almost 40 percent of Latin Americans live in poverty. In addition, social inequalities in Latin America are deeper than in any other region all over the world (BID 1998).

9

Globalization, Violence and Revolutions: Nine Theses

Adolfo Gilly

The tradition of the oppressed teaches us that the 'state of emergency' in which we live is not the exception but the rule. We must attain to a conception of history that is in keeping with this insight. Then we shall clearly realize that it is our task to bring about a real state of emergency, and this will improve our position in the struggle against Fascism. One reason why Fascism has a chance is that its opponents confront it in the name of progress as a historical norm. The current amazement that the things we are experiencing are 'still' possible in the twentieth century is *not* philosophical. This amazement is not the beginning of knowledge – unless it is the knowledge that the view of history which gives rise to it is untenable.

Walter Benjamin, 'On the concept of history', thesis VIII (1969 [1940]: 257, translation slightly modified)

I

'A state is a human community that, within a given territory ['territory' being a key element] successfully upholds a claim to the monopoly of legitimate use of violence', according to Max Weber's classic definition. Every state community or nation-state (to use modern terminology) inherently possesses a historically given relation of domination–subordination through which an elite exercises a monopoly on violence and rules over a stable mode of extraction and distribution for society's surplus product. I define revolution as a violent break of such a relation by the oppressed.

Each victorious revolution establishes a new relation of domination with a new elite, not the abolition of all forms of domination. This has been the norm for all known revolutions. If it is a social revolution, it also sets up new forms and justifications for the allocation and distribution of the social surplus product, beginning with rent and its by-products. The way the surplus is produced is not necessarily changed, as this is a function of a society's culture of production and level of technological development. Social and human relations (those which are not the state politic relation), do not change as much, as these are shaped and transformed through the long, slow course of history (Roux 1999: 47–56). The persistence of memory, and the material and non-material fabric and legacy of civilizations and life, endure across and beneath revolutions, wars and counterrevolutions.[1]

II

The oppressed and subaltern peoples of the rural world have been the main protagonists in twentieth-century social and national revolutions, often led by a fraction of the educated urban elite, the nucleus of a new revolutionary elite. The violent eruption of the peasantry and other rural people in these revolutions was driven not by a precise vision of a future world, but by the unbearable conditions of an existing one. 'The masses go into a revolution not with a prepared plan of social reconstruction, but with a sharp feeling that they can no longer endure the old society', notes Leon Trotsky in *The History of the Russian Revolution*. In the words of Walter Benjamin, violent force is nourished 'by the image of enslaved ancestors rather than that of liberated grandchildren' (1969: 260).

It is neither in the economy nor in the political but in history (in specific histories), and its networks of dependency and domination, that we may unravel the genetic code of given revolutions. This perception is shared in various ways by Barrington Moore (1978), E.P. Thompson (1991), James C. Scott (1990) and the 'moral economy' school, as well as by the subaltern studies group, and by various Mexicanist historians in the United States, of whom I shall mention only two who are no longer with us: Daniel Nugent (see Joseph and Nugent 1994) and William Roseberry (1994). They have all accepted Walter Benjamin's admonition to 'brush history against the grain' (1969: 257).

The national, agrarian, social revolutions of the twentieth century arose each time against the universal plunder embodied in the expansion of capitalist relations and destruction of an older human world of personal relations, against the transformation of use value into exchange value and against the commodification of every human relation.

Thus, if we heed the imaginary of their main actors, rather than their leaders, these revolutions confirm Walter Benjamin's insight: 'For Marx, revolutions are the locomotive of world history. But perhaps things are different. Perhaps revolutions are the way that humanity, riding on this train, reaches for the emergency brake' (1990: 1232).

It is not a matter of returning to the past. Those who rebel wish to avenge the oppression suffered by previous generations at the same time that they seek to break violently into their own future, a future which they can only imagine or glimpse through any of the forms of hope carved from the memories of past generations. 'The task to be accomplished is not the conservation of the past, but the redemption of the hopes of the past', as Max Horkheimer and Theodor W. Adorno write in the introduction to their *Dialectic of Enlightenment* (1997 [1944]: xv).

There exists in every social relation of domination and subordination, as both words imply, two active parts, each recognizing the other as its counterpart. This is therefore an active relationship. The element that denotes this activity is the *resistance* of the dominated, the crucial designation for the constant, multiform and changing friction between the two terms of the relation.

Resistance assumes specific forms in agrarian societies where domination – visible and recognized by all – takes the form of bonds of personal dependency. In modern society – the society of capital, the society of the self-valorization of value – domination masks itself as a relation between individuals who are free and equal before the law and property, in a community where exchanges are mediated by money and exchange value subordinates and subsumes use value, not as the substance of life or enjoyment but merely as material means for its instantaneous and unceasing digital metamorphoses. Mike Davis calls Los Angeles the City of Quartz to denote a place where such artificial transformations of value beyond any human control seem to dictate the terms of life.

For each of the forms of domination and subordination there exist a variety of forms of hegemony (the recognition – always subject to challenge – of the legitimacy of domination within the shared ideology of an illusory or imagined community), along with equally varied forms of spontaneous as well as organized resistance. However, only in exceptional cases does this resistance culminate in rebellion or revolution to break the existing bonds of dependency, either temporarily or permanently. In most cases, resistance leads, with varying degrees of awareness on either side, to a renegotiation of authority and its rules, of the accepted forms of legitimacy, and of the sometimes less apparent but always present way that surplus product is extracted and allocated (tribute, rent, taxes, prices, profit, surplus value).

Thus, we have a relation – *domination* and *subordination* (taking the form of legitimacy and hegemony) – accompanied by a friction that is integral to its existence: *resistance*, from which two variables can be derived – *negotiation* in normal times, and *revolution* in exceptional times.

III

Revolution is neither upheaval nor conspiracy, though these may be its attributes in specific cases. Revolution is, above all, organization and mobilization. Its basic organizational features are not conveyed by the political parties or movement elites that guide them. They already exist in people's everyday practices and social life. They are enriched by pre-existing realities and organized actions, as well as taking root in the long-established solidarity of the oppressed (indistinguishable from their everyday life, although that is far from being its only component) and an ancient hope for justice, which tends to be identical to their religious beliefs. The indigenous rebellion in Chiapas that began in 1994 is a case in point, according to the accounts of its main actors.[2]

Historical accounts by revolutionary elites about both national and social revolutions have either almost always discounted – they have literally not recorded – the 'autonomous realm' of subaltern politics or simply assumed that the politics of the vanguard was the conscious reflection of the unconscious movement of the masses.

A rebellion presupposes a common imaginary among those who rebel. This does not stem from the theories or programs of educated elites, who can only play this role if they are capable of perceiving and understanding this historically grounded imaginary and of harmonizing with it their own ideas and visions of the reorganization of society, whether religious, political or utopian. This is not a simple adaptation of ideas but an implicit dialogue, a negotiation and creation within the intense spiritual and intellectual activity of the revolution. Such is the way an original discourse is forged in every revolution or rebellious movement, at once old and new and shared by all: not the preservation of the past, but the redemption of its hopes in the novelty, discourse and actions of the revolution.

In this line of thinking, a redemption of hope does not imply the coming of a savior, but the advent of a time for redemption – the not-yet-arrived – as an achievement of the subaltern and oppressed. This implies thinking that in the relation of resistance – which is active by definition

– a certain vision (a perception, an unperceived imagination) is produced, the practical and unexpressed utopia of 'an upside-down world' that simultaneously feeds its explicit protests, angry cries and hidden discourses; this vision seeks to overcome the type of domination that resistance rejects without being able to suppress.

Within Marxist theory, Rosa Luxemburg (1968 [1912]) had one of the sharpest insights into the distinction between revolutionary elites and the people, who sustain them but at the same time retain their everyday spaces and ways of interacting, reflecting, discussing, deciding and acting. In the second half of the twentieth century Frantz Fanon (1959, 1961) also explored the relation between these domains as coexisting but not fusing with each other during times of revolutionary mobilization, and as distinct and separate in times of retreat.

In the case of India, Ranahit Guha has demythologized the national elite's representation of Indian nationalism as an enterprise in which 'the indigenous elite led the people from subjugation to freedom' (1988: 38). This representation is, in essence, the same device that sustains diverse narratives, including some leftist ones, about the official history of the Mexican revolution and its Cardenista outcome.

> What, however, historical writing of this kind cannot do is to explain Indian nationalism for us. For it fails to acknowledge, far less interpret, the contribution made by the people *on their own*, that is, *independently of the elite* to the making and development of this nationalism.... What clearly is left out of this un-historical historiography is the *politics of the people*. (Guha 1988: 39, 40; emphasis in original)

Guha goes on to explain that there was another domain of Indian politics during the colonial period apart from the politics of the nationalist elite, where

> the principal actors were not the dominant groups of the indigenous society or the colonial authorities but the subaltern classes and groups constituting the mass of the laboring population and the intermediate strata in town and country – that is, the people. This was an *autonomous* domain, for it neither originated from elite politics nor did its existence depend on the latter. It was traditional only insofar as its roots could be traced back to pre-colonial times, but it was by no means archaic in the sense of being outmoded.... As modern as indigenous elite politics, it was distinguished by its relatively greater depth in time and as well as in structure. (1988: 40, emphasis in original)

A vertical, hierarchical mobilization distinguished the politics of the elite, while a horizontal dimension was characteristic of subaltern politics. The former was mainly articulated within colonial or precolonial political institutions; the latter 'relied rather more on the traditional organization of kinship and territoriality or on class associations depending on the level of consciousness of the people involved' (Guha 1988: 40). Elite mobilization tended to be

> relatively more legalistic and constitutionalist in orientation, subaltern mobilization relatively more violent. The former was, on the whole, more cautious and controlled, the latter more spontaneous. Popular mobilization in the colonial period was realized in its most comprehensive form in peasant uprisings. However, in many historic instances involving large masses of the working people and petty bourgeoisie in the urban areas too the figure of mobilization derived directly from the paradigm of peasant insurgency (Guha 1988: 40–41).

Traditional organization tends to construct its structures of command according to its own parental rules and family or clan networks, from which the cacique, Cossack chief or godfather emerges as both protective and menacing figure, an almost indispensable mediator when agrarian society and the urban state negotiate. Left party local leaders may often be a soft version of these forms of authority based on personal and family influence.

Once a movement has passed its high point elite politics tends to deflect subaltern mobilization onto the institutional terrain of electoral politics: that is to say, towards the existing state apparatus. At the same time, the state is the terrain for the legitimization of this kind of politics and its bearers as the institutionally sanctioned leaders of the subaltern classes and groups, whether they rely on the subaltern to maintain their government or form an opposition party that seeks to displace the ruling group within the existing political institutions. In such a case we are not in front of a new relation of domination (a new state formation), but instead in front of the modification of the existing one as a consequence of subaltern mobilization.

Where do the ideas, imaginary and traditions of these movements from below come from? According to Ranahit Guha, on the whole their operating ideology

> reflected the diversity of its social composition with the outlook of its leading elements dominating that of the others at any particular time and within any particular event. However, in spite of such diversity one of its invariant features was the notion of resistance to elite domination. This followed from the subalternity common to all the constituent elements of this domain. (Guha 1988: 41)

In the case of these subaltern classes, 'The experience of exploitation and labour endowed this politics with many idioms, norms and values which put it in a category apart from elite politics' (Guha 1988: 41). Of course,

Guha warns us that these distinctive features of the politics of the people don't always surface in a pure form, but they do contribute to demarcating the subaltern political domain vis-à-vis the elite's.

In the new modernity of capital known as globalization, we may find these generic features in the most diverse and at times seemingly opposed subaltern resistance movements. It is possible that here – and not in the movement of global capital – are to be found the similarities by which resistance movements may recognize each other despite their externally visible differences.

As has always been the case, the available communications technology (in turn the press, telegraph, telephone, radio, video and Internet), if used appropriately, is able to facilitate the impact of social movements and influence their outcome, but this is no substitute for them. The real place of struggle, organization and strength against adversaries remains, as always, the social, physical and spiritual reality of human beings, which is produced and reproduced in the infinite texture of their everyday lives and dreams. The EZLN and the Zapatista indigenous people's rebellion remind us once more of this fact. It is far easier for the elite of the dominated to make use of the 'rational' technological tools of the dominating elite, than for the latter to understand and appropriate the customs and 'hidden relations' of the dominated.

The Internet has no value without this reality; or it may just become a tool for elites of all stripes to settle their own disputes, as has been the case on more than one occasion with the communications technologies of the past. In our enthusiasm for the real possibility of utilizing these new instruments in favor of mobilizations and rebellions, we must not forget that they are also newly available to the forces of domination: the owners of money, power, information, communication and arms. It is not in that 'virtual reality' but in the opposite domain where we can find, as Victor Serge would say, 'the birth of our strength'.

IV

In the beginning of the twentieth century, at the height of the *belle époque*, Rosa Luxemburg applied her keen vision in *The Accumulation of Capital* (1968 [1912]) to what was happening before everyone's eyes – theorists, analysts, writers and scientists alike: the relentless onslaught of capital on a global scale against natural economies (peasant communities, demesnes, bonds of personal dependency, non-capitalist social spaces), against simple mercantile economies (artisans and independent producers) and between capitalists. Colonial military violence, the burden of credit and taxation, and cheap merchandise were the weapons of this war without quarter waged in the colonies and in those European regions where natural economies still existed. For its own realization and reproduction, capital needed to accelerate the 'emancipation' of the natural wealth and labor forces of those closed places, destroying the obstacles to incorporation in the circuit of value. The weapon of choice was (and still is) spoliation through violence, actual or implied, just as has happened to the present day with the centuries-long process of *enclosure*.[3]

Surveying the entire century from the standpoint of its initial years, Rosa Luxemburg considered 'any hope of restricting the accumulation of capital exclusively to "peaceful competition", i.e. to regular commodity exchange', a mere illusion:

> Accumulation, with its spasmodic expansion, can no more wait for, and be content with, a natural internal disintegration of non-capitalist formations and their transition to commodity economy, than it can wait for, and be content with, the natural increase of the working population. Force is the only solution open to capital; the accumulation of capital, seen as an historical process, employs force as a permanent weapon, not only at its genesis, but further on down to the present day. From the point of view of the primitive societies involved, it is a matter of life or death; for them there can be no other attitude than opposition and fight to the finish – complete exhaustion and extinction. Hence permanent occupation of the colonies by the military, native uprisings and punitive expeditions are the order of the day for any colonial regime. The method of violence, then, is the immediate consequence of the clash between capitalism and the organization of a natural economy which would restrict accumulation. (1968: 369)

'Indian masses in the second half of the nineteenth century did not die of hunger because they were exploited by Lancashire; they perished in large numbers because the Indian village community had been demolished', wrote Karl Polanyi in 1944 (1957: 159–60, quoted by Davis 2001: 10).[4] This second half of the nineteenth century – the great era of European colonial expansion in Asia, Africa and the Middle East; the conquest of the 'wild west' in the United States, the penetration of modern capitalism into Latin American countries; the cruel era of colonial armies, external and internal; the massacres of indigenous peoples; the expansion of the railroad that brought soldiers, goods and the capitalist market; and the violent enclosure and expropriation of communal lands from the ancient and vast territories of the natural economy – brought with it tens of millions of deaths through military force and hunger, and innumerable natural and ecological disasters.[5]

This violence without limits, a violence through which the expansion of global capital was accomplished, did not escape the gaze of some, like Georges Sorel, but it did escape that of many European socialists and Marxists, which accounts for their indifference and lack of interest in a great revolution such as Mexico's, although the revolution caught the attention of anarchists in the US, Latin America and Spain.[6] At that time, according to Jean-Marie Vincent, there was a particularly poor understanding in most socialist circles regarding the role of violence:

> The seeming normalcy found in European capitalist societies blinds many Marxists to the hidden potential of violence. They refuse to appreciate how violence against the other is inscribed in social relations and everyday confrontations between individuals. Nor can they see how dubious is the legality which states observe in their repressive politics. The rule of law represents progress compared with the arbitrariness of absolutist politics. But at the same time it is a medium used to label and criminalize a segment of society in order to reassure the dominant classes and give them the illusion of superiority. More surprising still is how little attention is given to colonization, with its innumerable massacres and its ruinous impact across large sections of the planet. A not insignificant number of revisionists is even convinced of colonization's civilizing mission and is unshaken by the colonizers' racist postures. The radical left that disapproves of colonialism and imperialism often tends to downplay their importance (this is not the case with Rosa Luxemburg). The arms race in Europe and the periodic international crises between the great imperialist countries, are, in fact, a source of concern for many socialists, but they believe that they can ward off danger with pacifist campaigns and appeals to leaders for rational compromise. They even refuse to imagine that the world could collapse into barbarism or an orgy of violence. (Vincent 2001: 16)

This was nonetheless the destination for the splendors and glories of the *belle époque*, its *douceur de vivre* and luxury trains, extolled in Valéry Larbaud's unequalled *Ode*:

> Lend me your grandiose noise, your grand allure, so gentle,
> Your nightly glide across enlightened Europe, Oh luxury train!
> And the anguishing music that whispers in your corridors of golden leather
> While millionaires sleep behind lacquered doors with heavy copper latches....
> I felt for the first time the simple sweetness of living
> In a cabin on the Northern Express, between Wirballen and Pskow.
> We slid across prairies where shepherds
> At the foot of trees like hills
> Were dressed in crude and dirty sheep skins ...
> (A fall morning at eight o'clock, and the beautiful singer with violet eyes
>   was singing in the cabin next door)
>   (Larbaud 1983: 196–7)

On the other hand, this was the time of anarchism, when a train driver from Bologna named Pietro Rigosi, remembered in a Francesco Guccini song from the 1970s, unable to control his rage, hurtled his locomotive at full speed against an oncoming luxury train, 'a train packed with gentlemen'. 'I don't know why he did it', the Italian composer recounts, 'perhaps an ancient fury, untold generations calling for retribution, blinded his heart.'[7] His words sound a distant echo of Walter Benjamin's reasons. A few years later we would see in what a massive conflagration Europe's *douceur de vivre* would end, with its two contrapuntal violences: luxury from above, fury from below.

V

The creation of the modern colonial empires – as narrated from Joseph Conrad's *Heart of Darkness* to Mike Davis's *Late Victorian Holocausts* (2001) – came into being through slaughters more horrific than both world wars combined. These two atrocious wars over the division of colonial spoils and the global market – in whose very preparation and implementation additional dozens of millions died, including those victimized by Nazi extermination camps and Stalin's gulags – were the culmination of the colonial slaughters that gave rise to the spoils in question.

Starting with the first three successful great revolutions of the twentieth century – 1910 Mexico, 1911 China and 1917 Russia – an increasing tide of rural and peasant-based rebellions began to undermine and swallow the colonial empires of the nineteenth century, together with the *belle époque*. After World War II, the British, French, Dutch, Belgian, German, Italian, Japanese, Spanish and Portuguese empires collapsed. The scales tipped, perhaps, between 1948 and 1949, when the British withdrew from India and the Chinese revolution triumphed. During the second half of the twentieth century, a wave of colonial and agrarian revolutions defeated the imperial armies of France, Japan, Portugal and the US and constituted new national states. The nationalist elites in these states had to work out terms with the rebelling groups on which they had relied, accept roundabout ways and change the rhythm of the centuries-long process of destruction of the natural economy and expansion of money relations. But they did not propose to set forth in a new direction, nor would they have been able to.

From this point of view, the so-called cold war (1946–90) had nothing to do with the official version of a prolonged defensive struggle by the US against dictatorial and oppressive regimes, ending with the destruction of the Evil Empire and the victory of democracy in the final decade of the twentieth century. On the contrary, it was a war of the world of capital, headed by its military, industrial and financial center, the United States, against social, national and colonial revolutions across the five continents, to subordinate or destroy them. Its victory is that of the empire of exchange value, which seeks to invade and conquer even the most concealed interstices of life.[8] At the same time, it meant the dismantling or fragmentation of social pacts – 'communist' or Keynesian – imposed on the state by movements from below as dikes, temporary in the end, against the tide of exchange value. It is important to note that those states, under the common ideology of technical and scientific progress, were also participants in the dismantling of natural economies. Once a new level of accumulation and subsuming of knowledge to capital was reached, the ground was prepared for the next wave of capital expansion in the 1990s.

Today, the violence of money, moving itself with the speed and pervasiveness that the existing technology affords it, but also maintained as always by the ever-present and vigilant violence of arms, pursues without respite the commodification of every domain and interstice of society, the incorporation of all physical and mental labor to the process of self-valorization of value, and the extermination through poverty or war of whoever resists this plundering or fails to enter into the universal valorization of capital: peoples, ethnic groups, cultures, individuals.

Globalization is only the exacerbation of this universal plundering, a new offensive by the owners of money, power and knowledge (owners therefore of technology and weaponry), to incorporate both the sources of wealth – nature and human labor – without exception or reservation to the seemingly limitless world of capital. (Yet the limits of this world, as Luxemburg also foresaw, are implicit in the very relation of capital and the permanent resistance and rebellion of living labor against the tyranny of dead labor; but that is another story.)

With the advent of the capitalist restructuring that began in the 1970s and accelerated during the 1990s (that is, across the whole of the last quarter of the twentieth century), this offensive shattered the defensive and protective barriers raised by the oppressed during the first three-quarters of that century through their rebellions and their organizations. The tide of 1968 and the US defeat in Vietnam – an event unparalleled in the century and in US military history – together with the exhaustion of the long wave of expansion of the world economy, accelerated the technological (digital), legal, political and social offensive against the gains made by workers in Western Europe and the United States.

The military victory of the Vietnamese revolution, with logistical support from the Soviet Union and China, sounded the final alarm. The subsequent expansion of the US military industry, with its correspondent scientific and technological ramifications and spillovers would be the gravitational force determining the exhaustion and fall of the Soviet Union in the cold war race.

The G7 (Group of Seven) was set up in 1975. In the core countries, the process of capital accumulation entered a new phase, a change from the mode of regulation established after World War II. This offensive taking place within the boundaries of the greatest capitalist countries was the indispensable social prelude to the phase of unregulated worldwide capital expansion that was to follow, with its attendant 'unbearable misery of the world' (Poulin and Salama 1998) in which we live nowadays and that we now call globalization.

The current drunken gaze of the financial powers over this world is comparable only to the drunken spree of the *belle époque* that followed the Paris Commune, at the height of the pillage of colonialism, and ending in the carnage of World War I and the subsequent era of wars and revolutions.

VI

Because they have entailed an alteration and readjustment of the relations of domination between nations, as well as a threat to the legitimacy and stability of the structure of domination in neighboring nations, all modern revolutions have suffered violent pressures and external interventions. A list of examples would include Mexico (1910), Russia (1917), China (1949), Bolivia (1952), Korea (1953), Vietnam (1954), Algeria (1954), Guatemala (1954), Egypt (1956), Hungary (1956), Cuba (1959), Czechoslovakia (1968), Angola, Mozambique and Guinea-Bissau (1960–70s), Chile (1970–73), Iran (1979), Nicaragua (1979), El Salvador (1980) and Grenada (1983). This list could go on. In this sense, the history of revolutions is also the history of the external interventions staged to contain, disorganize and crush them.

Within this context of external violence, we must also consider the support and intervention, at times overt, from specific branches of the United States military apparatus, like the CIA, in the setting up and stabilization of military dictatorships in Latin America's southern cone (Argentina, Uruguay, Chile, Bolivia) as well as in their wars of extermination against rural and urban workers' networks and organizations, and against all leftist or democratic cultures. In these four countries, such organizations and networks were destroyed by force, and many of their leaders murdered during the 1970s and 1980s, together with thousands of labor organizers or ordinary citizens who were imprisoned, tortured, murdered or disappeared in 'death flights' (i.e. thrown alive from planes) or mass graves. How can we exclude this horrendous internal war, supported from abroad and exemplified by Operation Condor, from the general offensive staged by capital during the very same years? Similar support and counsel were dispatched against the Central American revolutions during the 1970s and 1980s. In Argentina and in other countries, French army officers who had been trained in the colonial wars of Indochina and Algeria proffered their technical advice as torture specialists. They were not the only ones to do so.

In the present age of globalization, this combination of economic and military force (economic pressure, harassment, undercover operations, blockades or military intervention) has become an institutionalized matter of fact: on one hand, we have the incremental expansion of NATO and the military initiatives that accompany it; and on the other, the role of universal policeman that the UN Security Council bestows upon the armed forces of the United States and its surrogate powers.

At the end of the year 2000, the Socialist International declared that it 'supports the use of "the right to intervention on humanitarian grounds", if carried out within the framework of international law, as an integral part of the struggle for democracy and human rights'.[9] Who defines how and in which cases this right is to be applied? The facts indicate that, in the end, whoever possesses military power gets to decide in which cases and to what degree a military force may exercise this ambiguous 'right to intervention'. Czechoslovakia in 1968, Afghanistan in 1980, Panama in 1989, the Gulf War in 1990 are clear cases in point. We have certainly strayed far from Max Weber's definition of the 'monopoly of the legitimate use of violence' as an attribute of a state community. Moreover, it would appear from its actions that the expansion of NATO, with or without the UN's blessing, is declaring the candidacy of its core force, the United States and the Pentagon, to exercise and legitimate this monopoly on a global scale.

VII

The two great wars of the twentieth century (1914–18 and 1939–45) shattered, modified and then reassembled in a new way the relations of domination between nations. Globalization does not involve the abolition or dissolution of these relations, but rather a new definition of their rules.

The mainstay of this redefinition is 'legitimate violence' as organized in national armies.

In other words, today's globalization would be unimaginable without the Pentagon, its military bases, its military industry, its information and communication systems, and its global arsenal, as the linchpin of global violence.

This new monopoly on the exercise of possible physical violence at a planetary level is the ultimate − though not the only − guarantee for the reproduction of the modern 'transnational community' of exchange value, whose legitimacy is maintained by a specific form of a 'community of money' that includes those who participate in the reproduction of value and excludes everyone else as pariahs, barbarians, marginals, excess baggage or disposable people. At the international level, labeling certain nations 'rogue states' is the correlate of the criminalization of entire sectors of national societies (the return of the 'dangerous classes').

At the same time the intense and never-ending spread of wage relations, under conditions imposed by the massive devaluation of a workforce that is ever less protected at the national level, generates the spontaneous and violent conditions for the unavoidable dispute of labor power against capital.

The constitution that is under way of this type of society may be regarded as an epochal break from all preceding periods. Bolívar Echeverría notes:

> Not only do the archaic forms of destructive violence not disappear or tend to disappear under capitalist modernity, they actually reappear refurbished in a terrain that is doubly auspicious: that of a scarcity that no longer has any technical justification, but that, following a 'perverse logic', must be reproduced. The histories of the proletariat of the eighteenth and nineteenth centuries, of the colonized peoples of the nineteenth and twentieth centuries, of the 'lumpen', informal or marginal classes, of 'minorities' of race, gender, religion, opinion, etc., are some among the many stories of the others/enemies that the 'national community' that was built by the owners of property around the accumulation of capital has seen fit to 'construct' in order to reaffirm itself. If told 'against the grain' − as Benjamin said a materialist should tell history − the astounding history of capitalist modernity, its progresses and its liberations, would show its somber side; its narrations would have to treat it, first and foremost, as the history of oppression, repression and exploitation, as the history of the countless holocausts and genocides of every type that have taken place throughout its centuries and, particularly, in this one that is about to end. (1998: 116)

The violence of capitalist modernity recapitulates and embodies its previous manifestations. But it also spreads an internal violence throughout contemporary society like an epidemic, a violence that is verbal and physical, virtual and material, and which, like money, tends to become a habitual and even acceptable way for human beings to relate to each other, as our natural bonds are ever more absorbed by the bonds of exchange value. At the same time, the capacity to unleash the destructive power of general or focused extermination is concentrated into one place. Perhaps this brutality, still contained but about to bloom in modern capitalist societies, was the same that Rosa Luxemburg foresaw as a possible future when she critically assessed the inhumane forms of expansion of capitalist relations in the colonial territories.

VIII

The norms of relations between nations and between citizens of a state community sanctioned at least formally in the Universal Declaration of Human Rights at the end of World War II have been obsolete since 1990.[10] The globalization of the domination of financial capital implies the imposition and legitimization of new rules for the relations between nations, between capitals, and between capital and labor, both within each nation and in the global market that imposes the norms followed by national markets.

This predominance of the world market over national markets is not new: it has been an intrinsic feature of the existence of capital ever since the sixteenth century. What is new is the tearing down of the protective barriers – always relative and porous – against this domination, barriers whose forms included the state monopoly of international trade established by the Russian revolution from its beginnings or the welfare state formations that came into being after World War II.

The present digital globalization knows no barriers, boundaries or limits. One of its great accomplishments has been the gradual incorporation, for the first time in history, of Russia's immense territories and China's unlimited human labor reserves into the market. Another has been the initial steps taken in the expropriation and commodification of the genetic code and the biological reproduction of the natural world, a kind of delirious culmination of the centuries-long process of the enclosure of common lands.

We stand before an epochal change. This international and societal mutation is sometimes referred to as 'deregulation'. At such an early stage of this new modernity of capital, it is difficult to divine what lies beyond the horizon, although history, theory and reason may allow us to begin to imagine it.

Capital's new form of domination does not eliminate but rather exacerbates competition between the different capitals, particularly among the financial conglomerates that dominate the capital market. This competition now encompasses the entire surface of the planet. In the history of capital, such recurring and periodic conflict has time and again been resolved through war. There is no reason to believe that weapons of mass destruction and new technologies have changed the terms of the relation among capital, military industry and war. This is confirmed by the new US anti-ballistic space shield, that dangerous mixture of Maginot line and nuclear delirium.

<h1 style="text-align:center">IX</h1>

If violence is an intrinsic component of competition between capitals, resistance is also a necessary corollary to capital's domination over human beings. From the resistance of living labor at the heart of the capitalist relation to the resistance of the still vast regions of human societies attached (underneath the universal domination of capital) to the material and spiritual forms of the natural economy, the abstract logic of self-valorization of value has not taken over, as would be its inner tendency, the will and the lives of human beings right up to their innermost reflexes.

No matter how defeated or dismantled the organized instances of resistance that arose throughout the twentieth century may be, the human experience of resisting, organizing, thinking and imagining an 'otherworld' – whether to negotiate one by one the forms of the new domination when it cannot be changed or whether to rebel against it when its inevitable future fissures permit – will not vanish. This has been the constant in all the revolts and rebellions of the subaltern and the oppressed, and there is no reason to think that this mode of being and existing of human beings in relation to the domination exercised over them has disappeared.

Only dead labor can exist without resisting, and while it neither thinks, organizes nor rebels, it doesn't produce surplus value either.

By definition, every resistance of classes, groups and subaltern communities against domination is a relation implying very diverse but real degrees of violence on both sides. Only after a new form of domination has been experienced will we be able to tell the kinds of organizations that will be generated by this ever-present and inevitable resistance. Whatever these may be, it is part of the human condition that no previous experience will be lost.

New relations among domination, resistance and violence are being forged within globalization. If this is the case, globalization brings with it the seed of new wars and revolutions in which violence, as ultimate reason, will redefine these relations. Any other assumption, given the current state of human affairs, lies within the realm of utter fantasy.

Notes

The translation of this essay from Spanish was a joint collaboration among Lucero Quiroga, J.-P. Reed, John Foran and Adolfo Gilly. The editor and the author are most grateful to the other three!

1. If it is so, every state community can be imagined as a great arch built over centuries, not harmoniously but through perpetual friction, conflict and negotiation (Corrigan and Sayer 1985; Gilly 1998).

2. See, for example, the interview with Subcomandante Marcos (1995a).

3. The process of enclosing common lands began in twelfth-century England and was virtually complete by the end of the nineteenth century, according to the *Encyclopaedia Britannica*'s entry on 'Enclosure'. The marginalization and suppression of local languages and linguistic unification under the language of the dominant nation-state paralleled this: inasmuch as the official language is the means of authority and cultural and commercial exchange in the space of the nation-state, regional languages tend to be those of the conspiracies or 'hidden discourses' of the oppressed.

4. In *The Great Transformation* Karl Polanyi emphasizes the process of destruction of the natural economy through the violent imposition of the capitalist market: 'The catastrophe of the native community is a direct result of the rapid and violent disruption of the basic institutions of the victim (whether force is used in the process or not does not seem altogether relevant). These institutions are disrupted by the very fact that a market economy is foisted upon an entirely differently organized community, labour and land are made into commodities, which, again, is only a short formula for the liquidation of every and any cultural institution in an organic society' (1957: 159, quoted by Mike Davis 2001: 10).

5. Including those carried out by the dispossessed. For example, in Algeria, in the region of Sétif – where the rebellion that foreshadowed the Algerian revolution erupted on 8 May 1945 – from 1880 onward the inhabitants had been setting aflame the woods confiscated by the colonial state for the benefit of French settlers (Benot 2001: 19).

6. It is worth noting that toward the end of the nineteenth century the organizations of artisans and workers created by anarchists and anarcho-syndicalists in Argentina and Uruguay called themselves Societies of Resistance, a term with ancient roots, not just a discovery of the moment.

7. The words to the song, in Italian and English, can be found at the website www.ifm.liu.se/~danbi/guccini.html. See also Salvatori 2001.

8. Echeverría summarizes what he refers to as 'the core of Marx's critical discourse' in these terms: 'Operating incessantly at the root of modern life, we find

an untiring mechanism that systematically subordinates the "logic of use value", the spontaneous meaning of concrete life, labor and human enjoyment, and the production and consumption of "earthly goods" to the abstract "logic" of "value" as a blind substance, indifferent to all concrete forms, that only needs to validate itself through a margin of profit in its capacity as an "exchange-value". It is the relentless reality of alienation, submitting the realm of human will to the hegemony of the pure "thing-like will" of the commodity world, inhabited by capitalist economic value' (1998: 63).

9. Meeting of the Council of the Socialist International, Maputo, 10–11 November 2000.

10. According to the Universal Declaration of Human Rights (article 25) 'Everyone has the right to a standard of living adequate for the health and well-being of him- or herself and of his or her family, particularly food, clothing, housing and medical care as well as the necessary social services. Everyone has the right to education, work and social security.'

The Political Economy and Geopolitics of Globalization: What Has Changed? What Does It Mean for the Future of Revolutions?

25 January 2001

John Foran Today's theme has two parts: First, what has changed in the world political economy, with its several components – the world economy, states and geopolitics? Second, what might this mean for the future of revolutions?

In terms of the world economy, I think it would be worth spending some time to trace its contours to some degree and ask if and how, in some important sense, it is radically different than in the past. We might begin with Perry Anderson's classic first editorial of the new series of the *New Left Review* (2000) because in it he does, whatever its faults, try to sum up the current conjuncture in terms of the world economy. Rather than talking about globalization and the world economy he talks about neoliberalism, something that a number of us also do. He locates this in the context of TINA – 'There is no alternative' – the sense that neoliberalism is the name of the game on a worldwide scale and that's precisely what is significantly different about the world today, mentioning a set of interlinked developments that are geographic illustrations of this.

Anderson's first observation is the reassertion of the primacy of American capitalism in all fields – economic, political, military and cultural: the sense that America leads the world's economy and that it dictates the terms for the rest. Second, surveying Europe, he raises the paradox of European social democracy coming to power and then enacting deregulation and privatization in ways that conservative governments previous to it have feared to do. Third, surveying Asia, he notes that Japanese capitalism has fallen into a deep slump and along with South Korea is being gradually pressured to submit to deregulatory standards with increasing unemployment; that China is eager to enter the World Trade Organization at virtually any price and is itself, of course, inviting in foreign capital and weeding out state industry; and that India is for the first time now willingly dependent on the IMF. And fourth, turning to the new Russian economy, he calls it the weakest link in the global market system and notes that in spite of catastrophic regression in production and life expectancy, there has been no popular backlash, and observes that there, too, privatization, including in land, is now in prospect.

Most of the Third World is missing here, to be sure. But Anderson does us the service of providing the start of a survey of developments in the world economy that he argues are significant, possibly unique and recent. What I would like to do, then, is open the floor for observations and thoughts about the nature of the world economy, that aspect of globalization today.

Jeffery Paige   Scarcely have I heard such a mischaracterization of the world economy. Indeed the exact reverse, I think, is true. Let me just go through it because it's remarkable. First of all the idea that American capitalism has achieved primacy in the world. This is true, I agree, as is Carlos Vilas's quotation from Henry Kissinger, that globalization is simply American domination. However, I think we should look carefully to Giovanni Arrighi and Beverly Silver's arguments that what this really represents is the last phase of a declining hegemony. In their recent book *Chaos and Governance in the Modern World System* (1999) they trace the rise of previous hegemonies, especially the British attempt. And at the end of each hegemony what you have is the current moment, where a tremendous development of speculation, the triumph of financial capital, conceals the fundamental weakness of the leading countries. Though the US is very powerful at this stage – what Peter Gowan calls the dollar and Wall Street regime economy – this conceals the fact that the United States economy is in fundamental difficulties, including the superinflated stock market, the absence of any effective saving, the tremendous trade imbalance, the hollowing out of the American industrial structure and the departure of capital abroad. The United States may be able to push its current financial levers to maintain its hegemony for a while longer, but the idea that it's suddenly consolidated is mistaken.

Second, the idea that somehow all the European welfare states have been eviscerated is simply not true. Sure the effort is being made, there is little doubt about it, but it simply hasn't happened except in Great Britain and the United States. In France there's been tremendous resistance. And I think the same is true in Germany, despite a lot of efforts in that direction. We have weakened welfare states in the Third World, but I don't think it's true in the First.

Asia is an interesting case. Yes, there's tremendous pressure in South Korea to sell off assets and to some extent that's happened. The interesting case is China. In all these triumphalist analyses of neoliberalism and capitalism, people always count China as one of the positive cases, but China has maintained the greatest state control over the economy. Foreign investment is highly limited. It's for export, through joint production agreements. The Chinese have very carefully regulated that and that's one of the reasons they've competed so successfully. Now, Anderson may be right that the World Trade Organization leads to a dramatic opening but I'd be very surprised if the Chinese do that.

Then the Russian economy: as Stephen Cohen has suggested, it's not in transition to anything. It's deindustrializing, as Michael Burawoy argues, who calls this process industrial devolution. Cohen calls it the first modern country to demodernize, to go back to the nineteenth century. This is not a triumph of capitalism.

And that finally brings us in turn to the Third World. There are whole areas of the Third World that are increasingly out of the control of capital – much of sub-Saharan Africa, much of Russia, much of the former Soviet Republics and so on. We seem to be increasingly moving into a period of instability and crisis in those countries. I would say the exact opposite of what Anderson is suggesting here. Wallerstein sees this as a tremendous opportunity; I think that we've got to cut through this kind of triumphalism. Why is everybody shouting so loudly that Marx is dead, that revolution is over, that capitalism is successful? Let's not confuse rhetoric with reality. I wish the world worked better, but it doesn't, and that's not the fault of the left. I'm not wishing this terrible world on anyone. We didn't create it. Capitalist planners created it. But it presents an opportunity for constructive alternatives for people, and what we need to be doing as intellectuals is thinking through whether those alternatives are revolutionary or something else. It's an extraordinary moment.

Valentine Moghadam I think that the world order really has changed, much in the ways that Perry Anderson has described. Certainly we do have the primacy of the US and of neoliberal capitalism. To me the downfall of Communism in the Soviet Union represented a tragedy of world historical proportions precisely because the US became the sole hegemonic power. And instead of a world with two economic systems and two political systems where countries can pick and choose, we have one neoliberal system run by the United States. The last battle of the cold war was fought on Afghan soil. The outcome of that battle of wills between the former Soviet Union and the Carter/Reagan/Bush administrations is also a tragedy that we're all suffering, including the US, having created a Frankenstein's monster in the form of the Taliban and Osama bin Laden. I do agree that the US is *the* hegemonic power, much to the detriment of lots of people around the world.

The European social-democratic parties have become extremely conservative. And I do not refer only to the UK Labour Party. Surely I was not the only one shocked that the German government – made up of Social Democrats and Greens – signed on to the NATO bombing of Yugoslavia. The whole political landscape of European social democracy has changed. Although we still have a social-democratic system in northern Europe and the continental welfare system remains very different from that of the US, there is more convergence than there used to be.

I remember when some world-systems analysts talked about Japan being the next hegemon. This has not happened. China definitely is marching in line. China gets the lion's share of direct foreign investment from the rich countries to the developing countries. India is a new neoliberal capitalist country. Russia is a mess. And so on.

I also agree with Jeff Paige that the year 2000–01 is very different from 1989–90. I think we can all remember the capitalistic triumphalism at the time. I don't think that's where everybody is today. People recognize that the system is in crisis, and that there are serious instabilities around the world. Folks at the World Bank and the IMF and the World Trade Organization understand this very well and have been trying to make some concessions to their critics. There *is* a crisis.

This is why Wallerstein calls this the age of transition, not the age of globalization. He thinks that there are some real possibilities and real prospects and I agree with that, too. What Perry Anderson has left out of his equation is of course 'globalization-from-below', the movements of resistance and anti-capitalism and anti-globalization. Now the precise form that this attack on globalization from above and the world neoliberal capitalist order will take is the major question for me. I think that there will be some kinds of coalitions of transnational social movements, transnational advocacy networks and transnational feminist networks, perhaps in alliance or in solidarity with the local struggles, the nationalist struggles, the labor struggles going on in different parts of the world.

One other point related to this is that there *is* a global capitalist or ruling class. The best theorist of this is Leslie Sklair, a British sociologist who has written on 'the transnational capitalist class' in his recent book of the same title (2001). We know who the major institutions are – the multinational corporations, the World Bank, the IMF, the World Trade Organization and, of course, the capitalist states who are doing the bidding of the local business classes. In response to this global capitalist class we see the formation of global and transnational social movement organizations that use the language of socialism and anti-corporate capitalism – the global economic justice movement, the transnational feminist networks, the direct action networks, the Third World Network and similar campaigns and organizations.

Douglas Kellner We do need to go beyond the triumphalism and defeatism both of capitalist and socialist forces, just as we need to go beyond the dichotomy of optimism and pessimism. If you look at things historically, it's ironic that Perry Anderson wrote *Considerations on Western Marxism* (1979), arguing that Korsch and Lukács in the 1920s and the Frankfurt School in the 1930s were basically describing the defeat of the left. If you look at the history of the twentieth century, you'll see that there's an up-and-down dialectic for both socialist and capitalist forces. At different times in the 1920s it looked like socialism was on the move – the Russian revolution, all the European revolutions. They were defeated and then came fascism, as Perry Anderson described. But then lo and behold in the 1950s and the 1960s and the 1970s you have the reorganization of capital in the welfare state, but also the resurrection of socialist movements and capitalism in crisis again. So it's probably a mistake to take a triumphalist or defeatist position just because of the ebb and flow of struggle.

You can see the restructuring of capitalism today as both a disorganization of capitalism and the reorganization of capitalism. On one hand, you can say, it's a period of instability and crisis, but also opportunity unfortunately for capital as well as for the left and oppositional forces. In the 1980s there was a book with the title *Disorganized Capital* by Klaus Offe (1985) coming out of the Frankfurt School, and another by Scott Lasch and John Urry titled *The End of Organized Capitalism* (1987), which basically saw welfare state capitalism falling apart. In retrospect we see this now as globalization and the restructuring of capitalism and post-Fordism – a turbulent restructuring of the state, of the economy, of the whole global order. During the 1990s the triumph of neoliberalism, the technocapitalist dot.com orgy, looked like a triumph of capitalism, and with the collapse of the Soviet Union and the socialist block after 1989, like the total victory of capital. Now we're seeing that there's been resistance to this from the beginning, a globalization from below.

The current political economy, therefore, is simply a turbulent one – a crisis of restructuring, of reorganization that is an open field. History is now in an open situation where there are possibilities of resistance, struggle, maybe even a rebirth of socialism. There are also great dangers that could take many forms. Capital could have a catastrophic collapse through world economic crisis – this is worrying me about the new Bush administration; there could be a new period of really virulent intervention. That there's the possibility that the Latin American movements in Venezuela, Ecuador, Colombia or Chiapas that we've talked about could meet with intervention from a very aggressive Bush administration. We just don't know which way that this is going to go, so it's very hard to characterize a moment that doesn't lend itself to either defeatism or triumphalism, and we need to see the chaotic disorganizing and reorganizing crisis tendencies of capitalism as we struggle for democratization and a more positive future also.

Farideh Farhi If studies of revolution have contributed anything to the social sciences it is this notion that the world was not simple, that revolutions do not happen because you have a clash of forces from below with those at the top. They are much more complex processes that involve nuances and a conjuncture – the bringing together of many different processes that presumably do not have anything to do with each other. I therefore have a hard time thinking of the kind of things that are happening in today's world only in terms of the clash of globalization from below and globalization from above. There is something else going on here; only if we are able to analyze it in a more nuanced way, can we begin to see its opportunities.

What happened in Seattle? It wasn't just a protest in the streets. Sure enough, the protest was there but it revealed something that was very important – that there was conflict within the WTO between the South and the North and in the new ruling class between Europe and the United States. Remember that the core proponents of globalization like Thomas Friedman would say that the hidden hand of globalization has to be backed by the American fist, a fist that presumably has to depend on political mobilization for war at home. Of course, after the 2000 election, I don't know what to say about American politics anymore. In order to defend its election process the only thing a country that is supposed to be hegemonic in the world could say to its own population was that 'We're better than Haiti and let's be happy about it.' They never said, we are better than Sweden. They said be happy because we're better than Haiti. This is the way they justify their political system to their own American population. Now there is something not working here that may be creating a crack. And maybe there are opportunities here. It seems to me that for a better understanding of the opportunities all these lines and how they are interconnected have to be better conceptualized, and I don't think Perry Anderson does that because I think the cracks are not shown.

Mary Ann Tétreault I wanted to come to emphasize the need to take a more historical approach and look at past hegemonies. Globalization in essence is the continuation of a life that ended in 1914 and picked itself up a little bit at the end of the First World War, collapsed again during the Depression, then was reformulated at Bretton Woods, which collapsed again, and since the early 1970s has been rolling along. So we're looking at the spread of capitalism that has been going on for at least 400 years, and that did have a collapse between 1914 and 1945, ending an earlier era where it looked as though life was going to improve forever. This very scary collapse took the form of a major war with two primary phases. And we could look now at the non-resolution of very similar problems. We have more technology now. We also have more personal empowerment. We have the very deleterious effects of that last spurt of colonialism from 1880 onward. In the past twenty years, as production has been put out all over the world, we have seen the compartmentalization and geographic scattering of production. But we had analogs to this at the end of the nineteenth century and the beginning of the twentieth century in the exploitation of the Third World as globalization deepened.

So we're looking at a kind of restructuring that was halted, when the kinds of political interventions that were made to support it were ineffective. The Soviets in the Soviet Union were not allowed to be socialist. They merely turned capitalism upside down and installed the same kind of primacy of the economy and the neglect of everything else. *I think we have a century of failed solutions.* And maybe that's also why we feel unoptimistic about revolution when we look at the revolutions that have been made. Farideh said when she was back in Iran there's a feeling of opening of political space. And I think that's always a very important part of revolutions. In future revolutions we'll need to see whether that space will close down in the same way – you know, in twenty or thirty years – as it did in these others. I think we need a total reimagination of how these kinds of social change take place.

Jeff Goodwin I agree that global capitalism is in some kind of crisis. It has certainly created tremendous privations for hundreds of millions of people. At last count there are about 800 million hungry people, mainly in Africa and Asia, in a world of six billion. This is surely a crisis. But the question here is how we get from this reality to revolution. Farideh Farhi is absolutely right that if there's anything we scholars of revolutions have learned over the years it's that there is no direct or simple connection between poverty or misery and revolution. The connection between poverty and revolution is highly mediated. There are many, many cases of tremendous human misery which have not led to revolutions. Worse, there are many instances in which capitalist crises have helped bring about fascism or authoritarianism. So we need to get at those mediating links between poverty and revolution and name them.

I don't think there's much debate among this group about the tremendous human costs associated with globalization. The more difficult question, however, is the political effects of globalization on both states and non-state actors. Alas, I don't see that globalization, despite the horrors it's creating, is simply opening up opportunities for progressive revolutionary struggles. I think the reality is much more complicated than this.

John Foran   Let me bring some closure to our discussion of the global economy. It's clear that, as Doug said, it's a moment of some chaos or turbulence or confusion of how to characterize it because I find myself agreeing with a good part of what I quoted from Perry Anderson, and the very trenchant critique that Jeffrey gave us, as well as Val's defense of Perry! The way I reconcile it is as follows: to ask what is going on in the world economy is not a simple question, but we're talking about a system still, obviously. And that system is a network of First World countries with the US first among equals, perhaps, if not hegemonic, combined with the multilateral institutions, finance capital, banks and transnational corporations. But of course it's not an extremely well-functioning system and it's one with a long-standing continuity with the past insofar as there are clear winners and losers, and it touches down in very particular ways. So, it's wrong to say that neoliberalism is a kind of homogeneous process because of the way it intersects with various local settings. But I think that within that continuity there are real changes afoot and we have to talk about how to characterize this emerging very strong network of power-holders, banks, states and corporations, national and multilateral.

What are the contradictions in this and how does it lead to prospects for revolutions? The bottom line, and here I've always disagreed with Jeff, is that we're talking about inequality, rising inequality, growing inequality between First and Third Worlds, within regions in both First and Third Worlds, and within nations. I know Jeff agrees with that but not on how that leads to revolutions, of course, and all the mediating steps in between. And we disagree about how important that is as a kind of prime mover. I see that as a prime mover, and if we talk only about the world economy, this process of crisis, restructuring and contradictions is a very strong argument for revolutions to come. Much more can and ought to be said, but at least we have made a start.

We should move on to the second of our three interrelated topics, and that is states. What is changing in terms of states today and what does that means for revolutions?

Valentine Moghadam Globalization and transnational social movements do not necessarily imply the eclipse of the state. State interests still matter in terms of international relations, and state policies are often targets of transnational advocacy networks. What is very interesting and sophisticated about transnational social movements and organizations, and in particular the transnational feminist networks, is that they are working simultaneously at the global level and at local, national and regional levels. For example, each of the transnational feminist networks that I study actually comprises individual women, groups of women and women's organizations from different countries that coalesce around a common agenda. Meanwhile, they are very active in their own countries, making very strong demands and claims on their governments and states. They understand very well the dialectical relationship between the global economy, the transnational capitalist class and their state, and they understand the way in which their governments are implicated in the making of the global economy and the implementation of the global economic neoliberal agenda in their own countries. Feminist demands are therefore directed at their governments and also at the international financial institutions and the World Trade Organization.

Jeff Goodwin In the literature on globalization there is an assumption by many that globalization *ipso facto* means declining state economic intervention. But we ought to be rather suspicious of that claim. There seems to be a sort of zero-sum assumption that if markets play a bigger role, then by definition the state has to play a smaller role. But I'm not at all convinced that there is such a zero-sum relationship between markets and state power. This is a claim that we should question. In my view, state intervention has not declined in this age of globalization so much as taken new and different forms. A state can restructure or even reduce its economic role, for example, even as it's developing new policing and surveillance capacities.

Mary Ann Tétreault I'm also very interested in the issue of how state intervention changes the nature of conflict in a state. If you look at the literature in political science, you see a growing involvement of the state even as it appears to look less involved. In other words, going back to the way Polanyi used 'the great transformation', it is the power of the state that enables a capitalist system to develop and grow, through the power of administration. And this links surveillance and markets very much because what the state is doing on the side is watching us and controlling us, but the state has done this initially through the creation of administrative systems for markets, the tax system and other indirect means of intervention.

Jane Collier   What seems truly new about the world is that the persons who are experiencing the most pain are people who feel the developmentalist welfare state that used to make life livable has deserted them. In the nineteenth century, the capitalist state broke in on communities that had their own safety networks through families and so on. But what makes the present different is the passage of a century of the dismantling of families, the dismantling of communities that could provide those kinds of safety nets. And what people have come to rely on is states that were going to provide health care, education or subsidies to be able to grow crops. This is now being taken away from them. It's something very new in the world that we haven't seen before that we really need to take into account.

Valentine Moghadam   Some of the globalization literature overemphasizes the so-called 'withering away of the state' and depicts the state as a hapless victim of globalization. But the state today can be seen more accurately as the handmaiden of capitalism and of the bourgeoisie. What has withered away after all? The welfarist and developmentalist states, to be replaced by neoliberal regimes in line with US-style capitalism. What is being constructed or restructured is precisely that classic capitalist state that Marx criticized so trenchantly. What is more, there are growing disparities within countries and across countries, which have been very well documented by conventional economists and world-systems analysts alike. This situation, I think, could lead to the re-emergence of the kind of class-based movements and revolutions that many people thought were a thing of the past.

Eric Selbin   I do think it's worth remembering that Thomas Friedman is right: it's about fists, or rather bombs and bullets. But even here there is a division in the ruling class. In the Bush administration think of it as the Powell faction, on the one hand, and on the other Richard Pearl, the

self-styled Prince of Darkness from the Reagan administration, who has
been giving interviews lately saying that this is not a moment of triumph,
this is a moment of great global crisis and we're going to have to something about it. So, people do recognize that the system is in crisis and
somebody is going to have to do something about it. And, of course,
being John Wayne, it's going to be us. But what all of this raises is, who's
going to do all of this? It's going to be states – that's who's got the armies.
They are a gun club, if nothing else, by and large. And I think that one
of the things that we're going to have to think through is this continuing
role of the state and how seriously we're going to take the state as we try
to talk about what this future of revolutions looks like.

Farideh Farhi As far as the question of the state and revolutions is
concerned it seems to me that the fundamental question that we face is
whether or not there are states left in the world that are still vulnerable to
revolution. And whether or not the ones that were vulnerable are all
gone, and whether or not that kind of globalization has occurred, the
processes that have been brought about by late capitalism have been in-
ventive enough to create a state structure that is less vulnerable to revolutions than it was before. It seems that almost everybody is saying that
democratization has created some sort of road block in front of at least the
old-style revolutions, as we have conceptualized them. The question is
whether or not these states – that we all know are not truly democratic,
but are creating a veneer of democracy or engaging in some sort of intra-
elite competition – are able to prevent that kind of breakdown that we
have seen in the past in terms of revolutionary situations. And my incli-
nation is to suggest that at least there are some states that are still vulnerable, that we have not got rid of all of them. You may not have them in
most of Latin America, but certainly in other parts of the world there are
still possibilities that something might happen. I cannot imagine a kind of
grand-style revolution, but even in Russia you have a situation that is very
very fluid and not totally invulnerable to a revolutionary situation at this
point. Revolutions do not happen that often in countries because they are
such traumatic experiences and people don't want to go through that
process, but certainly I would not call the contemporary Iranian state
invulnerable. And so I would still recommend a state-centered approach in
that sense. Let's not fall into the trap of suggesting that globalization in
general has made states less relevant. I think there are some places where
there's quite a lot of possibility, good or bad. And states are the focus of
the struggle because, ultimately, in most of the Third World the question
of the basic rules of the game has not been solved. And that's the primary

reason for revolutions to happen. They start with a political crisis. They may turn into something else more social, but in most places that has not been resolved. And revolution is still an option: the question is what kind of form it will take because of the collapse of the alternatives that used to exist in the world.

Eric Selbin Not only may there well be states out there that are 'still vulnerable' but there may well be states – Russia is an excellent example – that are about to become vulnerable after perhaps not having been so. I don't think anyone wishes revolution on others. But I think we can't rule them out, and I think to move too far away from states does so. I would add, though, that for a very long time there's been a transnational aspect to revolution among revolutionaries that is not beholden to states and even on occasion nationalities, in terms of stories and figures and borrowings from one revolution to another. There's a long tradition that is first seen in the 'European spring' of 1848, with people trying to copy each other and model each other: 'If they can do it there then we can do it here.' And: 'What strategies did they use? Well we can use these here.' An international revolutionary bricolage began to take shape, a combination of things that people were aware of and concepts that were not bound by any state. Though each case, each place, is particular, there arose connections there, across time, across space, across cultures, that matter. In that sense we focus too much on the state and the national necessarily in terms of studying revolutions. On the other hand, the focus of attention of revolutionaries who are trying to do something, in the short term, is still going to be primarily on seizing state power; and if it's not, then I think, as with Chiapas, a legitimate question then becomes, what's it about, what is it they want, and how do they think they're going to implement these things or do them differently without in some sense controlling state power?

Jeffery Paige One of the problems of many globalization studies is that they don't take into account an unevenness of process. Some states, the US for example, seem stronger and more effective, at least for the immediate future; European states seem very strong; African states seem to be in a period of dissolution; Latin American states have not gone that far but they've lost part of their financial autonomy. So I think there's a range of options here and it's not some single process. Second, it seems to me that we need to distinguish those sorts of changes loosely called globalization or neoliberalism, and the effective use of state power by popular movements to resist and restrain the effects of a globalized economy.

Because the transnational networks that are emerging are still building through existing states that have the possibility to mobilize popular groups resisting these sorts of changes.

And that brings me to my final point, an issue that has come up continually. What Carlos Vilas calls market democracy or what Bill Robinson (1996) means by polyarchy is a project pushed by the Clinton administration and international organizations to create a kind of veneer of democracy. Polyarchy simply means you have elections and limited political freedoms. And in the situation of many places in Latin America, you surely have those things but that does not mean the effective ability of much of the population to exercise democratic rights and participation. What difference does it make if people are too poor to participate effectively, to be concerned with their daily lives? If politics are too dominated by the local caciques or bosses? If violence can be used against much of the population? What possible difference does it make that Colombia is a democracy? There are no effective political rights or participation for anybody, people are being killed by death squads, the powers of the army grow apace, and so on. I don't think that these kinds of democracies in any way inhibit revolutions.

I want you to give you two examples. Cynthia McClintock (1998) points out something that we overlook about Sendero Luminoso – she notes that it is certainly a revolutionary movement although not one that many people would like to associate with. Peru had a democracy, not a military dictatorship, but a highly unrepresentative one in which much of the population, the indigenous population, had no effective rights. Indeed in much of Latin America now indigenous people are claiming these rights. The second example is Venezuela, which people are always talking of as a great democracy. This is a fundamental misconceptualization of Venezuela. Venezuelans did not mean by democracy a set of legal rights and obligations. They meant a collective sharing in oil revenues. So it's not really surprising that Hugo Chávez is in power and people in the North think this is a great change. It's not a great change, but it indicates that this sort of democracy is very vulnerable to change and Chávez represents a kind of revolutionary upsurge from below, initially extra-legal. So I don't think that polyarchies or limited market democracies are at all invulnerable to pressures from below. And I don't think that we should be seduced into thinking that this so-called Huntington wave of democracy is real. It simply is not in most places. There is a kind of real democratization in which groups have real social power – women, extremely poor people, desperately poor people, indigenous people, people now thrown out of the stable working class. If these people were to gain real democratic rights, real effective political participation, this could be a tremendously powerful force for change. And it would also tie into global movements for human rights and transnational networks that really are beginning to have an effect. If we want to talk about this in the context of revolution, it seems to me that we have to rethink many of our concepts of revolution because we have emerged from a world of oligarchic states which did not extend those rights, where the only recourse was often to a Leninist model.

But what if popular movements and human rights movements actually succeed in extending real effective democratic participation, where poor people, women and indigenous groups are truly able to have rights? Then we have the possibility of fundamental social transformation – which is what I think is always at the heart of revolution – through democratic means. And I think we have to be prepared to look at this new positive real democratization as a possibility for a new kind of transformation, and then maybe we can avoid the terrors of the huge human costs of traditional revolution.

Jeff Goodwin   I agree with some of these remarks up to a point. But let's consider Peru. First, no revolution occurred in Peru, of course, and Sendero Luminoso has been decimated if not destroyed. Moreover, I disagree entirely with Cynthia McClintock's claim that Peru was a democracy after 1980. Vast expanses of Peru were essentially placed under martial law for many years. There were no civil or political rights to speak of in these areas, and human rights abuses by the military were awful, the worst in the hemisphere in fact. Yet McClintock maintains that Peru was a democracy, mainly because there were elections. But elections aren't the same thing as democracy. Look at apartheid South Africa; look at Colombia today. At the very least, we have to ask 'democracy for whom?' There are political systems, such as the South African, the Peruvian and the Colombian, where there were or are effective political rights for certain groups only – whites in South Africa, elites and sectors of the middle class in Peru and Colombia. But in general terms it doesn't make sense to talk about apartheid South Africa, Peru or Colombia as democracies.

So McClintock's attempt to hold up Peru as a case that allegedly shows that revolutionaries can do pretty well under democratic conditions is not persuasive to me. Yes, revolutionaries can sometimes do well where there are elections – for example, Peru and El Salvador during the 1980s – but they do much less well where most people can actually exercise basic civil and political liberties. It's not surprising, given the lack of such liberties, that black South Africans and some of the rural poor in Peru and Colombia joined or supported revolutionary organizations.

I do agree that we need to think harder about how radical change can occur in democracies. And I'm not totally pessimistic on this score, as there clearly are cases in which large numbers of people (although not majorities) have been radicalized while living in democracies – for example, during the late 1960s in France, the US and especially Chile. Of course, these cases of mass radicalization under democracy are statistical 'outliers'. They're few and far between, for reasons I've discussed elsewhere. And we should also remember that these episodes of popular mobilization led to predictable counter-mobilizations, giving us Pompidou, Nixon and Pinochet. Still, I certainly agree that we need to think more about the parliamentary path to revolution as a possibility, however remote or contingent, or at least about how large populations are sometimes radicalized and mobilized in democratic contexts. But, to repeat, we certainly should not include Peru or Colombia as cases of revolutionary mobilization in democratic contexts.

John Foran Let's take up the proposition, or the reality, the fact, that the cold war is over and, therefore, here indisputably we are in a new situation. The question is, how do we characterize the present conjuncture in geopolitical terms? What does it mean for the future of revolutions? What, to make it specific, is US policy towards revolutions likely to be and how might revolutions fare in light of what you see that to be?

Valentine Moghadam I said earlier that the end of the Soviet Union and of communism have had devastating effects. The cold war period may have been a period in which many revolutions took place, but it was also a period in which many revolutions were attacked and failed, mainly because of the response of the United States. Let's revisit the Afghan revolution of April 1978. Afghanistan was the last battle of the cold war, as I mentioned earlier. The Shah of Iran, Zia al-Haq of Pakistan, and the United States almost immediately opposed the Democratic Republic of Afghanistan. Why? Solely because it was a left-wing government that was friendly with the Soviet Union. Even though its social program was one that was very progressive: land reform, women's rights, infrastructural development, bringing Afghanistan into the twentieth century. Now we're in a post-cold war period, more than ten years after the collapse of the Soviet Union, and the global political environment has changed. Perhaps this is what has made possible the resurgence and the re-emergence of this socialistic discourse that Jeffrey Paige has rightly referred to and that I have also discerned in the transnational feminist networks. Of course, the socialist-feminist discourse of the transnational feminist networks is in part a generational thing in that many of the leading figures are veterans of left-wing movements. But it's also true that young people, for example students who are involved in the anti-sweatshop campaigns, also utilize this discourse in an almost spontaneous manner. So perhaps the post-cold war, post-anticommunist environment is creating opportunities both at the global level and at the national level for these types of movements and organizations, and this kind of anti-capitalist and socialistic discourse.

Jeff Goodwin   I certainly agree that we've heard such anti-capitalist and socialist discourse, but I don't see how the United States government is creating space for revolutionary movements. Any time the US sees something, someone, some movement that opposes its perceived interests, it's going to let them have it full bore. Now, 'full bore' has admittedly taken on a new meaning in the post-Vietnam, post-cold war context. One good thing that came out of the US defeat in Vietnam is a significant shift in mindset not only among the general population but also in the Pentagon, a mindset that has become quite intolerant of US casualties in foreign interventions. So the massive deployment of ground troops is generally not viable at the present time. But 'smart bombs', B-52s and the high-tech gadgetry of the sort deployed in the Persian Gulf, Yugoslavia and elsewhere will be used against enemies. Or the US will simply pay corporations like Sikorsky and Bell to send military hardware in the billions of dollars to places like Colombia. This sort of intervention is going to continue, it seems to me, as long as there are no body bags. I don't see any weakening of US resolve when it comes to confronting and destroying its perceived enemies. So I just don't see much political space emerging from this quarter. On the contrary, it seems to me that with no countervailing power in the form of the Soviet Union, the United States has much more leeway for coercive action than before.

John Foran   The end of the cold war *has* been very hard for the people of Russia, certainly in material terms. It may hopefully have some other benefits in the long run for the Russian people. However, what it does mean on a larger geopolitical scale is that the Soviet model is gone in every respect. It's gone as an ideal, it's gone as a material source of aid to revolutionary states, and that's not a bad thing, I think, for the revolutionaries of the future. I think the US response will depend greatly on who these revolutionaries are and how they conduct themselves in all respects. Armed rebels in Colombia, Iraqi state intransigence, and since 11 September 2001 a worldwide terrorist threat – these will be intervened against. Democratic revolutionaries, though, may have a chance. This is something

I feel in my bones, I guess, about the future. And, ironically, in the same way that you argue that democracies are invulnerable to revolution, democratic revolutionaries may prove themselves less vulnerable to intervention than in the past. And it does have to do with the end of the cold war. It does have to do with the lack of the Soviet target standing behind revolutionaries. It might be that the Internet may help defend democratic revolutionaries; they may take it up as a weapon and find new responses. The international community might stay the hand of the United States under certain circumstances, again depending on the nature of the movements. And that's why the lesson of Chile is not that democratic revolutionaries will always be defeated. But if we project it into the future based on different circumstances, geopolitical among others, and on the side of revolutionaries in terms of strategy and means and approach, we could see something really different. I believe that somewhere, some day, there will be a revolutionary government elected and the question is, will the outcome be different? Optimistically, that possibility is there.

Eric Selbin   Based on a fairly small set of conversations with people in Central America and the Caribbean, I think there's actually a sense in which the Soviet model dies when Khrushchev's speech about Stalin gets out. For some revolutionaries around the world, at that point the relevant model, for good or ill, becomes Cuba, not the USSR. While the Soviets may be in the background and there may be notions of funding, I think there are actually a lot of people who are happy to dispense with the Soviet model, which seems confusing and increasingly burdened by the revelations that start to come out. The idea that there was all of this international support has long been overblown, a bill of goods sold to the population of the United States. But what this recent US election suggests is – just like people were smitten to some extent with Ronald Reagan because he represented some mythical era of the 1920s and 1930s that never existed – what goes along with that is an increased isolationism. I am amazed at the extent to which conservative Republicans in the small town where I live in Texas think we have no business being in Colombia. I've got neighbors that say 'I just don't see what business we got being down in Colombia.' There's a desire on the part of a lot of people in the United States to turn away from what they see as an increasingly complicated and complex world system that they're not sure what to do with. And so in part because of that, there is going to be more space. And without this sort of bogey man – 'if we don't go fight the rotten Commies behind every bush in Central America, the nukes are going to fly from the Urals' – without that threat, it gets tough. As revolutionaries figure out how to frame things differently and learn from their past mistakes, they're going to avoid walking into some of those traps. They're not going to run around like Sendero Luminoso talking about being the fourth sort of Marxism and waving those flags. But it doesn't necessarily mean they're going to change what they're up to. Increasing isolationism in the US, an unwillingness to sacrifice troops, particularly ground troops, which is what it's going to take to win in these kind of situations – if you put the whole package together there's more space.

Mary Ann Tétreault   When I look at the prospects for revolution and for global change in the world, I see this not only from the perspective of individual countries but also from a global systemic perspective. To me the end of the cold war has meant an increased prospect for the localization of politics, where you can have your own local politics with less direct intervention from the two superpowers.

Farideh Farhi   I never thought of the cold war as being particularly conducive or resistant to revolutions. I've tried to look at particular international contexts, moments where revolutions became more possible because of certain interactions which created those possibilities. In the case of Iran and Nicaragua, it was the Vietnam syndrome and the human rights discourse, trying to figure out some way of giving coherence to American foreign policy but instead producing an immobility, which created conflicts within various departments in the United States that prevented the US from directly engaging in countries where it had previously been very much involved. And had its foreign policy had some coherence, it probably would have followed in Iran the Brzezinski proposal of 'Let's go and kill 30,000 people and end the revolution right there.' But that was not the policy that was pursued. In the case of future revolutions, if there are going to be any, we have to look at the facilitating contexts that may possibly arise – the kind of conflicts that either occur within the United States because of disagreements about how to go about preventing a revolutionary group that is about to take over in countries of significance for US global objectives, or conflicts between the United States and Europe and between the United States and regional allies.

I would still argue that we have to conceptualize the United States as the main anti-revolutionary body in the world and accordingly give due attention to both internal and international dynamics that allow it to have a freer hand in its pursuit of global objectives. For instance, the bombing of Iraq in the early 1990s was made possible because of what had happened in the Soviet Union and the fact that the Soviet Union had disintegrated and simply abstained from opposing the decision. Clearly the US has had a freer hand in its use of force since then but not one that is totally unhampered. In the case of Iran, for example, it was clear that the Clinton administration was looking for any excuse to move to a confrontational stance. But the opposition from the region and from Europe prevented the administration from moving in that direction. Of course, these examples are not about revolutionary situations, but if you're going to conceptualize the United States as the main global player whose actions have local consequences, and in some areas such as the Persian Gulf its physical presence even makes it a local player, I think it's important to think of not only the broader international context, but the particular conjunctures – the nuances and the conflicts that exist both within the United States and outside – that allow revolutions to come about rather than saying that the cold war made it more likely or not, and draw conclusions accordingly about the post-cold war period.

Jan Rus We spent a lot of the morning talking about great revolutions and great social revolutions, but they were all revolutions contained within single countries and they were the nineteenth century's revolutions or revolutions that come out of rural places, people who were being crushed by modernization and rebelling against it. The problem is that we're using that model of revolution to talk about achieving justice and some kind of economic leveling out in *this* period, in a globalized world, where great powers control great spaces and have great ability to penetrate those spaces and keep track of them. And my sense is that the Chiapas revolution isn't exactly a chimera but that it's been way overconstrued. It comes after the fall of the Iron Curtain and the collapse of the Soviet Union and suddenly there's an example of what looks like another big social revolution rising up in a rural place, that looks like other social revolutions that we think we know about. It achieves great resonance in Mexico because all social classes have been in a depression since the beginning of the 1980s. It had resonance with urban middle classes as well as with Mexico's industrialists, who were being impoverished by the lowering of the barriers to trade. So you have this peasant reaction in a part of Chiapas which was a reaction to conditions that rural people all over Mexico have been suffering for a couple of generations. It gets much more resonance within Mexico because of the situation at that moment. And then it gets worldwide resonance and passes beyond Chiapas because of the situation of the world with respect to the struggle for equality and justice.

Now what that leads me to is the globalized economic system that we've been talking about, the OECD, the Group of Seven and other multilateral bodies. It's hard for me to understand how those are going to be overthrown by a social revolution of the old sort, of the nineteenth-century sort, the early-twentieth-century sort. It will take some other kind of movement for democratization, something like the civil rights movement, the suffragette movement or the movement against sweat-shops. We're talking about other ways to achieve the ends of a revolution without revolution in that old-fashioned sense being available to us. I don't think it was available, frankly, any place in Mexico. I don't think it's available any place in Central America. We need to find a new model of this rapid overthrow of an unjust political economy but we can't be count-ing on the Zapatistas and Che Guevara to provide that model. We need to be looking for another model of how it will work. The Zapatista rebellion in Chiapas is a noble and inspiring thing, but in a way it's a detour because it's not going to solve the larger question.

Eric Selbin   I think it's a detour but it catches a lot of attention because it is evocative. It does seem to suggest that there might be other possibili-ties. The problem that I run into is when I start trying to play out those other possibilities; they don't go very far, they don't go places.

Carlos Vilas   A lot of revolutions failed during the cold war, notwith-standing the support from superpowers. And a number of revolutions also succeeded, notwithstanding the opposition of superpowers. And it's a fact, too, that revolutions in Latin America date well before the cold war. For example, the Mexican revolution of 1910, the Guatemalan revolution of October 1944. The problem now is that what we see is this huge scope of social mobilizations without an evident articulating principle which could translate this social unrest into a political challenge. What is lacking at present is this articulating political ingredient which in summing up all these social movements involves the building of political power. And the second point is against whom are you going to mobilize this power you are building? Because in politics it's very important to accept that there are enemies. Who is the enemy right now? Davos, the World Bank, the IMF, the supposed local ruling class? Against whom are we going to mobilize this power we are building?

And finally, after this huge wave of revolutions, successful or failed, we have to accept that, for many people, revolution is a bad word. Right now in Nicaragua you had better not speak the word 'revolution'. You're not going to mobilize people in Central American under the banner of revolution but you can mobilize them under the banner of reconstruction after the earthquake in El Salvador. Trying to give aid to the people who really need it, not to the army. Struggling for jobs, for a decent environment, for women's rights, for children's rights. The struggles are there, but they are isolated struggles, sectarian struggles and the magic, as Commander Ruiz put it in Nicaragua, deals with this ability to accumulate different struggles, to articulate them into a political party, a front, a confederation of organizations. That's how revolutions started. We could look at Marcos in Chiapas. What has he achieved after seven years? He's made some good poetry, and he has survived. Second, he has been able to project their proposal to the whole world. This has not been enough to seize power, but I don't know if they wanted to seize it. They have survived. They have enriched the democratic demands of Mexican society. I will not discuss whether Mexico is right now a democratic society or not. There is more democracy now than ten years ago. And the Sandinistas have also contributed to this enhanced democracy in Nicaragua. Perhaps that was not their intention; nor was it Pinochet's to became the hero of economic modernization. He just wanted to get rid of Communism. Neither was it Lenin's intention to pave the road for Stalinism. He wanted socialism and democracy. In politics, things do not always turn out as we want. So the question is how or where are the ingredients in the current events that will lead, or should lead, or could lead to this articulation, this summing up of sectoral struggles in order to bring about progressive change, whatever its name is?

John Foran Thank you, everyone, for your collective contributions to several important sets of arguments about the economic, political and international geopolitical changes that globalization is arguably engendering, and about how these might affect the prospects for revolutions of the future, whether at the national or the transnational level. There can necessarily be no consensus or closure to such a discussion, but we will continue it when we take up the topics of culture and agency in the next thematic conversation.

PART III

Languages and Strategies
of the Future

The Demise of Bolshevism and the Rebirth of Zapatismo: Revolutionary Options in a Post-Soviet World

Christopher A. McAuley

Whatever our ideas about what was either attempted or achieved in the former Soviet Union and in the Eastern Bloc generally – socialism, state capitalism or totalitarianism – the demise of those revolutionary governments naturally forces us to rethink, among other matters, the ideologies, objectives and institutions of revolutionary societies. That is to say that with 'the passing of the illusion' – to borrow François Furet's (1999) title – of a communist utopia, we are moved to redefine and to reimagine the components of both successful and sustainable revolutions that avoid compromising human dignity for the sake of attaining particular material or ideological ends. From this perspective, the 'fall of the wall' may prove more promising and fruitful than the energy formerly spent on defending a political-economic system born of the Russian revolution but failing to fulfill its own proclamations and subsequent expectations. In this light, too, the original Zapatista movement, also born in the same decade that the Bolsheviks took power, may be the model to which future revolutionary movements return as the ongoing uprising in Chiapas suggests in more than just name. This chapter will explore the possibility of such a return and propose what may be the strategies that future revolutionary movements will need to adopt in order to undertake it. However, before addressing those themes, it may be useful to revisit the common political-economic conditions that prevailed in pre-revolutionary Russia and Mexico and the diametrically opposed ideologies that emerged between their most radical wings.

Intolerable Circumstances

Liberals and radicals in both countries agreed that the root of their myriad socioeconomic and sociopolitical problems was autocratic rule – dynastic in Russia, self-made in Mexico. To these ideologues, not only was rule under Porfirio Díaz and Nicholas II increasingly arbitrary, repressive and unjustifiable, but, at the turn of the century, also ineffective. At that juncture it was clear to virtually all Mexicans (save his most ardent supporters) that the economy that Díaz built was not only woefully dependent on the level of foreign demand for the nation's raw materials but equally so on the import of capital, foodstuffs and manufactured goods, particularly in the north (Hart 1992: 99), and, on occasion, American military personnel; while the debilities of tsarist Russia were most graphically revealed in the defeat of that nation's armed forces by a non-European people in 1905. Little wonder, then, that toward the end of the first decade of the last century, neither autocrat was able to use his old trump card to dissipate criticism at moments of political-economic crisis – appeals to nationalism – since the vast majority of Mexicans and Russians agreed that their respective heads of state were unable or unwilling to promote the best interests of the nation. In Adolfo Gilly's description of this new mass consciousness, nationalism lost its ability to 'obscure the relations of exploitation in the eyes of subaltern classes, and prevent or delay the self-identification and class solidarity which should normally result from the development of capitalist relations of production' (1983: 343). In place of autocracy, liberals and most radicals in both countries proposed that representative institutions and the introduction of basic civil liberties – freedom of speech, assembly and press, and male suffrage – should be part of the new political dispensation.

For obvious reasons, the extent of liberal–radical cooperation could neither be deep nor long-lived, for each constituency had vastly different diagnoses of its respective nation's political ills and subsequently proposed equally different correctives. In Mexico, many liberals were, like Francisco Madero, large landholders themselves, and therefore could not and did not seek to reverse the processes by which they expropriated village lands and/or those of individual, small farmers; instead they sought to rid agribusiness of cronyism and the state's privileging of foreign interests. Similarly, liberal Russian ministers like Stolypin and Witte sought to stimulate capitalist social relations in the countryside by 'allow[ing] individual peasants to opt out of their communes, and if their holdings were in separate strips, to demand that they be consolidated. This the government hoped would enhance agricultural productivity, as well as lead to the emergence of a prosperous rural middle class, which as in other countries should become a force for political stability and economic well being of the country as a whole' (Ulam 1981: 195). Their efforts were partially successful: by 1906, some 20 percent of Russia's peasantry had left the *mir* (Bideleux 1985: 16). These family farmers and 'engrossing' (to borrow a term from English agricultural history) peasants who remained in the *mir* purchased the bulk of the land that the Russian nobility put on the market after Emancipation (Wolf 1969: 63). By contrast, at the other end of the rural scale, it has been estimated that more than half of Russia's peasants 'could not support [themselves] from [their] land allotments' after 1900 (Riasanovsky 1984: 431).

Since liberalism in the countryside literally fed urban industry's appetite for human labor, industrial liberalism could not but mirror its rural counterpart. Accordingly, its concern was not the welfare of the industrial worker – who measured her/his quality of life in terms of higher wages, reasonable time for leisure, and the respect of his/her employer to negotiate as equals – but to substitute European and American ownership of Russia's and Mexico's mills, mines and railways with native capital. Thus, for all their railings against the injustices of the Porfiriato, Mexican liberals, to use their example, objected more to Diaz's relinquishment of 'control of some of the most important sectors of the economy [to] foreign firms' than to the political-economic methods he employed to make those sectors profitable (Katz 1981: 4). Political theory, not economic practice, was what separated the Maderos from the Terrazasas.

Radicals, on the other hand, of primarily the anarcho-syndicalist variety in Mexico and of the socialist mold in Russia, wanted to do away with the entire liberal capitalist order, both for its hypocrisy and its inadequacy. As they interpreted the social landscapes of their respective societies, radicals concluded that liberals paid lip service to universal equality before the law but were beholden to an economic system that widened socioeconomic inequality and enabled money to buy political influence, if not office. In place of the liberal capitalist order, anarcho-syndicalists envisioned a society of worker-constituted and controlled small communities, while socialists imagined a society governed by industrial workers (or by their non-working-class representatives), first through the useful remains of the bourgeois state and later in the form of communes, similar perhaps to those envisioned by anarcho-syndicalists but centralized rather than decentralized. Still, these are ideologies more appropriate for societies with numerically substantial industrial working classes, not for those in which the numbers of these is a mere fraction of their nation's total population: 600,000 out of 16 million Mexicans and 3 million out of 170 million

Russians *circa* 1910 (Wolf 1969: 20, 103; Riasanovsky 1984: 428). Yet, among radicals in both countries in the pre-revolutionary era, only Russia's Social Revolutionaries centered their political-economic program on peasant forms of social organization, the others thinking them 'impediment[s] to social and economic progress' (Ulam 1981: 138).

Bolshevism and Industrialization

It is one of the curious developments of the twentieth century that the Russian revolution was inspired by Marxism although the bulk of that country's population lived in the countryside and by agriculture. As we will recall, Marx was of the opinion that the industrial working class would spearhead the revolutionary transformation of capitalist to socialist society, first in the capitalist leader of the nineteenth century – Britain – and then in larger arenas. The fact, then, that Russia's industrial proletariat was numerically Lilliputian made that state an unlikely candidate for the type of socialist revolution that Marx had predicted. The wide gulf separating Marxist theory and the (potential) practice of socialism in what would become the Union of Soviet Socialist Republics was understandably worrisome to the Bolsheviks and largely explains why they first looked expectantly to the movement of German workers as a safeguard of their revolution before embarking on a crash industrialization program themselves (Ulam 1973: 265). Stalin's 'socialism in one country' slogan owes as much to the abortive German revolutions of 1918, 1919–1920 and 1923 as it does to Marxist social theory (Furet 1999: 125–31).

However, given that Marx posited that Western Europe's industrial proletariat would pioneer the societal transition to socialism, he was naturally a wanting guide through the maze of political-economic dilemmas encountered by socialist revolutionaries in marginally industrialized countries (Ulam 1973: 294). For the pressing decision that these men and women must take is to determine which segment of their population will be forced to make the greatest economic sacrifices for industrialization's capital requirements. British and other Western European capitalists, we will recall, had the resources of both domestic and overseas populations and lands (not to mention those where people displaced by capitalism's advance at home could be sent) from which to accumulate capital. Unlike those capitalists, however, socialist leaders in marginally industrialized countries do not have recourse to colonial and/or neo-colonial populations to supply that capital; thus, they must look inward. The choices there are ostensibly limited in countries characterized by huge agricultural populations, minuscule (even if highly concentrated) industrial sectors, and equally puny commercial sectors. Yet, as we suggested earlier, independent even of the social composition of the country in question, for many Marxists the choice is simple: given that they consider the industrial working class the basis of the socialist revolution, they naturally look to the agricultural sector to finance industrialization (Ulam 1973: 247–9, 292–306). Thus, Stalin's rash decision to collectivize agriculture (which he benignly described as the 'transformation of small and scattered peasants' plots into large consolidated farms based on the joint cultivation of land using new superior techniques') may have been madness, but there was clearly a method to it (as cited in Ulam 1973: 291). 'Stalinism', Ulam further remarked, 'came to mean many things, but chief among them was this relentless struggle to produce, to sacrifice everything but the dictator's personal power at the altar of industrialization' (1973: 293).

It hardly seems necessary to state that an economic development program such as this one perforce undermines supposedly democratic institutions in socialist societies. Many Marxists have indirectly admitted as much when they ceased to vaunt socialism as the only true democracy and turned their attention instead to socialism's economic prospects. This type of intellectual evasion of the total social meaning of socialism not only abets, but ultimately justifies the pseudo-dichotomy between political and economic socialism which, among other consequences, allows socialist leaders and intellectuals to postpone indefinitely the institutionalization of democracy while claiming that they do so in order to lay the material foundations of socialist society. On the self-serving nature of this type of socialist argument, Joseph Schumpeter had this to say:

> it is obvious that any argument in favor of shelving democracy for the transitional period affords an excellent opportunity to evade all responsibility for it. Such provisional arrangements may well last for a century or more and means are available for a ruling group installed by a victorious revolution to prolong them indefinitely or to adopt the forms of democracy without substance. (1950: 237)

Otherwise put, there exists the strong possibility in marginally industrialized countries which have undergone socialist revolutions that planners rather than workers will govern in the short, intermediate and long terms. Consequently, although nominally founded in the name of the industrial working class, socialist governments are not beyond mandating the adoption of management practices in industry even more coercive than those employed in capitalist leader nations to increase productivity (Bideleux 1985: 4, 10–11). Thus, it is not surprising to learn that Soviet workers were frequently paid 'piece-rate' wages and that the Soviet government enacted laws 'providing sanctions against absenteeism, lateness, unauthorized job mobility, and other breaches of labor discipline', without investigating their fundamentally political causes (Meyer 1965: 428).

A Dictatorship of the Peasantry

In contrast to the 'scientific' political-economic philosophy that inspired Russia's revolutionaries, the social philosophy that moved Emiliano Zapata and his compadres to revolutionary action was far simpler: the restitution of village lands stolen by *hacendados* and the provision of land to those families that had been, in one way or another, denied the ability to own any. No less important was, in John Womack's words, the Zapatistas' uncompromising insistence that there be 'local ... participation in national progress' (1970: 228). These goals (formally laid out in the Plan de Ayala of 1911 and in the Agrarian Law of 1915), though applicable to most of Mexico at the time that they were written (save some areas of the north), were originally drafted with the socioeconomic conditions of the state of Morelos in mind (Katz 1981: 7–22, 136–45, 283–4). There, sugarcane *hacendados* were continuing to expand cane cultivation on lands for which villages and numerous small proprietors held legal title, such that the overwhelming majority of household heads were drawn into the sugar industry as wage workers. So successful had these *hacendados* been in their campaign to expropriate peasant lands that they made Morelos into the world's third largest sugarcane producer at the time of the revolution (Womack 1970: 49–50). Thus, among other objectives, Zapatismo sought, in Adolfo Gilly's words, 'the revolutionary liquidation of the latfiundia ... the form in which capitalism existed in Morelos' (1983: 237).

However, Zapatismo was as much a political process as it was an economic program. For the handful of years that it survived despite being constantly under counterrevolutionary attack, Zapatismo revived the democratically conducted village assemblies which oversaw the surveying and marking of reclaimed village lands, settled boundary disputes between villages, and made general decisions on the 'disposition of local resources' (Womack 1970: 224). In addition, the revolutionary movement also established a party apparatus – the Consultation Center for Revolutionary Propaganda and Unification – which, among other functions, was to 'deliver lectures in the villages on the mutual obligations of revolutionary troops and pacificos;... give public readings and explanations of headquarters manifestoes, decrees, and circulars; and ... mediate feuds between chiefs, between chiefs and pueblos, and between pueblos (Womack 1970: 275). As Womack posits, the objective of the party and of other Zapatista institutions was 'to keep local people immediately and constantly involved in politics' (1970: 280). Here is how Gilly summarizes Zapatismo's political accomplishments:

> The Zapatist government did not merely constitute itself as a military command, to be maintained until the triumph of the armed struggle, but sought to become a genuine government in all spheres of activity, to construct in Morelos a new central state apparatus, fused with village self-government, that would prefigure a similar structure throughout the country. It passed and applied a series of decrees on the land, education, supplies, finances, the police and the army. After settling the crucial question of land distribution, it issued money, carried out public works, built schools, and so on. (1983: 287)

It is without exaggeration that we can call this a 'dictatorship of the peasantry'.

Gilly's endorsement of Zapatismo is not unqualified, however, and the manner in which he (and others) criticize the movement is important to our discussion of the future of revolutionary movements. For example, he faults Zapatismo for not having 'answered the crucial question of state power', which he attributes to the myopia and petty-bourgeois tendencies of peasant life (Gilly 1983: 78). He remarks that

> The methods were revolutionary, and the mass initiative posed a revolutionary challenge to capitalist power. But the peasantry could not rise to a nation-wide social perspective nor offer a revolutionary solution for the insurgent nation. A national revolutionary perspective, counterposed to the goals of the bourgeoisie, could only have come from the other basic class in society: the proletariat. Yet the proletariat lacked an independent leadership, party and class organization. (1983: 79)

To the proposition that successful revolutions require the combined efforts of agricultural and industrial workers, there is nothing to gainsay. However, in light of our reflections on the anti-peasant nature of industrializing socialist societies, Gilly's contention that working-class leadership of the proletariat–peasant alliance will improve the prospects for truly revolutionary change (that 'dramatically alters the prevailing economic system, and transforms the class structure as well as the patterns of wealth and income distribution') is in no way guaranteed (R. Ruiz 1980: 4). Based on our earlier remarks on the underpinnings of the former Soviet Union's economic development strategy, I think that it is fair to surmise that had it been possible for some portion of the Mexican working class to model itself after the Bolsheviks and had this party been successful, like the

Bolsheviks, in seizing state power, it is likely that this party would have subjected the Mexican peasantry generally to a political-economic regime as harsh or even harsher than that imposed by the *hacendados* of Morelos. In suggesting this hypothetical outcome of a socialist Mexican revolution, it is not my intention to negate either Gilly's contention or those of others who hold similar positions, but rather to underscore two points: one, that in 1910 there was not yet an example of a successful industrial worker–peasant allied revolutionary movement after which Mexican revolutionaries could have modeled their ideologies and actions; and two, that working-class-inspired socialist movements in predominantly agricultural societies suffer from their own myopia and petty-bourgeois biases. Though the context was admittedly different, it was Marx's own awareness of the social limitations of working-class movements in Western Europe that led him, in his final years, to turn to the possibility of peasant-inspired social movements in no less a setting than Russia (Hill 1986: 238–9; Bideleux 1985: 5–11).

Prospects for the Future

Having offered a brief survey of the two competing revolutionary models born in the second decade of the last century, I can now offer what I believe we may expect of future revolutions.

Like others who witnessed it, I believe that the era of the pro-industrializing/anti-peasant socialist revolutions died with the fall of the Soviet Union. In short, capitalists can achieve the same with greater effect. In its place, I share with Samir Amin the vision of the rise of autocentric (which he defines as the 'subjection of external relations to the logic of internal development')/pro-peasant revolutions à la Zapatismo, probably in countries or regions of countries in the throes of war (civil and/or of occupation) or of severe economic crisis or whose economic importance to the capitalist world economy is modest or marginal (Amin 1990: 158–9). Under these conditions, those prospective revolutionary movements might have greater room to maneuver than those areas more fully integrated into the capitalist world economy (Amin 1990: 159). Of Amin's six requirements for the pursuit of this type of political-economic development, I believe that two are most relevant to future revolutionary movements: the development of 'national and popular forms of social organization of production'; and the conception of industrialization 'as a support to progress in agricultural productivity' (1990: 161, 160). The first he described as peasant control over agricultural projects, genuine co-operatives (that are not the means of exaction on the peasants through administrative frameworks depriving the peasant of control over production), machinery for collective negotiation of agricultural prices, national control over industry, a national wages policy, redistribution of sources of finance over the country, and so forth. (Amin 1990: 161)

The main objective of the above policies is to establish the 'most equitable income distribution possible ... between the countryside and the town' by indexing non-rural wages to 'average rural productivity' (Amin 1990: 160). About the production of both the means of production and of consumer goods, Amin draws attention to

production of appropriate inputs (fertilizers, tools, for example), infrastructural work (irrigation, transport and so on), packaging and processing of products, among others. It also entails that this industry satisfy the non-food consumption needs of rural and urban workers, on as egalitarian a basis as possible and that, on the basis of this demand, an integrated chain of intermediate and machine tool industry is established to provide for efficient manufacturing production of consumer goods. (Amin 1990: 160–61)

Amin does not specify the requisite political institutions to implement an autocentric development program, but he insists that they practice 'participatory democracy' or the 'direct involvement of ... communities in preparing and managing small projects' (1990: 166). Participatory democracy is not only political insurance that 'Social relations [are] founded on workers' cooperation rather than their surrender to exploitation', but is furthermore the 'sole means within the national and popular society of ... isolating the internal capitalist relations of production from comprador integration in the world capitalist system and reducing external vulnerability' (Amin 1990: 181, 189). Put in more concrete terms, of all the revolutionary wings of both the Russian and Mexican revolutions, Zapatismo was the one that authentically contested despotic rule in these two peripheral capitalist societies on its social, economic and political bases. Zapatismo proved, moreover, that public ownership of capital is a necessary but insufficient condition for the making of socialist society, contrary to what the Bolsheviks led many to believe.

Though these projections may seem utopian at the dawn of the twenty-first century, it must be borne in mind that many African and Asian countries have social structures similar to those that characterized pre-revolutionary Mexico and Russia. The challenge, then, that will face the future revolutionary movements that I think it no exaggeration to say will inevitably emerge in the Afro-Asian world will be to avoid the pitfalls that we earlier highlighted in the Russian and Mexican revolutions: the privileging of the industrial sector over the agricultural sector, and the limiting of the purview of revolutionary institutions to select geographical areas. In order to skirt these political dead ends in the future, I believe that much will depend on the ability of the petty-bourgeois and working-class allies of what will largely be peasant-based revolutionary movements to shed their capitalist-derived notions of social progress and economic development. Without that ideological transformation, the age of revolution may well be over.

11

Is the Future of Revolution Feminist? Rewriting 'Gender and Revolutions' for a Globalizing World

Valentine Moghadam

In this chapter I return to my earlier theoretical work on gender and revolutions (Moghadam 1993, 1997). There I developed a model of gendered revolutionary processes and outcomes, by which bourgeois, socialist and populist revolutions are classified as egalitarian ('the women's emancipation model') or patriarchal ('the women in the family model'). I used this model to analyze the gender dynamics of, *inter alia*, the French revolution of 1789, the Bolshevik revolution of 1917, the Iranian revolution of 1979 and the East European revolutions of 1989. I now revisit this model in light of the multifaceted process of globalization, the end of the cold war and of anti-communism, the global spread of feminist discourses and the emergence of women's movements and organizations across countries and regions. I hypothesize that if revolutions or oppositional movements do not incorporate women and feminism, it will be to their disadvantage; they will be less likely to gain either national or international support. A contemporary example of the latter is Afghanistan. I hypothesize, too, that revolutions will occur because globalization – the present stage of capitalism – is resulting in increased inequalities globally and within societies (UNDP 1999). Oppositional movements are likely to emerge and to mobilize at both national and global levels, as we have seen with the anti-globalization protests of 1999–2001. Organization and mobilization could be facilitated by new civil-society-mobilizing structures and by the global infrastructure created by transnational social movements and global civil-society organizations associated with labor, women, human rights and the environment. Many of the organizations that comprise transnational social movements deploy a strong critique of global capitalism. Future revolutions, therefore, may evince socialist and feminist features alike.

Gender and Revolutions: Before and After Feminism and Globalization

In previous work, I have developed a model in which I classify revolutions by their (immediate) gender outcomes. This work was an attempt to bridge the divide between the feminist scholarship on women and revolutions and the more mainstream study of revolutions. In the former, women's roles in revolutions were recovered from historiographical obscurity and emphasized as important to the course and outcome of the revolution. Many feminist scholars also argued that revolutionary movements subordinate women's interests to 'broader' or 'basic' revolutionary goals, and that revolutionary states often marginalized or excluded women from power and enacted legislation that emphasized women's family roles. In contrast to the feminist scholarship, mainstream studies of revolution have tended to neglect women and gender issues; their description and analyses of revolutionary causes and outcomes focus on class, state and world-system as key factors. The approach in this chapter seeks to combine the attention to 'structure' that has been characteristic of the third generation of scholarship on revolution, and the more recent recognition of the salience of 'agency' that is said to be a defining feature of the emerging fourth generation of revolutionary studies (Goldstone 2001; see also Foran 1993, 1997b).

My earlier work on gender and revolution was thus an attempt to integrate gender analysis in the broader study of revolution, to recognize the social-structural salience of gender (like class), and to differentiate revolutions by their gender outcomes. It grew from the simple observation that almost all revolutions involve the participation of women in ways that disrupt pre-existing social relations of gender, and that revolutionary states are preoccupied with policies and laws pertaining to women and the family. In my review of the great social revolutions and various Third World populist revolutions, I found two types of revolution and their implications for women and gender relations.

One group of revolutions falls into the 'women in the family' or patriarchal model of revolution (the French revolution, the Mexican revolution, the Iranian revolution); while others illustrate the women's emancipation, or egalitarian model of revolution (the Bolshevik revolution and some Third World revolutions that were explicitly socialist, e.g.

Yemen and Afghanistan). These are ideal-types, and it should be noted that in each case there have been differential effects upon women, based on social class, race/ethnicity and ideological divisions among women. Nevertheless, and thus far, revolutionary discourses and policies pertaining to women, the family and citizenship seem to fall into these two categories.

The women's emancipation model says that the emancipation of women is an essential part of the revolution or project of social transformation. It constructs Woman as part of the productive forces and the citizenry, to be mobilized for economic and political purposes; she is to be liberated from patriarchal controls expressly for that purpose. Here the discourse is more strongly that of gender equality than gender difference. The first example, historically, of such a revolution is the Bolshevik revolution in Russia, which, especially with respect to its early years, remains the avant-garde revolution par excellence, more audacious in its approach to gender than any revolution before or since. Other revolutions that conform to this model – in some cases explicitly – include those of China, Cuba, Vietnam, Democratic Yemen, Democratic Afghanistan and Nicaragua (socialist or populist revolutions) and the Kemalist revolution in Turkey (a bourgeois revolution).

The women-in-the-family model of revolution excludes women from definitions and constructions of independence, liberation and liberty, and sometimes expressly designates women as second-class citizens or legal minors. It frequently constructs an ideological linkage between patriarchal values, nationalism and the religious order. It assigns women the role of wife and mother, and associates women not only with family but also with tradition, culture and religion. The historical precursor of the patriarchal model was the French revolution, which, despite its many progressive features, had an extremely conservative outcome for women. The French woman's chief responsibility in the Republic was to be the socialization of children in republican virtues. In twentieth-century revolutions that had similarly patriarchal outcomes for women – notably Mexico, Algeria and Iran – women were relegated to the private sphere despite the important roles they had played in the revolutionary movements. In these three cases, men took over the reins of power; associated women with family, religion and tradition; and enacted legislation to codify patriarchal gender relations. Feminist studies in the 1990s on postcommunist Russia and East Central Europe would confirm that the political and economic changes there, too, conformed to the patriarchal model of revolution (see Einhorn 1993; Moghadam 1993a).

What determines each type of revolution and its gender outcomes? Here ideology and social structure are equally salient. In general, where revolutionaries are guided by a modernizing and socialist ideology, the revolution is more likely to be emancipatory in gender terms. Where revolutionaries are guided predominantly by religious or nationalist ideology, patriarchal outcomes are more likely to occur. In addition, pre-existing gender relations (the position of women within the society and economy) and the place of women within the revolutionary move-ment strongly determine the gender outcome. Pre-existing patriarchal gender relations are often carried over in the post-revolutionary situation, despite temporary disruptions in the course of the revolution, when women take part in protests and struggles. This is less likely to happen, however, when a 'critical mass' of women have entered the public sphere in the pre-revolutionary situation, and when large numbers of women take part in the revolution and assume decision-making and leadership roles. Thus, structural determinants of gendered revolutionary outcomes seem to be: (1) pre-existing social structure and the nature of gender relations; (2) revolutionary ideology and the movement's goals; and (3) the extent of women's participation in the revolutionary movement and leadership.

Let us apply this model to the Iranian case. The immediate gender outcome of the Iranian revolution was a patriarchal and regressive one, in part due to the pre-existing social structure and the nature of gender relations. In the 1970s Iran was a modernizing society, but a very dualistic one, characterized by a growing modern middle class and working class alongside the older, more traditional and larger urban petty bourgeoisie and rural population. In the 1960s, partly as a result of the modernizing efforts of the Pahlavi state, women's access to education, employment and political participation improved, but these social changes, and the legal reforms that accompanied them, affected a relatively small proportion of the female population, mainly in the major cities (Tohidi 1994; Poya 1999). Moreover, the unprecedented physical and social presence of urban women of the 1970s was met by a backlash in the form of an Islamist movement that went on to overturn the Pahlavi-era legal reforms, insti-tute gender-discriminatory policies and emphasize women's maternal roles. Opposition to the new gender regime was limited, emanating mainly from women leftists and liberals of the small urban upper-middle class.

Another major determinant of this outcome was the ideology of the revolutionaries. This pertains particularly to the Islamic revolutionaries, who were the dominant force in the anti-Shah revolutionary coalition and who went on to build an Islamic state. Theirs was a religious and cultural-nationalist ideology that called for the re-establishment of the traditional Muslim family and codified a patriarchal gender contract premissed upon the male breadwinner and female homemaker ideal. (The longer-term outcome complicates this picture somewhat, but it is plausible to suggest that had Islamization not occurred, the rates of growth in women's social, political and economic participation that became evident in the late 1990s may well have occurred earlier and more rapidly.) In addition, although Iranian women took part in the massive street demonstrations, their slogans were those of the broader revolutionary coalition, and not those that might be more typical of women's interests (e.g. equality of women and men, women's autonomy and self-determination, full political and social citizenship rights, etc.). Most importantly, women were nowhere in the revolutionary leadership, which was dominated by clerics (exclusively male), male nationalist leaders and male leftists.

In fact, there was probably greater female participation among the left, but even so, women were a small minority among the guerrillas and the leadership. Many Iranian feminists have raised the question of why the left forces were so ambivalent on the woman question after the revolution, and why they were so hostile to feminism (Sanasarian 1983; Yeganeh 1982; Shahidian 1994; Paidar 1995; Moghissi 1999). I submit that it had to do first with the novelty of second-wave feminism in the 1970s, as well as the distinctions that were being made throughout the world between bourgeois or radical feminism versus working-class or socialist feminism, and between 'Western feminism' versus 'Third World feminism'. Second, it had to do with participation and representation: the overwhelming presence of men in left-wing organizations versus the limited presence of women. There were, of course, some well-known communist women among the fallen guerrillas as well as in the left parties that emerged during and after the revolution. And in the immediate post-revolutionary period, the National Union of Women was formed — but this occurred in the absence of a social movement of women. The novelty of feminism as an ideology, the novelty of autonomous women's organizing and, perhaps most significantly, the absence of a sizable female working class precluded any real influence on the politics and positions of the left organizations (in contrast, in the case of the Russian revolution, the Bolsheviks, especially Alexandra Kollontai, were organizing women workers as early as 1905).

In other words, I suggest that many earlier revolutions, including the relatively recent Iranian revolution, lacked the capacity to integrate women and gender concerns into their ideologies, goals, state-building and legal projects due to structural reasons — the nonexistence or relative novelty of feminism, the absence of an established women's movement or a critical mass of activist or 'public' women, the pre-existing strength of patriarchal gender relations and ideologies.

In an era of globalization and of global feminism, however, the social structural context in which future revolutions will occur has changed. Worldwide, a critical mass of activist women and women's organizations, including influential transnational feminist networks, as well as the diffusion of women's rights discourses worldwide, have changed the social relations of gender within societies and globally. Global feminism has emerged since at least 1985, when the Third UN World Conference on Women took place in Nairobi, and a number of influential transnational feminist networks formed. It has grown since 1995, when the UN's Fourth World Conference on Women in Beijing resulted in the adoption of a Platform for Action and commitments by governments to implement its recommendations for women's equality and empowerment (Moghadam 2000). Moreover, women's caucuses were active at all the UN conferences of the 1990s – the conference on environment and development in Rio in 1992, the human rights conference in Vienna in 1993, the population and development conference in Cairo in 1994, and the world summit for social development in Copenhagen in 1995. During 2000, women activists from around the world, and representatives of increasingly influential transnational feminist networks, took part in the five-year reviews of the World Summit for Social Development and the Beijing Conference, writing position papers, lobbying delegates and advocating stricter observance of timelines and benchmarks for implementation. It should be noted that many feminists active in Latin America, the Middle East, North Africa, sub-Saharan Africa and Europe, including founders of transnational feminist networks, are veterans of left-wing parties and Third World revolutions. A careful examination of their literature shows the revitalization of a socialist-feminist discourse (Moghadam 2001).

These domestic social changes and global processes have served to bring greater legitimacy to demands for women's participation, autonomy and citizenship. Now that feminist ideas have spread and women's rights are on global and national agendas, revolutionary movements and state-building projects of the new century are more likely to incorporate women and feminism.

Contemporary examples of revolutionary movements and states that have incorporated feminist or women's rights goals are South Africa's ANC, the Zapatista movement in Mexico and Northern Ireland's republican movement. In these cases, the revolutionary ideology and women's major roles in the movements are far more amenable to emancipatory gender outcomes, and in South Africa have led to the conscious integration of feminist claims in the legal and budgetary frameworks (see, for example, McWilliams 1995; Marcos 1995; Meintjes 1998; Ponce de Leon 2001).

These also are movements and states widely hailed as progressive through-out the world. The case of Islamist Afghanistan exemplifies this argument. It should be noted that the Taliban regime was a pariah state, shunned by the international community and recognized by only three states. Nor was the Taliban regime popular domestically – it had to impose itself on the Afghan population (that is, those who were not in exile). The inter-national isolation of the Taliban is a success story of the global feminist movement. In September 1996, when the Taliban came to power, the Clinton administration and governments around the world were close to recognizing the new regime. Concerted action on the part of expatriate Afghan feminists in the United States, Europe and Pakistan, along with protests by feminists around the world (e.g. the 'gender apartheid' cam-paign by the US Feminist Majority, feminist action in Italy and a petition drive by women's organizations in many countries) prevented recognition at the time, and subsequently prevented a planned oil pipeline deal.

It is too early to assess developments in Afghanistan, following the removal of the Taliban government and its repressive gender regime (Moghadam 1999a, 2002). But it is noteworthy that the post-Taliban government had to be responsive to international feminist concerns and include Afghan women in its decision-making bodies.

The lesson seems obvious. In an era of feminism and globalization, if revolutions or oppositional movements do not incorporate women and feminism, it will be to their disadvantage. They will be less likely to gain either national or international support.

On World Revolution

In their recent book, Terry Boswell and Christopher Chase-Dunn (2000) distinguish *social revolutions* and *world revolutions*. The first, they note, are class-based rapid transformation projects that build or strengthen states. By contrast, world revolutions are clusters of revolutionary activity and social movements, including separatist and colonial revolutions. This is an ex-panded definition of revolution, not as a singular, episodic event, but as a cyclical process that should also be viewed in historical perspective. In addition to mapping periods and sites of world revolutions, Boswell and Chase-Dunn argue that revolutions (both social revolutions and world revolutions) have a progressive nature to them, in that their demands and objectives tend to persist across time and space. This approach is a useful one. By blurring the distinction between revolutions and social movements and by examining anti-systemic activity in a world-historical perspective,

Boswell and Chase-Dunn point the way toward an understanding of the future of revolution in an era of globalization.

Economic globalization – or the current form of world capitalism – has led to much dissatisfaction and unrest, mainly due to growing income inequalities, declining labor standards, continuing economic difficulties and the emergence of new forms of global governance that appear hegemonic and undemocratic. But who will spearhead world revolution in the present era? Could left-wing political parties build alliances, along with trade unions, in a re-enactment of the early Internationals? Boswell and Chase-Dunn note that 'despite globalization, international political parties and labor unions have not been among those international organizations on the rise' (2000: 196). They conclude that 'a cluster of revolts in the semi-periphery, when matched with demands from core social movements and peripheral states, could suddenly make debated issues of global standards an obvious solution. This would in retrospect appear to be a world revolution, one that would initiate new movements for global change' (2000: 245).

To a certain extent, this is already occurring. It appears to take the form of (1) the cycle of anti-globalization protests that have appeared since 1999, involving organized groups from the global North and South; (2) the proliferation of transnational feminist networks that target capitalism and patriarchy (calling for economic justice and gender justice); (3) the global environmental movement, which demands sustainable human development rather than unfettered economic growth; and (4) sporadic struggles across the globe for workers' rights.

To their credit, Boswell and Chase-Dunn acknowledge the progressive nature of the women's movement, although they do not elaborate on its character, activities or demands. And they take seriously the importance of an alliance of global movements – labor, environmental and women's movements (2000: 245). Indeed, it is my view that a formidable alliance would be one between feminism and labor – that is, between the social movement of women and social movement unionism. Such an alliance is entirely possible, given global feminism's concern with the exploitation of female labor in the global economy (Ward 1990; Moghadam 1999), and given the growing participation of women in trade unions (Hastings and Coleman 1992; Cobble 1993; Martens and Mitter 1994; Chhachhi and Pittin 1996; Dannecker 2000). Trade-union women, and especially feminists within trade unions, could bridge the divide between the feminist movement and the labor movement. But such an alliance would call for a more activist and transnational labor movement than we have been accustomed to seeing in recent decades (see, for example, Moody 1997). Meanwhile, feminists have joined forces with environmental and human rights organizations in the campaigns against the vagaries of economic globalization.

Were there to be a formal alliance among the women's, environmental and labor movements, a worldwide socialist movement could emerge. For now, mobilizing structures are in place that could be extremely useful to world revolutionary activity. In particular, there exists a global infrastructure that is the result of at least three decades of social-movement organizing and interaction on the part of transnational advocacy networks and global social movements, including the women's, human rights and environmental movements (Smith, Chatfield and Pagnucco 1997; Keck and Sikkink 1998). Research, advocacy, lobbying and direct action are planned and coordinated through the use of information technologies, while the relatively low cost of international travel and relaxed visa regulations facilitate participation in major events or mobilization for protest actions.

And what of worker protests? It has been suggested that the era of revolution is over, partly because the so-called third wave of democratization prevents, hinders or attenuates revolution in the Third World. But does the third wave of democratization guarantee economic justice? Despite democratization, there have been growing income and social inequalities across countries and within societies (UNDP 1999; Bornschier 2001; Moghadam 2001), much of it due to liberalization and privatization, the hallmarks of economic globalization. Such inequalities have been the basis for class conflicts and revolutions in the past, and they remain salient today and for the foreseeable future. American unions were well represented in the anti-WTO protests in Seattle in late 1999. In May and June 2000 there were six general strikes against the effects of globalization and neoliberalism – in India, Argentina, Nigeria, South Korea, South Africa and Uruguay (Brecher, Costello and Smith 2000: 20). Workers went on strike in Turkey for more pay and for a voice in decision-making (Frantz 2000), and the same occurred in Iran (*Iran Bulletin*, various issues). In Greece, the federation of Greek telecommunications workers, representing 18,500 of the 19,700 workers in the Hellenic Telecommunications Organization (OTE), mounted a seven-day strike in autumn 2000 when the government announced it would cut its stake in the OTE and support privatization (Simkins 2000). In addition to triggering worker protests at the national level, the existence of inequalities – between classes, the sexes and countries – forms the basis of anti-globalization protests and informs the activities and objectives of the major transnational social movements.

What are the new conditions, therefore, that may result in revolutionary activity that is feminist, socialist and global?

- the worldwide growth of feminist discourse and of transnational feminist networks;
- the emergence of transnational advocacy networks and global social movements with a capacity to organize and mobilize effectively across borders;
- widening income gaps and social inequalities, and the emergence of grievances related to the failures of neoliberal capitalism.

In the past, revolutions were outcomes of processes related to the nation-state and domestic social classes. But in the twenty-first century and in an era of globalization, this may no longer be a necessary or sufficient feature of revolutions. The sort of organized transnational revolutionary activity that first emerged in the early twentieth century may become more wide-spread and successful in an era of global social movements with developed infrastructures. In recent years we see the expansion of criss-crossing trans-national advocacy networks and social movement organizations, many of which have explicit or de facto anti-capitalist and socialist discourses and objectives, in that they target the major institutions of capitalism in our time – multinational corporations, the World Bank, the IMF, the World Trade Organization. Together with nationally based revolts, such move-ments and organizations could lead to major social and political transfor-mations. The classical Marxist vision of a world revolution may actually be realized.

In assessing the future of revolution, therefore, we need to understand the constraints and opportunities associated with structure and agency – contradictions within the capitalist world-system and the prospects of existing social movements and class struggles. I end in agreement with a pertinent prediction by Immanuel Wallerstein: 'The modern world-system is in structural crisis and has entered into a period of chaotic behavior which will cause a systemic bifurcation and a transition to a new structure whose nature is as yet undetermined and, in principle, impossible to pre-determine, but one that is open to human intervention and creativity' (Wallerstein 2000: 249).

At the Crossroads of Globalization: Participatory Democracy as a Medium of Future Revolutionary Struggle

Abdollah Dashti

It is perhaps necessary to look at participatory democracy as a utopia, in the sense that it is not completely achievable, given various sociological and psychological limitations, but rather achievable in steps only, and certainly valuable as a tool in dealing with such problems as education ... and giving people a strategy for self-determination.

Martin Oppenheimer (1971: 280)

Several processes portend the end of the revolutionary era. The nation-state as the normative site of revolutions appears to be weakening as globalization renders its geographical and ideological borders more porous. The importance of class as an analytical tool and class struggle as a mobilization strategy for revolutionary movements is increasingly questioned by many analysts, especially those reflecting the wishes of the elite. The formation of trade blocs, possible unions (à la Europe) or military pacts carries the collusion to combat movements that might threaten their viability or perceived interests. The attenuation of the role of the state as a formal repressive apparatus and the expansion of organs of civil society diminish the effectivity of frontal attack on the state. The fall of 'communism' removed the larger discursive context within which popular revolutions can be acted out. And triumphalist discourses of capitalism in the aftermath of the collapse of 'actually existing socialism', promoted as proof of the futility of revolutions that conceived them, have dampened the ideology of revolutionary struggles. All these developments point to a scenario that closes the possibility of revolutions. Is there still a future for revolution?

Since many of the injustices that triggered past revolutions not only remain firmly in place but are growing, the short answer is a possible yes. Addressing or answering this question calls for developing specific geo-historically informed conceptualizations of the contemporary world. However, an adequate reading of the contemporary globalizing world and the possibility of revolutions hinges upon a comprehensive understanding of past revolutions that played a momentous part in shaping the present age.[1] Given the extreme fluidity and ambiguity of globalization, the accompanying question would be: What does the future of revolution look like? This chapter draws a preliminary general outline of a framework for exploring past revolutions and globalization to evaluate the possibility of future revolutions.

Wars of Maneuver

Let me sketch two revolutionary scenarios with varying degrees of possibility: one based on Gramsci's (1957, 1971) war of maneuver, the other based on his war of position. Most revolutions of the past have been won through the war of maneuver, as just battles in a still more protracted revolutionary war whose eventual success depended on a more intricate war of position to attain popular hegemony and sustain a revolutionary social formation, ideally advancing participatory democracy. There are still several cases where struggle for freedom and justice might operate, albeit with some changes, within the parameters of the war of maneuver, leading to some form of revolutionary transformation (I am thinking of Palestine, Chechnya, Abkhazia, Kosovo, Bosnia, Chiapas, Colombia, Algeria, Egypt, Afghanistan, the Kurds (especially in Turkey), the Basques, the Sikhs and Muslims in northwest China). But since globalization is increasingly diminishing the possibility of revolutions through the war of maneuver, struggle along that path in the future might not play as crucial a role it once did in catapulting revolutionaries to power. Most future revolutions will be fought through the war of position. A brief analysis of past revolutions helps us speculate better about future revolutions.

Like history itself, revolutions have been riddled with ironies. They have been clamorous commentaries on modernity's ideological attempt to shape the world in a certain way around unitary concepts – Reason, Progress, Culture, Democracy. They have also often been 'pathways to modernity' (Halliday 1999: 54), bloody interventions to resolve contradictions arising from uneven and fragmented processes of capitalist modernity. Trying to dispel modernity's philosophical quest for foundations, ironically revolutions themselves ended up being cast in a teleological mold – in that revolutions were viewed as inevitable. Trying to unravel the contradictions of uneven 'development' that capitalism couldn't assuage, revolutions ironically, despite their rhetoric, ended up helping capitalism not to contract but to expand.

Entangled in an interpretation of the logic of capital as homogenizing, most accounts of revolution have fallen prey to several shortcomings, including: (1) abstracting from the overall social structure one set of social relations – for example, economic, political or psychological – in terms of which that structure is read; (2) neglecting, until the 1979 Iranian revolution, the role of cultural/ideological practices; (3) failing to address the specificities of local forces and to account simultaneously for local, national and global forces; (4) lack of sensitivity to the dialectical relationship between agency and structure; (5) viewing revolutions as merely moments or methods of change (as does, for example, Aya 1979, 1984) rather than processes that precede and continue after the moment of victory; and (6) defining revolution as a radical, abrupt change in the overall structure of society, aiming at qualitatively transforming society's political, class and social order (as, for example, Skocpol 1979) while overlooking the historical possibility that changes in class structure, cultural meanings, ideological construct and 'ways of knowing' take place gradually (Appadurai 1986; Reddy 1986: 261–84). An integral definition of revolution should also include utopian visions projected in equality and justice avowed by revolutions.

The genealogy of revolutions needs a thesis that provides a picture of revolutionary transformations that doesn't stop with the analysis of causes alone, but delves into the mechanisms, directions, immediate achievements and long-term outcomes of revolutions. Such a picture only emerges from a meticulous examination of historical processes constituted by the interplay between actions and structural possibilities, and between local and global processes. A theory of revolution read in terms of social-historical contradiction helps extend the analysis of contention beyond the state apparatus, the main theme of conflict theories of revolution (see Halliday 1999: 161–5). Without an analytical framework accounting for contradictions, issues such as autonomy, solidarity, mobilization and damage that have concerned students of revolutions remain empty categories in themselves.[2]

Such conceptualization requires a historiography of the formation of contradiction as an arena in which social forces, bridled by structural constraints, acted out their cooperation or conflicts to promote or prevent a revolutionary victory. A cursory overview of past revolutions and their ensuing transformations via the war of maneuver lays bare the workings of five principal contradictions: political, national, class, intra-elite/economic and cultural. I will explore this idea with brief examples from two cases: Nicaragua and Iran.

Political contradiction stemmed from the illegitimacy of governance. In many revolutionary cases this tension between the state and society manifested itself in the protracted rule of externally sponsored dictatorial regimes. The imposition of the Somoza dynasty on Nicaragua by the US in 1933 and the reinstallation of the Shah in Iran in 1953 marked those regimes with illegitimacy, contributing to their eventual downfall. Those countries' liberal elites sought to mitigate dictatorial regimes by reforming the government. But most revolutionaries targeted the structure of the state itself, aiming to reconfigure radically the governing apparatus. In cases such as Russia, Cuba, Iran and Nicaragua, dictators summed up in a unified image the principal contradictions of their societies. Recognizing the importance of this image as a rallying point, some revolutionaries made strategic use of it. A few years prior to the victory of the Nicaraguan revolution, a group of Sandinista guerrilla fighters drew up a careful, and potentially successful, plan to assassinate the dictator Anastasio Somoza Debayle. When they went to seek the permission of Carlos Fonseca Amador, a founder of the FSLN and the commander-in-chief of the guerrilla forces, he strongly advised them against implementing the plan. He is reported as having argued that 'Somoza was like a precious gem around which all of our people's contradictions coalesced, within which national liberation and liberation from the dictatorship were intertwined, and in which the economic contradictions with the bourgeois sector of our country were concentrated' (quoted in H. Ruiz 1980: 14).

National contradiction dealt with the perception among many, predominantly intellectuals, that their nation wasn't entirely free because their national interests were subordinated to foreign powers' vital interests. Drawing the axis of opposition between what is national and what is antinational, this contradiction has been the most effective of the contradictions, in that its main motto of national dignity offered a better possibility of cutting across varied identities and of unifying many people behind national sovereignty, against foreign domination of their country. Perceiving the Somozas and the Shah as servants of US interests triggered an enduring wave of nationalist sentiments and practices against those regimes. However, under the canopy of the global power play of the cold war, and to ward off the destabilization of a given country within a global division of labor, nationalist movements around the world were crudely branded by dictatorial regimes as part of an international communist conspiracy, and hence themselves anti-national. As such, anticommunism served as the most convenient ideology for inverting or denying the national contradiction.

Derived from sharp differentiation between rich and poor and embodied in the contradiction between capital and labor, class contradiction generally corresponds to the contradiction between 'private appropriation' and 'socialized production'. When moral economies collapse and real-economik takes hold there develops a strong impetus for class contradiction to intensify. As modern capitalism penetrated more seriously into Nicaragua and Iran, especially in its early phase of primitive accumulation, and eroded moral economies without replacing them with any sort of safety net of its own, it rendered more intense the gap between rich and poor, facilitating the mobilization of the poor against the rich. For some revolutionaries who adhered more staunchly to the Marxist materialist conception of history, resolving the three contradictions of nation, class and state aimed to transform radically the whole society. The revolutionaries aimed to eliminate social class, the state and the nation, creating eventually a classless, stateless, borderless global world – a vision of globalization rather different from the current one. The creation of such a utopian cultural form as myth-like political ideology, doesn't manifest itself 'as a cold utopia or as a rational doctrine', writes Gramsci (1957: 135), 'but as a creation of concrete fantasy which works on a dispersed and pulverised people in order to arouse and organise their collective will'.

Intra-elite economic contradiction refers to an ongoing tension between factions of the bourgeoisie holding political power and politically marginalized factions of the bourgeoisie. In most cases, the ruling elite monopolized national resources, especially financial institutions and the military, as their private property, creating an oppositional elite. In Nicaragua the Somozas' monopolistic use of public resources became so outrageous that the opposition bourgeoisie accused them of engaging in 'disloyal competition'. Similarly in Iran the only way for the opposition bourgeoisie to build a profitable enterprise was to seek the endorsement of the shah's relatives. Learning how intra-elite divisions contributed to the overthrow of those regimes, the US managed to bring the revolutionary wars in El Salvador and Guatemala to a standstill by mediating the conflict between those countries' opposing bourgeois factions; it also managed to forge a counterrevolutionary coalition in Nicaragua to defeat the Sandinistas in the 1990 elections. Of course, a lack of embodiment of dictatorial imageries in a single person also played an important part in hindering revolutionary victories in those countries. Many revolutionaries failed to recognize the importance of this contradiction because they generally tended to view the bourgeoisie as a monolithic, coherent group with a unitary strategy for constructing capitalism in their countries.

Cultural contradiction embraces a whole range of conflicts arising from competing cultural claims, meanings, authority, production, consumption, identity and representation. Viewed not as a shared, coherent and timeless entity but as a contested, fragmented, fluid process and a site of struggle, culture closely articulates with new liberation movements woven around complex metaphors such as gender, race, ethnicity, ecology. As such, cultural contradiction has been the most complex and the most illuminating of all contradictions. It is the most complex because it doesn't lend itself easily to analytical exercises as the others do. It is the most illuminating because it casts light on how all other contradictions are played out in everyday life and how those contradictions crisscross. Cultural contradiction played a crucial role in mobilizing the population to overthrow regimes in Iran and Nicaragua, one which revolved around religion. In Nicaragua liberation theology challenged the official Church in perpetuating the corrupt rule of the rich at the expense of the poor. In Iran Shi'i Islam assailed Westernization and corrupt capitalism for destroying the fabric of Islamic values and ways of being. The use of cultural contradiction challenges the deployment of 'national culture' or 'populist culture' as an ideal seamless unity. Such populist projects have failed to cover up the antagonistic differences (gender, race, ethnicity) that exist among diverse segments of a population. Here is the arena where real alternative politics and ways of producing historical knowledge come into play. Counter-narratives and counter-practices help unravel, generate or heighten social contradictions to mobilize people for or against certain social issues, forces or institutions.

How useful is this framing of past revolutions as constituted by a varying combination of five principal contradictions for understanding the contemporary world and assessing the possibility of future revolutions? The thesis of contradiction encompasses the workings of major contradictions internal and external to a nation-state in two ways. Contradictions triggering revolutions, the specific form each contradiction took, the specific combination of contradictions, and which one(s) played the most important role in effecting a revolutionary victory or shaping the post-victory scene are all products of a historical interplay of local and global forces. Contradictions triggering revolutions in a given society also operated against the backdrop of the principal global contradictions, predominant in their particular epoch: most post-World War II anti-colonial struggles, national liberation movements and especially revolutions took place against the backdrop of the cold war and the tension between two globalizing processes: capitalism and socialism.

Thus, one way that contradictions manifested themselves as prime sites of the local–global nexus lies in the dynamic interaction between revolutions and counterrevolutions that contributed to shaping our contemporary world. Revolutions made for varying degrees of change beyond their national boundaries explicitly through state policies or active engagements, or through what Fred Halliday (1999: 228) calls 'the demonstration effect' of revolutions (as in the anti-colonial struggles or the aftermath of the Iranian revolution). Counterrevolution employed a variety of techniques to suppress, contain, reverse or preempt revolutionary movements, or, once in power, to overthrow revolutionary regimes. For example, in the mid-1950s, Ramón Magsaysay, who presided over the Philippines from 1953 to 1957, preempted the Huk revolutionary movement by implementing some of its programs such as agrarian reform. This probably served as a pilot study for the more ambitious and global project of the 'Alliance for Progress', unveiled by the US delegation at the August 1961 economic summit of the Organization of American States in Punta del Este, Uruguay. Initially designed as an aid package for Latin America and the cornerstone of Kennedy's policy to contain communism in Cuba and preempt revolutionary movements in Latin America, it soon formed the basis for launching a host of so-called 'bloodless' but colorful 'revolutions' ranging from the 'white revolution' in Iran to 'green revolutions' in Southeast Asia in order to prevent possible red ones.

The relation between the local and global runs both ways, for, ironically, revolutions have contributed to the rise of globalization in several ways. For capital to be able to survive the onslaught of revolution, it had to become more flexible. To prevent its outback bases from falling to revolutions, it had to install or support dictatorial regimes, touching off a counter-trend, the globalization of human rights issues. The prevalence of those dictatorial regimes as the guardians of the capitalist hinterland alongside bureaucratic totalitarianism practiced in 'actually existing socialisms' forced the West to play up its minimum basic liberties and electoral democracy, thereby contributing to the globalization of the discourse of democracy. Capital's flexibility, mobility and the speed with which it can move around the globe are making the world increasingly a smaller place. Partly a by-product of the arms race, militarism, counterrevolution and counter-insurgency of the cold war era, and initially developed by high energy physicists, the World Wide Web and new information technologies have brought about time–space compression and a new consciousness of the world as a singularly small place (Harvey 1990; Robertson 1992).

Wars of Position

To what extent these contradictions are still relevant in the era of global consumption is an open question. But globalization, especially of democracy, has effectively diluted political, national, intra-elite and, to a lesser degree, class contradictions. The latest discursive strategy whereby capitalism is trying to conquer the remotest corners of the world is through democracy, which crowns capitalism as the only way of being, overshadowing the previous subjugating techniques of missionization, capital investment and foreign aid. The preemptive removal of dictators in Indonesia and the Philippines, and attaching free elections as a precondition for international aid, may have decreased the likelihood of political and intra-elite contradictions. The intricate interdependence of nations has dulled the sharp division between the national and anti-national. Rather than sealing the end of revolutions, the removal of dictatorial regimes has opened a more intricate mode of revolutionary struggle based on the war of position as opposed to the war of maneuver. I foresee that future revolutions will be fought more on the domain of cultural than of other contradictions. An integral part of such struggle might be the formation of democratic cultural practices and alternative institutions, especially in education, that could reverse the historical trend in which 'behavior has replaced action', and 'society, on all its levels, excludes the possibility of action' (Arendt 1963: 40–41).

Although the transnational capitalist class (Sklair 1995) is promoting the globalization of democracy, the very process of globalization is in no way democratic. Let me distinguish three possible modes of globalizing the world: authoritarian, populist and popular. Giving the impression that globalization would benefit everyone, capital's authoritarian attempts at globalization through advancing a version authored exclusively by the capitalist class, or capital's attempts at populist globalization orchestrated by the capitalist class, through incorporating an assorted selection of ordinary people's values and concerns, either aim to gloss over class and other differences using nationalism, national cultural identity or even sometimes cosmopolitanism (or denigrating nationalism or cosmopolitanism if they go against its interests), or try to commodify cultural differences. Whereas diversity and difference are celebrated as hallmarks of democracy, one needs to question whether the celebration of difference by postmodernism and globalization isn't the same old trick, albeit in more sophisticated guise, of divide and rule. Whether obfuscating, commodifying or celebrating differences, globalization's tendency is to erase the past. But most people know what it means to lose the past. They know intuitively what

Bernard Cohn (1981: 244) wrote two decades ago: 'The capacity to control the past, by defining it as history, and to establish classifications, which differentiate Europeans from others are central to … revolutions and transformations.' To safeguard, recall, reinvigorate or reinvent the past calls for the establishment of direct democracy, and a definite rejection of authoritarian attempts at globalization and a transition from a globalization in common to a common globalization, or a move from populist to popular globalization, in which ordinary people become the authors of globalization.

Operating within new cultural-political spaces carved out by authoritarian or populist globalization, future revolutions should be fought more along the war of position with an important site of struggle organized around quality of life and alternative cultural meanings and practices of democracy, a democracy that surpasses the representative without debunking it but attempts to conquer gradually the difficult terrain of participatory democracy. We need to explore two questions as a preliminary step toward launching this war of position. How might subalterns be able to conquer and redefine the terrain of democracy that has hitherto been naturalized by the rulers and the rich as a technology of rule and the main bastion of political legitimacy? For how much longer can the rich, the powerful and the sage theorizing on their behalf continue to separate the notion of democracy from its economic and cultural dimensions?

The utopianism and the thought of unachievability entailed in participatory democracy have dissuaded many analysts from even speculating about it. I therefore suggest that we should look at attempts at participatory democracy not as a goal or ideal that can be reached easily but as a mechanism, strategy or site of struggle organized around a variety of popular coalitions and alternative institutions, especially alternative education, aiming patiently to gain further ground for popular action in order eventually to revolutionize society and render formal politics irrelevant. There are several instructive examples of attempts, however limited, at participatory democracy, two of which are the Zapatista attempt to safeguard alternative ways of being and Nicaragua under the Sandinistas. Those familiar with the Nicaraguan revolutionary case might agree that one of the main reasons behind the US plan to destroy that revolution was probably that revolution's asserted objective to implement a mode of people's power, which, if even only somewhat successful, could have challenged the circus of representative democracy in the US. This isn't of course to deny that bureaucratic authoritarianism was creeping into the revolutionary state. Nor is it to argue against the institution of electoral democracy, although as Ian Budge warns, 'From a participatory point of view, greater opportunities for debate and participation stimulate greater engagement. Representative democracy can well be seen as institutional-izing popular inertia through its limitation of such opportunities' (1993: 145–6). Rather, it is to insist that electoral democracy, to be revolutionary, must operate within a participatory democratic frame.

To develop a plan of action for a war of position around popular coalitions and alternative ideas, institutions and modes of being based on attempts at a participatory democracy that links the local to the global using advanced information technology, including the Internet, requires at least a long essay and is the subject of another paper. For Stuart Hall, 'The notion of the struggles of the local as a war of positions is a very difficult kind of politics to get one's head around; none of us knows how to conduct it. None of us even knows whether it can be conducted. Some of us have had to say there is no other political game so we must find a way of playing this one' (1997: 57). Though I agree with Hall about the difficulties of organizing struggles around a war of positions, I would like to suggest that we should be more daring in actually trying to think of the ways in which we can launch such a struggle. There is certainly much to learn from past attempts at popular democratic intervention throughout world history, from decision-making councils in many communities, to the agora and Paris Commune, to the uprisings of 1968 and demonstra-tions against world financial institutions and coordinating bodies in Seattle, Washington, the Hague and elsewhere.

Conclusion

At the same time that capitalist globalization has provided a more autono-mous space for electoral democracy to flourish, it is removing the dis-cursive context within which popular democracy can be achieved. Let me therefore end this chapter by reiterating the importance of participatory democracy as a critical arena for future revolutionary struggle. In most locations around the world where electoral democracy has currently be-come the predominant form of political organization, it constitutes the main enemy of participatory democracy and considers participatory democ-racy as its main enemy. Challenging the rule of representative democracy in narrowing the field of politics under global capitalism, participatory democracy as a cultural strategy opens the way to the formation of new identities and imaginations. In contradistinction to electoral democracy, which, while indispensable, has become primarily a political device and method for the reproduction of capitalism, participatory democracy may be viewed as an integral way of life. Reconstituting the social as relations of presence rather than representation, participatory democracy threatens the power relations and forms of subjectivity that are simultaneously the effects as well as the underpinnings of representative democracy. Given that to avoid a deep crisis the elite may be willing to redistribute temporarily everything but political power, a serious quest for participatory democracy might be one way to precipitate future revolutions.

Notes

This chapter is a revised version of a paper I presented to a conference on 'The Future of Revolutions in the Context of Globalization' organized by John Foran. I would like to thank John wholeheartedly for organizing that lively conference and for his generous and helpful comments on various drafts of this essay. I am also grateful to Ralph Armbruster-Sandoval, Jeff Goodwin, Eric Selbin, Mary Ann Tétreault and graduate students at the University of California, Santa Barbara, for their useful suggestions. My very special thanks go to Doug Kellner for his words of encouragement and insightful comments and suggestions.

1. 'A picture of the contemporary world, and of the international system in particular, that ignores this unfinished agenda' of the revolutions of modern history, claims Fred Halliday correctly, 'is not only incomplete, but fundamentally distorted' (1999: 3).

2. This analytical move accords with Anthony Giddens's (1984: 193) suggestion that the concept of contradiction should not remain the property of the field of logic alone, but be employed as an indispensable concept in social theory.

13

Globalization, Technopolitics and Revolution

Douglas Kellner

The coincidence of the changing of circumstances and of human activity can be conceived and rationally understood only as revolutionizing practice.

Karl Marx

A community will evolve only when a people control their own communication.

Frantz Fanon

As the third millennium unfolds, one of the most dramatic technological and economic revolutions in history is advancing a set of processes that are changing everything from the ways that people work to the ways that they communicate with each other and spend their leisure time. The technological revolution centers on computer, information, communication and multimedia technologies. These are key aspects of the production of a new economy, described as postindustrial, post-Fordist and postmodern, accompanied by a networked society and cyberspace, and the juggernaut of globalization. There are, of course, furious debates about how to describe the Great Transformation of the contemporary epoch, whether it is positive or negative, and what are the political prospects for democratization and radical social transformation.[1]

In this chapter, I will engage some issues involving globalization, technological revolution and the alleged rise of a new economy, networked society and cyberspace in relation to the problematic of revolution and the prospects for a radical democratic or socialist transformation of society. Globalization and the rise of a new computer and information-technology-based economy and society are interpreted in both popular and academic literature as a 'revolution' in which new technologies are transforming every mode of life from how individuals do research to how people communicate and interact socially. There is some truth in this notion, but it is also true that the technological revolution perpetuates the interests of the dominant economic and political powers, intensifies divisions between haves and have-nots, and is a defining feature of a new and improved form of global technocapitalism.

While there are novelties and discontinuities in the current configuration of economic, political, social and cultural constellations that constitute the contemporary moment, there are also continuities with the previous forms of 'modern' society to be noted. In particular, the 'new' economy exhibits crucial features of the 'old' capitalism such as the driving forces of capital accumulation, competition, commodification, exploitation and the business cycle. From this perspective, globalization and technological revolution are best theorized as forms of the global restructuring of capitalism in which technological development and a turbulent socioeconomic transformation are intrinsically interconnected.

As to whether globalization renders revolution in the classical Marxian tradition obsolete, I would argue that much significant political struggle today, especially resistance to globalization, is mediated by technopolitics. The use of computer and information technology is becoming a normalized aspect of politics, just as the broadcasting media were some decades ago. Deploying computer-mediated technology for technopolitics, however, opens new terrains of political struggle for voices and groups excluded from the mainstream media and thus increases potential for resistance and intervention by oppositional groups. Hence, if revolution is to have a future in the contemporary era it must incorporate technopolitics as part of its strategy, conceiving of technopolitics, however, as an arm of struggle and not an end in and of itself.

Consequently, in this chapter, I focus on the ways that an oppositional politics can use new technologies to intervene within the global restructuring of capitalism to promote democratic and anti-capitalist social movements aiming at radical structural transformation. I would argue that globalization and technological revolution are in some ways inevitable – barring an apocalyptic collapse of the global economy – but the forms that they take are not. That is, I think that the trends toward a more global economy and culture, a networked society, and the continued flow of commodities, images, cultural forms, technology and people across the globe will continue apace, as will intense technological revolution. Both take the form of what Schumpeter called 'creative destruction' and guarantee that the next decades will be highly turbulent, contested and full of struggle and conflict. But the forms that globalization and technological development will take are neither fixed nor determined. Hence, I would argue that it is perfectly reasonable to oppose corporate capitalist global-ization and its market model of society, its neoliberal laissez-faire ideology and its putting profit, competition and market logic before all other aspects of life. I will accordingly focus on the ways that technopolitics can be and is being used for anti-capitalist contestation, while noting the limitations of this conception.

Technopolitics and Oppositional Political Movements

Significant political struggles today against globalization are mediated by technopolitics – that is, the use of new technologies such as computers and the Internet to advance political goals. To some extent, politics in the modern era has always been mediated by technology, with the printing press, photography, film, radio and television playing crucial roles in politics and all realms of social life, as McLuhan, Innis, Mumford and others have long argued and documented. In representative democracies participation is mediated by technology, as the disastrous failure of voting machines and the vote-counting process in the 2000 US presidential election dramatized (see Kellner 2001).

What is new about computer and information-technology-mediated politics is that information can be instantly communicated to large numbers of individuals throughout the world who are connected via computer networks. The Internet is also potentially interactive, allowing discussion, debate and on-line and archived discussion. The Internet is increasingly multimedia in scope, allowing the dissemination of images, sounds, video and other cultural forms. Moreover, the use of computer technology and networks is becoming a normalized aspect of politics, just as the broad-casting media were some decades ago. The use of computer-mediated technology for technopolitics, however, opens new terrains of political struggle for voices and groups excluded from the mainstream media and thus increases potential for intervention by oppositional groups, poten-tially expanding the scope of democratization.

Given the extent to which capital and its logic of commodification have colonized ever more areas of everyday life in recent years, it is somewhat astonishing that cyberspace is by and large decommodified for large numbers of people – at least in the overdeveloped countries like the United States. On the other hand, using computers, transforming infor-mation into data-packets that can be sent through networks, and hooking oneself up to computer networks oneself, involve a form of commodified activity, inserting the user in networks and technology that are at the forefront of the information revolution and global restructuring of capital. Thus the Internet is highly ambiguous from the perspective of commodification, as from other perspectives.

Nonetheless, in many areas of the globe, government and educational institutions, and some businesses, provide free Internet access and in some cases free computers, or at least workplace access. With flat-rate monthly phone bills (which do not exist, however, in much of the world), one can have access to a cornucopia of information and entertainment on the Internet for free, one of the few decommodified spaces in the ultra-commodified world of technocapitalism.[2] So far, the 'information super-highway' is a freeway, although powerful interests would like to make it a toll road. Indeed, commercial interests are quickly converting it into a giant mall, thus commercializing the Internet and transforming it into a megaconsumer spectacle (see Schiller 1999).

Obviously, much of the world does not even have telephone service, much less computers, and there are vast discrepancies in terms of who has access to computers and who participates in the technological revolution and cyberdemocracy today. As a result, there have been passionate debates over the extent and nature of the 'digital divide' between the information haves and have-nots. Critics of new technologies and cyberspace repeat incessantly that it is by and large young, white, middle- or upper-class males who are the dominant players in the cyberspaces of the present. While this is true, statistics and surveys indicate that many more women, people of colour, seniors and individuals from marginalized groups are becoming increasingly active.[3] In addition, computers may become part of the standard household consumer package in the overdeveloped world, although studies are emerging that indicate that large numbers of individuals claim that they have no intention of purchasing computers and using the Internet. Yet in the light of the importance of computers for work, social life, entertainment and education, no doubt growing amounts of people will continue to go on-line. Further, there are plans afoot to wire the entire world with satellites that would make the Internet and new communication technologies accessible to people who do not now have a telephone, television or even electricity, and wireless, interactive technologies are touted as the next stage of networked communication.[4]

However widespread and common computers and new technologies become, it is clear that they are of essential importance already for labor, politics, education and social life, and that people who want to participate in the public and cultural life of the future will need to have computer access and literacy. Although there is a real threat that the computerization of society will intensify the current inequalities in relations of class, race and gender power, there is also the possibility that a democratized and computerized public sphere might provide opportunities to overcome these injustices. Cyberdemocracy and the Internet should be seen, therefore, as a contested terrain. Radical democratic activists should look to the Internet's possibilities for resistance and the advancement of political education, action and organization, while engaging in struggles over the digital divide. Dominant corporate and state powers, as well as conservative and rightist groups, have been making sustained use of new technologies to advance their agendas. If forces struggling for democratization and social justice want to become players in the cultural and political battles of the future, they must devise ways to use new technologies to advance a radical democratic and ecological agenda and the interests of the oppressed.

There are by now copious examples of how the Internet and cyberdemocracy have been used within oppositional political movements. A large number of insurgent intellectuals are already making use of new technologies and public spheres in their political projects. The peasants and guerrilla armies who formed the Zapatista movement in Chiapas, Mexico, beginning in January 1994, used computer databases, guerrilla radio and other media forms to circulate their ideas and to promote their cause. Every manifesto, text and bulletin produced by the Zapatista Army of National Liberation, who occupied land in the southern Mexican state of Chiapas, was immediately circulated through the world via computer networks.[5]

In January 1995, when the Mexican government attacked the Zapatistas, the latter used computer networks to inform and mobilize individuals and groups throughout the world to support them in their battle against repressive government action. There were many demonstrations in support of the rebels throughout the world. Prominent journalists, human rights observers and delegations traveled to Chiapas to demonstrate solidarity and to report on the uprising. The Mexican and US governments were bombarded with messages calling for negotiations rather than repression. The Mexican government was forced to back down and halt their repression of the insurgents. While carrying out various forms of subjugation, they continued to negotiate sporadically, with the post-2000 government of Vicente Fox continuing this pattern without resolution to the conflict.[6]

Seeing the progressive potential of advanced communications technologies in revolutionary struggle, Frantz Fanon (1967) described the central role of the radio in the Algerian revolution, and Lenin stressed the importance of film in spreading communist ideology after the Bolshevik revolution. Audiotapes were used to advance the insurrection in Iran and to disseminate alternative information by political movements throughout the world (see Downing 2000). The Tiananmen Square democracy movement in China and various groups struggling against the remnants of Stalinism in the former communist bloc used computer bulletin boards and networks, as well as a variety of forms of communications, to promote their movements. Anti-NAFTA groups made extensive use of the new communications technology (see Brenner 1994; Fredericks 1994). Such multinational networking and distribution of information failed to stop NAFTA, but created alliances useful for the politics of the future. As Nick Dyer-Witheford notes:

> The anti-NAFTA coalitions, while mobilizing a depth of opposition entirely unexpected by capital, failed in their immediate objectives. But the transcontinental dialogues which emerged checked – though by no means eliminated – the chauvinist element in North American opposition to free trade. The movement created a powerful pedagogical crucible for cross-sectoral and cross-border organizing. And it opened pathways for future connections, including electronic ones, which were later effectively mobilized by the Zapatista uprising and in continuing initiatives against maquiladora exploitation. (1999: 156)

Thus, using new technologies to link information and practice and to advance oppositional politics is neither extraneous to political battles nor merely utopian. Even if immediate gains are not won, often the information circulated or the alliances formed can have material effects. There are, moreover, striking examples of how Internet-centered organizing campaigns effectively worked against the institutions and corporations of capitalist globalization. Successful struggles against the Multilateral Agreement on Investment (MAI) in 1995–98 involved websites and e-mail campaigns against the US-supported effort to develop binding rules on how states treat foreign investors, and listservs linking the groups struggling against the 'agreement'. Obviously, the Internet alone did not defeat this initiative for capitalist globalization, but it enabled the non-government organizations fighting against it to circulate information, share resources and link their struggles (see Smith and Smythe 2000).

There have been many campaigns against the excesses of capitalist global corporations such as Nike and McDonald's. Hackers attacked Nike's site in June 2000 and substituted a 'global justice' message for Nike's corporate hype. Many anti-Nike websites and listservs have emerged, helping groups struggling against the global shoe and manufacturing corporation, which have forced Nike to modify its labor practices.[7]

A British group that created an anti-McDonald's website against the junk food corporation and then distributed the information through digital and print media has also received significant attention. This site was developed by supporters of two British activists, Helen Steel and Dave Morris, who were sued by McDonald's for distributing leaflets denouncing the corporation's low wages, advertising practices, involvement in deforestation, cruel treatment of animals and patronage of an unhealthy diet. The activists counterattacked and, with help from supporters, organized a McLibel campaign, assembled a McSpotlight website with a tremendous amount of information criticizing the corporation, mobilizing experts to testify and confirm their criticisms. The three-year civil trial, Britain's longest ever, ended ambiguously on 19 June 1997, with the judge defending some of McDonald's claims against the activists, while substantiating some of the activists' criticisms (Vidal 1997: 299–315). The case created unprecedented bad publicity for McDonald's, which was disseminated throughout the world via Internet websites, mailing lists and discussion groups. The McLibel/McSpotlight group claims that their website was accessed over 15 million times and was visited over 2 million times in the month of the verdict alone (Vidal 1997: 326). The *Guardian* reported that the site 'claimed to be the most comprehensive source of information on a multinational corporation ever assembled' and was part of one of the more successful anti-corporate campaigns (22 February 1996; www.mcspotlight.org).

Anti-Nike, anti-McDonald's and other websites critical of global capitalist corporations have disseminated a tremendous amount of information. Many labor organizations are also beginning to make use of the new technologies. The Clean Clothes Campaign, a movement started by Dutch women in 1990 in support of Filipina garment workers, has supported strikes throughout the world, exposing exploitative working conditions (see www.cleanclothes.org/1/index.html). In 1997, activists involved in Korean workers' strikes and the Merseyside dock strike in England used websites to promote international solidarity (for the latter, see www.gn.apc.org/labournet/docks/). Jesse Drew (1996) has extensively interviewed representatives of major US labor organizations to see how they were making use of new communications technologies and how these instruments helped them with their struggles; many of his union activists indicated how useful e-mail, faxes, websites and the Internet have been to their struggles and, in particular, indicated how such technopolitics helped organize demonstrations or strikes in favor of striking English or Australian dockworkers, as when US longshoremen organized strikes to boycott ships carrying material loaded by scab workers. Technopolitics thus helps labor create global alliances in order to combat increasingly transnational corporations.[8]

On the whole, labor organizations, such as the North South Dignity of Labor group, note that computer networks are useful for organizing and distributing information, but cannot replace print media, which are more accessible to many of their members, face-to-face meetings and traditional forms of political action. Thus, the challenge is to articulate one's communications politics with actual movements and struggles so that cyberpolitics is an arm of real battles rather than their replacement or substitute. The most efficacious Internet projects have indeed intersected with activist movements encompassing campaigns to free political prisoners, boycotts of corporate projects, and various labor and even revolutionary struggles, as noted above.

The Global Movement against Capitalist Globalization

One of the more instructive examples of the use of the Internet to foster global struggles against the excesses of corporate capitalism occurred in the protests in Seattle and throughout the world against the World Trade Organization meeting in December 1999, and the subsequent emergence of a worldwide anti-globalization movement in 2000–01. Behind these actions was a global protest movement using the Internet to organize resistance to the institutions of capitalist globalization, while championing democratization. In the build-up to the 1999 Seattle demonstrations, many websites generated anti-WTO material and numerous mailing lists used the Internet to distribute critical material and to organize the protest. The result was the mobilization of caravans from throughout the United States to take protestors to Seattle, as well as contingents of activists throughout the world. Many of the protestors had never met and were recruited through the Internet. For the first time ever, labor, environmentalist, feminist, anticapitalist, animal rights, anarchist and other groups organized to protest aspects of globalization and to form new alliances and solidarities for future struggles. In addition, demonstrations took place throughout the world, and a proliferation of anti-WTO material against the extremely secret group spread throughout the Internet.[9]

Furthermore, the Internet provided critical coverage of the event, documentation of the various groups' protests, and debate over the WTO and globalization. Whereas the mainstream media presented the protests as 'anti-trade', featured the incidents of anarchist violence against property, and minimized police brutality against demonstrators, the Internet provided pictures, eyewitness accounts, and reports of police viciousness and the generally peaceful and nonviolent nature of the protests. While the mainstream media framed the Seattle anti-WTO activities negatively and privileged suspect spokespeople like Patrick Buchanan as critics of globalization, the Internet provided multiple representations of the demonstrations, advanced reflective discussion of the WTO and globalization, and presented a diversity of critical perspectives.

The Seattle protests had some immediate consequences. The day after the demonstrators made good on their promise to shut down the WTO negotiations, Bill Clinton gave a speech endorsing the concept of labor rights enforceable by trade sanctions, thus effectively making impossible any agreement during the Seattle meetings. In addition, at the World Economic Forum in Davos a month later there was much discussion of how concessions were necessary on labor and the environment if consensus over globalization and free trade were to be possible. Importantly, the issues of overcoming divisions between the information-rich and the information-poor, and improving the lot of the disenfranchised and oppressed, bringing these groups the benefits of globalization, were also seriously discussed at the meeting and in the media.

More important, many activists were energized by the new alliances, solidarities and militancy, and continued to cultivate an anti-globalization movement. The Seattle demonstrations were followed by April 2000 struggles in Washington, DC, to protest the World Bank and IMF, and later in the year against capitalist globalization in Prague and Melbourne; in April 2001 an extremely large and militant protest erupted against the Free Trade Area of the Americas summit in Quebec City, followed by spectacular and dramatic demonstrations in Genoa in July 2001. It was apparent that a new worldwide movement was in the making, capable of uniting diverse opponents of capitalist globalization throughout the world. The anticorporate globalization movement favored globalization from below, which would protect the environment, labor rights, national cultures, democratization and other goods from the ravages of an uncontrolled capitalist globalization (see Falk 1999; Brecher, Costello and Smith 2000a).

The movement against capitalist globalization used the Internet to organize mass demonstrations and to disseminate information to the world concerning the policies of the institutions of capitalist globalization. The events made clear that the protestors were not against globalization per se, but were against neoliberal globalization, opposing specific policies and institutions that produce intensified exploitation of labor, environmental devastation, growing divisions among social classes and the undermining of democracy. The emerging anti-globalization-from-above movements are locating these problems in the context of opposition to a restructuring of a neoliberal market capitalism on a worldwide basis for maximum profit with zero accountability. The anti-capitalist movements, by contrast, have made clear the need for democratization, regulation, rules and globalization in the interests of people and not profit.

The new movements against globalization from above have thus placed the issues of global justice, democracy and the environment squarely in the center of the political concerns of our time. Hence, whereas the mainstream media had failed to debate vigorously or even report on globalization until the recent past, and rarely, if ever, critically discussed the activities of the WTO, World Bank and IMF, there is now a widely circulating critical discourse and controversy regarding these institutions. Stung by criticisms, representatives of the World Bank, in particular, are pledging reform. Pressure is mounting concerning proper and improper roles for the major global institutions, highlighting their limitations and deficiencies, and the need for reforms like debt relief for overburdened developing countries to solve some of their fiscal and social problems.

Hence, to capital's globalization from above, cyberactivists have been attempting to carry out globalization from below, developing networks of solidarity and propagating oppositional ideas and movements throughout the planet. To the capitalist international of transnational corporate-led globalization, a Fifth International, to use Waterman's phrase (1992), of computer-mediated and popular-based activism is emerging that is qualitatively different from the party-based socialist and communist Internationals. Such networking links labor, feminist, ecological, peace and other anti-capitalist groups, providing the basis for a new politics of alliance and solidarity to overcome the limitations of postmodern identity politics (see Dyer-Witheford 1999; Burbach 2001).

Technopolitics: A Contested Terrain

A key to developing a robust technopolitics is articulation, the mediation of technopolitics with real problems and struggles, rather than self-contained reflections on the internal politics of the Internet.[10] The Zapatista movement in Chiapas has been addressing problems of survival and transforming social, cultural, political and economic conditions, using new technologies as an instrument of political struggle. Likewise, the campaigns against major capitalist corporations and the institutions of corporate globalization are attempting to advance progressive political agendas and to engage key issues of the day.

The examples in this study suggest how technopolitics makes possible a refiguring of politics, a refocusing of politics on everyday life and using

the tools and techniques of new computer and communications technologies to expand the field and domain of politics. In this conjuncture,
the ideas of Guy Debord and the Situationist International are especially
relevant with their stress on the construction of situations, the use of
technology, media of communication and cultural forms to promote a
revolution of everyday life, and to increase the realm of freedom, community and empowerment.[11] To some extent, the new technologies *are* revolutionary; they *do* constitute a revolution of everyday life, but it is often
a revolution that promotes and disseminates the capitalist consumer society
and involves new modes of fetishism, enslavement and domination, as yet
but dimly perceived and undertheorized.

Clearly, right-wing and reactionary forces can and have used the Internet to promote their political agendas as well. In a short time, one can
easily access an exotic witch's brew of websites maintained by the Ku
Klux Klan and myriad neo-Nazi assemblages, including the Aryan Nation
and various militia groups. Internet discussion lists also disperse these views
and right-wing extremists are aggressively active on many computer
forums, as well as radio programs and stations, public-access television
programs, fax campaigns, video and even rock music productions. These
organizations are hardly harmless, having carried out terrorism of various
sorts extending from church burnings to the bombing of public buildings.
Adopting quasi-Leninist discourse and tactics for ultra-right causes, these
groups have been successful in recruiting working-class members devas-
tated by the developments of global capitalism, which has resulted in
widespread unemployment for traditional forms of industrial, agricultural
and unskilled labor. Moreover, extremist websites have influenced alien-
ated middle-class youth as well (a 1999 HBO documentary on *Hate on the
Internet* provides a disturbing number of examples of how extremist websites
influenced disaffected youth to commit hate crimes).

A recent twist in the saga of technopolitics, in fact, seems to be that
alleged 'terrorist' groups are now increasingly using the Internet and
websites to promote their causes. An article in the *Los Angeles Times* (8
February 2001) reports that groups like Hamas use their website to post
reports of acts of terror against Israel, rather than calling newspapers or
broadcasting outlets. A wide range of groups labeled as 'terrorist' reportedly
use e-mail, listservs and websites to further their struggles, causes including Hezbollah and Hamas, the Maoist group Sendero Luminoso in
Peru, and a variety of other groups throughout Asia and elsewhere. The
Tamil Tigers, for instance, a liberation movement in Sri Lanka, offers
position papers, daily news and a free e-mail service. According to the
Los Angeles Times, experts are still unclear 'whether the ability to

communicate online worldwide is prompting an increase or a decrease in terrorist acts'.

Different political groups are in fact engaging in cyberwar as adjuncts of their political battles. Israeli hackers have repeatedly attacked the websites of Hezbollah, while pro-Palestine hackers have reportedly placed militant demands and slogans on the websites of Israel's army, foreign ministry and parliament. Likewise, Pakistani and Indian computer hackers have waged similar cyberbattles against opposing forces' websites in the bloody struggle over Kashmir; while rebel forces in the Philippines taunt government troops with cellphone calls and messages, and attack government websites.

Concluding Remarks

The Internet is thus a contested terrain, used by the left, right and center to advance their own agendas and interests. The political battles of the future may well be fought in the streets, factories, parliaments and other sites of past conflicts, but political struggle is now mediated by media, computer and information technologies, and increasingly will be so. Those interested in the politics and culture of the future should therefore be clear on the important role of computer-mediated technopolitics and act accordingly.

Active citizens thus need to acquire new forms of technological literacy to intervene in the new public spheres of the media and information society. In addition to traditional literacy skills centered upon reading, writing and speaking, engaged citizens and public intellectuals need to learn to use the new technologies to participate in democratic discussion and political struggle.[12] Computer and digital technologies thus expand the field and capacities of the intellectual as well as the possibilities for political intervention. During the Age of Big Media, critical-oppositional intellectuals were by and large marginalized, unable to gain access to the major sites of mass communication. With the decentralization of the Internet, however, new possibilities for public intellectuals exist to reach broad audiences. It is therefore the responsibility of the active citizen to work creatively with these new technologies, as well as to analyze critically the diverse developments of the cyberculture. This requires dialectical thinking that discriminates between the benefits and the costs, the upsides and downsides, of new technologies and devising ways that the technological revolution can be used to promote positive values like education, democracy, enlightenment and ecology. Active citizens thus face new challenges, and the future of democracy depends in part on whether new technologies will be used for domination or democratization, and whether each individual will sit on the sidelines or participate in the development of new democratic public spheres.

I have not discussed the ways that technopolitics could be used to struggle not only against capitalism, but for socialism. I would argue that socialist ideas are still relevant to the politics of the contemporary era and that in particular Karl Marx's ideas, far from being obsolete, are still essential in developing critical theories of globalization, technology and capitalism in the current conjuncture (see Kellner 1995). It may be that only a socialist politics could overcome the digital divide, making accessible to all the benefits of the technological revolution. A socialist government could provide wireless communications in underdeveloped societies, making possible access to the Internet and use of new communications and information technology even to societies that are not yet wired, or whose telephone systems extend only to the privileged. Interestingly, citizens in societies like Korea, Japan and the Philippines make more extensive use of wireless communications than the US, with wireless messaging systems and Internet access made use of by the working classes as forms of popular communication.

This study has suggested that in the era of globalization and the Internet political struggles are at once local and global, that there are continuities and discontinuities with struggles and movements of the past, and that we can therefore continue to draw on the most progressive ideas of the modern tradition while also developing new concepts of politics and new strategies for social transformation. A revolution of the future needs to articulate models and ideals of a post-capitalist economy, a radical democratic polity, an egalitarian and socially just multicultural society, and diverse, free and open culture. Ideals of the past can and no doubt will enter into revolutionary thought of the future, but new ideals, values and forms of everyday life will no doubt emerge. The future of revolution is thus open and requires new theory and practice as well as appropriation of the best progressive heritages of the past.

Notes

1. This study and the concepts of globalization and technological revolution developed here are grounded in the studies of Best and Kellner 2001. By 'revolution', I am assuming a concept of fundamental economic, political, social and cultural transformation, such as was developed in the works of Herbert Marcuse. See Kellner 1984 and the six volumes of Marcuse's collected and largely unpublished papers that I am publishing with Routledge.

2. In most parts of the world, individuals must pay telephone companies for each unit of time on the Internet, giving rise to movements for an affordable flat rate for monthly Interact access; for discussion of the access movement in Britain, promises from the telecommunications companies to provide a flat rate in the immediate future, and speculation that access still might not be affordable for many, see the dossier in the technology section of the *Times* (London), 12 December 1999.

3. In August 1999, a widely publicized US Department of Commerce report contended that the 'digital divide' between the information haves and have-nots was growing; by November, there were critiques that the survey data were severely out of date and that more reliable statistics indicated that the divide was lessening, that more women, people of color and seniors were connected to the Internet, and that more than half of the United States was connected by late 1999. In 2000, several surveys indicated that the digital divide was mainly structured by class and education, and not by race. One should, however, be suspicious of statistics concerning Internet access and use, as powerful interests are involved that manipulate figures for their own purposes. Yet there is no doubt that a 'digital divide' exists and that various politicians, groups and corporations are exploiting this problem for their own interests.

4. On the growth of wireless, see the discussion in Best and Kellner 2001. It was announced in April 1997 that Boeing Aircraft had joined Bill Gates in investing in a satellite communications company, Teledesic, which planned to send up 288 small low-orbit satellites to cover most of the Americas and then the world by 2002. This project could give up to 20 million people satellite Internet access at a given moment; see *USA Today*, 30 April 1997. In May 1998, Motorola joined the 'Internet in the Sky' project, scrapping its own $12.9 billion plan to build a satellite network capable of delivering high-speed data-communications anywhere on the planet and instead joined the Teledesic project, pushing aside Boeing to become Teledesic's prime contractor (*New York Times*, 22 May 1998). An 'Internet-in-the-Sky' would make possible access to new technologies for groups and regions that do not even have telephones, thus expanding the potential for democratic and progressive uses of new technologies. On the other hand, there are reports that the corporations proposing such projects are not pursuing them and thus, once again, state intervention may be necessary to develop progressive technologies that will serve all.

5. On the Zapatistas, see Cleaver 1994; the documents collected in Zapatistas Collective 1994; Castells 1997; Harvey 1998; Burbach 2001.

6. In early 1998, however, Zapatista supporters were murdered by local death squads – which once again triggered significant Internet-generated pressures on the Mexican government to prosecute the perpetrators. Likewise, there has been ongoing government repression and sporadic violence, although, so far, the kind of massive repression of the movement favored by many in the Mexican military and political establishment has been avoided. I should also mention here the incredibly conflicting interpretations of the Zapatista movement by its supporters and detractors, and the problem that it has been given iconic significance, with all the attendant mythologization, in the contemporary era. For my purposes, it represents a strong example of how new technologies can be used as an arm of political struggle and how computer-mediated technologies can help generate global

support networks and circulate information of revolutionary struggles and movements.

7. For an overview of Nike, see Goldman and Papson 1998. For a dossier of material assembled on Nike's labor practices and campaigns against them, see the highly impressive website constructed by David M. Boje (cbae.mnsu.edu/~davidboje/nike/nikemain.html).

8. For an overview of the use of electronic communications technology by labor, see the studies by Waterman 1990, 1992; Brecher and Costello 1998; Dyer-Witheford 1999; Drew 1999. Labor projects using the new technologies include the US-based Labornet, the European Geonet, the Canadian LaborL, the South African WorkNet, the Asia Labour Monitor Resource Centre, Mujer a Mujer (representing Latina women's groups), and the Third World Network, while PeaceNet in the United States is devoted to a variety of progressive peace and justice issues.

9. As a 1 December 1999 abcnews.com story titled 'Networked Protests' put it:

> disparate groups from the Direct Action Network to the AFL–CIO to various environmental and human rights groups have organized rallies and protests online, allowing for a global reach that would have been unthinkable just five years ago.
>
> As early as March, activists were hitting the news groups and list-serves – strings of e-mail messages people use as a kind of long-term chat – to organize protests and rallies.

In addition, while the organizers demanded that the protesters agree not to engage in violent action, there was one website that urged WTO protesters to help tie up the WTO's web servers, and another group produced an anti-WTO website that replicated the look of the official site (see RTMark's website, http://gatt.org/; the same group had produced a replica of George W. Bush's site with satirical and critical material, winning the wrath of the Bush campaign). For compelling accounts of the anti-WTO demonstrations in Seattle and an acute analysis of the issues involved, see the documents collected in Danaher and Burbach 2000; and Cockburn, St. Clair and Sekula 2000. See Smith and Smythe 2001 for detailed analysis of the use of the Internet in the anti-WTO demonstrations; they located 4,089 websites with material specific to the Seattle WTO meetings and selected 513 to examine and classify.

10. See, for example, Mark Poster's 'Cyberdemocracy: Internet and the public sphere' (1995), which focuses primarily on the politics of social relations within cybercommunication (www.hnet.uci.edu/mposter/writings/democ.html). This topic, expounded upon in countless Internet discussion lists and publications, is interesting in its own right, but occludes the key issue of how Internet communication can be articulated with the 'real world'.

11. On the importance of the ideas of Debord and the Situationist International to make sense of the present conjuncture, see Best and Kellner 1997: ch. 3; and on the new forms of the interactive consumer society, see Best and Kellner 2001.

12. For further examples of how the Internet is being used in the US in a variety of social movements, see Kellner 1998; on some of the ways that citizens are participating in cyberpolitics in the US, see Hill and Hughes 1998. For the new forms of multiliteracy needed to use the new technologies for education, communication and politics, see Kellner 1998, 2000.

The Shaping of Revolutions by Culture and Agency and by Race, Class and Gender

26 January 2001

John Foran Race, class and gender – and culture and agency – while representing very different orders of things, possess an elective affinity that makes them plausible subjects for a thematic discussion. I want to trace briefly how this might be so. First we can note the rise of feminist analysis of revolutions, pioneered among others by Val Moghadam (1997), Karen Kampwirth (2002), Julie Shayne (2000) and now increasingly quite a few other people. So this puts gender far more squarely into the center of analysis than it has ever been. This is an irreversible process in the sociology of revolution that is under way.

The same can be said, but unfortunately to a far lesser degree, of the project of introducing race and ethnicity into the study of revolutions. One might speculate about the reasons for this, since there is, of course, a large and growing literature in sociology and in the US on the inter-section and connections among race, class and gender, which has not found its way into the sociology of revolutions. Very few people have tried to put these things together. One can, however, be more optimistic about the future of this kind of work, not least due to the rise of the Zapatistas into view in the field. I try to review some of this emerging literature on race, on gender and on class, and their intersections with respect to revolutions (in Foran 2001). Chris McAuley has also written on race and revolutions, one of the few pieces that takes up this topic comparatively (1997).

Alongside all of this, we have the 'cultural turn' which has taken place widely in the social sciences and increasingly in the sociology of revolutions, with contributions by Eric Selbin (1997), myself (1997), J.-P. Reed

(2000), Jeff Goodwin (Emirbayer and Goodwin 1996), and Farideh Farhi (1990) among others. The same is happening with respect to agency, and again the credit must be given to Eric Selbin and other people who have commented at this gathering, including Linda Klouzal, and the work of Jeff Goodwin and others (Goodwin et al. 2000) on emotions.

How to link all this together is clearly a wide open project. To my way of thinking, these are some of the hottest topics, at the cutting edge of the field of the sociology of revolution as it currently stands, ones that are starting to get attention and development, and will more so in the future. Therefore, it makes sense to try this afternoon to ask how globalization is shaping class, race and gender relations, a hugely impossible question. Second, to ask how culture comes into play under current conditions. And third what issues will revolutionary alliances have to solve in the future and how might they do so.

I propose that we take these matters up consecutively. So, part one is a very amorphous question: How is globalization shaping class, race and gender relations?

Carlos Vilas   I am really optimistic about this particular question because it is precisely when dealing with this set of identity issues that we can see the progress in revolutions. Thus revolutions today are more articulated, more complex than fifty years ago. The revolutionary agenda includes a number of questions, and approaches these questions in a more literate way, a more cultivated way, in terms of revolutionary culture.

Now we know that the goals of revolution and transformation go far beyond just productive issues, political institutions and the like. We know that there is a gender question in Latin America. We know that there is an ethnic or an ethnocultural question in Latin America. This makes a sharp contrast with how revolutions were conceived of fifty years ago, and this is a contribution of the very revolutions that took place in Latin America over all these years. It is also a contribution of what I should call the globalization of the idea of justice, which is the most progressive dimension of globalization – the exchange of domestic revolutionary processes with ideas and social movements, intellectuals, activists and or-ganizers all over the world. We cannot understand Latin American femi-nism without taking into account the articulation of Latin American women's movements with Spanish women's movements or US women's movements. These greatly enriched the Latin American revolutionary agenda, notwithstanding the fact that in many cases the initial contacts were very conflictive ones.

I could go further back. Marxism is not a Third World ideology. Someone brought Marxism to us, to Africa, to Latin America. In the case of Latin America, it was initially workers migrating from Europe. So, when dealing with these issues, we can see one of the best dimensions of globalization – the globalization of progressive consciousness. And I have no doubt that in the future – and this is not just speculating, I'm trying to make a linear projection of history – that in the future we will keep on advancing in this more complex articulated, integrative, balanced approach to revolutions. And the more we are able to include these dimensions, the more we will approach a positive solution to the problems we are facing.

I call this solidarity across borders. The original Marxist conception of international worker solidarity was launched in a world of nations, and European workers were deeply involved in national politics. After the Bolshevik so-called revolution, the Soviet Union promoted 'internationalism', which was in fact international support for their own foreign policy. Many progressive movements in Latin America tragically failed because of this alliance of national communist parties with the foreign policy of the Soviet Union. Now we are facing the possibility of real progressive internationalism because capitalist globalization makes possible, for perhaps the first time in history, a true progressive solidarity across borders.

Jeffery Paige Globalization is creating some contradictions in the categories of class and gender and this also creates some distinct problems from the way that the world has previously been organized, and therefore some opportunities. For example, the concept of class has been traditionally identified since nineteenth-century working-class struggles with the image of the European independent male wage earner. By its very workings globalization is beginning to break down that conceptualization: Who is the worker today?

First of all a worker is very probably a woman, as global capitalism takes advantage of traditional gender relations to impose a kind of regime of super-exploitation on the Third World and that means that male workers, industrial workers in the United States, have to engage with the issue of working conditions for women workers in Nike factories in Vietnam. So the whole concept of who a worker is, which was assumed in the market, is really under attack socially, conceptually and so on, providing the opportunity to reconceptualize it in ways that could possibly create solidarity across these categories. And I think the same thing is true for the national and ethnic issue.

Similarly, globalization is a notion of development of the South, of the Third World, but it also operates at home. One need only go to Los Angeles to see the development of sweatshops, reproducing themselves with Central American workers. This is another super-exploitation regime, but it also has possibilities in that many South-born workers have brought their politics with them, so when Justice for Janitors struggled in LA, there were many people from El Salvador and Nicaragua who were wearing red bandanas with Sandinista and other Central American slogans.

So there is a possibility for cooperation across these boundaries which never would have been possible in the past where people were definitively 'other' and their concerns were not our concerns. It's also true for the post-colonial intellectual or for people from the First World who are in the Third World, such that friendship and intellectual comradeship are developing across these boundaries and so that somebody from Iran who studies in the United States or becomes a United States citizen becomes part of this society. And therefore the boundaries between Iran and the United States break down in ways that change the longstanding assumption that the United States was a kind of European Protestant nation, even though it was always false, of course. But it's now being challenged in fundamental sorts of ways.

So, all of these things that start off as attempts to save labor costs or to superexploit workers, and so on, simultaneously provide rich opportunities for new forms of solidarity that did not exist in the past. What happens to them is a question of political agency. You can have a Pat Buchanan using them to generate xenophobic hatreds or you can have people arguing that the conditions of workers are the same here as abroad and representatives of the Third World here arguing for greater understanding, and so on. That seems to me a place where progressive forces, possibly revolutionary forces, come in.

Mary Ann Tétreault   I think that there are a number of reasons why it's difficult to get at this intersection of race, class, gender and other identities. One of the impacts of globalization has been to make more rather than fewer distinctions for the self part of an anti-globalization-as-homogenization project for a lot of people. This is very clear in feminism where there's been such a vast split into different feminisms that a person might want to have fifty qualifiers for what kind of a feminist she is. And this is very problematic when you're looking at some sort of basic level of global rights. I think that gender is a problem in the way that it intersects with these other identity categories. Even Marx, who was gender-egalitarian on one level, squashed any real speaking out and consciousness-raising in dealing with gender issues. And this certainly has been true in a lot of Marxist revolutions. Women are told, 'well you wait until afterwards'. These contradictions exist even in cases where, as a matter of fact, the revolutionaries themselves were interventionist for women; think of Zimbabwe, where the revolutionaries would go after husbands who beat up their wives and collect money and do other things to support families. This all bounced back very negatively on the women when the revolution was over. Or in Vietnam, where gender analysis was a way of examining class oppression, but people, workers, were insulted to be compared to women – who are inferior after all – whereas workers were seen as superior and full of agency.

Finally, one of the unresolved issues, certainly with respect to gender, and to some extent race as well, is the role of the state, whether it is the pre-revolutionary state or the post-revolutionary state, in making rules of the game that allow people to compete for what is valuable in society. Gender is very frequently a category of exclusion. Race is very frequently a category of exclusion. Class is very frequently a category of exclusion. And the intersection of these exclusions creates even more levels of excluded groups – it's a way of dividing and ruling. I think, if we could leap over this and make a stronger activist approach to these differences, that the capacity of the state to utilize these differences against us could be eroded and so enable us to use our solidarities for ourselves.

Valentine Moghadam Something that came to mind as Mary Ann was speaking about Vietnam: one of my favorite currency bills is one from Vietnam where the picture is of a woman in a factory. It seems to me that women were valued and recognized for their role in society and the economy. I have kept that bill.

I think that globalization has brought issues of class and gender to the fore in ways that had been eclipsed previously. The neoliberal economic environment is disliked because of its adverse effects on working people, working women, working families, and the poor. Incidentally, these are the categories used by the anti-globalization activists. The British development economist Paul Streeten (1997) has produced a useful matrix, a balance sheet of globalization with a list of social groups and geographic areas that benefit or lose out from globalization. As an aside, someone like me can be described as a beneficiary of globalization. But that's not good enough for me. And it's the same with many people in the anti-globalization campaigns. Their discourse is that globalization has been bad for workers, for peasants, for women, for the poor, and in that sense issues of class and gender are made prominent by globalization.

Now my wish, my dream, my vision, my fantasy, is that in the future the labor movement might look more like the feminist movement, that the labor movement will learn from the organizational style of the feminist movement and create the kind of transnational movement that feminists have succeeded in creating. The transnational feminist networks bring together women from different ethnicities, cultures, religions, countries and regions, who coalesce around a common agenda. Although they are involved in local or national struggles – as well as global issues – I would argue that they are not nationalists. In fact, their discourse is often explicitly anti-nationalist. One of the reasons that the early International fell was because the leaders of the unions and labor movements sided with their respective bourgeoisies. Women don't do that, at least not in the transnational feminist networks that I study.

So my hope is that in the future the labor movement might look more like the women's movement organizationally and also in terms of vision and ideology, and that there might be an alliance, a coalition of the women's movement and the labor movement. The bridge might consist of trade-union women, feminists who are working in the labor movement. I think that would be a very potent revolutionary anti-systemic movement in the future.

Mary Ann Tétreault   One of the things that's changing in many states, both developed and developing, is the struggle within states by groups that are defined differently from class – an upsurge of either ethnic politics or religious politics. And I think that there are a number of aspects of globalization that support this trend and, in consequence, mobilize support for the continuation of the development of global capitalism. Yet internally, states are still important. States do have the bombs. Control of the state is a useful thing to have, no matter who you are. These cross-narratives across groups within states seem to be less compelling, or at least they seem to be vulnerable to attack by way of dividing the state vertically so that you can then manage conflicts of interest within states, not as class conflicts, but as intergroup conflicts. So, in Rwanda, you can have Hutu killing Tutsi to discourage people from looking too closely at the top layer of Hutu who are controlling the state and controlling the economy, and yet who themselves are oppressed from outside because of the pressures of globalization on Rwanda as a whole. I think that the collapse of Yugoslavia can also be looked at in terms of differential levels of development among ethnic groups, and particularly regionalized ethnic groups, that then could be exploited by people who wanted to take over the state for reasons of their own, not to make a horizontal revolution but to displace many of the costs of globalization onto a different set of people who were not in their constituencies, and yet not disturb that basic pattern of class relations within their constituencies.

Kate Bruhn One of the themes here is whether or not class has disappeared as a major organizing identity, or at least been subordinated as such in these post-cold war movements, to be replaced by religious, ethnic, feminist or other types of identities. In the initial phases of the Zapatista movement, the first three or four documents that came out still had strong overtones of class discourse and dialogue, but this is one of the things that mysteriously disappears after about two or three weeks. All of a sudden there is a very postmodern, identity-based discourse in which the ethnic identity of the movement is stressed to a much greater extent than it was in the first two or three documents. And as time goes on, there is a clear effort by the Zapatistas to reach out to other groups, outside of their borders, on the basis of common identities that are not class identities, as in Marcos's statements about how 'I am a homosexual, I am a woman walking alone in the Metro', identifying himself with all of those who had been marginalized based on identities that were not really strongly tied to class. Now as you look at the Chiapas situation, it's clear that class is still playing a role, but it's not the mobilizing discourse.

Jan Rus The incorporation (or not) of indigenous people has long been one of the great issues in Latin American revolutions. One of the things that got me interested in indigenous history in the first place was Che's 1967 diary where he writes about how stupid the Indians were who wouldn't give him their chickens and pigs even though he was liberating them. He eventually had to liberate the chickens and pigs to feed himself, which is why the Indians turned against him. You have that sort of progression in Latin American revolutionary practice from seeing indigenous people as people who had to be incorporated by force into revolutions: even the popular revolutions didn't usually include indigenous people, who didn't participate even marginally in the national polities. And then we get to Guatemala where the guerrillas got better and better at learning native languages, but they were still the leaders and still the ones making decisions. There's a lot of argument about that now. And finally you get to the Zapatistas where supposedly what is being articulated is a native indigenous project, but the people doing the articulating are still not indigenous.

Carol Smith (1990) has written about the extent to which the survival of indigenous people in Latin America, and probably in the Americas in general, has occurred in small communities, enclosed in a kind of a nutshell of cultural rejection of what's outside. To the extent that they are participating now in larger revolutionary movements, that nutshell in which those cultures have preserved themselves and kept themselves apart has been breached. To the extent that there are indigenous leaders in the Zapatistas, they turn out to be people who have migrated around the country to work outside in factories. This cultural dimension is an awkward one because the revolutionary project, the revolutionary agenda, is something that's kept in the global by participants in the global outside of local society. It's not something that's kept in these traditional societies that are resisting.

And I'm a little afraid that what's going to happen is that we're finally including Latin American indigenous people in revolutions, when the agrarian societies in which they actually existed – viable up until the very recent past – will have stopped existing and they're going to be thrown into participating in bigger revolutions with everybody else. They never emancipated themselves within that old structure. So, the place of culture in revolutions, at least in Latin America, is a very mixed and painful one. You can join the revolution of larger society only when you're acculturated.

John Foran Acculturation, as you put it, doesn't necessarily mean a one-way street. Increasingly as we think about the future, we might think in terms of acculturation from below. Consider the influence of the Zapatistas on urban Mexico and in North America and Europe, or the autonomy movements in the Americas linking North, South and Central America and so forth. And finally, the need to address in all of this the existence and the struggles of other non-white populations in the Americas, and particularly Afro-Americans, Afro-Latin Americans in places like Cuba and throughout the Caribbean, including Central America and Brazil and so on, and how their struggles fit into these pictures in complicated ways.

Jan Rus I think the question for indigenous people is how do they go about making revolutions and societal changes that are their own, that come from themselves. They have to open their own spaces, without others speaking and acting for them, but how do they do this? Just as the question for feminists has been about women making a space for women, how do indigenous people acquire rights without having to become just like the dominant society first? How do you become the other from their position? I think this is still much more theorized in feminism, and in fact a lot of indigenous people – indigenous women – are looking to feminism as a place to begin. How do you acquire equality for spaces that are different within a larger collectivity without becoming subsumed by it? I'm skeptical of the romantic image of the Zapatistas' others, of their 'Mayanness' as an alternative to the West, that's been commodified in the

First World, in the United States. I think there's been a mistranslation of their desire for equality within, not isolation from, the larger whole.

John Foran   Literally they're not talking in the same languages (in Chiapas and North America). But there are two points to make. One is that there *is* suddenly a dialogue, however imperfectly mediated and however indirect it is, because in a sense you yourself, Jan, are mediating the dialogue in that context. And second, that difference between the realities on the ground in Chiapas and the perceptions of those elsewhere doesn't really undermine the impact that this rebellion can have elsewhere. It can have a positive impact even if it's a misunderstanding, even if it's an imperfect translation. It has a real effect also in the world. I think you're right – we don't want that to build misunderstanding upon misunderstanding – but that effect is already in itself a positive development. And further interaction and dialogue are wanted, I think, on all sides to build something even stronger out of all of that.

George Collier   One important development is the way global things are connecting to very local things in both directions. I think there is a real need – for lack of a better word – for ethnographic study of the kinds of cultural changes that are going on in landscapes like the Zapatista movement. That kind of ethnographic work can reveal or take note of really surprising things – for example, the use by indigenous people of the concept of intellectual property rights. This is something that has emerged on the Chiapas scene in the past couple of years. Recently there's been an effort by the state government to steal the Zapatista agenda, legislating indigenous autonomy, with the state circulating a draft law about indigenous cultural rights in one of the forums that they organized to hear what indigenous people had to say about culture. They expected people to talk about song and dance and the other things that are often thought of as culture. Instead, a group of shamans wanted to insist on understanding what were going to be their intellectual property rights for the herbal medicines that are potentially going to be used by pharmaceutical firms. There's actually a movement against a bioprospecting project that does plant collecting to determine their pharmaceutical value. Maya protest is characterizing this project as biopiracy, a characterization that has been picked up by the transnational circuits who were involved in the Seattle protests. And the Maya protest is coupled here with an indigenous concept, that of the *pukuh*, a native concept a bit like the evil spirits often associated with commodity fetishism, for example as described by Michael Taussig (1980) for Latin America. The Maya are referring to the bioprospectors as *pukuh* – evil spirits – and are asking First World people to think of the bioprospectors in these terms. For the indigenous Maya, the concept of the *pukuh* is also used to refer to the robots that they know are used in industrial manufacturing in First World places. Undoubtedly some Maya, such as those Jan Rus has worked with who have migrated in the international work circuits, have seen industrial robots. Some may have experienced the manufacturing that goes on with robotic industries. The point is that there is a kind of reverberation between the corporate notion of intellectual property rights, very much a First World thing, and Maya trying to use the concept for their own kinds of collective projects. And at the same time, there is some cross-fertilization of indigenous ideas in the notion of the *pukuh*, as a kind of evil-spirited thing, that is going on back into the First World communication. This is something quite new. It isn't the sort of thing that we were seeing, at least in any direct way, between the global, the transnational and the very local in the landscape that we worked within in the 1960s, when the flow of ideas, if any, was just from the First World to the Third World.

Valentine Moghadam   We've been talking a lot about Chiapas, an example of an indigenous movement that people sitting around this table find encouraging and progressive. But there are other indigenous movements with some kind of connection with globalization, perhaps not so clear a connection, or one that might be more problematical. What is our response to indigenous movements in Asia or Africa or the Middle East or the former Soviet Union? What is their connection to globalization given that they don't have that wonderful ten-point program that the Zapatistas have for the liberation of women? The Chechens don't have it. Even though a large proportion of the Tamil Tigers, including unfortunately the people who do suicide bombings, are women, they don't have a woman-friendly social program or an emancipatory program for women. Are they part of our revolutionary pantheon or not?

Eric Selbin   We just can't pick the cases that we like and that we're comfortable with. I wonder, for instance, if we're going to talk about gender and revolution, what do we do with a case like Sendero Luminoso, where clearly there is a tension to a set of factors that one could reasonably place under the rubric of gender but works out in some ways that make a lot of people uncomfortable? There are also some particularly interesting cases both in North Africa around Algeria in the early 1960s and later in sub-Saharan Africa. There's a point in 1969 where Amilcar

Cabral goes to the leadership in Cape Verde and gives an absolutely marvelous speech on 'Our party and the struggle must be led by the best sons and daughters of the people', arguing that women can't simply be appendages, and what is really intriguing about it is that this part falls flat with his audience. It would be very interesting to try and find the context to set that in.

Similarly, there is said to have been a crucial meeting that took place at one point among the leaders of SWAPO about what to do with white folks who have ended up in leadership positions? Apparently there was a terribly intense two- or three-day meeting which basically decided, 'well we haven't figured it out up to date and we didn't figure it out this weekend, so the hell with it'. And it would be a really interesting reversal or revision to see what must have been the tone and tenor for a set of black African revolutionaries trying to figure out what to do with some of their white comrades who had been with them for a long time.

John Foran   I'm mindful of John Walton's critique of the question and certainly it was a daunting task for me to find a way to pose the question. And I trusted, rightly, in the discussion going in many different directions as a way to generate ideas. Mindful of the critique, I will leapfrog over the even more impossible question of how culture comes into play under current conditions, and, in the spirit of sharpening things a little bit, shift us on to the third and final question that I propose for today: What issues will revolutionary alliances and coalitions across these and other categories – because there are other categories as well, including nationality among others – have to solve in the future and how might they do so? And you can take that as concretely or abstractly as you want. I'm asking specifically, what are the problems involved in forming revolutionary alliances? What issues would coalitions of different groups have to confront – specifically their differences – and how might they confront them? The topic in the larger sense is agency, building coalitions, and these categories that divide or differentiate or potentially work against inclusiveness in revolutionary coalitions. And culture does enter in here, for many people.

Jeffery Paige   Originally I submitted an abstract to this conference for a paper called 'Abstract subjects: class, race and gender and modernity'. In response to the frequent jokes about my 'postmodernity', I would say a more accurate view might be 'counter-modernity', because, unlike the postmodern postulates of role relativism and flexible identities, I think there is a revolutionary counter-modernity project. And it is not me deconstructing the categories of the global economy, but global capitalism that is doing it, providing, as I said, an opportunity.

The implication of this is that there are new difficulties of transcending these separate movements and these separate identities and the dilemmas and difficulties and intentions of identity politics that have congealed around the fact that we have separate social movements organized by class, the socialist movement, the labor movement, feminism around gender, and various civil rights and nationalist struggles organized around the issue of race. And these clearly share concerns, but I think it's extremely important that we go beyond them and seek a common positive agenda. What others, Jane Collier among them, were saying earlier on is very important, that this common agenda is not going to be *explicitly* feminist, but perhaps in the sense of developing some sort of caring or human ethos which unites people to transcend these categories. And here I am definitely going to deconstruct.

In the heritage of the liberal revolutions, there's a particular conception of who the subject was, including the subject of revolution, an idea that was taken over by Marxism. This was a person motivated by instrumental concerns, concerned with production and property, material well-being, whether it was the capitalist concern of increasing wealth or a socialist concern with redistributing it. The focus in the labor movement is on those things; even the concept of labor itself is the construction of a particular instrumental subject. It's the transformation of human beings into abstract labor and the taking away of their fundamental humanity.

The socialist movement acted as if we really had been turned into this abstract quantity of labor and demanded more rights for labor and so on, and there was a labor movement which forgot that the core of the problem was the transformation of people into labor. Now this is a process that's going on all over the world as people have been incorporated into the global economy. But they know they are being incorporated into something distant and different because they live in their own cultural worlds. There's an increasing discomfort in the developed world as well, marked by a change in consciousness among upper-middle-class people who don't want to be incorporated into this, who don't want to lose their humanity, and similarly for women who have approached this masculinized instrumental subject with some trepidation. We have to go beyond class, and I think the same is true for race: one of the difficulties is that people think we know what race is. We use a term which we know to be false. There are no human races; people do not differ on the basis of biology. In fact what we've done, unfortunately, is racialize people. We say that people have biological differences. These are dangerous tropes of irreducible human difference, and as long as we really believe that there are those irreducible differences, it will be very difficult for us to construct differences, and we'll debate the kind of things Eric was talking about between white people and black people, and so on.

These categories themselves are inherent in ideas about modernity. Even social scientists don't really know what we mean when we use these racist terms. I think we often mean kinds of cultural differences. By 'white', we too often seem to mean the modern instrumental subject and people who have those characteristics which are supposedly 'more white' than others. We really have to transcend those and recognize what we're talking about in order to construct a movement that will recognize the past differences that were created by racialized oppression. The paradox of the liberal revolutions was the creation of this instrumental independent subject. It's not just a question of liberating women from this. Why do most people, male people, want to be reduced to instrumental subjects?

Jane Collier To elaborate a little on notions of the self and what it might mean to be a human being, the creation of the modern liberal subject came about when landowners felt that subjection to the king wasn't going to take their property, that they had to take it into their own hands. And they created this liberal, equal subject that appealed to everybody, because everybody can imagine themselves as being this equal subject, and created this equal groundswell. And again, we might be getting to the point of wondering what the issue is, who are the bad guys. Maybe life as a rich capitalist isn't all it's cooked up to be if you have to live behind high walls and barbed wire and bodyguards and you can't send your children outside because they'll get blown up and kidnapped. You can't live a life. So maybe the upper classes, whose lives at least in some places in the world are fairly restricted, will be part of a reconception of what it means to be human, to be able to live a life that is not behind high walls and bodyguards and guns. Cultural changes will come about because the elites have experienced a need for a change. And we might want to think about what globalization is doing to the lives of the wealthy of the world who have to live behind high walls and barbed wire.

Jeffery Paige The task of the revolution, of a positive agenda, is to construct some idea of a common humanity, a global humanity that transcends these artificial categories. David Harvey reminded me in a talk that the idea of species-being in Marx was an idea of an ethos of caring, an ethos of constructive concern for other human beings, as human beings and as part of nature. And it seems to me that that really ought to be our focus and we should avoid the kind of false universalism of the Enlightenment which says only the instrumental Western male subject is human. The success of the movement depends on substituting that notion of worldwide common humanity to transcend the categories of gender and the categories of race. And I think in the current context, because of the changes introduced by global capitalism itself, it's an agenda that might actually work. It might make it possible for us to mobilize for social change on the basis of a common ethos and common ideology.

Mary Ann Tétreault That's all well and good, but I also think in many ways it's sort of like peace, love and granola, and that when we're trying to mobilize across these lines, one of the things that we tend to elide is how strongly such divisions are imbricated in all social structures. And how much of what we're talking about is redistribution that we need to confront directly. An example that is but isn't economic: there's a famous quotation from Golda Meir that says that there will be no peace in Palestine until Palestinian mothers love their children as much as Jewish mothers love their children. There, I think, is a sign of the difficult task of intersubjectivity. These cleavages are real in how they are perceived and how they're embedded in people's minds. Yes, we need revolutionary rhetorics and discourses to overcome them but it's not an easy task. And I think that we also have to confront directly what A has and what B doesn't.

Jeffery Paige Peace, love and granola? Actually you provide an example in support of mine. Somebody who had a human ethos could never make a racist, disparaging remark like the one that you just quoted. That's exactly the kind of thing we have to struggle against. And I never suggested it would be easy. I'm not suggesting a love fest; I'm suggesting we make a political agenda of getting rid of these categories and attacking statements like that, those horrifying racist things wherever they appear. We not only have to attack the state; we have to attack our categories and our own consciousness in order to make possible political mobilization to deal with the real structural differences that exist among these. So I don't want to ignore that at all. That was not my intent. But I think, first, that until people see Palestinians and Jews as human beings, they're not going to be concerned about alleviating the material deprivations. That was my point.

John Foran I'm glad you clarified that because that was my reaction also; that you were saying that, 'well we have to adopt a kind of color-blindness', and that that's the same thing as anti-racism, which it isn't. And without an anti-racist struggle embedded within the revolution, you're not going to have a multiracial alliance, revolutionary or otherwise. So, I'm glad for the clarification because I think there was some misunderstanding.

Let's talk about actual revolutionary coalitions. When a huge broad population coalesces because of a common enemy, when they succeed in seizing power, of course the next step is the problem of what to do then. You get rid of the Shah and then suddenly you fragment into all sorts of different views about what should come next. Keeping those coalitions together, that is the problem. And it is really a question of learning from the past because the past is littered with failures to achieve this.

Farideh Farhi   Coalitions come about because we have a clear view of who the enemy is. When the enemy becomes crystallized to the point where you can actually create those coalitions, it becomes a common enemy. And of course it is so much easier when it's only one person: just cut the head off and we take care of it. The agreement − that momentary agreement that comes about before everything falls apart − is on the basis of that crystallized enemy. Unfortunately revolutions go astray when we become 'captured by the enemy'. That is to say that we become so obsessed by the enemy that we cannot let go. And in our fight against the enemy, we end up expunging so many others from our coalition and from the body politic. We have an expression in Iran that, of our two attempts to liberate and democratize Iran, in the first one we were captured by the British enemy, and in the second one by the American enemy. Twenty years afterwards, we are still saying that to America and kicking people out of the body politic on the basis of being servants of America.

So it's difficult to envision a positive politics without going through the first step of clarifying what the enemy is in that particular context *but then* being constantly mindful of not taking the next step. That is, thinking in terms of what all these things entail, watching our step continuously and reminding ourselves of what has happened in our past. And that was what I was trying to say in terms of more attention to means.

Valentine Moghadam   There is obviously a real danger of a collapse of alliances and coalitions, whether these be revolutionary or otherwise, when the participants in these alliances and coalitions have not had the opportunity, or for various reasons they have been unwilling, to negotiate their differences, their different views and visions. The example par excellence of this was the Iranian revolution, which a number of us have described as a populist revolution. The revolutionary coalition consisted of competing groups with quite different agendas. But they never sat around

a table to work out their differences and come up with a common program or agenda. Instead, the populist revolutionary discourse was very
ambiguous; the one agreement, as Farideh said, was that the target was
the person of the Shah.

In light of the outcome of the Iranian revolution, people might be
more attentive to issues of clarity, negotiations, compromise, consensus.
They may be less willing to engage in alliances and coalitions without
working out and negotiating differences in a more explicit fashion. To
give one example, transnational feminist networks have taken part in the
broad coalitions and alliances against the World Bank, the IMF, the WTO
and the campaign to end the Third World debt. But DAWN [Develop-
ment Alternatives with Women for a New Era] has been very deliberate
in using the slogan 'economic justice and gender justice'. Their manifesto
(found in Sen and Grown 1987) starts out by saying something like 'we
call for an end to the oppressions based on class, race, gender, etc.' But
DAWN made clear its uneasiness with the Catholic groups that have taken
part in Jubilee 2000 and the campaign to end the Third World debt.
DAWN is concerned that Catholic groups might be unwilling to concur
on feminist reproductive health and rights issues, in particular abortion
and contraception. This difference did not lead DAWN to pull out of
these campaigns but they have been explicit about their uneasiness. In the
future, groups will have to take each other more seriously. Women's groups,
groups that are concerned about human rights, environmental issues,
workers' rights and so on, will have to negotiate their politics, visions and
tactics before the movement really expands and moves forward.

It seems to me, too, that the future will see fewer patriarchal revolutions because of the social structural and ideological changes that have
taken place – the growth of global feminism, of women's organizing and
mobilizing on a global scale. Let's not forget that the isolation of the
Taliban is a success story of global feminism. The Clinton administration
was very close to recognizing the Taliban regime in the fall of 1996. It was
concerted efforts on the part of Afghan feminists working with the Feminist Majority and NOW in the United States, not to mention the action
alerts and petition drives by feminists in Italy, France, Spain, Pakistan and
elsewhere, that led to non-recognition of the Taliban by all but three
governments – those of Saudi Arabia, Pakistan and the United Arab
Emirates. This isolation of the Taliban as a result of global feminist activism
has some larger theoretical and political lessons.

Jeff Goodwin   As a number of people have pointed out, revolutionary
coalitions have generally formed in opposition to clear, unambiguous and

palpable enemies that are typically personified by a single despot. Such coalitions have largely been 'negative' coalitions; that is, they've included many very different groups that have come together on the basis of a common ideology or political vision. I think part of the difficulty in confronting globalization and neoliberalism is that it is not a centralized project but a hydra-headed beast. And it's not clear where this beast is actually located. Where is the Winter Palace that we're going to storm?

There are so many agencies involved in the project of globalization – from transnational corporations and banks to universities to governments to transnational institutions like the World Trade Organization. Moreover, the responsiveness of these various agencies to pressure and protest varies considerably from one institution to the next, from one national context to the next. This means that it's highly unlikely that we'll witness, on a global level, the type of unambiguously exclusionary and violently repressive response to popular mobilization which has typically helped to congeal revolutionary coalitions. As a result, I'm very pessimistic about the possibility of a revolutionary transnational coalition against globalization. The terms of globalization will be fought out at various levels. But I don't think we'll see a transnational revolution against global capitalism of the sort that Marx foresaw.

To those who spoke earlier about the idea of deepening democracy, or of participatory democracy as a potential foundation or ideological glue for a revolutionary coalition against globalization, I must say that I am skeptical that this sort of language can actually work, given, once again, the very different agencies involved in this project, the very different issues at stake and demands being made by particularly situated people. I'm skeptical, in short, that a truly revolutionary coalition is possible under present circumstances. We will see issue-oriented coalitions on some questions, more radical mobilizations on other issues, but not, I think, a single revolutionary coalition against global capitalism as such.

Eric Selbin I think Val's right that coalitions are going to recognize that they can negotiate and bargain with each other as they come together because people's best hopes are going to be to put these coalitions together. And I think there is a set of 'mundane' issues such as: Is it going to be armed struggle or not; and if it is, when and where and how? Who is going to pay for this? What's going to be our strategy if it's not armed struggle? If we ignore them, we're ignoring a real world element, a part of meaningful conversation or negotiations between various groups that are trying to figure out how to approach this problem, as any coalition tries to figure out what it will look like.

Carlos Vilas   By the end of 1958, the revolutionary coalition in Cuba included almost every segment of Cuban society, even the haute bourgeoisie, which had to join with the 26 July Movement after the failure of the April 1958 general strike. The same thing was seen in Nicaragua. It was clear that in the struggle against Somoza there were two coalitions, the Sandinista one and the conservative, bourgeois one. Somoza made a mistake by killing the head of the conservative coalition. From that moment on, there was no alternative to the revolutionary coalition that was led by the Sandinistas. The problem arises anew today for a coalition of sectoral movements – human rights, environmentalists, gender and so on. How are we going to think of such a coalition without thinking of some kind of conversion from social protest to political propositions and without thinking of some kind of leadership? This is difficult, but it is not impossible.

So the question for me is to figure out what kind of coalitions will need to be built in order to confront neoliberalism and globalization. Who is going to lead this process? Because unless one of these many actors is able to lead this process, as coalitions come and go, it will be very difficult to reach a plausible solution. Up to now we were trained to think of the working class as the leading actor of revolutionary transformation. This is no longer true. Perhaps it has never been true. But who are the would-be leaders, who could teach us how to build this coalition, around what goals? Again, I have no answers.

Abdollah Dashti   I agree that we need some sort of leadership that will differ from what we saw in the past revolutions from Cuba to Nicaragua or even back to Russia. I think the time for that is gone because they led to bureaucratization and hierarchy. So we have to think about some new form of leadership which would prevent that, avoiding it in the future. The way to do it is some sort of democracy. How can we eliminate hierarchization in leadership but at the same time have direction? Today's spontaneity should be combined with some organization, with a new leadership that can incorporate different interests – feminists who are part of it, gays and lesbians who might be part of it, different racial groups that might be part of it. So it's not that sort of unitarian leadership that we have had in the past.

Carlos Vilas   This authoritarian ingredient has to do with the terms of the struggle. If you are in hiding, if you are clandestine, it's very hard to be democratic in discussions. If in addition you are committed to military struggle because you are facing an authoritarian state, it is even more difficult. It would be great now if these coalitions and these leaderships could be built in a legal setting, in the open sun. Nevertheless, there is always an ingredient of authority, not necessarily authoritarianism. Democracy at this level has to do with discussions, with participation, with a moment. After the very moment that a decision is made, once the decision is made, it is like an order.

George Collier   One answer that comes out of looking at the tenacity of the Zapatista movement is to have many irons in the fire, many kinds of network. The Zapatistas have had several agendas. There is an agenda which is to end the PRI's domination of Mexican politics, and the fact that there has been an election where the PAN won undercuts a lot of support within Mexican society that might otherwise have continued. Now the Zapatistas have to regain the stage of support within Mexican society, which is probably why they're about to stage this march to Mexico City, the theater that captures the popular imagination. The Zapatistas have also had the agenda of indigenous rights, and that entails the coalitions that expand to various kinds of movement in the Americas that grow out of the quincentennial movement, which the Zapatistas did not found but built upon and used. And, of course, the other agenda has been the anti-neoliberal agenda, which they've worked on through these national and international meetings and 'encounters'.

These are, in a sense, speaking to different constituents that the Zapatistas can juggle and play together in interesting ways as the hydra-headed character of the contemporary moment shifts. And so, one of the answers may be that when the goal is not to seize the state any more but to work on several fronts to bring about all kinds of progressive social change, successful alliances will be networked together in interesting ways such that when one dimension of those networks for one or another reason declines in its potency for the moment, other dimensions can be brought to the fore.

The Zapatistas have not always been as inclusionary as the world likes to see them. They've been able to get away with things. An example is in the negotiating of the San Andrés accords. They did invite various indigenous groups to participate in the discussion of what was going to be on the agenda of the San Andrés accords, but when it came actually to negotiating with the government the Zapatistas excluded a very significant number of indigenous groups from the bargaining process and went ahead and negotiated things on their own. They could in a sense get away with that because of the power of other kinds of alliances and networks that they had established, which made them the spokespeople for the indigenous movement whether other groups liked it or not.

John Foran   One of the things that I take away from this discussion is that the history of revolution shows in some sense a progression from the elite kinds of revolutions (as Jane mentioned) against monarchs to lower-class revolts of all kinds, to an autonomous women's movement within the revolution in the last decades, to an emerging indigenous movement along-side and in some sense at the head of the movement today. And now you have to match this up with a hydra-headed enemy that Jeff Goodwin so well described and ask where you are. And without being able to offer any answers, what I heard and agree with is that there is a set of problems at stake here: there is an organizational question, there are strategic questions and problems, there's a vision question and problem, even a question about whether one should have a vision or whether a vision motivates people, and there's an increasingly new question about the goal or target of such struggles. There's also a leadership problem about which we have various points of view, as it should be. So that's a lot of questions and problems.

It seems that if you try and think about all of this, it's clearly difficult and you can come up with various answers. The anti-globalization movement in North America and the Zapatista movement are facing this now. These are questions that are therefore hanging in the air. And they point us toward tomorrow's papers and final thematic discussion, so maybe on that note we'll stop.

PART IV

From Afghanistan to the Zapatistas

14

Globalization and Popular Movements

John Walton

The Argument

In the short space available, I shall argue three related points: that revolution is a historically changing phenomenon, that today's developing world is undergoing a transition from developmentalism to globalism, and that this sea change affects the nature of political contention as it is expressed in varied forms ranging from popular protest and social movements to rebellions and revolutions.

In *Reluctant Rebels* (1984), I argued that the anti-colonial rebellions and Third World revolts of the mid-twentieth century, while different in many respects from the 'classical' revolutions in Europe and China from the late eighteenth to the early twentieth centuries, were no less revolutionary when judged by their extensive mobilizations and transformative results. Without repeating the steps of the argument, the point was that classical and developmental revolutions were different kinds of 'national revolts' capable of instructive comparison but historically distinct types. The modern Third World revolutions, for example, arose in efforts to expand popular democracy, contended with a powerful colonial or neo-colonial state, involved important urban–rural links, were precipitated by state attempts preemptively to suppress political movements, and in the end achieved results comparable to 'successful' revolutions.

Events that I have studied in the ensuing years now lead me to conclude that a new global political economy has taken shape since the 1980s and that we are already discovering changed forms of political contention, new struggles over globalization that, so the hypothesis goes, will be reflected in continuing conflicts including future revolutions. This discussion will first characterize the changes of the last twenty years and their effect on forms of political contention in the developing countries, and then draw out the implications of this transition for future revolution.

The Transition from Development to Globalization

Throughout the developing and former colonial world the postwar years witnessed the creation of new states and the expansion of older ones for purposes of economic development. Industrialized countries around the world turned to the decolonizing states for geopolitical allies and trade partners. Indeed, the 'Third World' was formed in this context of cold war rivalry, multilateral sponsorship, development assistance and economic incorporation. Developing-country governments began to invest in their own economies and regulate them in the interests of planned growth. State-owned enterprises were established to help direct this process, provide economies of scale, assure the development of essential industries, and deal on an equal footing with multinational firms. Planned investment included large infrastructure projects – dams, roads, reclamation, electrification and ports. Most important, the new 'developmentalist state' (Cardoso and Faletto 1979: 143; McMichael 2000: 39) was distinguished from earlier state forms by its strategy of social intervention in support of the social wage, public ownership, central planning, social security, health care, workers' compensation, minimum wage and trade-union rights. The developmental state was capitalist and dependent on trade and aid from Western industrial nations, but it also attempted to husband national capital in a set of policies that included import-substitution industrialization, capital and exchange rate controls, industrial protection and joint investment ventures (Cardoso and Faletto 1979; Rueschemeyer and Evans 1985; Migdal 1988; White 1988).

Consistent with their dependent and capitalist features, developmental states displayed a clear urban bias (Lipton 1977). Public investment in health, education, architecture, infrastructure and enterprise went disproportionately to the big cities alongside state and corporate headquarters. Urban bias was implemented through a dense network of policy and legislation. For example, developmental states often overvalued the exchange rate in a policy that favored consumption of imported goods (including food) and disadvantaged (mainly primary product) exports. Urban consumers were subsidized, giving the appearance of generalized development and restraining upward pressures on wages and improvements in the standard of living (de Janvry 1981). A social pact was created between the state and low-income groups based on patron–client exchange – regime support for a set of urban collective goods and services ranging from land and housing to subsidized food and public employment (Cornelius 1975; Ross 1975). The developmental state certainly cultivated other forms of lucrative patronage for upper-income groups, but its strategy rested on a new social pact with the growing numbers and political potential of the urban masses.

During periods of economic growth and generous international lending, developing countries successfully maintained the welfare state apparatus. Many Latin American states, for example, adopted national health and social security programs. States weathered oil price shocks and recession in the 1970s by borrowing heavily to support public services and popular consumption. External debt soared, requiring new loans to pay old ones. By the early 1980s, when the international financial system recognized the debt crisis, urban groups had become accustomed to basic state guarantees. Over the course of a generation a 'moral economy of the poor' (Thompson 1966) had evolved on the premiss that hard work and political loyalty were rewarded by an urban homestead and employment opportunities. The social pact prevailed in most instances, although developmental states were not averse to repression when demands outpaced the ability to satisfy too many constituents at once. Social inequality and official arrogance were tolerated by the poor majority owing to a combination of force and favor. But the system was predicated on reciprocity among interacting participants – stable under the conditions described but also delicate.

Contentious politics under the developmental state period typically operated within a patron–client framework. This pattern suits the logic and practice of the developmental state for two reasons. First, clientism offers a less costly alternative for redress of grievances, which suits the purposes of both the state and the urban poor. Second, it works effectively in times of economic growth, state expansion and social mobility. Joan Nelson's comprehensive book subtitled *Politics and the Urban Poor in Developing Nations* identifies four 'patterns of participation': ethnic associations, political parties, special interest groups and patron–client links, the latter being 'the most universal' (1979: 383). In a more recent review of this research, Gilbert and Gugler (1992: 180) conclude that the 'recurrent theme' is the politics of co-optation. Bryan Roberts notes that 'there were several factors making political and civil rights [conflict] less salient in Latin America during the period of import-substitution industrialization from the 1940s to the 1970s. Chief amongst them, I suggest, was the social mobility that accompanied urbanization and economic development' (1995: 194).

Political contention does take place in the developmental state, particularly in struggles over collective goods – public services such as land titles, housing, transportation, education, health and infrastructure (streets, sewers, electricity). The logic behind this proposition derives from the conditions of dependent development. Material welfare is uppermost in the intentions of migrant and rapidly urbanizing populations. In the cities of developing societies large segments of the population experience chronic poverty with limited (geographical and intergenerational rather than individual) mobility opportunities. To the extent that these groups are absorbed into the urban economy it is principally through the underemployed informal tertiary sector where protest organizations (e.g. trade unions) and repertoires (e.g. strikes) are in the main not present. Neighborhoods and communities are the more common locus of mobilized action and urban services are the currency of political exchange – public goods such as water, electricity and transportation that improve the material condition of households by reducing their expenditures.

Comparative evidence supports this reasoning. In Africa, Peil and Sada observe that industrial workers are conservative, collective action is covert, and 'though radical outbursts occur they tend to be rare' (1984: 265). Political participation finds other expressions: 'individuals and groups are probably most active at the defensive and allocative levels, in appealing for or against government action or proposed action (e.g. a request for a new market or against the destruction of a squatter settlement)' (1984: 342). In Latin America,

> the cross section of the urban population offered by squatter and other settlements can be compared to advantage with that provided, for example, by trade unions. In the transitional economies of Latin America, established industrial, construction, and transportation workers – especially those belonging to unions – represent a much restricted sector.... Lower-class settlements not only represent the most varied and highly focalized cross-section of the urban poor but also, and perhaps most importantly, embody the most vital manifestations of their political action. Organized land invasions, to cite only the best known case, represent viable instances of political struggle ... rather than occupational or income needs, it is the demand for housing that has most effectively politicized the poor. (Portes and Walton 1976: 74)

Drakakis-Smith observes that political movements of the urban poor are usually expressed in 'non-institutional' forms such as rent strikes or squatting rather than through institutional channels provided by trade unions and political parties.

The more institutional options are often the least effective form of action.... Trade unions can be very ineffective vehicles for political protest by the poor, few of whom have the sort of employment which leads to union membership.... As a result of this ineffectiveness, many of the urban poor have recourse to less 'acceptable' methods of involvement.... The most visible type of action in this context is perhaps the seizure of land by squatters. (1987: 51–2)

Finally, Gilbert and Gugler note three patterns of political conflict; among them 'a broad, class-conscious movement of workers is very much the exception', while struggle for land is 'the most conspicuous political action of the urban masses' and street demonstrations, riots and insurrections play an important role (1992: 192, 200). Comparing the first two periods, under liberal modernism conflict is low, political contention is channeled through developing institutional mechanisms, and contention centers on private goods such as wages or rents. In the developmental state, conflict is moderate, channeled by patron–client mechanisms with occasional eruptions of popular insurgency, and focused on collective goods.

Globalization and Countermovements

Neoliberal globalization is a process that began in earnest around 1980, rather than an accomplished fact at the turn of the century. It is, as the term implies, a new international regime that governs, with varying degrees of success, the economic and political relations among world states and populations. The regime consists of three components. First, it is a coordinating institutional complex of multilateral organizations, notably the International Monetary Fund, World Bank and World Trade Organization, linked to member governments, international banks and private associations such as the World Economic Forum. Second, the regime is orchestrated by a set of policies that promote market economies, free trade, unimpeded capital and investment flows, and elimination of obstacles to free markets such as labor codes, environmental protections and state subsidies (e.g. of food). Governments and institutions that constitute the globalizing regime sometimes differ sharply on the substance and implementation of neoliberal policy, but their differences concern how, not whether, to foster globalization. Third, globalization, like its predecessor development, is an uneven process over time and space. It moves by fits and starts. States are incorporated in different forms and degrees. Contentious politics appear at these uneven junctures. The changing whole is best understood through 'incorporating comparisons' of how its components fit together, cohere, and conflict (McMichael 1990; see my discussion below).

Neoliberal globalization generates a distinct configuration of winners and losers. Power shifts in the direction of multinational institutions and corporations. International bankers, exporters, regionally differentiated and integrated businesses, and electronic financial services are among the winners. Potential losers include welfare states, weak exporter countries, labor, environmental interests, middle classes in national enterprise, and notably the urban poor once incorporated by the developmental state. Contentious politics may arise in any of these settings depending upon particular combinations of circumstance, which we propose to identify.

Mridula Udayagiri and I have developed this argument in connection with a set of case studies devoted to (1) global austerity protests (or IMF riots), (2) social movements in response to neoliberal reforms in India, (3) democratization in Mexico, and (4) the recent wave of anti-globalization protests ranging from the WTO to sweatshops (Walton and Udayagiri 2000). In that paper, we compare the varied forms of anti-globalization contention, explore common mechanisms surrounding their expression, and consider interrelated patterns of causation. We begin with one broad claim: the developing world has experienced a sea change in the role of government, the aims of development, its winners and losers, its privileged policies and popular entitlements, and in the moral economy that suffuses this world. Something new is afoot in the globalizing world and in the notions people have of the situation they are in.

The argument may be summarized in several related propositions. Foremost, we argue that a new and growing form of contentious politics has infused the international system during the last twenty years as the result of a number of closely related trends toward economic and political restructuring. These trends and events include Third World debt crises, internationally orchestrated structural adjustment programs, expansion of trade and investment under deregulated terms, the rise of global administrative agencies and agreements, and the international popular response to these developments. It is, in brief, an era of neoliberal policies and global countermovements. This does not mean that international system politics is the only important form of contention in the modern world or that global countermovements are unprecedented. It does mean that new forms of protest have burgeoned from a narrower precedent and that global countermovements are becoming more important in the daily affairs of world populations, particularly those of the advanced countries once buffered from international inequalities and underdevelopment.

If the first proposition is valid, then it follows that our research methods and theoretical explanations must change apace with emerging forms of contention. Analyses must be cast at the global level, an argument made long ago by world-systems theory but still incompletely realized. Study of global countermovements must begin with the international political economy, the conditions and constraints it sets, and then move to regional, national and local phenomena, always under the assumption that system levels influence one another reciprocally. Put more succinctly, the global system and its distinct components must be understood through 'incorporating comparisons' (McMichael 1990). This is not to minimize the importance of states and localities or of political and cultural forces. But it does caution against the common tendency for students of contentious politics to fall back upon the models and embedded concepts of national politics and intrasocietal conflict in which select 'international variables' are brought into conventional nation-centered approaches. Incorporating comparison, by contrast, focuses on the international system, how it develops and changes by incorporating new arenas and sectors, how national and local societies change with enveloping ties to the system, and how in turn they set conditions on the system (e.g. as Mexico precipitated an international financial crisis in 1982 with great consequences for the system, Mexico and scores of developing countries).

Our case studies provide illustrations of incorporating comparisons. We argue for an underlying set of forces that affect differentially those groups, classes and populations of the international system. The underlying forces are, once again, the internationalization of capital and concomitant deregulation of welfare and developmental state protections in all their particular manifestations (e.g. multinational corporate power, trade competition, subsidy cuts, privatization of essential services, relaxation of environmental and labor standards, and so on). In different ways and different places, those forces affect such varied groups as Indian farmers, Latin American slum dwellers, European greens and US labor unions. Not only do the constituencies affected by globalization vary widely; their protest repertoires range from riots and street demonstrations to sustained social movements and international coalitions linked by high-tech communication. This range reflects predictable differences in political skills, resources and opportunities commanded, for example, by Third World shantytowns in contrast to US and European environmentalists. Yet the powerless are on the move. India's urban and rural poor mount serious social movements while Mexican voters mobilize to overturn a corrupt government. The more likely hypothesis about countermovement repertoires is that they are socially structured rather than consciously selected. The case of Mexican democratization (and relatively infrequent austerity protest) supports this interpretation. In a time of economic crisis and political unrest, elements of Mexico's developed civil society turned (among other initiatives) to electoral politics because of its extensive reach and symbolic tolerance under the one-party state.

In this nested set of explanatory factors, we come ultimately to the intersection of actors and conditions, protesters and perceived agents of their grievance. The case studies suggest a pattern in these global counter-movements. Actors are confronted abruptly with threats to their well-being, typically economic threats (jobs, wages, subsidies, protections) but also environmental, political and symbolic threats (environmental depredation, GMOs, corporate power, undemocratic processes). The threatened value in each case is a former entitlement (Sen 1981), typically a form of protection ensured by the state (e.g. food subsidies, labor legislation, environmental protection). The fact that entitlements have been to some extent guaranteed by the state means, in turn, that they have been won in previous struggles and negotiations, that they have become embedded in the social pact between states and citizens, and that they are woven into the moral economy of particular societies. Entitlements are more than interests or demands that might go unmet in the political process. They are experienced as rights and their potential loss as injustice.

Entitlements derive from states and in these instances have well-defined origins in the welfare states of the developed countries and developmental states of the former Third World. As our case studies demonstrate, nation-state entitlements sometimes conflict with the logic of global neoliberalism: in WTO rules that nullify endangered-species or labor laws in the United States, in European Union fiscal restraints that penalize French transport workers, and in IMF structural adjustment programs that raise prices to middle-class consumers and eliminate food subsidies in the developing world. In the rapidly globalizing world of deregulated trade and investment and incipient political organizations charged with implementing neoliberal policies, the rights of international populations are ill-defined, unrepresented, without redress.

But this spreading state of affairs presents a great paradox. Neoliberal economic reforms imply, even require, political reforms. Historically, capitalism is rooted in free labor, state-regulated competitive markets and bourgeois democratic governance. Global capitalism similarly requires open markets ruled by neoliberal policies and international agencies (the IMF, the WTO) as well as representative governments that incorporate citizen-consumers and eliminate rent-seeking autocrats. As the progressive Mexican opposition leader Porfirio Muñoz Ledo said, 'this government has to understand that it cannot move forward with an economic opening of the country without a political opening as well'. The new social pact replacing developmental-state patronage rests on the promise of democratization

– and so the concerted international effort to promote multiparty states and basic human rights. To be sure, these reforms are far from secure, even within the new global governing bodies like the World Trade Organization. But the Seattle demand for democratization of the WTO (and then President Clinton's acknowledgement of its logic) precisely demonstrates the paradox playing itself out at many levels of the global system. The point is not that a new set of democratic entitlements has been achieved, but rather that one is in contention.

The broader lesson is the emergence of a new global political consciousness along with (complementing, opposing, negotiating) the new global economy. We do not know exactly where this dialog is headed, whether the ideology of free trade and emerging markets will prove more compelling than its counterpart which attempts to define a coherent code of global justice embracing indigenous people, peasants, the urban poor, labor, democrats and dolphins. On one hand, the last twenty years have witnessed perhaps the most vigorous expansion of international capitalism and its enabling political framework in history. On the other hand, the same years have seen the remarkable growth of highly competent groups working for human rights, environmental conservation and people's protection. There is a new terrain of contentious politics where the stakes are higher and promises greater.

Implications for Revolution

Revolutions in the developing countries, like the larger political economy in which they are embedded, are increasing influenced by the forces of globalization and specifically by the international neoliberal policy regime and responses to it. The implications of this fact are manifold and direct. Globalizing forces will precipitate revolutionary situations and play a larger role in their development. Restructuring changes in international trade, debt management and welfare state responsibilities will shape political movements. This, of course, has been the case previously. But recently it has been more extensive and more consequential. Internationally designed structural adjustment programs, for example, represent a new level of intervention in developing state policy. Activities sanctioned by the WTO have become volatile issues for mobilized groups of Indian farmers and workers.

Similarly, social and revolutionary movements in the developing world will contend with international actors in the form of multilateral agencies (IMF, WTO), states (the G7), multinational corporations (like Monsanto in the Indian state of Karnataka), and popular organizations (People's Global Action, Global Exchange, etc.).

International policies and actors also introduce new ideologies. Neo-liberal doctrine that celebrates the effects of market forces is the strongest of these influences because it supports and works through a global insti-tutional framework. But a number of popular doctrines are being elabo-rated and enacted in the areas of human rights, environmental standards, women's rights, an international labor code, recognition of indigenous peoples and even discussions of an international code of justice. Anti-globalization movements are elaborating these principles while building alliances around their inclusive tenets.

If we invert the lens and examine revolutionary situations on the ground, then we should discover new ways in which globalization affects these movements by contrast to their predecessors in classical and develop-mental revolutions. Such, at least, is my hypothesis. Experts may make the argument relevant in cases such as Chiapas and the recent Indian move-ment of Ecuador. We are witnessing, moreover, new internationally sanctioned forms of state change that might be called 'revolutionary elec-tions'. Popular movements in conjunction with international reformist intervention successfully force elections and replace oppressive regimes. Indonesia is the best recent example of this phenomenon that also resembles the 'Yellow Revolution' in the Philippines. Whether a new form of globalized revolution is emerging remains an open question. But given the demonstrated influence of globalization on popular movements, it is a compelling question.

Marching with the Taliban or Dancing with the Zapatistas? Revolution after the Cold War

Karen Kampwirth

1994 was the year when the first two post-cold war guerrilla movements emerged, on opposite points of the planet. The first of those movements, the Zapatista Army for National Liberation (Ejército Zapatista de Liberación Nacional, or EZLN), seized seven cities in one of the poorest and most oppressed corners of Mexico – the southern state of Chiapas – during the early hours of the new year. The most significant of the cities taken by the rebels was San Cristóbal de las Casas, the capital of indigenous Chiapas, a colonial-era town still characterized by colonial-era politics.

It was a woman, Major Ana María, who led the takeover of San Cristóbal. Subcomandante Marcos, the chief spokesperson for the rebels, described what happened:

> Only the indigenous men and women under her command are witness to the moment in which the Major, a rebel indigenous Tzotzil woman, takes the national flag and gives it to the commanders of the rebellion.... Over the radio, the Major says: 'We have recovered the Flag. 10–23 over'.... It is 0100 hours of the new year for the rest of the world, but she has waited 10 years to say those words. She came to the mountains of the Lacandón Jungle in December of 1984, not yet 20 years of age and yet carrying the marks of a whole history of indigenous humiliation on her body. In December of 1984, this brown woman says 'Enough is Enough!' but she says it so softly that only she hears. In January of 1994, this woman and several thousand indigenous people not only say but yell 'Enough is Enough!', so loudly that all the world hears them. (Marcos 1996)

In November of the same year, a different sort of guerrilla group emerged, this one composed entirely of men. The Taliban (literally, the religious students), made their first public appearance as they rescued a caravan of Pakistani officials, stopped by bandits while traveling near the city of Kandahar, Afghanistan.

> About 2,000 of the students, who soon came to call themselves Taliban … went to Kandahar and freed the convoy from the bandits. A legend sympathetic to the Taliban, and possibly true, recounts that two girl refugees, prisoners of a local commander and ill-treated by him, were freed by the Taliban. Then they went on to capture Kandahar.… Compared with past armed bands the Kandahar population had known, the students behaved in an exemplary fashion. When they cleared the gunmen from the roads, they merely disarmed them instead of killing them. They then sent them on their way, saying in effect, go and sin no more. (Cooley 1999: 143)

If the dozens of earlier twentieth-century guerrilla movements had been largely creations of the cold war, devised by the Soviet Union and its satellite states, then those movements should have ceased to emerge after the cold war ended, silenced like puppets after the death of the puppeteer. Clearly nobody had explained that theory to either the Zapatistas or the Taliban. At the most basic level, the emergence of the Zapatistas and the Taliban tells us that revolutionary movements are quite possible in the post-cold war world.

The Zapatistas and the Taliban are similar in a number of ways. Both took up arms to promote agendas that were revolutionary[1] in that they required the transformation (rather than the reformation) of economic life, political life, ethnic relations and gender relations. They both arose in peripheral spaces, angered by their marginalization and yet fairly free to organize due to that marginalization. In the Zapatista case the peripheral space was the Lacandón jungle in the eastern end of the state of Chiapas. In the Taliban case the peripheral spaces were the refugee camps for Afghan refugees in Pakistan, and specifically the madrassas, or Koranic schools, associated with those camps. Both were aided by international forces: international civil society in the case of the Zapatistas, and regional powers, especially Pakistan and Saudi Arabia, in the case of the Taliban.

Yet the two post-cold war guerrilla movements were dramatically different in terms of their goals and their organizing styles. While the EZLN promoted national democratization and autonomy for indigenous Mexicans, the Taliban promoted Islamic authoritarianism and rule for the majority ethnic group, the Pashtun. While both were initially formed in atmospheres where radical religion thrived (the liberation theology movement in Chiapas and politicized Sunni Islam in the refugee camps), the EZLN would be a secular organization, while the Taliban would be highly religious. While the EZLN was remarkably open for a guerrilla organization, the Taliban were highly secretive. Though both initiated their public lives through the armed seizure of cities, they would move in different directions with regard to violence. The EZLN would begin a cease-fire after less than two weeks of fighting, initiating years of negotiations with the government, while the Taliban would become increasingly violent. No longer content merely to disarm sinners, Taliban leaders institutionalized punishments like stoning, dismembering or decapitating those who failed to live up to their version of Islamic virtue.

In this chapter, I will present a brief overview of the local, national and international roots of these two guerrilla movements, along with a consideration of their goals,[2] suggesting that both the Zapatistas and the Taliban provide clues to the future of revolution. But they are not the only possible models for future guerrilla movements. Indeed, if the causes of future movements will be largely national and local, as was the case for the Zapatistas and, to a lesser extent, for the Taliban, then the future may bring as many models of revolution as there are models of local injustice.

Revolutions during the cold war were fueled and shaped by the international politics of that era, but the cold war was not their only cause, or even the most fundamental one. Did international relations play some role in shaping revolutionary outcomes during the cold war? Absolutely. Will international relations continue to play a role in shaping outcomes in the post-cold war world? The cases of the Zapatistas and the Taliban suggest the answer is also yes: to a fairly minor extent in the case of the Zapatistas; to a much more significant extent in the case of the Taliban. But to say that international relations have and will shape outcomes is not the same as to claim that they are the fundamental cause of revolutionary situations. Given the low probability of success and the very high cost of failure (frequently death), few individuals will tie their fates to revolutionary movements for abstract, far away, international concerns. They do so instead for concrete, intimate, personal reasons – reasons that are experienced first and foremost at a local level. The cases of the EZLN and the Taliban suggest that we have hardly seen the last revolutionary movements. Yet the EZLN and the Taliban also suggest that the twenty-first-century style of guerrilla struggle may differ dramatically from that of the twentieth century; neither the EZLN nor the Taliban chose to frame their grievances in the language of Marxism-Leninism, as did so many guerrilla groups during the cold war.

The Taliban

In 1996, two years after they first appeared in the southern city of Kandahar, Taliban troops took control of the capital, Kabul. By the summer of 1998, they had consolidated their control over more than 90 percent of Afghanistan. In late 2001 the Taliban was to lose its control over the country as a result of the US-led campaign of aerial bombardment in the wake of the 11 September 2001 attacks.

During the years of Taliban power, few countries recognized them as the legitimate rulers of Afghanistan. But that lack of international recognition did not keep them from implementing a revolutionary agenda: banning nearly all forms of entertainment, from kite flying to household pets, imposing swift and violent punishments on suspected criminals, requiring men to grow beards under threat of beating or prison, expelling women and girls from school, forbidding females from receiving health services except from the few female medical workers, forbidding women from working in most professions, and requiring them to hide from any unrelated men (in the street, by wearing the tent-like burqa; in the house, by painting over first- and second-floor windows). Under the Taliban, daily life was turned upside down.

While some elements of the Taliban's agenda had their origins in Pashtun village life, the Taliban did not simply restore past practices. Instead, they imposed new ones in the name of the past. How the Taliban came to seize control of Afghanistan and institutionalize an imagined past was a story with strong international elements, a parable of the cold war and post-cold war. In this respect, their history differed tremendously from that of the Zapatistas. While the EZLN could have easily emerged had there never been a cold war, it is impossible to imagine that the Taliban could have become all they became in a more peaceful international context.

To tell the story of the Taliban, one needs to consider an earlier attempt at revolution, and the rapid involvement of the Soviet Union and the United States in that revolution. In 1965, the People's Democratic Party of Afghanistan (PDPA) was founded by students at Kabul University, in an effort to accelerate the pace of reform of traditional Afghan society. In 1978, the predominantly Pashtun PDPA seized power, possibly with the backing of the Soviet Union, and instituted what was called the Saur, or April revolution: instituting a literacy campaign for men and women of all ages, prohibiting forced marriage and limiting the practice of brideprice, restricting the size of landholdings and rural debts.

Many people resented these attempts by the urban leaders of the PDPA to transform rural life. Even the seemingly innocuous literacy campaign was experienced by some people as an example of great disrespect: older people were humiliated by being taught by the young, while many objected to the use of male teachers to instruct girls and women.[3] In the midst of a growing Islamic resistance to the PDPA, and internal disputes within the revolutionary government, President Nur Muhammad Taraki was assassinated in September 1979. In response, the Soviet Union invaded Afghanistan in December of that year, marking the beginning of a decade of civil war between the Soviet-supported revolutionary government, and the mujahidin, supported by a number of regional powers and the United States.

The many factions of the mujahidin shared a common hatred for the Soviets and a commitment to some sort of Islamic rule for Afghanistan. But they were divided by geography (whether they were based in Afghanistan or in the refugee camps in Pakistan and Iran), and were also divided into at least eight different organizations. These internal divisions meant that, after the withdrawal of the Soviets in 1989, the mujahidin were not able to form a coherent government. As a result, the civil war of the 1980s effectively continued into the 1990s, when the Taliban appeared. Their efforts to impose order upon Afghan society were welcomed by many, exhausted after years of war.

While some members of the Taliban had fought with the mujahidin or even with the Soviet-backed government, the Taliban was hardly a continuation of the mujahidin, and certainly not of the PDPA government. Instead, the majority of the Taliban traced their origins to the madrassas, the Koranic schools based in Pakistan that provided a religious education for boys from the refugee camps, an education comprising years memorizing the Koran in Arabic (which few of them understood), free from the corrupting influence of women. In that secluded atmosphere, those boys, resentful of the forces that had sent their families into exile, prepared to return to the country they did not remember, to impose what they thought were the values of the villages they had never known.

Without the involvement of the Soviet Union, the United States and regional powers, the war of the 1980s and early 1990s would probably have been far less prolonged and less brutal. To the extent that the Taliban emerged because of that conflict, the story of the Taliban is a cold war story. But the cold war was formally over by the time the Taliban made their first appearance, and in fact they were not financed primarily by the remaining superpower, the United States, but rather by Pakistan and Saudi Arabia.

While the cold war was over by the mid-1990s, international relations obviously did not come to an end, and the Taliban showed that regional powers were just as capable of supporting revolutionary movements to promote their own national and international interests as had been the superpowers. The Taliban also benefited from the rivalry of international oil companies that hoped to build pipelines across Afghanistan. The apparently smooth transition between the politics of the cold war and the post-cold war was overseen by preeminent cold warrior Henry Kissinger, former Secretary of State of the United States, who attended a 1995 signing ceremony between the Taliban and the US oil company UNOCAL, a company for which he was consulting, apparently allowing him to earn a bit of pocket change in his retirement.

The interest of US corporations in Afghanistan may have explained the Clinton administration's initial acceptance of the Taliban government. In the bipartisan consensus that US business interests could override concerns for democracy and human rights, it seemed that the US foreign policy of the post-cold war period would be much like that of the cold war. And yet the world had changed. By the 1990s, new technology like the Internet, the rise of an international human rights movement, and the significant organizing capacity of feminist organizations meant that the Taliban would not long enjoy the acquiescence of the remaining superpower. While the Clinton administration was silent on the Taliban's treatment of women through 1996, it became vocal once the US women's movement, and many of Clinton's strongest supporters in Hollywood, became mobilized. By 1999, 'US policy appeared to have come full circle, from unconditionally accepting the Taliban to unconditionally rejecting them' (Rashid 2000: 182).

The actions of the Clinton administration suggested that, in a globalized world, groups like the Taliban will not be entirely free to promote right-wing revolution. The Bush administration's unofficial war against the Taliban in the months that followed the bombing of the World Trade Center and the Pentagon would seem to be still stronger evidence that right-wing revolutionaries will have a hard time in the post-cold war world. And yet George Bush had been silent regarding the Taliban up until 11 September. Had the Taliban refrained from trying to export their right-wing revolution, or from supporting groups like al-Qaeda, they would probably still be free to impose their version of Islamic rule on their own people. Even in a globalized world, the most extreme revolutionaries may have room to manuever as long as their actions only affect their compatriots.

The Zapatistas

By the end of the twentieth century, the Zapatistas hardly controlled any territory in a formal sense. From that perspective, the Zapatistas were far less successful than the Taliban, though of course success must always be measured in terms of original goals. In these terms, the Zapatistas enjoyed some successes during their first public years. By the beginning of the twenty-first century, daily life in Mexico as a whole, and especially in Chiapas, had changed in important ways: with the Zapatistas' encouragement, the women's movement had grown and consolidated, a nationwide indigenous rights movement had emerged, 80 percent of the predominantly indigenous municipalities of Chiapas had declared their autonomy from the federal government, and in 2000, for the first time in over seventy years, a presidential candidate from an opposition party won.[4]

On a negative level, the years of the public rebellion were years in which the state of Chiapas became increasingly militarized, accompanied by the emergence of semi-clandestine paramilitaries that carried out some of the most extreme violence of the 1990s. Yet despite the low-intensity warfare that was waged against the Zapatistas and their supporters during the 1990s, and despite the fact that the Zapatistas gained very little in formal political terms, support for the Zapatistas seemed to grow in rural Chiapas during the final years of the decade.[5]

While the Taliban would probably not have emerged in the way they did in the absence of the forces of cold war and post-cold war international relations, the Zapatistas emerged for reasons that were largely domestic. Inadvertently, the stage was first set for the rise of the movement by the Mexican government itself when, starting in the 1950s, in response to demands for land reform, government officials encouraged colonization of the Lacandón jungle in the eastern third of the state of Chiapas. By late in the century, at least 150,000 land seekers had migrated to the Lacandón, mainly from the predominantly indigenous highlands of Chiapas, but also from every other state in the Mexican union. It was in the jungle that new multilingual communities were created, communities in which residents were left to make a living off the jungle soil largely on their own, with very little support from the Mexican state, the sort of abandonment that caused some resentment. Unlike elsewhere in Mexico, where the state typically had a strong presence through intertwining clientelistic networks, in the Lacandón jungle the main institutional presence was not the state but, rather, the Catholic Church.

From the late 1960s onward, the archdiocese of San Cristóbal, under the leadership of Archbishop Samuel Ruiz, was highly involved in serving indigenous communities, including those in the jungle. Outreach to the indigenous residents of Chiapas included the traditional ritualistic work of saying mass and providing sacraments, but it went well beyond that. For the archdiocese's work was informed by the thinking of the liberation theology movement, for which true Christianity involved challenging social injustice in this world, rather than meekly waiting for justice in the next world. Many of the thousands of men and women who were first mobilized by the Church went on to become active in a series of peasant and indigenous rights groups that were active in the last quarter of the twentieth century. Perhaps more than a few were eventually to find their way to the EZLN. The church did not create the EZLN any more than the Mexican state did, but it helped set the stage.

The predecessor of the EZLN, a group called the Forces of National Liberation (Fuerzas de Liberación Nacional, or FLN) was founded in the northern city of Monterrey in 1969. FLN activists were typical of guerrillas of that era. 'They were all male, in their 20s, passionately anti-Soviet (therefore as well hostile to the Mexican Communist Party), passionately pro-Cuban and Guevarist, most of them from locally respected families, and graduates of the State University of Nuevo León' (Womack 1999: 190).

In 1980, after having formed active cells in six states (including Chiapas) plus Mexico City, the leadership of the FLN wrote and published forty-two pages of statutes 'to regulate its new clandestine forces and organize them into the already then named Zapatista Army of National Liberation' (Womack 1999: 191). Those statutes suggest that the FLN saw itself as a typical guerrilla movement of its day. It opposed 'U.S. imperialism, the Mexican bourgeoisie and its puppets who form the bourgeois Mexican state'. Like its fellow Latin American guerrillas, it promised to utilize a 'political-military' strategy, including 'the creation of mass organizations' under the guidance of a guerrilla force that would act as 'the vanguard of the revolution'. That revolution, in turn, would be framed by 'the science of history and society: Marxism-Leninism, which has demonstrated its validity in all the victorious revolutions of this century' (Womack 1999: 192–4).

In the 1980 statutes, the rural branch of the FLN was already called the Zapatista Army of National Liberation, the EZLN. By the time the guerrillas went public in 1994, the name 'FLN' had been dropped altogether. But more had changed than the name. Gone were the references to Marxism-Leninism, to the bourgeoisie as the enemy, to the vanguard party that would guide the revolution. Why did the classically Marxist FLN evolve into the unorthodox EZLN? In some sense it had to evolve in that way; emerging in an atmosphere of significant political and religious pluralism, the EZLN could not be doctrinaire if it was to survive. When the outsiders from the FLN arrived in the Lacandón jungle in 1983, they had little choice but to adapt to local needs and local customs. The locals wanted literacy training, lessons in Mexican history, and help in setting up armed self-defense patrols. So that is what the FLN organizers initially provided, though none of those items was on their own agenda.

At the same time, locals very clearly did not want the outsiders to do anything that would threaten their customs. At first the Zapatistas seemed to be just such a threat. When the Zapatistas behaved in a way that would have been typical of clandestine guerrilla armies – preparing food and weapons under cover of darkness – many thought they were engaging in witchcraft. To try to avoid frightening the people they hoped to recruit, the FLN leaders had to act more openly within the community. Given the statutes of the FLN, written just three years earlier, it seems clear that the first Zapatistas to organize in the jungle would not have independently chosen such an unorthodox agenda and organizing strategies. But they did not have to accept the new agenda and strategies. They could have refused to take the lead of the locals, either trying to impose their agenda on the jungle residents, or leaving in search of a new place to organize. Instead they stayed, becoming less Marxist and more indigenous in the process.

So the very local needs of everyday life in the jungle could explain the evolution from the FLN to the EZLN. Another source of clues may be found in Mexican politics, at both the state and the national level. While the Taliban were a national movement (though the guerrillas obviously enjoyed more support in some parts of the country than in others), the EZLN was a movement with a strong base in only one of the thirty-one states in Mexico. Even if all residents of Chiapas were to support the rebels (which was far from the case), the Zapatistas could never hope to overthrow the Mexican government on their own.

The Zapatistas (like all guerrillas) made a series of demands of the state, even if they did not aim at overthrowing the state overtly. The party that controlled the Mexican state, the Party of the Institutional Revolution (Partido de la Revolución Institucional or PRI) was well entrenched and could claim a revolutionary heritage of its own. Having evolved out of the Mexican revolution of 1910–17, by the time the Zapatistas emerged on the public scene the PRI had ruled over national politics, without interruption, for nearly seventy years. If the PRI's rule was dictatorial, and many would say that it was, it was an inclusive dictatorship, maintaining control with some combination of multiple carrots and selective sticks.

But the very real democratic elements within the Mexican regime (especially since the highly contested election of 1988) and the PRI's preference for controlled inclusion over exclusion help to explain why the Zapatistas chose to forge a new sort of guerrilla movement. It is an armed force, to be sure, but one that is less doctrinaire, and more inclusive, than the Taliban or any of its fellow Latin American revolutionaries. This is logical enough given that the EZLN emerged against a regime that utilized a combination of authoritarian and democratic tactics with which to maintain its power; a traditional military organization would have had little chance of engendering the popular support needed for the Zapatistas to succeed.

While the roots of the Zapatistas were far more local than those of the Taliban, Zapatismo was influenced to some extent by international factors. The day the Zapatistas chose to emerge on the national and international stage – 1 January 1994 – was also the day the North American Free Trade Agreement (NAFTA) went into effect. Many have suggested that this shows that the NAFTA was one of the Zapatistas' primary concerns, that the rebellion was caused in part by this treaty that set the terms of economic globalization in North America. But the Zapatistas' main concern was not NAFTA itself, for if it had been they would have emerged a few months earlier, just before the close vote in the US Congress. An old-fashioned guerrilla war in modern Mexico would have quickly destroyed the myth that Mexico was almost a member of the First World, and would have just as quickly destroyed NAFTA's chances in the US Congress. Choosing 1 January as the birthday of the rebellion was more important for attracting international media coverage (which it did well) than for speaking to the members of the EZLN. This is not to say that an increasingly globalized political economy played no role in leading to the rebellion, but the real sore point, mentioned over and over by Zapatista supporters, was not NAFTA itself but rather part of the preparations for implementing the treaty: President Salinas's decision to revise article 27 of the constitution, thus ending the promise of ongoing land reform that had been an important source of legitimacy for the ruling party since early in the twentieth century.

At the level of discourse, it seems that the Zapatista army, one of the first major guerrilla movements to emerge in the post-cold war world, was shaped by that new world. For the Zapatistas the discourse of Marxism-Leninism was no longer as compelling as it had been for earlier guerrillas, who had something to gain through appropriating a Marxist discourse and analysis – namely, the material and ideological support of Cuba, and possibly that of the Soviet Union. During the cold war, seeking support from fellow revolutionaries by using their language was a smart and even necessary move (whatever the actual beliefs of the guerrillas), for Latin American guerrillas could count on rapid and often violent opposition from the US government, sometimes even to attempts at moderate and legal reform.

Such outside factors probably will not shape the calculations of the Latin American revolutionaries that follow the Zapatistas if they noted the Clinton administration's apparent lack of interest in the Zapatista rebellion. The passing of the cold war means that revolutionaries will have a harder time finding outside governmental allies, but that they will confront fewer outside enemies. So international alliances help explain the nature of Zapatismo from 1994 onward in a negative way: in the absence of strong opposition from the US government and in the absence of the socialist paradigm that framed opposition politics during the cold war era. They also help explain Zapatismo in a positive way; for speaking to the international left, through the Zapatista websites or the multiple international assemblies that would be held in Zapatista territory, required speaking an international language, and one of those languages was feminism.

As it turned out, international feminism would shape the fates of both the Taliban and the EZLN. The strength of the international feminist movement was clearly illustrated at the dawn of the new century, when the Clinton administration was forced to withdraw its initial support for the Taliban. Feminists had a less direct but not necessarily less profound impact on the Zapatistas, at least implicitly shaping their stated goals, goals which had evolved far from those of their Marxist-Leninist predecessors, goals which had little in common with those of radical Islamic revolutionaries like the Taliban. This is not to say that all feminists embraced the EZLN. Some Mexican feminists opposed the EZLN on the grounds that it was a military organization largely headed by men. Yet many Mexican feminists did support the EZLN, for it shared an array of goals with most feminists, promoting the rights of the traditionally excluded: indigenous people, women and even (at least in some communiqués) sexual minorities.

Conclusion

To return to the question that is the title of this essay: will the revolutionaries of the post-cold war world tend to march (as have the Taliban), or will they tend to dance (as have the Zapatistas)?[6] The answer, I think, is that they will be doing both things, though certainly not at the same time, and probably not in the same place. For there is little about the process of globalization or transformation of the bipolar world that requires a particular set of revolutionary demands or a single style of revolutionary politics.

In contrast, during the cold war period, the rivalry between the United States and the Soviet Union meant that a certain style of revolution tended to be strongly favored, with guerrilla groups across the Third World using the discourse and imagery of Marxism-Leninism (Colburn 1994). Indeed, the EZLN could trace its origins to a guerrilla group, the FLN, that fitted into the Marxist-Leninist mold. Yet even guerrilla groups that identified as Marxist-Leninist varied, and not all revolutionaries during the cold war identified as such. After all, the revolution that began in Iran in 1979 was a cold war-era revolution as much as those that identified as Marxist-Leninist.

What seems to matter for revolutionary groups is the existence of a mobilizing ideology. Marxism-Leninism could continue to play that role, though that is not nearly as likely now that guerrillas have little to gain, in material terms, by using such language. In the case of the two post-cold war movements I have evaluated here, religion has served, at least in some stages of organization, as a mobilizing ideology. Religion and nationalism (especially in countries with revolutionary traditions to draw upon, like Mexico) are well suited for mobilizing, for they tend to cut across an array of other social cleavages.

Social isolation – in the sense of conscious political exclusion by ruling governments or outside powers – is another factor that allowed for the rise of the Zapatista and Taliban movements, as indeed it contributed to the rise of many guerrilla movements in earlier decades. Isolation in the Lacandón jungle of Chiapas, or in the religious schools within the Afghan refugee camps in Pakistan, had an important effect on the thinking of people who lived in those peripheral spaces. It either simplified or sharpened that thinking (depending on one's perspective) into clear categories: right and wrong, oppressed and oppressor, us and them. Isolation allowed revolutionaries to develop and promote solutions to the injustices of the world, solutions that required transformation, not reform. Isolation allowed for the radicalization of common sense.

In the cases of both the Zapatistas and the Taliban, gender is a salient issue in a way that was not the case for most cold war-era movements, informed by an ideology, Marxism-Leninism, in which gender relations were treated as a residual category. It seems likely that the world has not seen the last of anti-feminist movements like that of the Taliban, since anti-feminism can be a good outlet for men who feel excluded: women are present in all societies and may be fairly easily scapegoated since they often are significantly less powerful than men. In contrast, it is extremely unlikely that we will ever see a feminist guerrilla movement, or any guerrilla movement that places full gender equality at the center of the revolutionary agenda (instead of somewhere down the list as has the Zapatista movement). For feminism does not lend itself to the same sort of stark 'us and them' thinking that is consistent with guerrilla thinking informed by Marxism-Leninism, nationalism or politicized religion. Other than those very few (possibly non-existent) feminists who seek full sexual segregation, there is no way for feminists to impose their agenda entirely through force. While the state may play an important role in defending gender equality, to a significant extent gender equality needs to be negotiated between women and their friends, co-workers, fathers, brothers, husbands and boyfriends. That sort of complicated negotiation is probably the thing that armed guerrilla movements do least successfully. So, in the twenty-first century, women will continue to join those guerrilla movements that will have them, but they will not do so primarily to promote feminist agendas (although organized feminism may emerge in the aftermath of such movements, as it did in Nicaragua and El Salvador).

While there is no reason to expect the rise of feminist guerrillas, we should expect that the intimate details of daily life and not the abstract notions of geopolitics will be the major factors that motivate the would-be revolutionaries of the twenty-first century. Whether or not they succeed may be explained in part by international relations: by the role of transnational civil society or that of the governments of other states. But the question of success is meaningless until critical masses of people choose to tie their fates to one revolutionary project or another. Those choices will be largely shaped by the local and the national – that is, by people's lived experiences and the meaning they give to their grievances. So we should expect that there will be more guerrillas like the Taliban, like the Zapatistas, and perhaps like some yet to be imagined group. Revolutionaries will continue to emerge as long as capitalism, globalization and the poverty of democracy continue to generate injustice, as seems likely.

Notes

1. According to some understandings of revolution, the Zapatistas but not the Taliban would be considered revolutionaries because the Zapatistas promote the transformation of society so as to increase social equality while the Taliban reject social equality as a value. In other words, the Zapatistas would be considered revolutionaries because they are progressive, while the Taliban would be considered counterrevolutionaries because they are reactionary. I think this objection is problematic, for it often means that movements are labeled revolutionary if the analyst finds their goals palatable, or counterrevolutionary if those goals are distasteful. But as long as scholars consider that a revolution triumphed in Iran in 1979, a revolution that certainly did not promote social equality, then I think we have to identify the Taliban as revolutionaries as well, no matter how repugnant we find them.

According to other understandings of revolution, neither the Zapatistas nor the Taliban could be considered revolutionary, but for different reasons. The Zapatistas would not be considered revolutionary because they have not seized state power (nor do they seek to do so). The Taliban, who seized the Afghan state, would not be considered revolutionary because they seized the state for counterrevolutionary reasons (to end and reverse the revolutionary movement led by the Marxist PDPA in the late 1970s and 1980s). This objection is rooted in Marx's understanding of revolution: a violent upheaval that leads to a new stage in history, accompanied by a new balance of class power, and a new mode of production. It is based on a view of history as progress, for without a concept of forward movement, it makes no sense to contrast a forward-moving revolution with a *counter*revolution.

By considering that both the Zapatistas and the Taliban should be analyzed as revolutionaries, I reject both the personal preference standard that I think is implicit in counting the Zapatistas but not the Taliban as revolutionaries, and the idea of history as forward movement that I think is implicit in calling the Taliban counter-revolutionaries.

2. In a short essay, I can hardly do justice to the complicated histories of either the EZLN or the Taliban. On the Zapatistas, see Collier 2000, 1994; Guillén 1995; Harvey 1994, 1998; Kampwirth 2002; Legorreta Díaz 1998; Lloyd and Pérez Rosales 1995; Tejera Gaona 1996; Womack 1999. On the Taliban, see Cooley 1999; Maley 1998; Marsden 1999; Matinuddin 1999; Moghadam 1999a; Rashid 2000. This chapter has been informed by all these sources, along with over four months of fieldwork in Chiapas in 1994, 1995, 1997 and 2000.

3. Elsewhere, literacy campaigns have highlighted both the affection and the resentment felt toward revolutionaries. During fieldwork in Nicaragua, the literacy campaign was consistently mentioned to me by Sandinista supporters (and some who opposed the Sandinistas) as the most beautiful moment of the revolution. But the literacy campaign was also seen by some Sandinista opponents as an example of the revolution's destruction of traditional values, as a time when young people lost respect for their parents, and when rural people suffered the humiliation of city dwellers imposing an unwanted agenda on their lives.

4. It would be an exaggeration to suggest that the EZLN was responsible for the election of Vicente Fox in July of 2000; in fact the rebels had indirectly thrown their support behind the other major opposition candidate for president, Cuauh-témoc Cárdenas. But the crisis in the Mexican southeast, along with terrible internal divisions within the PRI, were factors that informed President Ernesto Zedillo's decision to support the electoral reforms that made Fox's victory possible.

5. In April 2000 I went to Chiapas, expecting to find that support for the EZLN had fallen, given that the state was more militarized than it had been during my previous visit in 1997, and given that, I presumed, life had become more difficult for Zapatista supporters. To my surprise, none of the people I inter-viewed agreed with that hypothesis. To the contrary, from what they had seen, the EZLN had gained more supporters than it had lost. One reason may have been that the EZLN had made efforts to recruit in new communities. Another was that it was much easier to seize land in areas controlled by the EZLN than in areas controlled by the PRI. While the PRI could offer an array of clientelistic benefits, those projects tended to run out eventually, while land seemed far more permanent.

One woman who had done development work in indigenous communities for decades told me that in 1994 and 1995 the people she knew seemed to be passing through very hard times; the pressures of war meant that they were not able to feed or clothe themselves or their children as before. But after 1995, many of them looked better, often even better than before 1994. While they were hardly rich, many were surviving well, suggesting that they could wait out more years of war. A final reason many women supported the rebels was because, if their men supported the EZLN, they felt obliged to let their wives attend Zapatista-affiliated gatherings and conventions. The chance to visit new places, in some cases including the ocean, and to be treated with respect and affection when they arrived, was identified by many women as an improvement in their lives.

6. While the Zapatistas have certainly danced in a metaphoric sense when compared with more puritanical guerrillas like the Taliban, they have also danced in a literal sense at many Zapatista gatherings.

16

The Zapatista Rebellion
in the Context of Globalization

George A. Collier and Jane F. Collier

The Zapatista rebellion deserves its reputation as the most powerful force for democratization in Mexico. Since 1994, electoral reform, which began in the Salinas presidency of 1988–94, has advanced even further. The decades-old hegemony of Mexico's ruling party, the Partido Revolucionario Institucional (PRI), has crumbled. Opposition parties have gained in state and federal elections, most recently in July 2000 with Vicente Fox's winning of the presidency for the Partido de Acción Nacional (PAN) and Pablo Salazar Mendiguchia winning the governorship of Chiapas a month later in a coalition of opposition groups. Civil society has flourished, responding to the Zapatistas' call to revitalize Mexico's democratic life and social organization. The Zapatistas have sparked new attention to gender rights. The independent labor movement, to which Zapatistas had ties before the rebellion, has advanced. Peasant and indigenous Mexico, which appeared at risk of extinction after the 1992 'reform' of the agrarian law, has been reinvigorated in a new national movement for indigenous rights and autonomy (see Collier and Quaratiello 1999 for analysis of the background to the rebellion and developments since 1994).

Equally important, the Zapatistas have come to stand for radical challenges to globalization. The rebels have convoked international gatherings in the Chiapas hinterlands to weigh alternatives to neoliberalism, and have contributed to the critiques of globalizing institutions such as the World Trade Organization and the World Bank. Yet in significant ways, both democratization and Zapatista anti-neoliberalism grow out of the very processes of globalization that the Zapatistas have challenged.

Although Mexico's signing of NAFTA was not the cause of the Zapatista rebellion in Chiapas, which erupted the day NAFTA was scheduled to be put into effect, the rebellion's timing and course reflect global processes. Its principal causes, we suggest, lie in the 1980s, when the world's financial planners mandated austerity and the dismantling of Third World protected economies as a remedy for over-extended transnational petrodollar loans. The cutbacks in social services required by structural adjustment policies stimulated political opposition, which the Mexican government met by increasing militarization. By the 1990s, however, when the Zapatista rebellion actually erupted, the world's financial planners, while remaining true to their goal of facilitating global flows of capital and goods, had shifted the emphasis of their policies from dismantling trade barriers through international agreements and structural adjustment policies to strengthening the legal protections needed to shield foreigners from the social unrest unleashed by economic restructuring. Although globalizationists continued to focus on constraining states they viewed as too strong and protectionist, they now began to worry about how to strengthen states viewed as too weak and corrupt to provide the legal protections for persons and property necessary for transnational capital flows. With this shift – or, more accurately, addition – of emphasis, international financial planners thus hoped to strengthen state law in order to provide legal channels – specifically democratic elections and human rights commissions – for defusing the social protests triggered by economic restructuring and military abuses. If the Zapatista rebellion was 'caused' by global restructuring in the 1980s, its course and prospects have been shaped by international discourses of democracy and the rule of law in the 1990s.

The First Zapatista Demands

Because of its novel use of the media and the Internet, the Zapatista rebellion has been portrayed as the first 'postmodern' revolution (which it may well be).[1] Ironically, however, it began in many respects as a demand for a return to the past. The Zapatistas who rose up in armed rebellion on 1 January 1994 were deeply nationalistic. In their first communiqués, the leadership called on Mexicans to help restore the sovereignty lost by Mexico's having embraced economic restructuring and NAFTA. The communiqués also emphasized the Mexican state's responsibility for the social rights that citizens everywhere should expect from their governments. Finally, the Zapatistas protested the increasing use of the army for maintaining social order, although this aspect of their rebellion has received less attention in the media. All three facets of Zapatista nationalism, which surely were intended to resonate with concerns of other Mexicans, can be understood as responses to the dismantling of Mexico's developmentalist state after the debt crisis of 1982.

On the one hand, the Zapatistas castigated the government for opening the nation's resources to foreign depredation. With the restructuring that followed the 1982 crisis of Mexico's external debt, the government privatized and sold off national industries and removed historic protections dating back to the 1917 Constitution and their forceful implementation in the 1934–40 presidency of Lázaro Cárdenas to limit foreign ownership and competition. The decision to end the agrarian reform and to allow privatization of agrarian resources that previously had been treated as 'social property'[2] not only angered peasant groups with unresolved land claims but threatened to open the countryside to exploitation by transnational agribusiness. Moreover, by disbanding credits and infrastructural supports for peasant agriculture, and by phasing out price supports under the terms of NAFTA, the government appeared willing to sacrifice rural producers to unfair competition from imported and subsidized United States crops, particularly corn.

At the same time, the Zapatistas called for bona fide rather than sham implementation of the social pact that for half a century had held Mexico together – until internationally imposed austerity and the government's embracing of neoliberalism removed the state's capacity and will to sustain it. Within the corporatism that had grown out of Mexico's mid-twentieth-century import-substitution industrialization, sectors with antagonistic interests had at least held recognized places within the overarching institutionalized revolutionary party (the PRI). Manufacturers as well as workers in the formal sector or in state bureaucracy, and rural peasants as well as ranch owners in the countryside, could expect to have their demands heard in the future, if not heeded in the present. And even though many state programs for education, health, housing and development barely reached the countryside, especially in landscapes such as Chiapas, marginalized peoples had been promised that such redistributive services would reach them someday. But these hopes were dashed by economic restructuring. Even as declining real incomes plunged 50 percent of the Mexican population below the poverty line, austerity dismantled or gutted many public services. In Chiapas, for example, where public health services had begun to develop cadres of primary care workers for indigenous hamlets, even the token salaries for such workers dried up after 1983, and the primary care program collapsed. Moreover, the few resources that continued to flow into Chiapas were often distributed in a partisan fashion to reward government supporters and punish opponents (see Collier 1994), thus exacerbating the gap between rich and poor peasants that had been growing due to unequal opportunities for supplementing peasant production with off-farm income.

Finally, the Zapatistas called attention to the increasing militarization of Chiapas through their attack on the army base at Rancho Nuevo, and by kidnapping Absalón Castellanos Domínguez, the former army general who had been made governor of Chiapas in 1982, just as Reagan had declared Mexico's southern border an area of strategic concern and stepped up US training of Mexican military officers and supply of equipment for surveillance and counterinsurgency (see Schultz 1997; Harvey 1998; Collier and Quaratiello 1999). Although the Mexican government had portrayed the buildup of troops in Chiapas during the 1980s as a response to the civil war in Guatemala and the consequent flood of refugees across Mexico's southern border, the troops in Chiapas were increasingly mobilized less to protect Mexico's borders from external enemies than to quell internal dissent and protect landowners. The use of the army against peasants accused of land invasions in Chiapas grew dramatically after 1980 (see Burguete Cal y Mayor 1987). In 1993, for example, the army reportedly attacked a Zapatista training base and harassed Indians in two communities where soldiers had been killed. By calling attention to continuing military abuses of Mexican citizens, the Zapatistas hoped to create support for returning the military to the role it was supposed to play in defending the state from foreign enemies rather than being used against citizens.

If the Zapatista rebellion responded to the deteriorating promise of a Mexican state historically stronger than any nation to the south, it also differed from previous Central and South American revolutions by avoiding some of the apparent mistakes made by earlier Guatemalan, Salvadoran and Andean revolutionaries. The Zapatistas did not allow themselves to be cast as an ideologically rigid or vanguardist movement that excluded anyone who disagreed with them. Instead, they succeeded in portraying their rebellion as inclusive; as willing to accept anyone who shared their nationalist goals regardless of social or cultural differences. For example, the Zapatistas not only included women (as had the Sandinistas in Nicaragua); it accorded them special rights and included their concerns in Zapatista demands. Nor did the Zapatistas force indigenous recruits to discard their ethnic dress. They even welcomed mestizos into their ranks, treating them as indigenous people who had been stripped of their culture. The Zapatistas also portrayed their movement as non-hierarchical — as heedful of their responsibilities to the grassroots and as determined to 'govern by obeying'. For example, their spokesperson, Subcomandante Marcos, consistently cast

himself as subordinate to the comandantes of the revolutionary high command, even as the entire movement cast itself as responsive to the will of
the people, expressed through public assemblies. Finally, the Zapatistas
played to the media from the beginning. Their willingness and ability to
take their cause to the newspapers, television and Internet has often been
portrayed as the most innovative aspect of their rebellion.

Negotiating the Zapatista Demands

Although the Zapatistas who issued the first communiqués demanding
that the government fulfill its promises to provide land, housing, work,
health services and education, as well as justice and democratic representation, were invoking at least some of the old language and expectations
of corporatist pacting, their demands were heard in the context of the
1990s, when transnational financial institutions had switched from attempting to dismantle protectionist states to trying to quell the popular unrest
generated by structural adjustment policies. The Zapatistas, once they
agreed to negotiations, thus found themselves being offered the two
'solutions' advocated by transnational capital: 'fair elections' to replace
government pacting, and the 'protection of human rights' to replace
government services and to handle criticisms of the military's role in
suppressing domestic unrest.

The Zapatistas lost the military battle. They had to retreat into the
jungle only a few days after they emerged from it. More seriously, they
also lost the battle against the militarization of the countryside. The uprising
in fact gave the Mexican government an excuse for increasing the deployment of troops. Reports suggest that today about 40 percent of Mexico's
troops are stationed in Chiapas. The military presence is ubiquitous.

The Zapatistas won the media battle, however. The small group of
masked and poorly armed soldiers, emerging from the jungle on New
Year's Day, captured national and international attention and sympathy.
One reason the Zapatistas' strategy of appealing to the media worked so
well was that Chiapas had become host to independent and non-
governmental organizations sympathetic to the plight of the peasant and
indigenous poor. The Catholic Church, which under the direction of
Bishop Samuel Ruiz had organized the 1974 Indigenous Congress, provided a channel for other groups seeking to help marginalized communities. When the international financial community imposed austerity on
the Mexican government after the debt crisis of 1982, the state's retreat
from social services opened even more space for churches and other non-

governmental groups to move in. These non-governmental organizations spread word of the Zapatista uprising around the world.

National and international sympathy for the Zapatista cause – along with the Mexican government's fear of being accused of genocide – prevented the government from using military force to eliminate the Zapatistas. The government thus agreed to negotiate. But once the Zapatistas entered into negotiations with government representatives, they found themselves forced to debate on the new terrain established by transnational capital. However much the Zapatistas and their sympathizers might have wanted to revive the old protectionist state committed to development, the globalization of trade and financial services, combined with the 'demise of communism', made that impossible. The debate thus turned on how the new alternatives offered by international capital – 'fair elections' and 'human rights' – were to be interpreted.

By 1994, the Mexican government was already touting 'electoral reform'. After the 1988 election, which almost everyone believes was 'stolen' by the PRI's presidential candidate Carlos Salinas de Gortari from the real winner, the left-of-center PRD's Cuauhtémoc Cárdenas, the ruling party tried to restore national and international confidence in the Mexican government by establishing conditions for 'fair elections' in the future. The Zapatistas, however, had many reasons to doubt the government's good faith. Election processes in Chiapas were probably the most corrupt in the nation, and the increasing militarization of the region gave little reason to hope that Zapatista sympathizers could reach polling places or have their votes counted if they did. The Zapatistas thus snubbed Cuauhtémoc Cárdenas in 1994, when he urged them to trust the electoral process. Rejecting not only the limited 'electoral reforms' offered by the government, they rebuffed the entire existing political party system. They convoked their first 'Aguascalientes' gathering of civil society to advocate instead a new constitutional convention to rewrite the Mexican Constitution. After Mexico's ruling PRI party won the 1994 presidency in what were probably the least corrupt elections to that date, the Zapatistas advised their supporters to boycott further elections (paramilitarization of Chiapas after 1994 probably also contributed to abstention by groups who feared reprisal if they voted against the PRI). It is widely believed that the abstention of Zapatista sympathizers helped the PRI to win local elections in Chiapas in 1995 and thereafter, when the PRD might well have gained critical ground (Viquiera and Sonnleitner 2000). The Zapatistas, however, were unrepentant.[3]

By 1994, the Mexican government had also responded to international pressure to 'protect human rights' by establishing a National Human Rights

Commission in 1990 (see Keck and Sikkink 1998 for a discussion of the role of civil society in developing human rights advocacy and for the developments linking human rights to indigenous rights activism in Mexico). The states, including Chiapas, followed suit, establishing their own local commissions. Chiapas also became host to at least thirteen non-governmental organizations dedicated to the protection of human rights (see the organizations listed in Collier 2000a, which conveys the rapidity and extent to which the rights discourse swept even into such landscapes as Chiapas). The conception of 'human rights' advocated by these institutions, however, has tended to confine its emphasis to the civil and political rights of individuals. Most human rights work, for example, has denounced torture and illegal detentions by state security forces. The Zapatistas, and many of their sympathizers, however, had taken advantage of the discourse of human rights to argue for broader interpretation of the United Nations conventions that Mexico had signed to include the economic and social rights of citizens. Although most of the early Zapatista demands for state services were embodied in the United Nations International Covenant on Economic, Social and Cultural Rights (1966),[4] Zapatista efforts to recast human rights as economic and social rights have apparently met the same silent resistance that has befallen other attempts to invoke them.

But the Zapatistas did encounter widespread support when they began advocating indigenous rights and autonomy. The indigenous rights movement, which had been growing for two or three decades, received a tremendous boost from the protests of the 1992 Quincentennial of the 'discovery' of the Americas and from recognition in Mexico that many of the victims of rural repression were indigenous. By 1994, indigenous peoples around the world, as well as in Chiapas, had been active in lobbying the international community for recognition of their rights, including their right to cultural difference. After the 1994 PRI presidential victory, as support waned for the Zapatista proposal to convoke a new Constitutional Convention, the Zapatistas turned to indigenous rights and culture and to 'autonomy' as their central demand. The first, and only, accords thus reached by the Zapatistas and government representatives at San Andrés in 1996 concerned issues of 'indigenous rights and culture'.

The Current Stalemate

Although government representatives signed the San Andrés accords on indigenous rights and culture, the national government refused to ratify them. This has led to a stalemate. There is a military stalemate because neither side can afford to attack. Although the Zapatistas have refused to surrender and lay down their arms, they are also vastly outnumbered by government troops. The government, in turn, practices restraint because the Zapatistas' ability to mobilize international sympathy, combined with the government's fear of having to fight a genocidal war, ensures that any attack could turn into a public-relations nightmare.

The more interesting stalemate, however, is political. When the Zapatistas began to set up autonomous municipalities in areas they control, the state government responded by declaring the Zapatista bodies illegal and by establishing new municipalities of its own design. Although the national government refused to ratify the San Andrés accords, President Zedillo urged outgoing PRI governors to enact state legislation on indigenous rights before they left office. In 1999, for example, the interim PRI governor of Chiapas drafted his own law on indigenous rights and culture, which he pushed through the state legislature despite vocal opposition from minority parties. Both sides claimed to be implementing the San Andrés accords, but the governor's version, at least, subverted the accords in several crucial respects. Whereas the accords call for the government to 'recognize' the rights of indigenous 'peoples', the governor's law 'grants' rights to indigenous 'communities'. And whereas the San Andrés accords call for indigenous representatives to participate in drafting the laws to implement the accords, the PRI governor's laws were drafted by his lawyers, who later 'consulted' with groups of Indians convened for the purpose (see Speed and Collier 2000 for discussion of the Chiapas government's use of human rights discourses to limit indigenous autonomy).

The military and political stalemate in Chiapas has rendered at least half of the state ungovernable, and therefore unwelcome to transnational capital.[5] If one of the Zapatista aims was to prevent international capital from raiding local resources, they have been successful. A glossy coffee table book that the PRI governor prepared to attract international investors now looks like a joke – albeit a sick one – in that the book ignores the peasant and indigenous half of the state sympathetic to Zapatista demands. But the Zapatistas have so far failed in their two other aims. The level of government services continues to be low, particularly in the poorest regions where Zapatista support is the strongest. The Zapatistas have, in fact, prohibited their supporters from accepting government money. And although the Zapatistas welcome help from NGOs, the PRI government mounted an anti-foreigner campaign that made it difficult, if not impossible, for foreigners (and sympathetic Mexicans) to help build the schools and hospitals that Zapatista communities need. Finally, the Zapatistas contributed to, rather than restrained, the militarization of the region. Half of the state is presently ungovernable because violence is endemic.

Violence is endemic in Chiapas because one of the PRI government's responses to critiques of military abuses was to arm and support paramilitary forces in communities with many Zapatista sympathizers (Harvey 1998: 232–6). Most of these communities were already divided into opposing factions by economic processes in the 1980s that not only increased the gap between rich and poor peasants, but that made wealth dependent on cultivating PRI officials rather than on wooing local followers. As a result, the government found allies, many of whom were already acquiring arms on their own, ready to participate in a seeming policy of low-scale counterinsurgency to wear down the Zapatistas and their sympathizers.

Prospects

The horizon for the region's future is not entirely bleak. On the local and regional levels, there are hopeful signs that indigenous groups are backing away from divisive conflicts by crafting coalitions across religious and political divides for governing themselves. On the national level, the defeat of the PRI in the 2000 presidential elections offers the incoming president, the PAN's Vicente Fox, an opportunity to break the Chiapas stalemate by returning to real negotiations with the Zapatistas, broken off since 1996. Fox professed to seek a settlement with the Zapatistas that would honor the San Andrés accords. Pablo Salazar Mendiguchia, who won the state governorship with the support of a coalition of opposition parties, also pledged to seek a resolution that would honor the accords. Yet in April 2001 the Mexican Congress initiated constitutional reforms on behalf of indigenous rights that ignored key San Andrés provisions for autonomy. This setback led the angered Zapatistas to break off contacts with the government. But renewed pressure from indigenous rights advocates may yet lead to revisiting of the constitutional reforms. An exit strategy for the Zapatistas could thus emerge around government recognition of Zapatista demands for autonomy and cultural rights, coupled with the pulling back and scaling down of the Mexican military and the laying down of Zapatista arms.

Whatever Chiapas resolution Mexico's new leaders manage to craft, however, seems unlikely to change Mexico's trajectory of commitment to restructuring and globalization. While Vicente Fox's cabinet appointments underscore a willingness to build a broad governing coalition, his government continues to stress the business and foreign investment policies of his PRI predecessors. Given this commitment, Fox's promise to provide 'every individual with equal opportunities to overcome poverty by their own initiative' appears naive at best (*New York Times*, 25 November 2000: A6). The Fox government has been preparing the 'Plan Puebla Panama' (PPP) to link southern Mexico into free trade initiatives with Central America, even as the Zapatistas declare that the PPP shall not pass through indigenous territory (see www.ciepac.org 'Plan Puebla Panamá Primera Parte', Boletín 'Chiapas al día' No. 233 CIEPAC of 7 March 2001). At this point, the best that the Zapatistas and their sympathizers can hope for is that they will be granted the autonomy to shield their homelands from being swamped in the wake of globalization.

It remains to be seen whether in the emergent global order the indigenous peoples of Chiapas can forge alliances with groups elsewhere to form blocs capable of negotiating in global markets over forests and agrarian resources, cultural and intellectual property rights and possibly autonomous jurisdictions to harbor financial services. Already, indigenous groups in Chiapas have demanded control of archeological sites (including world-famous Palenque)[6] and have allied with Canadians to denounce bioprospecting of native herbal remedies as 'biopiracy' in coalition with other protestors of the Seattle WTO meetings. Alliances with other Native American groups also suggest such possibilities. In a world with many parallel realities – informal versus formal, underground versus legal – might there not be space for an autonomous indigenous reality?

Notes

This chapter draws on research by G. Collier, supported in part by the John D. and Catherine T. MacArthur Foundation, Program on Peace and International Co-operation, for research on 'Differentiation, Radicalization, and the Emergence of the Zapatista Rebellion in Chiapas', as well on support from the National Science Foundation (grants BNS 8804607 to G. Collier for a study of 'Agrarian Change in Southeastern Mexico'; SBR-9601370 to G. and J. Collier for 'Monitoring Rapid Social Change in Southeastern Mexico'; and SBR 97–10396 to J. Collier for 'Mapping Interlegality in Chiapas'). We thank the participants of the Wellesley College seminars on 'The Zapatista Rebellion in Chiapas' and 'Human Rights and Globalization' for discussion contributing to the development of this chapter. We are grateful for advice from John Foran, Tim Harding, Jan Rus and other participants in the conference on 'The Future of Revolutions in the Context of Globalization' leading to this volume.

1. Burbach (1994) made the first argument for the Zapatistas as postmodern. Ronfeldt et al. (1998: 9) assert that the Zapatista rebellion involved a new kind of 'social netwar', facilitated by the information revolution, using 'network forms of organization' to mobilize support from dispersed groups in an 'internetted manner'

rather than by conventional military or guerrilla means. Castells (1997) discusses the Zapatista rebellion as the emergence of a postmodern identity in the global order.

2. Salinas's 'reform' of Article 27 of the constitution ended Mexico's agrarian reform and angered peasants in Chiapas, who were responsible for 30 percent of the country's outstanding agrarian claims. Equally important were efforts under PROCEDE (the Programa de Certificación de Derechos Ejidales y Titulación de Solares Urbanos) to complete the national cadastral registry and to document secure title to landed property, as urged by international advisors as a prerequisite to investment in the countryside. While some peasant groups in other areas have taken the option to privatize and individualize collective holdings, this has not happened in Chiapas. Rather, since 1994, the state government has pressed forward in binding negotiations with peasant groups to resolve the backlog of land claims, primarily by purchasing land to give to claimants as private holdings. So far, the government has ignored the Zapatista call for a restoration of the agrarian reform.

3. After the recent presidential and Chiapas gubernatorial elections, in which abstention in Chiapas was about 50 percent, the Zapatista support group Enlace y Contacto por la Consulta Nacional Zapatista declared the elections anti-democratic and illegitimate, primarily because Fox and Salazar plan to continue neoliberal policies despite having won barely 15 percent of the support of the voting-age population (report according to Melel Xojobal Internet service of 26 September 2000 as originally reported in *Excélsior*).

4. UN Doc. A/6316 (Blaustein et al., 1987: 20–27). On the Zapatista demand for land, Article 1 Section 2 states that 'all peoples may, for their own ends, freely dispose of their natural wealth and resources. In no case may a people be deprived of its own means of subsistence'. On the demand for housing and nutrition, Article 11 Section 1 holds for the 'right of everyone to an adequate standard of living for himself and his family, including adequate food, clothing and housing'. On the demand for work, Article 6 Section 1 sets forth the 'right of everyone to the opportunity to gain his living by work which he freely chooses or accepts'. On health, Article 12 Section 1 concerns the 'right of everyone to the enjoyment of the highest attainable standard of physical and mental health'. On schools, Article 13 Section 1 declares the 'right of everyone to an education'. The demands for justice and democratic representation are covered in the 1948 Universal Declaration of Human Rights (UN Dec. A/810) and the 1966 International Covenant on Civil and Political Rights (UN Doc. A/6316).

5. While transnational investors have not expressed interest in developing the Zapatista areas of the state, they have planned projects in other areas of Chiapas. For example, a United States firm, Genesee and Wyoming, and the new governor of Chiapas, Pablo Salazar, recently announced an accord in which the firm will invest $50 million in modernizing the rail lines extending down Chiapas's Pacific coast to facilitate economic development and introduction of maquiladora industry (as reported in the Melel Xojobal Internet service of 29 January 2001).

6. The demand to control administration of archeological sites was made by groups also demanding cabinet positions in Salazar's state government, according to the 25 September 2000 Internet bulletin of Melel Xojobal, as originally reported in *Expreso*.

17

Overthrowing the Fathers: Prospects for Revolutionary Transformation in the Twenty-first Century Arab Gulf Monarchies

Mary Ann Tétreault

Rebellions against authoritarian rulers are nothing new (e.g. Crossan 1998; Tilly 1975) but revolution is a modern phenomenon (Goodwin 1997). It encompasses mass-based protest and, when successful, produces novel social arrangements and even 'new men'. 'The new age now begins', said successful revolutionaries in eighteenth-century North America; their twentieth-century Soviet counterparts set out to create a new Soviet man. Times changed literally when calendars were reworked and/or reset in eighteenth-century France and twentieth-century Cambodia, and new institutions came into being (Arendt 1963; Skocpol 1979). Thus, to make a revolution is not simply to protest injustice through violent social action. Revolutionaries attack the present order from the conviction that funda-mental change is both necessary and possible (Anderson 1991; Rist 1977; Scott 1998) and then make that change happen when the old order is defeated. Aristotle's vision of political change was of regimes developing and decaying in a kind of life cycle: revolution as the turning of a wheel. The vision of modern revolutionaries is not merely to turn Aristotle's – or Nietzsche's – wheel but to get behind it and steer their states and societies into a new political universe.

For much of the twentieth century, the political universe on this planet was organized under two frameworks. Following the successful Soviet revolution, an authoritarian party state with a centrally planned economy took root in the old Russian empire and became the template for com-munist revolutions from above and below in Eastern Europe, Asia and other developing areas. Elsewhere, capitalist globalization among states displaying a wide range of regime types continued after World War I but was virtually halted by the Great Depression. At the end of World War II, the implementation of a fixed exchange rate regime and Keynesian economic policies in the US and its allies slowed the rate of globalization but wild swings in commodity prices, the collapse of the exchange rate regime and recurrent debt crises signaled the erosion of these firewalls. Globalization accelerated markedly during the 1970s and raced even faster after the Berlin Wall fell in 1989, marking the end of the cold war. As Western investors scrambled to penetrate economies formerly closed to them, the image of rigid alliances characterizing great power interpretations of world politics during that period (Draper 1984) gave way to perceptions that at least some politics might indeed be local after all.

The Persian Gulf monarchies are part of a region that, while deeply embedded in cold war politics, retained its status as a hyper-globalized area of the world throughout the twentieth century. The Middle East as a whole includes many states manufactured by twentieth-century war, revolution and decolonization (Ayubi 1995; Fromkin 1989; Jackson 1990). However, their strategic location and sovereignty over so much of the world's proven hydrocarbon reserves have ensured the continued involvement of major powers in the domestic political and economic arrangements of oil-exporting states. Though the Persian Gulf has been influenced by European imperialism from the time of the Portuguese onward, informal cliency has been the primary relationship between its states and outside powers for more than a hundred years (Gasiorowski 1991; Tétreault 1991). A cliency relationship is primarily strategic and therefore at least partially mutual in that each side controls resources deemed critical for the survival of the other. The strategic value of the global hydrocarbon industry for the major Western powers lies in its role as the engine driving their military machines and domestic economies. These states form partnerships with oil-exporting countries that rely on the resulting hard cash, military protection and access to weapons and technology to stabilize their regimes. Money and guns are not sufficient to ward off successful revolutionary challenges, of course, as the example of Iran illustrates. However, on the whole, these, combined with skillful rulers and cautionary examples from the experiences of post-revolutionary neighbors, have deflected and defused most revolutionary political movements in the Gulf states (Gause 2000; Tétreault 2000), much to the surprise of both scholars and activists (Kostiner 2000).

Models of Stability and Change in the Persian Gulf

Here I define revolution as a rapid change in the institutions and dominant ideologies governing the relationships of a people to their state, such that the legal, social and cultural bases of the governing classes, the status of subjects/citizens and customary relations among members of society are fundamentally altered. Such changes always are mediated by force whether or not they are effected through violent means. By this definition, both the 1688 'Glorious Revolution' and the 'velvet revolution' characterizing the transition of several Communist regimes to post-Communism in the late 1980s and early 1990s – the original appellation refers to Czecho-slovakia – qualify despite the relatively low level of violence in their enactment.

I concentrate on the prospects for revolution in those Persian Gulf states that have not yet experienced a modernizing revolution, states whose governments are dominated by members and agents of ruling families and whose regimes are autocratic in that the decisions of the rulers trump popular opposition whether that opposition is offered within the frame-work of legally constituted domestic institutions or not. By this definition, even Kuwait, which has a liberal constitution and an elected legislature, has a pre-modern regime (Gause 1994; Herb 1999; Tétreault 2000). How likely is it that these traditional[1] regimes – including Saudi Arabia, Bahrain, the United Arab Emirates (UAE), Qatar and Oman – will undergo rapid, force-mediated and fundamental social transformation as opposed to gradual, legally mediated political change in the twenty-first century? One answer is offered by the *rentier* state theory.

> A rentier is ... more of a social function than an economic category.... The distinguishing feature of the rentier ... resides in the lack or absence of a pro-ductive outlook in his behavior. [With respect to the rentier state] there is no such thing as a pure rentier economy.... Second ... a rentier economy is an economy which relies on substantial *external rent*.... Third, in a rentier *state* – as a special case of a rentier economy – only a few are engaged in the generation of this rent (wealth), the majority being only involved in the distribution or utilisation of it.... Fourth, a corollary of the role of the few, in a rentier state the *government* is the principal recipient of the external rent. (Beblawi 1990: 86–8, emphasis in the original)

The rentier state is envisioned as having successfully disconnected the state apparatus from domestic checks on autocratic behavior (Aarts 1992; Aarts et al. 1991; Chaudhry 1997; Migdal 1988; al-Naqeeb 1990). Even with respect to traditional elites, the families ruling the Gulf monarchies control sufficient resources to bribe most of their populations into quies-cence. The pact between Kuwaiti rulers and the merchant clans they supplanted as the nation's dominant class gives the rulers primary author-ity in politics in exchange for creating protected enclaves in the economy for the merchants (Crystal 1990). The mechanisms of political dominance by the other Gulf monarchies operate similarly, and are reinforced by religion and traditional cultural practices (Gause 1994). The rentier state thus resembles early modern states in Europe that were founded on relationships between rulers who monopolized force and selected clients who offered other services in exchange for 'protection rents' (Tilly 1985). Gulf rentiers feature innovations such as foreign patrons and clients that include substantial segments of the popular classes. Such 'externalization' is especially useful regarding the popular classes. With variations arising from different ratios between national populations and oil revenues, Gulf monarchies have used oil revenues to create an extra-national proletariat. Unlike the socialist discourse framing the revolution that created the People's Democratic Republic of Yemen, a discourse of citizen entitle-ments masks class divisions among Gulf country nationals, dampening revolutionary ardor as well as encouraging loyalty to ruling families and their regimes (Crystal 1990; Longva 1997).

The primary flaw in the rentier state model is that it is static. The interests of rulers and population groups are assumed to be stable and the continuation of rentier regimes merely a matter of maintaining the flow of rentier income to the regime's clients. However, as I demonstrate below, both are oversimplifications of reality. Ruling families experience secular changes in their composition, such as in the number and quality of potential rulers and ministers. Some also incorporate significant internal differentiation that could itself be destabilizing. Population groups also change, not merely with respect to their resource endowments and politi-cal capacities, but also in the structure of interests producing coalitions among social groups and between clients and rulers. Some of the prob-lems with the rentier state model are dealt with in the second model, which envisions the Gulf monarchies as family corporations (Herb 1999).

The 'dynastic monarchy' model suggests that the Gulf monarchies are unusually resilient as compared to other monarchies because of the structure of interests within the ruling class. In dynastic monarchies, titular rulers are chosen by consensus from among powerful ruling family mem-bers while others occupy strategic sites in the state apparatus. Errors in judgment resulting in an obviously incompetent ruler are rectified by the same procedure taken in reverse. Ruling family control of key positions in the state apparatus closes off structural bases for potential revolutionaries. All this allows intra-elite competition for positions of power and authority while maintaining a basic level of ruler competence, adding directly to security and indirectly to legitimacy. Traditional practices like *shura* (con-sultation with ruler-selected 'wise men' of the community), the *majlis* (an assembly that can be informal and voluntary or formalized and elected) and the *diwaniyyah* (regular home-based men's meetings where rulers and their surrogates can take soundings of a broad cross-section of popular opinion), also boost legitimacy while providing critical intelligence and structural opportunities to coopt or deflect dissent (Gause 1994; Herb 1999; Tétreault 2000). Although this model does not envision divergent interests within the ruling class itself, unlike the rentier state model it does outline plausible means for countering adverse impacts of shifting bases of popular support for these regimes.

John Foran (1997) offers a universal model of social revolution that improves on the explanatory power of both the rentier state and the dynastic monarchy models as descriptors of regime stability by incorporating a role for culture and the importance of ideas in fueling movements for revolutionary social change. Foran argues that five interrelated causal factors typically accompany successful cases of social revolution. Four are structural: dependent development; a repressive, exclusionary and personalist state; an economic downturn; and a reconfiguration of external political constraints. The fifth combines ideology and culture: 'the elaboration of effective and powerful political cultures of resistance' (Foran 1997: 228). Three of the structural factors are embedded in the rentier character of the Gulf monarchies. *Dependent development* is integral to the architecture of incorporation into global capitalism of all the Persian Gulf hydrocarbon-exporting rentier states whose national incomes are almost totally determined by global markets in oil and gas (Ayubi 1995; Chaudhry 1997; Luke 1985; al-Naqeeb 1990; Tétreault 2000, 2000a). These states are politically vulnerable to dissent during *economic downturns* triggered by falling prices or falling demand for oil and gas because the structural adjustment imposed by plummeting state revenues exposes the fault lines of exclusion that otherwise are concealed behind lavish distribution programs. Collapsing oil prices in the mid-1980s increased competition for state resources among Gulf citizens and also between citizens and resident Palestinians, then a key expatriate population with claims on the state superior to those of other, even other Arab, expatriate groups (Hunter 1986). In Saudi Arabia, the oil price collapse affected not only Saudi domestic politics but also Yemen's. A sharp drop in Saudi foreign aid and employment of Yemeni nationals forced adjustments that led directly to the 'reunification' of North and South Yemen and then to the violent absorption of the south's 'modern' and socialist elements by an authoritarian, tribalist regime (Chaudhry 1997). Adjustment also politicized divisions within the populations of the rentier states themselves, many playing out as gender conflicts masking increasingly visible sectarian rivalries, class antagonisms and a growing hostility between neoliberal modernizers and Islamists of various political and economic persuasions (Chaudhry 1997; Tétreault 1999, 2000).

The dynastic monarchy model diverges from Foran's by suggesting that ruling family monopoly of authority over selection of the head of state and control of key governing institutions is both necessary *and sufficient* to defeat would-be revolutionaries. Here, *exclusionary rulership* by a dynastic corporation is posited as having structural advantages in preventing revolution that outweigh the negatives arising from its autocratic character, a position that runs counter to the general consensus among sociologists of revolution, which is that exclusionary rulers are the most vulnerable to overthrow (see the discussion in Foran 1997a: 793, and in the works referenced there). This assertion rests on two assumptions. One is that the greatest threat to regime stability comes from exclusionary practices inside rather than outside of the ruling family, whose powerful members in dynastic monarchies are not excluded from political power or from access to rents generated by the state.[2] The second is that the consultative mechanisms sketched above are powerful mobilizers of support from the popular classes. Even though the vulnerability of elites to their blandishments is limited, dissenting elites are constrained by ruler co-optation of mass publics from mobilizing the 'broad multi-class alliance against the state' (Foran 1997a: 793) required for a successful revolution.

State autocracy also rests on rentierism because external revenues free governments from having to compromise with domestic social forces (Aarts et al. 1991; Crystal 1990; Tétreault 2000; Tilly 1985). There is, in addition, a connection between rentier-state status and vulnerability to *world-systemic openings*. The patron–client relationship is one of mutual strategic dependence. This leaves clients vulnerable to patron failure such as occurred when the US failed to prevent the invasion of Kuwait by Iraq in 1990 (Smith 1992). A similar kind of failure could provide a systemic opening critical to revolutionary success, as some argue happened in the case of Iran (e.g. Foran 1993; Munson 1988).

Neither the rentier state nor the dynastic monarchy model incorporates ideology or culture specifically as an ingredient of regime stability. Yet in every one of the Persian Gulf countries, at least one *political culture of resistance* already is a potent social force whose authority, resources and reach have mushroomed in the past decade. This is (neo)fundamentalist Islam. Religious revivalism is a worldwide phenomenon mobilizing millions into political activism in developed and developing countries. Radical and conservative Islamist movements speak in similar idioms to 'articulate the experiences ... of broad segments of many groups and classes ... and [produce] effective and flexible analyses capable of mobilizing their own forces and building coalitions with others' (Foran 1997: 229). Especially since the Iranian revolution, what (neo)fundamentalist Islam in the Gulf monarchies speaks includes 'bitterness' at the moral and material failures of their governments.

Islamist movements have grown in size and power since the collapse of oil prices in the mid-1980s and the various means chosen by oil-exporting states to deal with the resulting fiscal crises (Chaudhry 1997; Hunter 1986; Tétreault 1999). The Second Gulf War (1990–91) contributed to the legitimacy of Islamist movements in Arab Gulf states, not only because it pitted Arab against Arab, thereby destroying the powerful myth that had located Arab nationalism at the core of domestic opposition movements (Tétreault 2000b), but also because the war itself brought US and other coalition troops onto Saudi Arabian territory. This allowed radical Islamists to charge the Al Sa'ud with having abdicated their authority as guardians of the two holy places by turning their protection over to foreigners (Roy 1999).

At the same time, governments throughout the Middle East have promoted the fortunes of Islamism through their own efforts to 'Islamize' the state. This began in the 1970s in response to domestic demands for democratization (e.g. Tétreault and al-Mughni 1995) and in reaction to the radicalization of the Iranian revolution (Roy 1999). During the 1980s, Islamization was used to defuse popular opposition to cuts in entitlements (Chaudhry 1997; Hunter 1986). Middle Eastern governments not only sought allies among the clergy but themselves used religious rhetoric and symbolism to bolster their beleaguered regimes. Although it was impossible to 'build an "official Islam" from scratch ... all the [Middle Eastern] states endeavored to co-opt traditional ulama by trading political support for conservative Islamization, importing Islamic law into positive law and enforcing religious censorship' (Roy 1999: 114) and also by legislating restrictions on women's rights (Tétreault 2000).

But rulers were unable to *monopolize* the political benefits of growing popular religiosity. Indeed, Islamization added to the authority of the clergy and also boosted Islamist opponents of the political and clerical establishments. Islamist and establishment clerics sought their own allies among conservative tribalists. In Kuwait, the combined results of officially supported religiosity, and 'desertization' – the importation of tribal values into the political and social mainstream through the wholesale naturalization and enfranchisement of newly sedentarized bedouins in the early 1980s – expanded the political base of the religious opposition. It also eroded the base of the urban liberals who could have provided a counterweight to growing Islamist power (Ghabra 1997), marked by Islamist successes in colonizing agencies of the state. Throughout the Middle East,

Islamism became the chief avenue for mobilizing marginal social groups into politics. This contributed to the heterogeneity of religious movements and sometimes to their radicalization (Roy 1994, 1999, Tétreault 2000). The resulting fragmentation of religious authority, however, coupled with the memory of how Iran's revolution was captured by radical clerics, limits the ability of Islamist-led forces to mobilize the same sort of broad-based coalition against the Arab Gulf regimes that Iranian revolutionaries managed to do against the Shah.

Prospects for Revolution in the Persian Gulf States

Here I assess the prospects for revolution in the Persian Gulf states using the categories from Foran's universal model, evaluating each in terms of its applicability to the Gulf monarchies. I conclude with a discussion of special factors, the most important of which are demographic, likely to affect the timing, scope and manner of regime transition, and focusing on the unique rather than the universal aspects of these cases.

Dependent development and vulnerability to economic downturns

All of the Gulf monarchies are classical examples of dependent develop-ment. Since the oil revolution of the early 1970s, they all have become more rather than less dependent on oil revenues despite the accumulation by Kuwait and the UAE of financial assets to hedge against oil price fluctuations by providing a source of post-hydrocarbon rentier income (Tétreault 1995, 2000a). The domestic politics of the Gulf monarchies offer repeated examples of domestic dissent when oil incomes stagnate or fall (Gause 1994, 2000). Significant domestic unrest in Kuwait is associated with falling oil revenues and the financial depredations by ruling family members that are also consequences of straitened state incomes (Tétreault 1999, 2000a). Key regime constituencies were effective in resisting attempts to restructure distribution programs in Saudi Arabia after the collapse of oil prices in the mid-1980s (Chaudhry 1997). All the Gulf regimes made substantial efforts during the oil price collapse that followed the Second Gulf War to mollify social groups demanding more openness and partici-pation (Gause 1994). Perhaps the clearest example occurred in Bahrain, where economic restructuring was so obviously biased against the Shi'i majority that an opposition movement including large numbers of the Sunni middle class mobilized to demand the reinstatement of parliament.

The new Bahraini National Charter and prospects for the return of elective representation are due not only to the death of the old ruler, who took a hard line toward the opposition, but also to a financial position improved by energy price increases (Katzman 2000).

A repressive, personalist, exclusionary state

The Gulf states are mixed with regard to their repressive and exclusionary character. Qatar is democratizing rapidly under an amir who deposed his traditionalist father in 1995, much to the chagrin of neighboring governments that were experiencing difficulty managing domestic dissent. Throughout the region, potentially dangerous non-family dissidents are seldom executed but often exiled – examples include the Saudi Osama bin Laden and the Kuwaiti Abdullah al-Nafisi. Some dissidents leave on their own. Overall, repression generally is inconsistent and inconsistently applied. Co-optation is the preferred method for defusing dissidence.

The local print press operates under varying degrees of self-censorship and sometimes under official censorship as well. Penetration by non-local media, chiefly via satellite television and Internet access, is accelerating. A new Qatari television station, al-Jazira, has electrified Gulf politics through satellite broadcasts of programs structured as debates. However, these debates are highly managed, not only because al-Jazira is owned by a member of the ruling family but also because the doctrinaire ideologies of program hosts and managers tend to dominate program content even on 'call-in' shows (Fandy 2000). Growing numbers of satellite television stations and access to them have increased viewers' exposure to news and entertainment originating outside their countries but they have not proven to be the revolutionary instruments that foreign observers had at first anticipated.[3] Even entertainment programming may have effects that diverge from expectations. For example, Kuwaiti parents watching television with their children employ Western shows as occasions to reinforce local values (Wheeler 2000).

Alternative media outlets present both opportunities for religious mobilization and focal points for Islamist opposition.[4] However, the targets of Islamist attacks tend to be individuals: poets, novelists, commentators – even information ministers – rather than the media themselves. The supply of media products continues although individual human beings may be cruelly treated. These ugly personal attacks deflect religious and non-religious dissidence away from regimes and also discourage alliances between secularist 'moderns' and religious 'traditionals' that could present effective challenges to governments.

Cultures of resistance

Islam and Islamism constitute the core of cultures of resistance to the state throughout the region, but the effectiveness of religious mobilization in this very religious part of the world may be limited. Benedict Anderson (1991) argues that revolution is propagated by example, and many feared that Iran's example would bring religiously based revolutions to other traditional regimes in the Persian Gulf. Yet, as I noted above, the violent excesses of Iranian Shi'i Islamists during the revolution's consolidation phase, and the violence associated with their aspiring Sunni imitators in Algeria and Afghanistan, were repugnant to many citizens of Arab Gulf states. A similar repugnance earlier limited the capacity of Arab nationalists to mobilize revolutionaries rather than mere dissidents. 'Yes, I would like to see us unify into a single Arab nation', one of these dissidents told me in the spring of 1990. 'But this has to be done voluntarily, by voting, not like in Iraq or Syria.' Kuwaiti Islamists I have interviewed talk similarly about adopting shari'a voluntarily, not in the sense of the old joke about the definition of democracy by Algeria's Islamist party (one man, one vote, one time) but rather as a reflection of expectations that fundamental political change should be chosen and not imposed.

Whether this emphasis on choice is principled or tactical, it shows the influence of liberal values on the ethical frameworks of some Gulf citizens. Modernization is more than 'development'; it changes minds by encouraging desires for private rights as well as for individual autonomy and political liberty (Ezrahi 1997; Taylor 1999). This self-referential orientation is the primary threat presented by modernity to 'traditional' cultures and social organizations as well as to traditional (and modern) political regimes. Islamist top-down agendas and confrontational styles are distasteful to many modern 'Gulfies'. The appeal of Islamism as a political orientation is strongest among people who define themselves as 'traditional'; on the one hand to the sort of young men from respectable and even wealthy families who, in imperial Europe, would have been sent to make their fortunes in the colonies and, on the other, to those subject to discrimination – many of the latter young men from the popular classes whose future prospects are endangered by economic liberalization.

Sectarianism limits the appeal of Islamism in Sunni-governed states with substantial Shi'i populations. The prominence of shari'a in Islamist platforms invites consideration of whose version of shari'a would be implemented following an Islamist victory. Minority sectarians, like their majoritarian counterparts, may be mobilizing populations in favor of a greater incorporation of religious values into state law and policy, but their approach also includes privatization. Like 'secular' moderns, religious minorities also seek to put at least some elements of religion off-limits as legitimate idioms of political discourse (Tétreault 2000). Religious principles constitute a strong basis for a culture of resistance in the Gulf states. However – and ironically – religion's effectiveness is limited by the prior successes of religious movements that are themselves repressive, exclusionary and, in some cases, personalistic.

A world-systemic opening

The identity of the Gulf monarchies as clients of militarily powerful states outside the region promises, but does not guarantee, external intervention should radical forces threaten to overthrow them. The most reliable assistance available from outsiders takes the form of military and security assets transferred from patron to client states (Gasiorowski 1991). Now, large cash incomes and the marketization of global relations enable these states to get such 'cliency instruments' in the market, a more reliable source than their patrons and one less likely to impose political conditions. The Second Gulf War is often cited as demonstrating that the Gulf monarchies survive only because of external intervention, but this is a facile and politically motivated assertion, especially if these client states are threatened by revolution rather than invasion. Even during the Second Gulf War, it took six months and billions of dollars in side payments to organize and deploy a force to roll back the Iraqi occupation of Kuwait (Tétreault 1993, 1995, 2000). At the very same time, Serbian and Croatian forces invaded Bosnia, murdering civilians and burning their houses down in full view of television cameras, and torturing and raping them in concentration camps, photographs of which adorned the front page of the *New York Times*. Later, in 1994, Hutu factions in Rwanda mounted a genocidal campaign against their Hutu opponents and the Tutsi minority, killing between three-quarters of a million and a million persons in only three months. In contrast to the Iraqi invasion of Kuwait, both of these cases could be and were framed as domestic conflicts, giving rise to lengthy debates about the ethics of external intervention in the affairs of a sovereign state in UN bodies and the policy councils of Western governments. This persuades me that direct intervention by external patrons of the Gulf states should not be seen as an automatic or particularly effective response to revolutionary movements in the region. If a movement were to be led by a dissident from within a ruling family, it would be difficult for outsiders to discriminate between attempted revolution and a palace coup. A mass-based uprising would evoke domestic opposition in the US and elsewhere to a decision to intervene against an arguably democratizing social movement. Either would slow the mobilization and deployment of external forces, which, in any case, would meet with significant opposition in the target country. Thus, the likelihood that the regime and its domestic client base could be preserved is very small.

Indeed, local and regional configurations of power are more likely than external forces to aid or check revolutionary movements in the Arab Gulf states. What the Second Gulf War did show was the absence of revolutionary sentiment in Kuwait despite more than a year of extensive and passionate popular mobilization against the regime (Tétreault 2000). Saddam Hussein probably anticipated a fairly easy takeover of Kuwait precisely because he confused dissidence with revolution. In contrast, in Bahrain prompt Saudi intervention in the form of police assistance of various kinds bolstered the regime against a broadly based local pro-democracy movement, giving the ruling family time to develop strategies to deal with dissidents and to devise policies of accommodation (Katzman 2000). The Gulf monarchies see dissidence among Shi'a as evidence of external intervention from Iran. No doubt the 'Iranian' taint galvanized both the ruling family of Bahrain and their Saudi allies. But as this example illustrates, effective state-sponsored intervention is more likely to be pro-government than pro-revolutionary.

Other factors

Demographic forces add to the relative vulnerability of Gulf monarchies to revolution. More than half of the citizen population in these states is under 25 years of age. Meanwhile, the large proportion of foreign workers in Gulf labor forces disguises the loss of the safety valve they represented twenty years ago because so many now hold jobs that are low-status and poorly paid. The growing flood of indifferently prepared young citizens onto labor markets with fewer jobs they can do or would be willing to accept is the forerunner of structural unemployment that inevitably will be unequally distributed across social groups because of unequal status and economic resources. Islamist leaders attract followers by demanding more jobs and housing, larger subsidies and family allowances, and by offering an attractive theory explaining why young men suffer so unjustly. Their calls for gender segregation in liberal states such as Kuwait, or their promises in conservative states such as Saudi Arabia to keep women secluded so that they cannot compete with men for scarce educational opportunities and jobs, attract angry young men with few opportunities (al-Mughni 1993, 2000). Large numbers of unemployed youth are a danger in any country and the Gulf monarchies are no exception. Yet whether they could be incorporated into a revolutionary coalition is debatable as long as state revenues are sufficient to pay them off and they continue to be allowed to engage with impunity in occasional vigilante acts – but not against the regime.

The population explosion is also evident among elites, for whom ambition and competence present a 'Goldstone' (1986) situation: too many worthy candidates for limited high-status, high-income and/or *interesting* positions. Some ruling family members leave their countries to make careers of criticizing the policies of their elders at home. Junior members of the al Sabah family have tried to run for parliament only to be checked by the amir. Other family members gratify their competitive and acquisitive impulses in shady financial dealings, whose exposure diminishes support for their families as national leaders. The first two courses of action reflect the modernity of the younger generation and the limits to the attractiveness of bit parts in dynastic family romances. The third shows how difficult it is to restrict the damage that even traditionalists inflict when they do not play their assigned roles properly.

An adequate supply of competent and reliable family members is required if ruling families are to protect their power and authority. The long reign of Sultan Qabus has brought prosperity to Oman but the lack of a named successor from a very small ruling family could lead to problems when the Sultan dies. Qabus's concentration in recent years on inaugurating more broadly representative institutions in Oman, along with his decision to leave a letter naming his choice of successor should his family be unable to settle on a candidate within three days of his death, show both the adaptability of dynastic monarchy and its dependence on far-sighted leadership (Kechichian 2000). In Kuwait, however, where the merchant class pioneered using women as place holders (al-Mughni 1993), the fact that some believe the leaders of a very large ruling family to be contemplating the same strategy for itself (pers. comm.) shakes one's faith in the superior stability of dynastic monarchy.

Another lost opportunity for political stabilization in Kuwait is represented by the marginalization of upper-class dissidents. Buying off or exiling Islamist and secular dissidents from the middle classes has met with mixed results. Attempts to discredit merchants associated with the political opposition in Kuwait have been more successful but the election of young, attractive members of merchant families to parliament could blur traditional antagonisms between elite and non-elite Kuwaitis. To envision upper-class dissidents on common ground with middle-class counterparts is not unreasonable, particularly if the regime deals with its current difficulties by increasing rather than reducing exclusion, and by repressing its Islamist critics in a way that alienates its popular base. Under such circumstances revolution is possible but the fact that these elites have much to protect makes reform the more likely course of action, especially if they can ally themselves with the progressive middle class to fend off an Islamist challenge.

Conclusions

The Arab monarchies of the Persian Gulf have surprised observers for years by their preposterous persistence (Anderson 2000). The rentier state and dynastic monarchy theses explore conditions under which these regimes might become vulnerable to modernizing revolutions, although neither examines the impact of modernity on the structure of domestic interests or state capacity. Circumstances that would simultaneously reduce state incomes and expose weakness or divisions within the ruling class could provide a political space for revolutionary transformation. However, the greater danger lies outside the boundaries of individual states, with militarily powerful neighbors who covet their riches and with a deteriorating situation in Israel–Palestine that could spread violence and political unrest elsewhere in the Middle East.

Consequently, while I believe that war is a constant possibility, revolution seems less likely. Indeed, I suggest that prospects for revolution, which, although small are not non-existent, should diminish further as rising generations replace elders whose ideas of themselves as the rightful occupants of fixed places in social and political hierarchies encourage intransigent positions and justify provocative behavior. The reconfiguration of power bases and national borders already under way globally might themselves or in combination with revolutionary social movements produce a violent rearrangement of the Persian Gulf states. But if this does not occur, today's Gulf monarchies may well be able to move relatively peacefully from their substantially traditional present identities to the postmodern future without ever having had to become modern themselves.

Notes

1. 'Tradition' and 'traditional' are loaded words in the Persian Gulf. They both describe social and political practices that shore up existing power hierarchies and those – such as Islamist demands for the implementation of shari'a – that challenge

them. The growth in Islamist movement activity has made 'traditional' a code for 'anti-Western', and thereby for opposition to democratization and also to global-ization. Yet the heterogeneity of tradition makes it available to a wide range of actors arguing both for and against political and social change. For example, Sultan Qabus of Oman used tradition to 'chastise' those who opposed his appointment of women to the Majlis, critics who themselves had appealed to tradition in their demands that women be confined to the home (Kechichian 2000: 206).

2. In practice, this is not entirely true because the pool of candidates for the top job is limited to particular family lines. In Kuwait, for example, only the direct descendants of Mubarak (ruled 1896–1915) are eligible constitutionally to become amir (prince). Informally, the range of candidates is straitened even further by intra-family alliances and rivalries.

3. For example, Fandy (2000) emphasizes the persistence of the 'anywhere but here' principle of criticizing only foreign governments and cultures by national media, and the lack of trust in expert systems throughout much of the Middle East, which makes political activity via electronic and print media less important than face-to-face encounters. In Kuwait, Wheeler (2000) observes that mediated and unmediated discourses occur together, citing daily upsurges in Internet use at the same time of day that family visiting and *diwaniyyah* attendance are at their height.

4. Fandy (2000: 388) notes that al-Jazira represents a new alliance in the Middle East between Ba'thist nationalists and Islamists.

PART V

Will the Future Be Better?

18

Magical Realism: How Might the Revolutions of the Future Have Better End(ing)s?

John Foran

Most of the contributors to this volume have focused on the questions posed at the outset: Under the emerging conditions of capitalist global-ization, is the age of revolution over? If so, why? If not, what might the revolutions of the future look like? I have stated in the Introduction and elsewhere (Foran 1997) that I foresee revolutions occurring well into the future and arising in the not-so-distant future, at that. This chapter there-fore asks the question: How might the revolutions of the future – what-ever form they take – have better outcomes? That is, what have we learned from the revolutionary record to date that might be of use to revolution-aries in the near to middle-run future (say, the next half-century)? This is perhaps an even trickier field to enter. It begs questions such as: Why would a supposedly neutral scholar try to assist revolutionaries? Why would revolutionaries listen to a First World ivory tower (OK, concrete block) self-styled intellectual? Isn't this an exercise in revolutionary romanticism or – worse – exoticism? And the ominous one: Couldn't states use this information against revolutionaries? I will return to these matters in the conclusion. For now, let us survey the record of twentieth-century revo-lutions to see what their lessons might include.

The Angel of History and the Lessons of the Past

The twentieth century we depart has been the age of revolutions, in Skocpol's sense of 'rapid, basic transformations of a society's state and class structures ... accompanied and in part carried through by class-based revolts from below' (1979: 4; in my view still the most useful definition of revolution). From the Russian events of 1917 that so profoundly shook the world, to the great Third World social revolutions in Cuba and China (and the lesser ones – in transformational terms – in Nicaragua and Iran, among many other places) and the anti-colonial revolutions in Algeria, Vietnam and southern Africa; from the shorter-lived but no less remarkable democratic revolutions in Chile under Allende and May 1968 in France and the more enduring revolutions of 1989 in Eastern Europe, to the current struggle in Chiapas, the historical record is rich in dramatic experiences of ordinary people undertaking extraordinary collective acts.

In previous work I have argued that five interrelated causal factors must combine in a given conjuncture to produce a social revolution: (1) dependent development; (2) a repressive, exclusionary, personalist state; (3) the elaboration of effective and powerful political cultures of resistance; and a revolutionary crisis consisting of (4) an economic downturn and (5) a world-systemic opening (a let-up of external controls). The coming together in a single place of all five factors leads to the formation of broad revolutionary coalitions which have typically succeeded in gaining power – in Mexico, China, Cuba, Iran, Nicaragua, as well as in Algeria, Vietnam, Zimbabwe, Angola and Mozambique, and revolutions that were ultimately reversed in Guatemala, Bolivia, Chile and Grenada.[1]

What are some of the lessons we might cull from the revolutionary record in light of this theory of causes? Let me try stating a few in propositional terms:

- Revolutions have typically been directed against two types of states at opposite ends of the democratic spectrum: exclusionary, personalist dictators or colonial regimes, and – more paradoxically – truly open societies where a critical left had a fair chance in elections.
- They have usually been driven by economic and social inequalities caused by both the short-term and the medium-run consequences of 'dependent development' – a process of aggregate growth by which a handful of the privileged have prospered, leaving the majority of the population to their hardships (each group relative to its social location).
- They have had a significant cultural component in the sense that no revolution has been made and sustained without a vibrant set of political cultures of resistance and opposition that found significant common ground, at least for a time.
- They have occurred when the moment was favorable on the world scene – that is, when powers that would oppose revolution have been distracted, confused or ineffective in preventing them.
- Finally, they have always involved broad, cross-class alliances of subaltern groups, middle classes and elites; to an increasing extent women

as well as men; and to a lesser degree racial or ethnic minorities as well as majorities.

Once in power, a series of related difficulties have typically arisen, which result from the continued significance of the patterns above for revolutionary transformation:

- Truly democratic structures have been difficult to construct following revolutions against dictators, while democratically chosen revolutionaries have been vulnerable to non-democratic opponents, internal and external.
- Dependent development has deep historical roots that are recalcitrant to sustained reversal, however much the material situation of the majority can be improved in the short and medium run.
- The challenge of forging a revolutionary political culture to construct a new society has generally foundered rapidly on the diversity of subcurrents that contributed to the initial victory, compounded by the structural obstacles all revolutions have faced.
- Few revolutions have been able to withstand the renewed counterrevolutionary attention of dominant outside powers and their regional allies.
- Given the above, the broad coalitions that have been so effective in making revolutions are notoriously difficult to keep together, due to divergent visions of how to remake society and unequal capacities to make their vision prevail; meanwhile women and ethnic minorities have consistently seen at best limited reversal of patriarchy and racism after revolutions.

The reader will be able to fill in many of the concrete examples that underlie the above propositions (as well as thinking of counter-examples and other propositions, no doubt).

In addition to these linked causal and outcome issues, there seem to be recurrent trade-offs or contradictions in the revolutionary record as well. For example, the participation of massive numbers runs up against the leadership's need to take decisive measures to deal with all kinds of problems once in power; this in part explains the often bloody narrowing of substantively democratic spaces even as so many previously disenfranchised members of society are gaining new rights and opportunities. When movements have been radically democratic, as in France in 1968 and Chile in the early 1970s, they have had troubles articulating a program acceptable to all parties at the debates, and withstanding illegal subversion from the right. Similarly, a series of economic trade-offs are associated with many revolutions, particularly in the Third World: impressive gains in employment, wages, health, housing and education have after short periods been eroded by internal economic contradictions (demand-driven inflation, limited human and material resources, labor imbalances) and powerful international counter-thrusts (boycotts and embargoes on trade, equipment, loans). As if these political and economic contradictions are not daunting enough, massive external violence has often also been applied, whether covert or openly military in nature, further undermining prospects for democracy and development.

These patterned realities have produced disappointing outcomes, including authoritarian, relatively poor socialisms in Russia, China, Cuba and Vietnam (the only revolutions to last much longer than a generation, except for Iran, where the degree of economic change has been limited); violent overthrows of revolutionaries in Guatemala, Chile and Grenada; slow strangling of change leading to political reversals in Mexico (by 1940), Bolivia (by 1960), Manley's Jamaica and Sandinista Nicaragua; and blocking the path to power altogether in France 1968, El Salvador in the 1980s, China in 1989 and Iraq in 1991, among many other places. This is not to mention the containment of social revolution in the form of far more limited political revolutions in places like the Philippines in 1986, Zaire in 1996 and, in a different and complex way, in the Eastern European reformist capitalist revolutions and the spectacular overthrow of apartheid in the 1990s. No revolutionary movement of the twentieth century has come close to delivering on the common dreams of so many of its makers: a more inclusive, participatory form of political rule; a more egalitarian, humane economic system; and a cultural atmosphere where individuals and local communities may not only reach full self-creative expression but thereby contribute unexpected solutions to the dilemmas faced by society. In this sense Benjamin's image of the angel of history being swept forward by the storm of progress willy-nilly into the future, its face turned to the catastrophic debris of the past, appears an apt one. Yet the past may hold other messages for the future, if we know how to read them.

Magical Realism: How Might the Future Be Different?

What, then, is to be done? In the knowledge that a definitive answer to such a question would be presumptuous (even were it possible), I would like to suggest what I see as some alternatives to the comparative-historical record to date. Insofar as these observations recall aspects of the actual historical record and introduce some emerging practices – notably from Chiapas – they are grounded in a collective creative process, open to all to extend and continue.

The magic of political cultures

In the post-1989–91 conjuncture, it is a truism that there exists a crisis of the left. At the same time, as Forrest Colburn has argued sensibly and hopefully, it is only *after* 1989 that 'A new revolutionary political culture may emerge, one that may prove more capable of fulfilling its promises' (1994: 17). The Zapatistas have offered some radically new ways of doing politics to the revolutionaries of the future. Javier Eloriaga, a member of the National Coordinating Commission of the FZLN (the unarmed, civil-society political wing of the Zapatista movement), notes that 'they say we are dreamers or fanatics. The institutional left continues to regard politics as the art of the possible. And Zapatismo doesn't. We have to do politics in a new way. You can't accept only what is possible because it will bring you into the hands of the system. This is a very difficult struggle. It is very, very difficult' (quoted in Zugman 2001: 113; this section on the Zapatistas' own views draws primarily on this remarkable work).

Sergio Rodriguez, founding member of the FZLN (and before that, a leader in the Trotskyist Partido Revolucionario de Trabajadores), raises the issue of whether this new form of political action can be harnessed and organized (even as he speaks eloquently of its transformative power):

> When the Zapatistas came to Mexico City [at the time of the National Con-sultation of 1999] and traveled all over the country, I remember being in the Zocalo where people were saying goodbye to the Zapatistas. There were these mothers with young people and children who accompanied the Zapatistas to the vans. I realize that there, in that moment, something was being created. I don't know what to call it. I don't know how you could organize it. I don't know how it would be expressed politically. But this relationship is more than thousands of speeches and discourse and propaganda. This is a life relationship. They lived together. They talked and spent time together. Two different com-munities lived together. There was a chemistry there that is impossible to break down. I think that someone would have to be totally blind or have a lot of bitterness not to see this. Luis Hernandez once said that Zapatismo is a state of being. In the beginning of the century, when the socialists and the anarchists organized clubs and strikes they said that socialism was a way of life. Zapatismo is like that too. It is a way of expressing yourself. It isn't just economic or social or political or cultural. It is that and more. Organizing it is very difficult, maybe impossible. I say that it is there. It is an underground relationship between communities. And it creates a very powerful force.... In very few countries is there a force that is so strong. It isn't what we dreamed of in the sixties. It isn't

pure and orthodox. But I think that it is better the way that it is. (quoted in Zugman 2001: 124)

Core Zapatista principles include: *mandar obedeciendo* ('to rule, obeying' – that leaders serve at the pleasure of the community and its struggle, not vice versa); *para todos todo, nada para nosotros* ('for everyone, everything, nothing for ourselves'); 'walking at a slower pace' (i.e. the recognition that change is a long and slow process, not secured with the mere seizure of power or electoral victories); and, indeed, 'not aspiring to take political power'. This last raises an intriguing question for us to ponder. As the second declaration of the Lacandón jungle put it in 1994: 'This revolution will not end in a new class, fraction or group in power, but in a free and democratic space of political struggle' (EZLN 1994, quoted in Zugman 2001: 74; the quotation can also be found in Vazquez Montalban 2000). But what does this mean and how is it to be done? For Subcomandante Marcos, 'This democratic space will have three fundamental premises that are already historically inseparable: the democratic right of determining the dominant social project, the freedom to subscribe to one project or another, and the requirement that all projects must point the way to justice' (Marcos 1995: 85). The dethroning of the ruling PRI, Mexico's seventy-year-old 'perfect dictatorship', in the July 2000 elections contains many lessons, no doubt, of which one is the success of the Zapatistas in altering the political landscape of Mexico. Though too many observers see their role in this historic event as minimal, it would be hard to imagine the collapse of authoritarianism without the insurgency in Chiapas under-mining the government's legitimacy. The new government of Vicente Fox immediately offered to resume negotiations, which the Zapatistas equally quickly accepted; talks soon broke down again as Mexico's two dominant conservative parties, the PRI and Fox's PAN, proved recalcitrant. The rebels now face new challenges, but seem to me all the more well-positioned to meet them in a more democratic, or at least more fluid, political climate (see Ross 2000, 2000a; Weiner 2000).

One innovative Zapatista practice is embodied in the phrase *dar su palabra* (literally, to have one's say). This refers to a dialogue in which everyone present participates, in which the value of the unique vantage point of each member of a community and the insights this affords is appreciated. It usually means taking far longer to arrive at a collective decision, but it also ensures that decisions arrived at have maximum input from the community they will affect, and (hopefully) a stronger consensus (or at least a more open sense of disagreements) behind them. As the Zapatistas put it, the goal is to build 'a world where many worlds fit'

(Zugman 2001: 110). Meanwhile, Mexican artist and scholar Manuel De Landa may have provided the beginnings of an answer to the daunting organizational question, again from observing Zapatista practices: he uses the term 'meshworks' for self-organizing, non-hierarchical and hetero-geneous networks (De Landa 1997; a remarkable book brought to my attention by Escobar and Harcourt 2002). This is a lead worth pursuing, and it has taken shape in the United States around the anti-WTO and G8 demonstrations in Seattle and Washington, DC, in November–December 1999 and April 2000, respectively, soon followed in the fall of 2000 in Prague and Melbourne and the summer of 2001 in Genoa (this list will grow). The combination of 'having one's say' and organizing meshworks has an important US antecedent, the direct action movements of the 1980s that fought nuclear weapons, US involvement in Central America, and the prison industrial complex, among other issues. Their tactics of nonviolence, consensus decision-making and fluid leadership, so effective at the local level in the initial phases of radical mobilization, ran into complex difficulties when the time came to build a national-level move-ment encompassing diverse groups, and led to tensions at the local level within groups between old and new activists, producing leadership burn-out and membership dropout (Borgers 2000, citing Epstein 1988).

These limitations must be confronted in the future, if revolutions are to succeed. Revolutionaries may be well positioned to negotiate the problem of *levels* of struggle, as they straddle the boundary between grassroots and global conflict. This raises the question of the supposedly declining signifi-cance of the nation-state in the new global conjuncture: while its powers and competencies have certainly come under strong pressure from global financial institutions and the transnationals, it yet remains one of the most likely sites for revolutionary activity, as the terrain on which political democracy, economic development and oppositional alliances meet and play themselves out. The new communications technologies are another contested arena linking levels, strikingly evidenced by the Zapatistas' use of both fax and Internet. The anti-globalization protests in Washington, DC, in April 2000 were in part organized by a website maintained by the group A16, for several months prior to the mobilization.[2] Whatever their potential for enhancing the repressive powers of states and corporations, such technologies also represent tools for the education of and communi-cation among social forces from below to foster meshworks of what we might call 'netizens' (a term coined in Hauben and Hauben 1997). Deep and clear thinking about all these matters is required work for would-be revolutionaries (see the wise reflections on the potential of the new tech-nologies by Douglas Kellner in this volume).

Finally, under the heading of magical cultures, we arrive at the frontier of emotions to ask, what do we know about the social psychology of liberation? Here, four US women, cultural producers and activists, have insights that recognize the power of this dimension of social change better than most theorists. Photographer Paula Allen and playwright Eve Ensler, in *The Feminist Memoir Project*, celebrate the strength that can be drawn from this source: 'Being an activist means being aware of what's happening around you as well as being in touch with your feelings about it – your rage, your sadness, your excitement, your curiosity, your feeling of helplessness, and your refusal to surrender. Being an activist means owning your desire' (Allen and Ensler 1998: 425). Alice Walker writes in *Anything We Love Can Be Saved: A Writer's Activism*:

> There is always a moment in any kind of struggle when one feels in full bloom. Vivid. Alive. One might be blown to bits in such a moment and still be at peace. Martin Luther King, Jr., at the mountaintop. Gandhi dying with the name of God on his lips. Sojourner Truth baring her breasts at a women's rights convention in 1851.... To be such a person or to witness anyone at this moment of transcendent presence is to know that what is human is linked, by a daring compassion, to what is divine. During my years of being close to people engaged in changing the world I have seen fear turn into courage. Sorrow into joy. Funerals into celebrations. Because whatever the consequences, people, standing side by side, have expressed who they really are, and that ultimately they believe in the love of the world and each other enough *to be that* – which is the foundation of activism. (1997: xxiii)

Poet Adrienne Rich cautions that this power, arising in individuals, must become a social, interpersonal force to realize its potential to shake the world:

> When we do and think and feel certain things privately and in secret, even when thousands of people are doing, thinking, whispering these things privately and in secret, there is still no general, collective understanding from which to move. Each takes her or his own risks in isolation. We may think of ourselves as individual rebels, and individual rebels can be easily shot down. The relationship among so many feelings remains unclear. But these thoughts and feelings, suppressed and stored-up and whispered, have an incendiary component. You cannot tell where or how they will connect, spreading underground from rootlet to rootlet till every grass blade is afire from every other. This is that 'spontaneity' that party 'leaders,' secret governments, and closed systems dread.[3]

The revolutionaries of the past and present have been enormously creative and expressive at critical junctures, as celebrated in the May '68 slogan 'Power to the imagination!' While we are thankfully far from some new hegemonic reigning oppositional culture, the revolutionaries of the future will likely forge multiple new amalgams of old and new ideas, ideals and ideologies in the best sense. I have argued that love and dreams need to be woven into the fabric of such globalized political cultures of resistance (Foran 2002).

The 'realities' of the political economic

Articulating an economic alternative to neoliberalism seems a fool's quest these days. Yet tapping the magical possibilities of a political culture of liberation might help make progress on this. One principle for such a political economy might be called, simply, the economics of 'social justice'. Recalling the principle of *para todos todo, nada para nosotros*, a woman who is active in the FZLN notes:

> in the Zapatista movement, people are working for something much broader than themselves ... for a change that will benefit everyone. I mean the Zapatistas don't have anything to hand out to people. There is no housing or powerful political positions to obtain. This isn't for your own benefit. It is a benefit for the whole country. It is for all the people who have been fucked over like the indigenous people. (FZLN member interviewed by Zugman 2001: 126)

Social justice has been the foundation of the economic side of revolutionary political cultures the world over, assuming many local expressions – 'Land and Liberty' in Mexico in the 1910s; 'Bread, Land and Peace' in 1917 Russia; 'Equality', from 1789 France to 1990s South Africa; 'Socialism with a Human Face' in 1968 Czechoslovakia; 'Dignity' in Chiapas; 'Fair Trade' and 'Democracy' in Seattle. Thus, defining what it means must be specific to particular times and places. Inventorying these and assessing what common meanings social justice has had across cases is a project of some urgency for activists and scholars of revolution, an important task for others to pursue.

A second need is that of protecting revolutions in a hostile world-system. The impact of the new global conjuncture is difficult to grasp fully, but it is far from uniformly dampening. The end of the cold war may in fact have opened up opportunities for revolutionaries to operate if the other four factors are in place, precisely because the countries in question can no longer be treated as pawns in a larger geopolitical struggle between the United States and the Soviet Union. Democratic revolutionaries and nonviolent movements in particular may find new spaces in which to maneuver. The United States also lost something with the end of the cold war: no longer (or not yet) certain of the bases of its global political–economic strategic vision, it may also be loath to intervene in conflicts in certain parts of the Third World, at least with overwhelming military force. The US under Clinton sought to expand corporate power with free trade agreements and aid to foreign militaries to fight 'drug wars' (aimed at guerrillas in Colombia and elsewhere), a 'strategic vision' of sorts. The post-2001 Bush–Cheney administration with realpolitiker Condoleezza Rice as national security advisor and throwback cold warrior Donald Rumsfeld as secretary of defense, and only Colin Powell as secretary of state to moderate them, surely *wishes* to be more aggressive militarily, but will it carry the needed weight, locally or internationally, to target democratic, nonviolent challengers to the global logic of economic injustice? (for early analyses of the ambiguous (if ominous) direction of US global strategy, see Perlez 2001; Lemann 2001). I should note that this chapter was completed well before the events of 11 September 2001; the logic and analysis of this section still seem accurate to me, as the Taliban do not fill the requirements of being democratic, nonviolent *or* revolutionary. The danger, of course, is that in the new counterrevolutionary discourse of US power, the term 'terrorist' will become a proxy for 'communist' in a new post-cold war world, and aimed at the real targets – national (and now global) revolutionaries.

The US pursuit of an obscenely expensive and chimerical space missile 'defense' system suggests that the imperial grand intent remains intact, but at the same time alienates allies as well as would-be adversaries, and may indicate a greater willingness for easy symbolic expressions of global power than any real ability to halt local rebellions effectively as they arise. The disarray of all leading First World nations in the face of imaginative anti-globalization protests since 1999 may also portend the limits of US power. This claim, too, needs updating, as the WTO's decision to hold its November 2001 meetings in Qatar made on-site protest impossible. But the movement's imagination will surely catch up with this ploy, and even with it the continued relevance of the WTO was just barely accomplished by the delegates, who understood that failure to agree on further discussions would mean the organization's end. The meaning and legacy of the Battle of Seattle were also clearly at stake, as the US representative claimed that the meeting had 'removed the stain of Seattle'. Even the *New York Times* questioned this, notably with its headline 'Measuring Success: At Least the Talks Didn't Collapse' and comment that 'Seattle, and subsequent protests at other international gatherings, have shown the potency and the breadth of opposition to free trade and the concept of globalization' (15 November 2001). Of course, I may well be wrong to discern openings here. The revolutionaries of the near-term future may themselves soon enough provide clues to the answer; my point is that their actions will surely influence the degree and type of interventions they face.

One way forward would be to build on the lessons of the radically democratic revolutions of the past. In counterpoint to Jeff Goodwin's insight that 'The ballot box is the coffin of revolutionaries' (1998: 8), democracy in its many forms may become one of the best weapons of the revolutionaries of the future. Though May '68, Allende, Tiananmen, Mussadeq, Arbenz and Manley all experienced defeat, they gave us a form that the radical reformers and revolutionaries of today in Chiapas, Iran, Uruguay, Brazil, South Africa, Seattle and beyond are already imaginatively appropriating and trying to deepen.[4] Among these movements are to be found new goals, tactics and coalitional possibilities as well as anti-hierarchical and creative political cultures, a sort of message to the future. As Alain Touraine said of it: 'The May Movement was a thunderbolt announcing the social struggles of the future. It dispelled the illusion that improvement in production and consumption result in a society in which tensions replace conflicts, quarrels replace disruptions, and negotiations replace revolution' (Touraine 1971: 79–80, quoted in Poster 1975: 371). All such democratic revolutionary movements can yield valuable lessons in fighting a *structure*, though this is harder than overthrowing a dictator. Out of the ashes of past failures may yet grow the seeds of future gains.

By Way of Concluding Thoughts (for Now)

'Magical realism', then, is a poetic way of referring to and relying on the immense creative potential of people the world over to construct what Perry Anderson once called a 'concrete utopianism' (in Elliott 1998: 168), or what David Harvey has recently named a 'dialectical utopianism' (2000) and Daniel Singer a 'realistic utopianism' (1999).[5] That this must be more socially inclusive than it ever has been in the past seems crucial, as FMLN representative and former guerrilla Lorena Peña puts it in the Salvadoran context: 'A proposal of the left that doesn't integrate the elements of class, gender and race, is not viable or objective, and it doesn't go to the root of our problems' (quoted in Polakoff 1996: 22). That it must somehow also prove capable of forging strong and imaginative consensus agreements around complex, cross-cutting issues makes the task even more formidable. The proper response to the pessimists of the dispirited acronym TINA – 'There is no alternative' – of course is TATA: 'There are thousands of alternatives!'[6] It appears to me that only a radically deepened, participatory process can unite these several dimensions, informing magical political cultures, making visible an economics of social justice, and (just maybe) disarming the US and other global interventionist forces.

We end, then, with a new set of paradoxes and challenges:

• to find a language capable of uniting diverse forces and allowing their not necessarily mutually compatible desires full expression;
• to find organizational forms capable of nurturing this expression and debate as well as enabling decisive action when needed, both locally and across borders;
• to articulate an economic alternative to neoliberalism and capitalism that can sustain itself against the systemic weight of the past and the pervasive and hostile reach of the present global economic system;
• and to make all this happen, in many places and at different levels (local, national, 'global') over time, working with both the deep strengths and frailties of the experiences and emotions of human liberation.

In negotiating the contradictory currents of the future, we must somehow be magical as well as realistic, finding a path marked by pleasures as well as perils.

As for the right of academics to intervene in the transformation of the world, I stand with John Dewey, who felt that our task is not just to map out patterns of causal regularity in social processes but to exercise more intelligent control over them – that is, to help solve problems.[7] It seems well beside the point to be overly concerned with leaving behind one's objectivity, worrying about romanticizing revolutionary violence, or being reluctant to share one's ideas with like-minded others. Nor do I fear that any of this talk could fall into the wrong hands; a greater and more realistic fear is that it will not fall into the right ones. In any case, as Marx urged exactly 150 years ago in 1852 (another epoch in which few saw a bright future for revolutions), let us 'find once more the spirit of revolution, not make its ghost walk again' (Marx 1972 [1852]: 438). As usual, Marx was at least half right: both spirits and ghosts will be needed tomorrow.

Notes

I thank the participants in the Future of Revolutions workshop project for feedback on this text, and especially Eric Selbin for his detailed comments. The essay has also been improved by discussions of it with my students at Smith College in fall 2000, as well as on panels at the Marxism 2000 conference, American Sociological Association meetings, and Latin American Studies Association meetings in 2000 and 2001.

My title takes its inspiration from Selbin (1997a), who elaborates upon the theme of 'magical revolutions' (Selbin 1999: 145). Like Selbin, I am using the term here purely in a suggestive sense, as a possible means and method of acting in the world. It also owes something to Perry Anderson's notion of moral realism: 'What revolutionary socialism above all needs today is moral realism – with equal stress on each of the terms' (1980: 206).

In homage to the late Daniel Singer's wonderfully subversive and optimistic political writing and its impact on my own radical sensibilities, I should like to dedicate this essay to his memory.

1. The fullest elaboration of this argument to date is my 1997a essay. The strange functional equivalence of dictatorships and democracies to explain the cases of Guatemala under Arbenz and Arévalo, Chile under Allende, and Jamaica under Manley is discussed there.

2. I learned this from one of my students, Sarah Macdonald, at Smith College in the fall of 2000. Among many websites, see www.a16.org.

3. I found this quotation by Adrienne Rich, significantly enough, as the epigraph to a book on the Zapatistas: Katzenberger 1995.

4. The intense struggle for democracy in Iran is worth following closely, as are the electoral fortunes of the Frente Amplio–Progressive Encounter alliance in Uruguay: see Moghadam 1999b, as well as other essays published in the same special issue of the *Journal of Iranian Research and Analysis* on the former, and Zibechi 2000 on the latter. Another key case is the left-led municipal government of Porto Alegre, Brazil.

5. One is strongly tempted to contrast unfavorably Anderson's pessimistic turn by the year 2000 – 'The only starting-point for a realistic Left [note term] today is a lucid registration of historical defeat' (Anderson 2000: 16) – with the conclusion to Harvey's book, a playfully imaginative vision of a post-capitalist utopia named 'Edilia' (2000: 257–81).

6. I first heard the term used by Robert Ware at the Marxism 2000 conference at Amherst, Massachusetts, in September 2000, who was quick to point out that he hadn't coined this wonderful rejoinder.

7. This notion of Dewey's was conveyed to me by Mustafa Emirbayer (2000).

How Might the Revolutions of the Future Have Better Outcomes?

27 January 2001

John Foran   In this final conversation I'd like to pose the question that underlay my desire to do this project with you. For me, that question is: *Can* a better world be constructed? If so, how much better? How much is possible, and what are the limits to change? In addition to the issue of how you view the future there are also questions of strategy involved in getting from here to there: How will it come about, and in what time span do you see whatever you propose happening?

It's my belief that we can of course live in a better world. And that it's high time for academics interested in social movements and revolutions to devote more energy than we have to achieving this. Though I don't put my faith in academics being the main architects of a better world, they have as much right as anyone to contribute to this project.

Why am I optimistic? First, the current world economy doesn't work. It will get worse, not better, left to the forces of globalization from above. I can see that much about the future with some certainty. Second, people resist, period. People will learn, also, to do things differently, somewhere, some time in the future, than we have heretofore; we learn from the past. Finally, opportunities will arise and a movement or movements will find a way to go through the eye of the needle into a better world. This is a set of propositions of faith as much as analysis, but rooted in analysis as much as faith, too.

How much better can things become? A half century, a fifty-year period, is about as far as I can imagine forward. And whether we'll get all the way to the kind of world I have in mind in that period I think is doubtful, but not impossible. I'm speaking about fundamental social transformation. I'm speaking about social and economic justice of the kind that I mentioned in my chapter. Serious redistribution on all levels. A world of ecological sustainability. A world of equality, dignity and love: I take some of this from feminism and anti-racism. A world that is fully democratic and participatory, small 'd' democratic; we have to think about that word, no doubt, and find better words if we don't like that word for its other connotations. And a world that is culturally liberatory.

That is the sort of vision that I have in mind as possible. How will it happen? I'm not going to solve that question, much as I'd like others to. Clearly it's going to happen over a long time. It's going to involve a series of steps, from Gramscian maneuvers out of a patient accumulation of forces that have, as Bob Marley puts it in 'Redemption Song', 'emancipated themselves from mental slavery'. As he goes on to say in that song, 'how long shall they keep our profits while we stand aside and look?' And in TATA I trust: I believe that 'There are thousands of alternatives'. I believe that I don't have to solve these problems alone. I believe that there will be a collective process that I hope we'll all contribute to, and many, many people will contribute to, that will somehow get us there, wherever *there* may be.

Carlos Vilas After this really intensive few days my perspective of revolution is as a specific political strategy to obtain certain goals. It's a painful strategy for revolutionaries, counterrevolutionaries and people caught in the middle. That's why we all agree it's a strategy of last resort, when there is no alternative to it. Now this implies there is not only one way to obtain results. There is no necessary correlation between revolutionary efforts and revolutionary outcomes. Success is not inevitable, and there is no relation between the costs of seizing government and the outcome of effective social transformation. The scope and the building up of a coalition to seize power is not necessarily the same as conducting social change afterwards because there will arise different opinions. The very day after the revolution takes power, the discussion about democracy begins. My second point is that we must pay attention to the institutional, political, social and ideological settings in which revolutions are developed and conducted. Future revolutions will have to confront United States military opposition. This has been the experience of popular revolutions and unfortunately I do not see why the future will be different.

Are there really going to be more revolutions in the future? I think there will be more mobilizations, people's revolts, upheavals and protests, which may or may not lead to revolutions. If not, I think that we're going to face perhaps the worst of possible worlds – increasing social degradation, inequality, anger. There is an evocative phrase in the Bible: 'they were thrown to the night, where everything is darkness and gnashing of teeth'. I think this is apt: if we don't have effective revolutions we will see increasing violence against the poor due to neoliberalism. As I don't like this scenario, I prefer the previous one. Yes, there might be more revolutions in the future, with different endings.

George Collier   At the end of our contribution Jane and I speculated that it's possible that one of the outcomes of the Zapatista rebellion is that the state will concede a certain degree of autonomy and then just leave those landscapes for indigenous people to fend for themselves – although we also talk about the possibility of parallel worlds or parallel universes. Might there be sort of archipelagic alliances across different kinds of autonomous regions, not necessarily within the framework of any given national state, but across states? And does that offer any kind of space in which alternatives to neoliberalism can take shape? We tend to think of ways of the future within the framework of our own times where the nation/state is the kind of the paradigm for things, but it's not the only paradigm for organizing societies.

Tim Harding   I think we should address the question of how future social revolutions could have better outcomes and how we could facilitate such outcomes. One of the things that makes a revolution oppressive is the need to survive in a hostile world facing armed intervention. One of the things that makes it easier for a revolution to take power is blocking foreign armed and financial intervention aimed at defeating the revolution. So those of us that live in the United States can play a role in joining the movement to stop the US from supporting repression, working to abolish the infamous School of the Americas (recently renamed). We can discredit the propaganda which says that neoliberalism is inevitable, is the only way, and we can counteract the myth that it brings democracy and freedom to people around the world. To the extent that we're successful working inside the United States, we can really help to change the course of revolutions and help them to be able to be more democratic.

On the other end, what we see emerging now, and I think for a while it is going to be the case, is that the radical social movements that confront neoliberalism come from the people that are most marginalized by this process, the poorest of people, including peasants, provincial workers and indigenous people. But unlike the situation of such struggles in the past, it seems that such groups now have taken on a world vision with a sophistication which wasn't as present before. Organizations like the

Movimento dos Sem Terra (MST, Landless People's Movement) in Brazil, the Zapatistas in Mexico and the Ecuadorian indigenous movement CONAIE are connecting their specific demands with those of the vast majority of their society. The challenges they pose to neoliberal restructuring can, they point out, only be successful by restructuring society in the interests of everyone. So they are holding out a hand and providing leadership for a national alliance to change society. And one of the reasons that has happened is that so many young people that came from the base of such movements, when they got education or training and a chance to go outside of the community, are instead coming back to the community and re-identifying with it. Indigenous people with university education no longer cease to identify as indigenous. Peasant and indigenous groups invite people from other countries to come to their educational programs and meet each other at international peasant and indigenous congresses. All this gives them an international sophistication and a set of allies around the world, which is a very hopeful development. It is easier for us to meet with them and learn from them. All of these positive processes give us much to look forward to.

Jeff Goodwin Even talking about the relatively near future – the next ten to twenty years – is difficult. There is always the possibility, indeed the likelihood, of contingent, unpredictable, unforeseen events that will completely alter our sense of what's going to happen next and what possibilities there are. But, if only as a projection of current trends, I would predict something like the following. I think there will be a proliferation of movements – not a single movement – against global capitalism and the neoliberal version of global capitalism in particular. This is an easy prediction because in many ways this process is well under way and has been for ten or twenty years. I see no reason to think that this resistance to neoliberalism will stop or reverse itself. I think we will see local, national and transnational forms of mobilization in these struggles. I think protests will range from the episodic and the spontaneous to the prolonged and well organized. I think they will be ideologically plural and very diverse. Many of these movements will take on nationalist or ethnic forms. Some will be feminist. Some will take on a religious coloration. Most will be populist; a few will be socialist. But some of these movements will also be reactionary and authoritarian. I don't think we can rule out the possibility that many responses to globalization will be of this nature. But I think most such movements will probably be emancipatory and implicitly socialist in the sense of demanding public or social control or at least regulation of economic affairs. Sometimes these struggles will be violent, sometimes not. A few of these movements, but I think only a few, will entail revolutionary struggles for state power; this will happen in contexts of extreme want and repression, as a last resort, when there's no other way out. But I think most of the movements by far will focus on single issues or sets of issues concerning, for example, the rights of labor, women, ethnic minorities, the environment, health care and so forth. And most will try to force power holders, including state officials, either to withdraw from certain domains or to redeploy power in different and presumably more democratic and accountable ways.

I think these struggles against globalization will both depend on and foster changes in popular consciousness and culture. This will sometimes occur quite quickly, but usually through a long and relatively slow process of cultural transformation. And, importantly, I think that these struggles will invite and provoke intense resistance – resistance not only from states and power holders but also from popular or populist countermovements that will seek to prevent or even roll back social change in the name of tradition, religion or the popular will.

So what I see in the immediate future are proliferating political and cultural conflicts increasingly articulated around issues of global capitalism and inequality – hence increasingly transnational conflicts. These conflicts will often lead to concessions from power holders but will be unable to destroy or displace capitalism at a global level. I hope I'm wrong about this, but I would be delightfully surprised if more than relatively modest concessions are possible in the foreseeable future.

Misagh Parsa It seems to me that there have been three sets of conflicts going on throughout human civilization: the economic conflicts that Marx identified, the political conflicts that others talked about, and then a third one of status and cultural lifestyle. On the issue of economic conflicts engendered by globalization, we're going totally in the wrong direction. Inequalities everywhere have been rising and disparities growing, not just between regions, developing countries and developed countries, but also among regions and within countries. And there's not much you can do in the current situation about this. We will be dealing with such issues in the years – maybe in the centuries, or even millennia – to come.

The second set of issues is illustrated by what happened in Eastern Europe, where political democracy was totally ignored, where the people with power, the Soviets, told them what they were supposed to do. In this respect humanity is actually going in a better direction. But the collapse of the Soviet Union and the end of the cold war leaves this big monster, the United States of America. Though I've benefited so much from coming here, I can never ignore or forget what this country has done to the rest of the world. Look at all the dictators – Suharto to Marcos, to the Shah, El Salvador, Somoza, the School of the Americas, Guatemala, all the CIA involvement, Peru – the United States has been a major partner to crimes against humanity. At least when Suharto was being overthrown, the United States kept quiet and finally said 'it's time for you to go'; this was a great success for humanity. The United States at last may not have some of the old reasons to repress people in the Third World. They might say, 'well, we were unfortunately involved in Guatemala and the CIA was a major partner to all the crimes that occurred'. There are now cases where the United States has admitted some involvement – even in the 1953 coup d'état in Iran, they say, 'well we played a role, and it was bad, it wasn't nice'. There are some positive changes happening and this may help future democratic socialists, if they survive this period of neoliberalism.

Finally, there's another set of conflicts having to do with my own background, being a religious minority in a country like Iran, which helps understand not just religious or ethnic minorities, but also issues of women, gays, lesbians and so forth. In this area we're actually seeing some progress in some parts of the world, though not everywhere. So, there's a lot of work to be done; this recent wave of democracy and democratization, plus the neoclassical market and the notion of expanding the pie to make it available to everybody, I don't think is going to solve problems. I think there will be future conflicts, violence or perhaps revolutions, but I'm hoping that socialists who are interested in transforming the world will not ignore the issue of democracy.

Valentine Moghadam   These are certainly interesting times – times of crisis and instability and lots of possibilities. I'm beginning to wonder whether concepts of democracy, human rights, workers' rights and women's rights may become unifying revolutionary slogans of the future, in a shift from the concept of the dictatorship of the proletariat. In American English 'freedom' was associated with the right, the CIA, and Freedom House, but something has happened in the past fifteen or twenty years. When Jimmy Carter first came up with his idea of a human rights-based US foreign policy, many on the left were suspicious and skeptical. It seemed so hypocritical. But in the past twenty years, human rights and similar concepts have been very effectively appropriated and given real meaning by the left. And in fact the left has managed to show how empty and hollow these concepts and terms were when utilized by conservatives and rightists. These concepts, as they are being utilized today by the transnational advocacy networks, the unions, feminist organizations, human rights organizations and environmentalists, have real meaning and could really mobilize reform and some revolutionaries around the world. Perhaps.

My second point concerns the kinds of movements that we'll be seeing in the future. I believe that there will be a myriad of types of movements. I'm not going to write off social revolutions – that is, nationally based revolutions – because we still have states, inequalities and ruling classes at the national level. But the social revolutions of the future might utilize those concepts of human rights, women's rights and so on in ways that they did not in the past. Moreover, these revolutions might be better networked with international solidarity movements and organizations, like the transnational social movement organizations and institutions of global civil society. In other words, revolutionary activity in a particular country might be less isolated, less vulnerable than in the past, in part because it will be much better networked and linked with international civil society organizations and solidarity campaigns that might do support work on their behalf in a more effective way than in the past. What I think might also be different with social revolutions in the future is that they may entail less violence. Of course that depends on how the state and the ruling class respond to these types of movements and revolutions. It's possible that social revolutions of the future may look like the 1989 revolutions in Eastern Europe and Russia minus the patriarchy. Parenthetically, the velvet revolutions were pretty patriarchal, as they resulted in a serious loss of political power and a decline in the economic status of women in those countries. Future revolutions might also look a little bit more like Allende coming to power, minus the Chilean military and the CIA. Our charge was to be visionary and that's what I've taken advantage of. I think there is something to be said for being a little utopian, and to retain some ideals and aspirations. But I think that there is a material basis for what I envision.

Finally, I believe that we bear a special responsibility as progressives in the United States because the United States and its two parties have been major actors on the international scene in very problematical and negative ways. I was quite distressed when American leftists and feminists were divided over the 2000 election, and when those of us who supported Nader were attacked for undermining Gore's prospects. The question seemed so ridiculous. How any progressive could possibly vote for any presidential candidate of the Democratic Party is just beyond me. American progressives have the responsibility to push for a third party, a fourth party, a fifth party, any alternative to the Democrats and the Republicans in order that there be real change in this country and in order that there be greater possibilities for real change around the world. We need – and Gore would never have been able to do this – serious redistribution of wealth and some serious reallocation of resources and priorities and ultimately a demilitarization of the US.

John Walton   Well, this is going to be a bummer after that. I was about to say, when we ask what we can do, we need to be much more realistic about what our institutional locations are and our particular skills and so on. In other words, the things that we can realistically do are more delimited, they are more within these kinds of settings in which we work. It would be advisable if many of our number gave up their university sand traps and their dental plans and joined the revolutionary movements. But short of that, I think there are concrete things that can be done.

If there were more attention to revolutionary and other outcomes generated by forms of political contention – that is, to begin to look at the whole arena of how changes, both good and bad, get produced – we may expand considerably the knowledge of how desirable results get produced. That's always been a bone of contention that I've had with the sociology of revolution which dismisses mere rebellions without really examining this question of how fragile is this notion of successful revolution. And I can point to lots of revolutions that were as successful at least as the so-called bona fide revolutions. If we begin to expand that arena of thinking about results, it can have useful effects.

The other point is that I think that a lot of what we do can be revelatory and liberating. Here's a quick anecdote. In the late 1970s, I was at a meeting where Richard Mueller, the co-author of the book *Global Reach* (1974) spoke about the book for the first time. It had just appeared, and he spoke in Austin, at the University of Texas, to a large group which included many Latin American people involved with developmental efforts in a variety of ways. This was a marvelous occasion because all of a sudden many of us understood for the first time how multinationals worked in a sort of nuts and bolts fashion. Mueller got into this discussion of transfer-pricing, saying 'now here's how it works: They put a certain value on this box, they send it to Panama, they take the stuff out of the box, they send the empty box down with the overvalued thing, and then they send it back. In these ways, they avoid tariffs and they conceal the volume of capital that is being repatriated.' Now I understood how the mechanisms of this system worked. And I know many of the Latin Americans went home with a lesson as to how to think about policies for the regulation of multinational enterprises. Our work can sometimes provide that revelatory and strategic sort of information to the extent that we endeavor to build that into our own analyses, so we shouldn't minimize some of the contributions that can come from work of this kind.

Jeffery Paige   The question of this conference is, do revolutions have a future? I want to pose another one. Do we have a future without revolutions? And my answer is no. Let me explain why. First of all I think that in some ways we have spent too much time focusing on individual revolutions. Jeff Goodwin points out that in the epoch from 1789 to 1848, there was only one revolution, and literally he's correct. But more importantly, during that period, the *concept* of democratic revolution motivated people everywhere. Even when it didn't occur, they were fighting for it, they were involved in projects of human liberation. The same thing is true for the socialist revolutionary movement, beginning after 1848 and intensifying after 1917. We're too willing to accept the liberal construction of the *defeat* of those movements. The socialist movement in its democratic fight for the welfare state vastly improved the situation of most people. And the Communist movement, too, scared the life out of the world capitalist class, forcing them to make concessions everywhere. Those struggles were not entirely in vain, and I think to have some project of that kind motivates and leads forward struggles of all kinds.

I'm also optimistic about the future. Another age of revolutions started in 1968 when we saw the beginning of the deconstruction of many of the categories left from earlier revolutions – those ancient ones of gender, race, sexual orientation, cultural difference, of civilization versus barbarism. I think that in itself is a step forward. It requires additional struggle and direct action but it also provides additional possibilities. Many movements and struggles are ongoing right now: the environmental movement worldwide, the worldwide feminist networks and a renewed labor movement including not only the poorest laborers but even the AFL–CIO in the United States, the human rights movement, the indigenous rising, the anti-WTO protests and so on. Indeed there's even a beginning of a global coordination of these events evident in the WTO protests. They have not come together in a single project but that's something that can be done, and indeed we should be contributing to it. We should not quit the university and go out in the streets; we should seize places like Dartmouth College and use them for revolutionary purposes by constructing an image of a more equal society.

What's the basis for this? I think the object of this revolution should be an image of human beings in which every single person on earth is included, from indigenous people in Chiapas to the people at Dartmouth College – everyone, without exception. I don't think there's any other basis for a revolutionary movement, one that doesn't count particular people out as enemies of the state or class or racial enemies and so on. Indeed, I think this will have a great appeal, and of course it's something we have to struggle for because we're divided in all kinds of ways and we'll have to struggle against all these forms of division to think of everybody in the world as human beings. We're all in it together, which implies a global consciousness.

Finally I think we're going to require a restructuring of global capitalism. Indeed, I think global capitalism in its current neoliberal incarnation is finished. It is spinning out of control, collapsing into disorder almost everywhere, and I think the smarter capitalists are going to realize this if they haven't done so already. One of the things that we haven't discussed here, strangely enough in a conference on revolution, is capitalism. In the previous incarnation of revolution, we were going to get rid of it. I'm going to say something that may be heretical here: I don't think anybody thinks like that any more. The interesting thing about capitalism is that it's an immensely malleable system. It coped with welfare states. It coped with good benefit programs for workers. It coped with no benefit programs for workers. We have to think of restructuring this system for human beings to take control of it. You can just as well run it with affluent consumers in Chiapas as desperately poor people working in maquilas. And I think we have the intellectual tools to do it. So increasingly, in part as a response to this conference, I don't think there is any hope except for profound revolutionary transformation of this type, global in inspiration.

Abdollah Dashti   Will the revolutions of the future be better? I would say yes, but it's not a given. And how much better? Again that depends on strategies, coalitions and several other issues. As to when, I'm less optimistic than Jeffery Paige, I think probably it will take a little longer time because, as he says, capital is so flexible. If our final goal is to eliminate capitalism — and here I disagree because that's really the only way that we can have a complete liberatory system with the sort of democracy that I have in mind — that sounds very utopian at this point. Nor am I able to rule out the chance of some sort of fascism, perhaps not the one that we saw before World War II, but when capitalism enters its next crisis, what will happen then? So part of our strategy must be to try to prevent that from happening.

In all the revolutions of the past, democracy was the final goal. I think it should be part of the *means*. One of the institutions that capitalism is using in order to control globalization at this point is democracy. It's not that we should reject progressive electoral democracy; the irony is that socialism, for which democracy was an integral part, became synonymous with authoritarianism, totalitarianism. The whole thing shifted historically at some point. So we need to build strategies and alternative institutions like the media to retake the concept. I'm afraid I'm not optimistic that we will achieve this in as soon as fifty years because it's a very hard battle ahead of us.

Mary Ann Tétreault   I agree that one of the things that Americans need to do is to focus on the United States and organize here. I think there are enormous numbers of very disaffected people who are much more mobilized now than possibly they were before November 2000. We have to start at home, not just looking to stop the United States messing up other peoples' revolutions, but maybe also to see what we can do here. One of the things that is hardest to do here is to reach across into groups that we don't have a lot of sympathy with. How can we have the kind of democracy that we're talking about where nobody is left out if we can't even talk to such people, if we have no common ground at all? Transversalist techniques – for example, the way the Northern Irish women have been working them out – are very, very crucial. And we need to develop 'them' as individuals in our own minds and lives, and not just assume that 'those people over there' will find and cultivate the common ground. We're talking about a plan for personal action.

I am not an optimist. I think we should be getting ready because I do think there will be a crisis. I'm very worried about, for example, another world war, something very unpleasant to think about. Hopefully I won't live to see it, but this has been haunting me for the past ten or fifteen years. Maybe we'll be lucky and we won't have a world war. Maybe we'll just have a phenomenal environmental catastrophe, which at least won't polarize us in the same way and won't affect things in quite the same way although it would have a similar capacity to kill. I think we need to be prepared to move in the case of a crisis, to make it work for us, and anticipate that crisis, as ugly as any kind of crisis is to think about, by planning ahead.

Finally, I don't think there ever is an end to revolution. I think that, in many ways, the condition of human beings is that we have to do things over and over again. It's so interesting to be here with so many people who have been involved in movements in so many places. When we die, how many people will we leave behind who have been very involved with these movements? Maybe that's why people need to do things over and over. What we want to achieve in concrete terms is not likely to be the same as what our children will want. So we shouldn't be thinking that revolutions are over but rather that we're leaving a legacy of how to make revolution something that is more permanent. The idea of searching for social justice is not something that you have; it's something that you have to work for all the time, forever. That's what being a human being is basically about.

Farideh Farhi   Everything has almost been said. I just want to reiterate one thing in response to the question of how it will happen. And it seems to me that, in keeping with what Jane suggested before and Val also and now Jeff, there are a lot of ideas that have been around for a long time that we have assumed are part of the globalization project, appropriated by capitalism, and therefore we have rejected them. These are now starting to be reappropriated and turned into something else. Obviously democracy is at the center of this; we are entering a period where this kind of language can bring a lot of progressives together all over the world. To me it's not a surprise that the same language is coming back in the United States. After the Florida elections, we are finding out the United States is not such a democratic country and a lot of votes are not counted. I don't see any reason why the population generally, and progressives in particular, should not be involved in the process of rewriting the rules in such a way that more people can be involved in the voting process. The same thing that is going on in many countries. So I get a little bit worried when someone suggests in a sort of easy way, let's forget about what happened in Indonesia, let's discount what happened in the Philippines. Despite the fact these elections are clearly not in some ways reaching the kind of results that we would like, I think it's also important that the mobilization that occurs in that process creates a lot of networks that may turn into something else. The results may not be immediate, but people are inspired by this idea of bringing more transparency to and having more input in the political process and ultimately more power in the process of negotiation that goes on regarding specific issues. There's revolutionary or progressive potential in all of this. These mobilizations create a potential for a kind of organizing, or a reality for a kind of organizing that did not exist before.

Eric Selbin   Let me try to pick up on some of what's been said so well already. One has to do with the special responsibility of the US and for us not to seek our salvation in places that we've been degrading and debasing and abusing. And that we need to take responsibility both for the behavior of the United States elsewhere but also for saving ourselves, for lack of a better term. Others have made the point about how smart capitalists are and whether or not there's some world capitalist class or global capitalist class pulling strings. Capital has proved far more enduring and far more adaptable than a lot of people ever expected. In the short term, maybe the best we can hope for is as things continue to worsen, as we see the Brazilianization of the rest of the globe, that we may well see a short-term move by capital to try to address some of the gross inequities according to a Scandinavian model. That's going to raise some interesting points because it will be capital seeking to prevent things getting to a breaking point. I think the time span for something significant is sooner rather than later.

I share what Val said about her belief that it's not the end of social revolutions. I see, from ancient China and ancient Persia, in some of the cultures in sub-Saharan Africa, around Spartacus and Rome, and the Bible, depending how you read and interpret it, on and on and on there are phenomenal stories of the struggle for justice and hope. And it seems to me that however deeply flawed the revolutions we talk about are, one of things that cuts across a number of these cases and part of their incredible staying power is this element of hope. And I suppose my unwillingness to abandon the concept of social revolutions resides in the hope that I have for myself and my children, found also in so many of the people that I've talked to in Central America and the Caribbean. It's my fascination with that hope that keeps me holding on to the concept of social revolutions.

Jan Rus   I wanted to say something as a North American looking back at the United States from Mexico. The strangest thing coming back here all the time is how complacent this place is: the view that nothing changes, that stability is natural, a force of nature, and that the Constitution is like the law of gravity – that things can't be changed. And I'm put in mind of how Ceausescu probably felt when he went out on the balcony and somebody booed and then there was silence and then in a couple days he was dead. Social systems can turn on a dime. When I look a bit deeper I see incredible instability and chaos lying underneath this apparent stability which people accept here so complacently.

I've heard that the equivalent of the gross national product of the United States flashes through the world's financial markets every two days. That's financial power, monetary power, that is just completely out of control. Then there is the chance of climate and environmental catastrophe. I remember the slogan in the 1970s of 'One, two, many Vietnams'. When you think about the United States being able to repress the world, the chance for a lot of things happening once things get out of control is also there. People on the left, progressive people in our lifetime, since World War II at least, have lived through this period of really relatively great stability, in spite of the instability in the rest of the world. Progressive politics has been something kept alive by faith more than because there was a place, an opportunity to apply it. And I think there are probably great opportunities coming.

They may be negative opportunities in a sense. Some of the future may already be visible in Latin America, in Mexico, for instance, which is going from having one of the smallest proportions of its population of working age in the world, only 30 percent, over the last twenty years because of a huge population explosion, to having one of the largest percentages of the population working age – it's going to something like 65 percent by 2015. We have the hollowing out of manufacturing in the United States, with manufacturing moving away to other countries. So there are two limiting cases. One is that the air slowly goes out of neoliberalism and US hegemony because it can't be sustained in the face of the unrest of populations. And the other one is for crises. In either case, there's pain coming. If it goes out slowly there will be pain because there will be union fights, labor fights, local fights. If it goes out quickly the pain can go as far as Mary Ann's vision of big wars. In either case, the cold war, oddly enough, is going to have been the time of stability for people who live in these privileged states. Now I think we're about ready to be pitched into the ocean with everybody else.

Ralph Armbruster   How do we really bring about social change today in a world that's globalized? In other words, how do people fight back around the world? I think a lot of people make the assumption sometimes that there's some kind of overarching beast out there called globalization, a structure that determines every outcome; that we can't do anything, we just have to then throw our hands up; that we don't have the ability to bring about any change whatsoever.

In the old days, in the revolutionary moments of the past, the war of maneuver would be directed against the nation-state: the national liberation movements, the socialist movements or whatever, would take over the state. But now the state is not really viewed as an effective place to try to bring about social change for a number of different reasons: because of capital mobility, because of globalization. If the nation-state is not really the site of struggle any longer, what is the site of struggle? Who is the enemy? Do we have multiple enemies or is there a single enemy? Where before it was 'let's take over the state and let's bring about revolution, let's bring about socialism and an egalitarian society and inequality will melt away', now it's 'what are we really going to do because the nation-state really isn't a unit of struggle any longer, supposedly.' So who is the enemy now? Is it capitalism? Is it the WTO? Is it corporations? Is it the GAP?

Is it Nike? Is it Phil Knight, Bill Gates? Who are we talking about, who are we battling? It's unclear in this war of position who is really out there to do the battling around. These two things are tied together: if we don't know what the war of maneuver is, we don't really know how to fight this war of maneuver, nor do we know how to fight a war of position.

The battle in Seattle is talked about in almost messianic terms: 'Remember Seattle.' It's going to be like that twenty years from now. And it *is* important. It was obviously a very important event. Revolution to a certain degree today is almost like 'moon talk'. I have students in my class whom I ask, 'what do you want?' 'Oh we want a revolution.' Do you want to go out to the everyday people and say, well what do you want, do you want to create a revolutionary society? That doesn't really make sense to them, so you need to have some kind of popular or populist discourse about how to bring about social change. One of the things that was really interesting that came out of Seattle was this discourse about democracy. 'This is what democracy looks like.' That was one of the major chants in these demonstrations. These chants are great because there's something hidden in them, there are discursive things going on in these chants that make sense to a certain degree. I mean, when you're out there chanting it, it feels really great; of course you're not there thinking about these theoretical things, you're thinking about how we're going to battle against the enemy. Yea, we're really battling against the enemy. 'There ain't no power like the power of the people 'cause the power of the people don't stop.' So there's something hidden in that. The people have the power to bring about these social changes. Hidden in that is a kind of democracy trope about how we really bring about social change. It's not really talking about revolution, it's not talking about socialism, it's talking about the discourse of democracy.

So the war of position, here in the United States, is the kind of thing that rallied disparate groups together – labor unions, environmentalists, gay and lesbian folks, students, religious people, all these different people came together, 50,000 people, the Zapatistas were even there – these disparate multiple identities that can usually never get their act together. Here's the collective action of all these different forces, coming under the banner of democracy. The structures weren't determining the outcome that day. People were fighting back. The WTO was shut down for five hours. And now the WTO is in disarray to a certain degree.

My point is about democracy as a rallying cry. This fits into US discourse to a certain degree. People understand that. So they understand what happened in Florida as an affront to democracy. The voting was shut down there, it wasn't just pregnant chads or hanging chads or any of this other business. It was that people really didn't have the right to vote and so not every vote counted. That struck people that at a visceral level. 'Something is wrong here, we don't really have a democratic society.' I think back to the 1960s: one of the things that started it was that a few students at Berkeley found they didn't have the right to set up a table to say we're concerned about the war. And then the University of California administration said we're not going to give you a freakin' table. So that one little battle over a table became a battle about free speech. It became a battle about democracy. It became this kind of chant about participatory democracy. So here's a trope that was used in the 1960s, about participatory democracy: How do we try to radicalize all of our social institutions to make sure that everybody has a voice in trying to make decisions? Thirty years later, what are we fighting for? What folks were rallying for back then – democracy. How do we really fight back against globalization? One of the possible ways to do that, if we can't really identify this kind of enemy through this war of maneuver, may be through the war of position. Maybe the terrain of struggle is through the cultural struggle or ideological struggle to define what we mean by democracy. We say that we have a democratic society, but do we? How are we really going to create democracy here in the United States and abroad?

John Foran   On these immense questions I think we're ready to close. I'm not sure how to thank you all. It's really not clear what I should say. I'm very inspired by what we've done and by you and by your ideas and your kindnesses. And I dare say I feel we have created a community of sorts in these three days which surpasses any expectations, high as they may have been, that I could have had for our gathering. And I shall certainly, for my part, try to make the volume that will embody this meeting live up to this spirit and collective creation and to draw your ideas together, different as they may be, and to do them all some justice. So with that you have my thanks and we come to a close.

Utopian Realism: The Challenge for 'Revolution' in Our Times

Fred Halliday

John Foran Fred Halliday kindly agreed to write this Afterword for the volume. The reader will readily note the degree of engagement, salutary caution and forthright criticism expressed herein. It only makes me regret the more that he – along with Adolfo Gilly, Karen Kampwirth and Noel Parker – was unable to be present at our discussions, for this would have led to even livelier exchanges, no doubt! In the end I am not so sure that our disagreements are as wide as they may seem, though there were many points of view expressed, and still others not represented, as is inevitable. I am most grateful to Fred for beginning, therefore, the further discussion of the issues raised by the book: his reflections are the kind of provocative – and provoked – response I hope there will be much more of as we move into the future we speak of. May they be the first of many after words.

The chapters that comprise this volume occasion two, contrasted, responses in a reader who did not participate in the discussions leading to its preparation, but who has sought, over some time, to address the issue of revolution in our times. The first response is a shared sense of interest, both analytic, in terms of the political sociology of revolutions, and ethical, in rejection of what contemporary capitalist modernity has on offer. Yet this common response is accompanied by a second one, of some unease, at what seems to be a too easy acceptance of the continued pertinence of a 'revolutionary' project, and a rather too rapid escape from discussing the negative lessons of the past century of violence, upheaval and mismanagement associated with revolutions. To a European reader, faced with a history both of revolution and of radical social democracy, this unease is reinforced by a questionable silence on what radical, but reformist, politics offer, as much in the developed world as in regions such as Latin America where strong democratic traditions and movements of civil society are to be found. In what follows, I would like to address both of these responses, and the tension, potentially a creative one, between them.

As many contributors to this book remind us, radical change is not just an aspiration, but a product of the tensions contained within the society we live in. Begin where all projection of, and engagement with, revolution should begin, the analysis of the contemporary world: the starting point, both for the analysis of revolutions and for the anger of those who undergo the risks and sacrifices of revolt, is rejection of the present. Marx's *Capital* famously focused not on the imagination of a new order – nor did his work as a whole concentrate, very much, on the forms of ideology or organization appropriate to revolutionary activity – but on the society and economy in which he lived. Lenin gave more attention to questions of revolution, but whether on the matter of the state, or on the foreign policy of a revolutionary regime, his prescriptions were notoriously inconsistent. His major contributions remain analytic – *The Development of Capitalism in Russia* (1900), *Imperialism, the Highest Stage of Capitalism* (1916). Revolutionary analysis of the post-1945 world centered on the international economy, on imperialism, dependency and the structurally unequal world that was being created. The analyses here equally comprise a many-sided, rich and, rightly, uneasy reflection on the contemporary world, on 'globalization' in its many manifestations. The starting point for an analysis of revolutions and their future has, therefore, to be the world we live in: the critique of ideology, the structures of exploitation, the balance of social and political forces, the forms of organization and power available to each side. It has, as E.H. Carr argued, to be utopian in aspiration but realist in analysis and in program: keeping both of these requirements in view remains the greatest challenge to any critique of the given (I have developed this further in Halliday 2000: ch. 10, 'For a Radical Universalism', and in Halliday 2000a).

This starting point underlines two very central constants in any analysis of revolution, much evident in these pages. This involves a necessary, recurrent, imbalance. First, we are much more certain about the structures, and inherent inequities, in the present system than we are about the alternatives, and the ways to get there. Second, in assessing the future and how contemporary society may produce an alternative order, we are engaged in a venture that is necessarily imprecise; our ability to predict revolution is imprecise not contingently – that is, because we do not have enough information, or theory, or are not smart enough in the ways and cunning of world history – but necessarily, because prediction about macro-

historical processes, and ones involving the clash of collectivities and
interests, is uncertain. Revolutionaries, notably Marx and Engels themselves,
as much as the non-revolutionary positivists that dominated late-twentieth-
century social science, sought for a secure, 'scientific', approach to the
movements of society, but this has remained, for left and right alike, a futile
venture. The very crisis about the certainty and predictive ability of much
of what is termed 'natural' science that is evident today should make us
even more careful. We do not know because given the complexity of
factors we cannot know, and because in this as in other respects human
will is central.

These recurrent elements in the analysis of revolution contrast, however, with a degree of change in how revolution is considered in different
times. A reader of the essays contained in this book would, for example,
note a number of continuities, but also discontinuities, with what would
have been written by a similar group of people, say, forty years ago. On
the side of continuity there is a deep, and documented, sense of the
inequality of capitalism, and of the international character of its exploitative system. Equally, on the ethical side, there is an anger, linked to a
belief in the ability of human beings collectively to resist oppression, at
the society, the myths and mystifications, the very intrinsic exploitation
perpetrated by that system. An internationalism, of analytic framework
and solidarity, would also be common to both times.

On the other hand, there are some striking differences. In the first
place, a generation or two ago the academic discussion of revolution was
at a much more elementary stage. Discussion of revolution today involves
an awareness of discussion of the state, of ideology, of global structures of
power and wealth that greatly enhances our understanding. The political
sociology of revolutions as an analytic field is very much the product of
the past twenty years. If we have gained, we may, however, have also lost
certain things. One of them is a sense of the drama of events themselves:
in our respect for 'scientific' and 'structural' accounts, it is tempting, but
often presumptuous, to dismiss the work of historians on revolution. Their
works capture much of the uncertainty, the tension and the ethical atmosphere, as well as the hopes, of political upheaval. We should, in more
sociological and comparative vein, build on those narratives, be they de
Tocqueville or Trotsky, and that is what has often occurred.

There is also much less reflection now than was the case a generation
ago on who the historical bearers, the agents, of revolutionary change will
be. The classic answer was in terms of organizational form and class: the
revolutionary party or vanguard, the working class and various, optional,
allies – peasants, intellectuals, in the case of Yemen revolutionary fishermen.

Today discussion shies away from this: the party is displaced by a vaguer invocation of social movements and coalitions, class has been given a secondary place in radical discourse, for better or worse. The development of analysis in terms of gender and race has been diffused by an indeterminacy, at times a *bricolage*, of radical agents. Moreover, there is much less certainty about what the alternative order should be. This too may be a liberation, from naivety or collusion with authoritarian statist regimes, and it may meet the need for predictive uncertainty identified above; but it also allows of evasion, with regard to the practicability of alternative orders, and, even more importantly, with regard to their desirability. The assumption that any, or all, visions of an alternative would be preferable to that which exists is, in the life of societies as of individuals, open to challenge.

Here it is worth noting how a significant part of the left formed in the 1960s, in both Europe and North America, has remained stuck in a rejectionist project that is, aesthetic intricacies aside, barren: one can indeed distinguish between those of the 1968 generation who have matured, and those who have not. Thundering denunciations of 'reformism' and 'betrayal' by unreconstructed radical thinkers and journals, stirring as they may occasionally be, are not bases on which to denounce all alternative critiques of, and proposed solutions to, the present world. A discussion of revolution that fails to address the demand for realism, and that dismisses radical and sustained non-revolutionary alternatives, may be sectarian. Of all the vocabulary of revolution and cold war that we are well rid of, my prime candidate is the word 'correct'.

These shifts in historical and analytic perspective, of the kind reflected in these pages, are compounded by another trend in contemporary activist critiques of the capitalist order, one that is also sometimes reflected in the social sciences and contemporary politics, as much as in the discussion of revolutions, namely a retreat from the radical rationalism that underlay earlier discussion of revolutions. Several contributors to this volume also note this problem. A generation, or three, ago, it would have been taken for granted that revolutions were considered on the basis of a modernist project. Indeed the fundamental case for revolution, from 1789 to 1989, was that modern society itself produced such contradictions that a new order was both desirable and possible: it would be produced by the conflicts of the existing order. Revolution fulfilled, rather than opposed, the economic, social and political project of modernity. Today this is, in many ways, contested. Modernity itself as a goal, and as a grand historical narrative, is in question. Radical challenges to the existing world system take the form of a variety of movements, many of them legitimating themselves by references to communal values, religion, tradition, not to say more or less utopian engagement with nature, animals, the spiritual and so forth. To someone formed in earlier debates, it is striking how much of what was formerly called 'anarchism' has returned, apparently in acceptable mode. Within the internationalism that is today so readily invoked by radical and revolutionary currents the world over, there are often strong elements of nationalism, relativism and irrationalism. This may be defensible (in my view it is most certainly not), but it marks a clear break with the intellectual framework that guided revolutionary and internationalist thinking from the French revolution onwards. It is here, indeed, that one of the more pertinent, and unsettling, implications of 11 September may be found: al-Qaeda represented an extreme of violence, racism and social reaction but, in an angry, and in some respect nihilistic denunciation of the West, particularly of the USA, it spoke for ideas that pervade much of the world today.

All of this has occurred, of course, in a historical context that is itself profoundly changed. The two most obvious dimensions of this changed context are, on the one hand, the collapse of the Soviet project and the erosion of the other remaining socialist regimes, notably China; and, on the other, the spread of what is generically termed 'globalization'. It is often easily asserted, but not too easily demonstrated, that these two processes are connected: the roots of the Soviet collapse lie in longer-term changes within that society, in part a product of its success in the educational field, and in the limited impact of the Bolshevik revolution on the world as a whole; globalization is much more a product of the changes – regulative, productive and technological – which matured within developed capitalist society in the early 1990s. Taken together, however, these changes constitute a new global conjuncture – one which, as the authors of this volume so well demonstrate, has created a world that is more unequal than ever. It is never going to be possible definitively to establish how far globalization is something new, how far a continuation of earlier forms of global inequality, going back through formal colonialism to the expansion of the world market since 1500. What is, however, evident is that for all that this is indeed new – in terms of capital and trade flows, deregulation and information technology – globalization builds not only on forms of structural inequality in the world, but on attitudes, domestic state structures and adaptive capacities and incapacities within every one of the two hundred societies in the world. We know better than Lenin than to say that anything is the 'highest state' of anything else: that globalization is the latest stage of world capitalism remains, however, indisputable.

This changed context, intellectual and historical, leads to a set of questions about revolution and to the possibilities of change in the contemporary world. Each of these is addressed in the essays above, and will remain central to any future discussion of this question. The first, the question that revolutionary analysis begins with, concerns the political sociology of modern society: capitalism is, if nothing else, a system in constant change and this applies to the elements that comprise any analysis of revolution – the class structure, ideologies, state formations, technologies of this system. 'Revolution' may be invoked as a constant possibility these past two centuries, but it must depend on very different forms of organization and actor, and be carried out under different ideological guises. Some of the contributors discuss the relevance of technological change, especially information technology, to radical movements: as they rightly point out, whether these benefit the opponents of capitalism more than the benefactors is an open question. Protesters can communicate with each other, but so can states, whose capabilities of surveillance and counter-action are greatly enhanced. Analysis of communication and of the media also requires analysis of how the very culture and mental approach underlying these forms of communication affect the ability to sustain critical thinking: a vacuous consumerism, and individualized engagement with the PC, are far from the forms of collective action classically associated with revolution. One of the most pervasive, and demobilizing, aspects of contemporary society is a radical, often narcissistic, individualism that rejects collective responsibility or engagement.

A political sociology of contemporary society also requires a critical analysis of democracy itself: several contributors assert, rightly, that democratic societies are resistant to revolution. Yet this critique of democracy may indulge the latter too much, since it does not adequately challenge one of the abiding illusions of contemporary liberalism, one that matched the historical illusions of communism, namely the belief that the system is 'irreversible', a permanent attainment. The democracy of Europe and North America is not only flawed, oligarchic by its very capitalist nature where money determines so much electoral practice, but may also be in the long run unstable. It is an illusion held as much by opponents as by proponents of capitalist democracy that the democratic system we have will last indefinitely: it may not. Here perhaps contemporary criticism misses something that would have been much more in the minds of critics a generation ago, namely the ability of our societies not to produce a radical challenge from the left, but to produce authoritarian movements from the right. That potential, stoked by nationalism, economic instability and aspirants to authoritarian power, has never gone away and may well return in a new, more strident, form. That possibility has been significantly enhanced by recent events, anti-migrant sentiment in many European countries, the authoritarian and unilateralist reflexes in the US since 11 September.

A second issue central to discussion of revolution today is that of the historic legacy of revolutions. Writers on revolution like to invoke Marx's observation about the weight of past generations lying on the minds of the present; it has been often stated that all revolutions invoke symbols and claims derived from the past, real or imagined. The revolutionaries of the twentieth century all looked, in some degree, backwards: Lenin and Trotsky to 1789, Mao and Ho to 1917, Castro to the 1890s, Khomeini to the seventh century. The present discussion of revolution seems, at first sight, not to do this. Political sociologists do look at earlier revolutions, but this is without practical import. Discussion of the possibility of change, particularly that linked to the anti-globalization movement, seems to be curiously ahistorical.

The price of this is, however, that not only is inspiration from the past muted but, equally, lessons are not learnt. Here something curious seems to have happened since the collapse of communism: the amnesia of neoliberal discussion, which consigns all that was associated with the communist experiment to the dustbin, seems to be replicated in the case of the radical movements of today. But to do this is questionable. In this latter respect, there are dangers, of an amnesia that is long on enthusiasm but short on responsibility and realism. For the fact is that the history of revolution in modern times is one not only of resistance, heroism and idealism, but also of terrible suffering and human disaster, of chaos and incompetence under the guise of revolutionary transformation, of the distortion of the finest ideals by corrupt and murderous leaders, and of the creation of societies that are far more oppressive and inefficient than those they seek to overthrow. The anti-globalization movement makes much of revolutionary internationalism: this is not some benign panacea, but a complex, often abused, transnational practice (Halliday 1999).

All of this entails confronting something that revolutionaries have always assumed but too often failed to discuss: the ethics of revolution. Denunciation of the given and invocations of an ideal other are not enough (Geras 1989). To grasp this involves a shift beyond the political sociology of revolutions, an academic pursuit that focuses in large measure on the incidence of revolutions, to an analysis of the consequences and longer-term records of revolutionary states. In the course of recent years, in writing my own work on revolutions, I have had reason to visit a number of cities that had served as the centers of world revolution and, if not revolution, anti-imperialist radicalism: Beijing, Havana, Tripoli, Tehran. These were the culminations of upheavals that had produced revolutionary regimes by some strange numerical consistency in, respectively, 1949, 1959, 1969, 1979. In every case, one could still discern the outlines of the original revolutionary project: a rejection of exploitation, foreign and domestic, a commitment to the transformation of society, internationalist support in rhetoric and deed for those resisting oppression elsewhere. But in the 1990s this had all faded: these were not the wave of the future. Whatever else, it could not be said that the initial revolutionary project was in good shape: few in these countries now believed in the ideological project that had initiated the revolution; corruption and inefficiency were widespread; there was a pervasive desire for change, towards a more open, liberal, society; the initial internationalist appeals had faded. Revolution had, in effect, become tired. It was indeed capitalism, not revolutionary socialism and third-worldism, which in the 1990s formed the global vision of the future.

This haphazard and impressionistic response has, however, to be compounded by a reflection on the overall legacy of the century of revolutions: neither form of amnesia − counterrevolutionary or revolutionary − is acceptable. Indeed, amnesia invites the repetition of another common saying with regard to revolutions, that those who ignore history are doomed to repeat it. Here perhaps is one of the most worrying aspects of the contemporary radical movement, be it in its national or internationalist forms: the failure to reflect, critically, on the past record of revolutionary movements. This pertains to models of alternative political and social orders. It pertains to the dangers inherent in any utopian, radicalized, mass movement that lacks clear forms of authority and decision-making. It also involves the espousal, spirited but ominous, of alternative social orders that could work only if imposed by an authoritarian state. A pertinent contemporary example is that of radical environmentalism: the program of de-industrialization, and restricted consumption and travel, entailed by such ideas could only be established, and maintained, by a coercive state. In the international sphere, the simple invocation of solidarity may too often conceal interests of power, and manipulation. In the days of authoritarian Communist Parties, but equally in that of national and communal movements today, unconditional solidarity with repressive organizations may be at odds with any commitment to emancipatory values.

Such a critical reflection has to apply, too, to the individuals often invoked for contemporary purposes: Lenin was a visionary, but also a cruel, pompous bigot; Che was a man of heroism and solidarity, but his economic programs were a disaster and his austere romanticism at times led to cruelty; Mao freed a quarter of mankind from imperialism, but also repeatedly plunged his society into barbarous conflict and social experimentation; Khomeini overthrew the Shah, but his social and political program was reactionary and repressive. A similar pause in romanticization might be applicable to some of the supposed components of the anti-globalization front today: few might defend Saddam Hussein, Kim Jong-il or Ayatollah Khamenei, but there is perhaps too little questioning of the commitment to emancipatory values of the PKK in Turkey, Sendero Luminoso, the FARC in Colombia, the Chechen rebels, to name but some. The Zapatista movement has become for many an icon of hope: but, as contributors to this volume make clear, it is not always itself a model of democratic practice. More importantly, one has to ask if this is the most important experience in the Latin America of the 1990s to study: it is part of, but only one part of, a broader crisis of the authoritarian PRI regime that beset Mexico and resulted in the rise on the one hand of the PRD and on the other of the election of Fox in 2000. An open assessment of challenges to authoritarian, and neoliberal, policies in Latin America in the 1990s would also examine democratization in Brazil and Chile, and the experience of social movements, be they of women, workers or indigenous peoples, who engaged with reformist states.

This need for a critical retrospective on the historical legacy of revolutions is, however, linked to another, perhaps even more pressing, issue, one that pervades the pages of this book, namely the relation of revolution to liberal democracy as a whole. Several contributors point out that where liberal democracy is established revolution is off the agenda. But this reflection may be taken further to ask the question of whether, faced with the alternative, one or other outcome is preferable. The implication of much 'revolutionary' writing over the past century has been that liberal democracy is to be denounced, and those who engage with and in it are reformists, dupes, or, in older language, 'class traitors'. Such a view lives on, in some of the contributions to this book, as in parts of the left. Yet this contrast of reform with revolution is not some eternal polarity. It too needs to be set in historical context, and seen for what it is, a product of the particular context of the twentieth century, starting with the split between the moderate and revolutionary factions of the socialist movement in 1914. The costs of this division are evident enough, and it would be desirable, in the aftermath of the collapse of the revolutionary socialist models, to re-examine it (Therborn 1989).

Part of this re-examination would involve a questioning of the automatic antinomy of reform and revolution present in much contemporary and recent writing, and of the assumed contradictory relation of revolutionary ideas to those of another critical, and internationalist, trend produced by modernity: liberalism. This has immediate implications for the discussion in this book. In particular, it relates to an issue that is widely present in contemporary academic and political discussion, but that writers on revolution tend to avoid, namely the question of rights. The language of rights was long denounced by the left, and its revolutionary part, as a bourgeois myth, except where it was for tactical reasons deemed pertinent to use it, as with regard to workers' rights, or the right of nations to self-determination. The record of the revolutionary tradition, once it came to power, is a very mixed one: a strong commitment to certain social and economic rights, whose abolition by neoliberal policies many in the former Communist states regret; and a sustained, cruel and dogmatic denial of political rights, collective and individual. Yet the program of rights embodied in national, regional and international codes is, as much as any flamboyant radicalism, both a critique and a program that confronts the contemporary world. Faced with the record of the Communist tradition on rights on the one hand, and the aspirations of liberalism on the other, this disdain for rights, and the related adherence to a denunciation of reformism and liberalism, should be questioned. Invocations of a romanticized 1968, of the nicer cases of armed struggle, or of Seattle may be fine for mobilization: they are not a serious answer to the problems of the contemporary world.

It is here that theoretical reflection and world historical change may, in some measure, come together, as is the purpose of this book. That the existing system of power and wealth in the world is exploitative and cruel is undeniable. That there is widespread anger and will be more so in the future is equally so. But the question remains as to what is the best means, ethically and realistically, to deal with it. The assumption that revolution is inevitable is as questionable as the assumption that it is desirable. Indeed the very category of 'Revolution' with a capital 'R' may turn out to be a product of a particular phase of modernity, associated with the two centuries following the twin revolutions, political and ideological, of the late eighteenth century. What this debate rests on is the ability of radical critique to wrest the initiative within a world of growing inequality and rancor, and to fulfill the promise, in terms of economic distribution and the implementation of rights, which modernity has always propounded. The outcome of this is by no means certain, but it would be mistaken to assume that the more radical alternative is necessarily preferable.

Bibliography

Aarts, P. (1992) 'Democracy, oil and the Gulf War', *Third World Quarterly* 13 (3): 525–38.

Aarts, P., G. Eisenloeffel, and A.J. Termeulen (1991) 'Oil, money, and participation: Kuwait's *Sonderweg* as a rentier state', *Orient* 32 (2): 205–16.

Abuza, Z. (1996) 'International relations theory and Vietnam', *Contemporary Southeast Asia* 17 (4): 406–19.

Ahmed, R. (1999) *Taliban: Islam, Oil and the New Great Game in Central Asia*, London: I.B. Taurus.

Alarcon Glasimovich, W. (1992) 'La democracia en la mentalidad y prácticas populares', in W. Alarcón et al., *¿De qué democracia hablamos?* Lima: DESCO, pp. 9–47.

Albrow, M. (1996) *The Global Age: State and Society Beyond Modernity*, Cambridge: Polity.

Allen, P. and E. Ensler (1998) 'An activist love story', in R. Blau DuPlessis and A. Snitow (eds) *The Feminist Memoir Project: Voices From Women's Liberation*, New York: Three Rivers Press, pp. 413–25.

Al-Mughni, H. (1993) *Women in Kuwait: The Politics of Gender*, London: Saqi Books.

—— (2000) 'Women's movements and the autonomy of civil society in Kuwait', in R.L. Teske and M.A. Tétreault (eds) *Feminist Approaches to Social Movements, Community, and Power*, volume 1: *Conscious Acts and the Politics of Social Change*, Columbia: University of South Carolina Press, pp. 171–87.

Al-Naqeeb, K.H. (1990) *Society and State in the Gulf and Arab Peninsula: A Different Perspective*, trans. L.M. Kenny, London: Routledge.

Althusser, L. (1969) *For Marx*, trans. B. Brewster, London: Allen Lane.

Amin, S. (1990) *Maldevelopment: Anatomy of a Global Failure*, London: Zed Books.

Anderson, B. (1991) *Imagined Communities: Reflections on the Origin and Spread of Nationalism*, revised edition, London: Verso.

Anderson, L. (2000) 'Dynasts and nationalists: why monarchies survive', in J. Kostiner (ed.) *Middle East Monarchies: The Challenge of Modernity*, Boulder: Lynne Rienner, pp. 53–69.

Anderson, P. (1979) *Considerations on Western Marxism*, London: Verso.

────── (1980) *Arguments within English Marxism*, London: New Left Books.

────── (2000) 'Renewals', *New Left Review*, second series, 1 (January–February): 5–24.

Anderson, P. and P. Camiller (eds) (1994) *Mapping the West European Left*, London: Verso.

Anderson, S. and J. Cavanagh with T. Lee and the Institute for Policy Studies (2000) *Field Guide to the Global Economy*, New York: New Press.

Appadurai, A. (1986) 'Introduction: commodities and the politics of value', in A. Appadurai (ed.) *The Social Life of Things: Commodities in Cultural Perspective*, Cambridge: Cambridge University Press, pp. 3–63.

────── (1996) *Modernity at Large: Cultural Dimensions of Globalization*, Minneapolis: University of Minnesota Press.

Appiah, K.A. (1992) *In My Father's House: Africa in the Philosophy of Culture*, New York: Oxford University Press.

Arendt, H. (1965) *On Revolution*, London: Faber & Faber and New York: Viking.

Arrighi, G. (1994) *The Long Twentieth Century*, London: Verso.

Arrighi, G., T.K. Hopkins and I. Wallerstein (1989) 'The great rehearsal', in T. Boswell (ed.) *Revolution in the World-System*, Westport, Conn.: Greenwood, pp. 19–31.

Arrighi, G. and B. Silver (1999) *Chaos and Governance in the Modern World System*, Minneapolis: University of Minnesota Press.

Aya, R. (1979) 'Theories of revolution reconsidered: contrasting models of collective violence', *Theory and Society* 8: 39–99.

────── (1984) 'Popular intervention in revolutionary situations', in C. Bright and S. Harding (eds) *Statemaking and Social Movements: Essays in History and Theory*, Ann Arbor: University of Michigan Press, pp. 318–43.

Ayubi, N.N. (1995) *Over-stating the Arab State: Politics and Society in the Middle East*, London: I.B. Tauris.

Barnet, R.J. and R.E. Müller (1974) *Global Reach: The Power of the Multinational Corporations*, New York: Simon & Schuster.

Bartkus, V. (1999) *The Dynamic of Secession*, Cambridge: Cambridge University Press.

Basualdo, E. (2000) *Concentración y centralización del capital en la Argentina durante la década del noventa*, Buenos Aires: Universidad Nacional de Quilmes/FLACSO/IDEP.

Bates, M. (1996) *The Wars We Took to Vietnam: Culture, Conflict and Storytelling*, Berkeley: University of California Press.

Beblawi, H. (1990) 'The rentier state in the Arab world', in G. Luciani (ed.) *The Arab State*, Berkeley: University of California Press, pp. 85–98.

Benjamin, W. (1969) [1940] *Illuminations*, New York: Schocken Books.

────── (1990) *Gesammelte Schriften*, volume I, part 3, Frankfurt: Suhrkamp.

Benot, Y. (2001) *Massacres coloniaux: 1944–1950. La IVè République et la mise au pas des colonies françaises*, Paris: La Découverte.

Best, S. and D. Kellner (1997) *The Postmodern Turn*, New York and London: Guilford Press and Routledge.

────── (2001) *The Postmodern Adventure*, New York and London: Guilford Press and Routledge.

BID (1998) *América Latina frente a la desigualdad*, Washington: Banco Interamericano de Desarrollo [Interamerican Development Bank].

Bideleux, R. (1985) *Communism and Development*, London: Methuen.

Blackburn, R. (1991) 'Fin de siècle: socialism after the crash', in R. Blackburn (ed.) *After the Fall: The Failure of Communism and the Future of Socialism*, London: Verso, pp. 173–249.

Blaustein, A., R.S. Clark and J.A. Sigler (1987) *Human Rights Sourcebook*, New York: Paragon House.

Booth, J. and T. Walker (1993) *Understanding Central America*, second edition, Boulder: Westview Press.

Borgers, F. (2000) 'War of the flea, war of the swarm: reflections on the anti-globalization movement and its future', *Voice* (University of Massachusetts, Amherst) XIV (ii): 18–9.

Bornschier, V. (2001) 'Changing income inequality in the second half of the 20th century – preliminary findings and propositions for explanations', paper presented at the meetings of the International Studies Association, Chicago.

Boswell, T. and C. Chase-Dunn (2000) *The Spiral of Capitalism and Socialism: Toward A Global Democracy*, Boulder: Lynne Rienner.

Brandt, P. (1995) 'Ethnic passions: considerations on a fundamental problem of humanity and the humanities', in N. Sørensen (ed.) *European Identities: Cultural Diversity and Integration in Europe since 1700*, Odense: Odense University Press, pp. 189–201.

Braudel, F. (1984) *The Perspective of the World*, volume III: *Civilization and Capitalism, 15th–18th Century*, New York and London: Harper & Row and Collins.

Brecher, J. and T. Costello (1998) *Global Village or Global Pillage: Economic Reconstruction from the Bottom Up*, 2nd edn, Cambridge, Mass.: South End Press.

Brecher, J. with T. Costello and B. Smith (1999) *Global Village or Global Pillage? How People around the World are Challenging Corporate Globalization*, film made by the World Economy Project of the Washington-based Preamble Center.

Brecher, J., T. Costello and B. Smith (2000) 'Globalization from below', *The Nation*, 4 December: 19–22.

——— (2000a) *Globalization From Below*, Boston: South End Press.

Brennan, T. (1997) *At Home in the World: Cosmopolitanism Now*, Cambridge, Mass.: Harvard University Press.

Brenner, J. (1994) 'Internationalist labor communication by computer network: the United States, Mexico and Nafta', unpublished paper.

Bruhn, K. (1999) 'Antonio Gramsci and the *palabra verdadera*: the political discourse of Mexico's guerrilla forces', *Journal of Interamerican Studies and World Affairs* 41 (2): 29–55.

Budge, I. (1993) 'Direct democracy: setting appropriate terms of debate', in D. Held (ed.) *Prospects for Democracy: North, South, East, West*, Stanford: Stanford University Press, pp. 136–55.

Burbach, R. (1994) 'Roots of the postmodern rebellion in Chiapas', *New Left Review* 205: 113–24.

——— (2001) *Globalization and Postmodern Politics: From Zapatistas to High-Tech Robber Barons*, London: Pluto.

Burguete Cal y Mayor, A. (1987),' Chiapas: Cronología de un etnicidio reciente (Represión política a los indios 1974–1987)', unpublished manuscript, Academica Mexicana de Derechos Humanos, A.C.

Cardoso, F.H. and E. Faletto (1979) *Dependency and Development in Latin America*, trans. M.M. Urquidi, Berkeley: University of California Press.

Castañeda, J. (1993) *Utopia Unarmed: The Latin American Left After the Cold War*, New York: Vintage Books.

———— (1995) *The Mexican Shock*, New York: New Press.

Castells, M. (1997) *The Power of Identity*, volume 2 of *The Information Age: Economy, Society and Culture*, Cambridge: Polity.

CEPAL [Economic Commission for Latin America and the Caribbean] (1998) *Panorama social de América Latina*, Santiago de Chile: CEPAL.

Chaliand, G. (1977) *Revolution in the Third World: Myths and Prospects*, Hassocks: Harvester.

———— (1990) 'Historical precedents', in S. Schutz and R.O. Slater (eds) *Revolution and Political Change in the Third World*, Boulder: Lynne Rienner and Adamantine, pp. 19–28.

Chaudhry, K.A. (1997) *The Price of Wealth: Economies and Institutions in the Middle East*, Ithaca: Cornell University Press.

Chhachhi, A. and R. Pittin (eds) (1996) *Confronting State, Capital and Patriarchy: Women Organizing in the Process of Industrialization*, London: Macmillan.

Chossudovsky, M. (1998) 'Global poverty in the late 20th century', *Journal of International Affairs* 52 (1): 292–311.

Churchill, J. (1995) 'Mayan rebellion? Guatemala and Chiapas', *Small Wars and Insurgencies* 6 (3): 357–74.

Cleaver, H. (1994) 'The Chiapas uprising', *Studies in Political Economy* 44: 141–57.

Cobble, D. S. (ed.) (1993) *Women and Unions: Forging a Partnership*, Ithaca: ILR Press.

Cockburn, A., J. St. Clair and A. Sekula (2000) *Five Days that Shook the World: Seattle and Beyond*, London: Verso.

Cohn, N. (1990) *Pursuit of the Millennium: Revolutionary Millenarians and Mystical Anarchists of the Middle Ages*, revised edition, New York: Oxford.

Colburn, F. D. (1994) *The Vogue of Revolution in Poor Countries*, Princeton: Princeton University Press.

Collier, G. (1994) 'The new politics of exclusion: antecedents to the rebellion in Mexico', *Dialectical Anthropology* 19 (1): 1–44.

———— (2000) 'Zapatismo resurgent: land and autonomy in Chiapas', *NACLA: Report on the Americas* XXXIII (5) (March/April): 20–25, 47.

———— (2000a) 'Emergent identities in Chiapas, 1986–1993', paper prepared for the meetings of the Latin American Studies Association, Miami.

Collier, G. and E. Quaratiello (1999) [1994] *Basta! Land and the Zapatista Rebellion in Chiapas*, revised edition, Oakland: Food First Books.

Concheiro-Borquez, E. (1996) *El gran acuerdo: Gobierno y empresarios en la modernización salinista*, Mexico City: Ediciones Era.

Cooley, J. (1999) *Unholy Wars: Afghanistan, America, and International Terrorism*, London: Pluto Press.

Cornelius, W. A. (1975) *Politics and the Migrant Poor in Mexico City*, Stanford: Stanford University Press.

Corrigan, P. and D. Sayer (1985) *The Great Arch: English State Formation as Cultural Revolution*, Oxford: Blackwell.

Cox, R. and D. Skidmore-Hess (1999) *U.S. Politics and the Global Economy: Corporate Power, Conservative Shift*, Boulder: Lynne Rienner.

Crossan, J. D. (1998) *The Birth of Christianity: Discovering What Happened in the Years Immediately after the Execution of Jesus*, San Francisco: HarperCollins.

Crystal, J. (1990) *Oil and Politics in the Gulf: Rulers and Merchants in Kuwait and Qatar*, New York: Cambridge University Press.

Danaher, K. and R. Burbach (eds) (2000) *Globalize This! The Battle Against the World Trade Organization and Corporate Rule*, Monroe: Common Courage.

Dannecker, P. (2000) 'Collective action, organization building, and leadership: women workers in the garment sector in Bangladesh', *Gender and Development* 8 (3) (November): 31–8.

Darnton, R. (1989) 'What was revolutionary about the French Revolution?' *New York Review of Books* 35 (21–2): 3–6, 10.

Davis, M. (2001) *Late Victorian Holocausts: El Niño Famines and the Making of the Third World*, London: Verso.

Dawley, A. (1976) *Class and Community: The Industrial Revolution in Lynn*, Cambridge, Mass.: Harvard University Press.

de Janvry, A. (1981) *The Agrarian Question and Reformism in Latin America*, Baltimore: Johns Hopkins University Press.

De Landa, M. (1997) *A Thousand Years of Nonlinear History*, New York: Zone Books.

Denemark, R., J. Friedman, B. Gills and G. Modelski (2000) *World System History: The Social Science of Long-Term Change*, London: Routledge.

Diniz, E. (2000) 'A busca de um novo modelo econômico: padrões alternativos de articulação público–privado', *Revista de Sociologia e Politica* 14: 7–28.

Doniger, W. (2000) 'Can you spot the source? Harry Potter and the prisoner of Azkaban', *London Review of Books* 22 (4): 25–6.

Doremus, P., W. Seller, L. Pauly and S. Reich (1998) *The Myth of the Global Corporation*, Princeton: Princeton University Press.

Downing, J. (2000) [1984] *Radical Media*, second edition, London: Sage Press.

Drakakis-Smith, D. (1987) *The Third World City*, London: Methuen.

Draper, T. (1984) 'Falling dominoes', *Present History: On Nuclear War, Détente, and Other Controversies*, New York: Vintage, pp. 89–105.

Drew, J. (1999) 'Global communications in the post–industrial age: a study of the communications strategies of U.S. labor organizations', Ph.D. dissertation, Graduate School, University of Texas.

Du Bois, W.E.B. (1965) [1946] *The World and Africa*, New York: International Publishers.

Dunning, J. and K. Hamdani (eds) (1997) *The New Globalism and Developing Countries*, Tokyo: United Nations University Press.

Dyer-Witheford, N. (1999) *Cyber-Marx: Cycles and Circuits of Struggle in High-Technology Capitalism*, Urbana and Chicago: University of Illinois Press.

Echeverría, B. (1998) *Valor de uso y utopía*, Mexico: Siglo XXI Editores.

Einhorn, B. (1993) *Cinderella Goes to Market: Citizenship, Gender and Women's Movements in East Central Europe*, London: Verso.

Eisenstadt, S. (1999) *Fundamentalism, Sectarianism, and Revolution: The Jacobin Dimension of Modernity*, Cambridge: Cambridge University Press.

Elliott, G. (1998) *Perry Anderson: The Merciless Laboratory of History*, Minneapolis: University of Minnesota Press.

Elliott, L. and D. Atkinson (1998) *The Age of Insecurity*, London: Verso.

Emirbayer, M. (2000) 'Mechanisms of fantasy, mechanisms of passion: the role of emotions in political life', talk at the University of California, Santa Barbara, 17 May.

Emirbayer, M. and J. Goodwin (1996) 'Symbols, positions, objects: toward a new theory of revolutions and collective action', *History and Theory* 35 (3): 358–74.

Engels, F. (1980) [1894] 'Acerca de la cuestión social en Rusia', in K. Marx and F. Engels, *Escritos sobre Rusia*, volume II: *El porvenir de la comuna rural rusa*, Córdoba: Cuadernos de Pasado y Presente, pp. 85–93.

Epstein, B. (1988) 'The politics of prefigurative community: the non-violent direct action movement', in M. Davis and M. Sprinker (eds) *Reshaping the US Left: Popular Struggles in the 1980s*, London: Verso, pp. 63–92.

Escobar, A. and W. Harcourt (2002) 'Conversations towards feminist futures', in K.-K. Bhavnani, J. Foran and P. Kurian (eds) *Feminist Futures: Re-imagining Women, Culture and Development*, London: Zed Books.

Estay, J. (2001) 'El Acuerdo de Libre Comercio de las Américas (ALCA): La integración latinoamericana y los retos para una inserción internacional alternativa', at www.iade.org.ar/esp/pag/conjunto.html

Evans, P. (1995) *Embedded Autonomy: States and Industrial Transformation*, Princeton: Princeton University Press.

———— (1997) 'The eclipse of the state? reflections on stateness in an era of globalization', *World Politics* 50: 62–87.

———— (2000) 'Fighting marginalization with transnational networks: counter-hegemonic globalization', *Contemporary Sociology* 29 (1): 230–41.

EZLN (1994) 'Segunda declaración de la selva lacandona', EZLN communiqué of 10 June 1994.

———— (1996) 'First declaration of *La Realidad* against neoliberalism and for humanity', originally published in Spanish, *La Jornada*, 30 January 1996.

Ezrahi, Y. (1997) *Rubber Bullets: Power and Conscience in Modern Israel*, Berkeley: University of California Press.

Falk, R. (1999) *Predatory Globalization: A Critique*, Cambridge: Polity.

Fandy, M. (2000) 'Information technology, trust, and social change in the Arab world', *Middle East Journal* 54 (3): 378–94.

Fanon, F. (1959) *L'an cinq de la révolution algérienne*, Paris: Éditions Maspero.

———— (1961) *Les damnés de la terre*, Paris: Editions Maspero.

———— (1967) *For a Dying Colonialism*, New York: Grove Press.

Farhi, F. (1990) *States and Urban-Based Revolutions: Iran and Nicaragua*, Chicago: University of Chicago Press.

———— (2000) 'The third republic and the changing dynamics of post-revolutionary politics in Iran', paper presented to the meetings of the International Studies Association (March).

Fazio, H. (1997) *Mapa actual de la extrema riqueza en Chile*, Santiago: ARCIS/CENDA.

Foran, J. (1993) 'Theories of revolution revisited: toward a fourth generation?' *Sociological Theory* 11 (1) (March): 1–20.

———— (1997) 'The future of revolutions at the fin-de-siècle', *Third World Quarterly* 18 (5): 791–820.

———— (1997a) 'The comparative-historical sociology of Third World social revolutions: why a few succeed, why most fail', in J. Foran (ed.) *Theorizing Revolutions*, London: Routledge, pp. 227–67.

———— (ed.) (1997b) *Theorizing Revolutions*, London: Routledge.

———— (2001) 'Studying revolutions through the prism of race, gender, and class: notes toward a framework', *Race, Gender, Class* 8 (2): 117–41.

———— (2002) 'Alternatives to development: of love, dreams and revolution', in K.-K. Bhavnani, J. Foran and P. Kurian (eds) *Feminist Futures: Re-Imagining Women, Culture and Development*, London: Zed Books.

Franco, C. (1993) 'Visión de la democracia y crisis del régimen', *Nueva Sociedad* 128: 50–61.

Frantz, D. (2000) 'Turkey struggling for solutions to economic crisis', *Chicago Tribune* (5 December).

Fraser, N. (1997) *Justice Interruptus*, New York: Routledge.

Fredericks, H. (1994) 'North American NGO networking against NAFTA: the use of computer communications in cross-border coalition building', XVIIth International Congress of the Latin American Studies Association.

Friedman, J. (1994) *Cultural Identity and Global Process*, London: Sage.

———— (1998) 'Indigenes, cosmopolitans and the discreet charm of the bourgeoisie', *Grænser for Globalisering*, Copenhagen and Aarhus: Dansk Ethnografisk Forening, pp. 1–20.

Fromkin, D. (1989) *A Peace to End All Peace: The Fall of the Ottoman Empire and the Creation of the Modern Middle East*, New York: Avon Books.

Fuentes, C. (1996) *A New Time for Mexico*, trans. M.G. Castañeda and C. Fuentes, New York: Farrar, Strauss & Giroux.

Fukuyama, F. (1992) *The End of History and the Last Man*, New York: Free Press.

Furet, F. (1999) [1995] *The Passing of an Illusion: The Idea of Communism in the Twentieth Century*, trans. Deborah Furet, Chicago: University of Chicago Press.

Galeano, E. (1998) *Upside Down: A Primer for the Looking-Glass World*, New York: Metropolitan Books.

Gamson, W. (1975) *The Strategy of Social Protest*, Homewood: Dorsey.

Garton Ash, T. (1999) 'Ten years after', *New York Review of Books*, 18 November.

———— (2000) 'The last revolution', *New York Review of Books*, 16 November.

Gasiorowski, M. J. (1991) *U.S. Foreign Policy and the Shah: Building a Client State in Iran*, Ithaca: Cornell University Press.

Gatsiopoulos, G. (1997) 'The EPR: Mexico's "other" guerrillas', *NACLA Report on the Americas* 30 (4): 33.

Gause, F.G., III. (1994) *Oil Monarchies: Domestic and Security Challenges in the Arab Gulf States*, New York: Council on Foreign Relations.

———— (2000), 'The persistence of monarchy in the Arabian peninsula', in Joseph Kostiner (ed.) *Middle East Monarchies: The Challenge of Modernity*, Boulder: Lynne Rienner, pp. 167–86.

George, S. (2002) 'Another world is possible', *The Nation*, 18 February.

Geras, N. (1989) 'Our morals: the ethics of revolution', in *Socialist Register 1989*, London: Merlin Press, pp. 185–211.

———— (1998) *The Contract of Mutual Indifference: Political Philosophy after the Holocaust*, London: Verso.

Ghabra, S. (1997) 'Kuwait and the dynamics of socio-economic change', *The Middle East Journal* 15 (3) (Summer): 358–72.

Ghose, A. K. (2000) 'Trade liberalization, employment and growing inequality', *International Labour Review* 139 (3): 281–306.

Giddens, A. (1984) *The Constitution of Society: Outline of the Theory of Structuration*, Berkeley: University of California Press.

———— (1989) *Sociology*, Cambridge: Polity Press.

Gilbert, A. and J. Gugler (1992) *Cities, Poverty, and Development: Urbanization in the Third World*, second edition, Oxford: Oxford University Press.

Gills, B. (ed.) (2000) *Globalization of the Politics of Resistance*, New York: St. Martin's Press.

Gills, B. and J. Rocamora (1992) 'Low intensity democracy', *Third World Quarterly* 13 (3): 501–25.

Gills, B., J. Rocamora and R. Wilson (eds) (1993) *Low Intensity Democracy: Political Power in the New World Order*, London: Pluto.

Gilly, A. (1983) *The Mexican Revolution*, London: Verso.

——— (1998) 'Chiapas and the rebellion of the enchanted world', in D. Nugent (ed.) *Rural Revolt in Mexico: U.S. Intervention and the Domain of Subaltern Politics*, Durham, N.C.: Duke University Press, pp. 261–333.

Goldman, R. and S. Papson (1998) *Nike Culture*, Thousand Oaks, Calif.: Sage.

Goldstone, J. A. (1986) 'The English revolution: a structural-demographic approach', in J.A. Goldstone (ed.) *Revolutions: Theoretical, Comparative, and Historical Studies*, New York: Harcourt, Brace, Jovanovich, pp. 88–104.

——— (1991) *Revolution and Rebellion in the Early Modern World*, Berkeley and Los Angeles: University of California Press.

——— (1995) 'Predicting revolutions: why we could (and should) have foreseen the revolutions of 1989–1991 in the U.S.S.R. and Eastern Europe', in N.R. Keddie (ed.) *Debating Revolutions*, New York: New York University Press, pp. 39–64.

——— (2001) 'Toward a fourth generation of revolutionary theory', *Annual Review of Political Science* 4: 139–87.

Gómez-Peña, G. (1995) 'The subcomandante of performance', in E. Katzenberger (ed.) *First World, Ha, Ha, Ha! The Zapatista Challenge*, San Francisco: City Lights, pp. 89–96.

Gonzalez-Casanova, P (1998) 'La explotación global', *Casa de las Américas* 212: 6–18.

Goodwin, J. (1994) 'Toward a new sociology of revolutions', *Theory and Society* 23 (6) (December): 731–66.

——— (1997) 'State-centered approaches to social revolutions: strengths and limitations of a theoretical tradition', in J. Foran (ed.) *Theorizing Revolutions*, London: Routledge, pp. 11–37.

——— (1998) 'Is the age of revolution over?' paper presented at the meetings of the International Studies Association Meetings, Minneapolis (March).

——— (2001) 'Is the age of revolution over?' in M. Katz (ed.) *Revolution and International Relations: A Reader*, Washington, D.C.: Congressional Quarterly, pp. 272–83.

——— (2001a) *No Other Way Out: States and Revolutionary Movements, 1945–1991*, Cambridge: Cambridge University Press.

Goodwin, J. and A. Green (1999) 'Revolutions' in *The Encyclopedia of Violence, Peace, and Conflict*, volume 3, San Diego: Academic Press, pp. 241–5.

Goodwin, J., J.M. Jasper and F. Polletta (2000) 'The return of the repressed: the fall and rise of emotions in social movement theory', *Mobilization* 5 (1): 65–84.

Gott, R. (2000) *In the Shadow of the Liberator: The Impact of Hugo Chávez on Venezuela and Latin America*, London: Verso.

Gramsci, A. (1957) *The Modern Prince and Other Writings*, New York: International Publishers.

———— (1971) *Selections from the Prison Notebooks of Antonio Gramsci*, Q. Hoare and G. Nowell Smith (eds and trans.), New York: International Publishers.

Green, C. (1998) 'The Asian connection: the U.S.–Caribbean apparel circuit and the new model of industrial relations', *Latin American Research Review* 33 (3): 7–47.

Greider, W. (1997) *One World, Ready or Not: The Manic Logic of Global Capitalism*, New York: Simon & Schuster.

Guedes, A. (2000) 'Repensando a nacionalidade de empresas transnacionais', *Revista de Sociologia e Politica* 14: 51–60.

Guevara, E. (1970) 'Proyecciones sociales del Ejército Rebelde', in *Obras del Comandante Ernesto Ché Guevara*, volume II, Havana: Casa de las Américas, pp. 1–32.

———— (1985) [1960] *Guerrilla Warfare*, Lincoln: University of Nebraska Press.

Guha, R. (1988) [1982] 'On some aspects of the historiography of colonial India', in R. Guha and G.C. Spivak (eds) *Selected Subaltern Studies*, New York: Oxford University Press, pp. 37–44.

Guillén D. (ed.) (1995) *Chiapas: una modernidad inconclusa*, México D.F.: Instituto Mora.

Hahnel, R. (1999) *Panic Rules: Everything You Need to Know About the Global Economy*, Boston: South End Press.

Hall, S. (1991) 'Old and new identities, old and new ethnicities', in A. D. King (ed.) *Culture, Globalization and the World-System*, Basingstoke: Macmillan, pp. 41–69.

———— (1992) 'Introduction: identity in question', in S. Hall, D. Held and T. McGrew (eds) *Modernity and Its Futures*, Cambridge: Polity, pp. 274–316.

———— (1997) 'Old and new identities, old and new ethnicities', in A.D. King (ed.) *Culture, Globalization and the World-System: Contemporary Conditions for the Representation of Identity*, Minneapolis: University of Minnesota Press, pp. 41–69.

Halliday, F. (1999) *Revolution and World Politics: The Rise and Fall of the Sixth Great Power*, London and Durham, N.C.: Macmillan and Duke University Press.

———— (2000) *The World at 2000*, London: Palgrave.

———— (2000a) 'Reason and romance: the place of revolution in the world of E. H. Carr', in M. Cox (ed.), *E.H. Carr: A Critical Reappraisal*, London: Palgrave, pp. 258–79.

Handler, R. (1994) 'Is "identity" a useful cross-cultural concept?' in R.R. Gillis (ed.) *Commemorations: The Politics of National Identity*, Princeton: Princeton University Press, pp. 27–40.

Harris, R. (2000) [1970] *Death of a Revolutionary: Che Guevara's Last Mission*, revised edition, New York: Norton.

Hart, J. M. (1992) *El Mexico revolucionario: gestacio y proceso de la revolucion Mexicana*, Mexico, D.F.: Alianza Editorial.

Harvey, D. (1990) *The Condition of Postmodernity*, Oxford: Blackwell.

———— (2000) *Spaces of Hope*, Berkeley and Edinburgh: University of California Press and Edinburgh University Press.

Harvey, N. (1994) *Rebellion in Chiapas: Rural Reforms, Campesino Radicalism, and the Limits to Salinismo*, Transformation of Rural Mexico Series, number 5, San Diego: Center for U.S.–Mexican Studies.

———— (1998) *The Chiapas Rebellion: The Struggle for Land and Democracy*, Durham, N.C.: Duke University Press.

Hastings, S. and M. Coleman (1992) *Women Workers and Unions in Europe: An Analysis by Industrial Sector*, IDP Women/Working Paper 4, Geneva: International Labour Organisation.

Hauben, M. and Hauben, R. (1997) *Netizens: On the History and Impact of Usenet and the Internet*. Los Alamitos: IEEE Computer Society Press.

Hawken, P. (2000) 'Skeleton woman visits Seattle', in K. Danaher and R. Burbach (eds) *Globalize This! The Battle Against the World Trade Organization and Corporate Rule*, Monroe: Common Courage, pp. 14–34.

Hechter, M., T. Kuran, R. Collins, C. Tilly, E. Kiser, J. S. Coleman and A. Portes (1995) 'Symposium on prediction in the social sciences', *American Journal of Sociology* 100 (6) (May): 1520–1626.

Held, D., A. McGrew, D. Goldblatt and J. Perraton (1999) *Global Transformations: Politics, Economics and Culture*, Cambridge: Polity.

Herb, M. (1999) *All in the Family: Absolutism, Revolution, and Democracy in the Middle Eastern Monarchies*, Albany: SUNY Press.

Higonnet, P. (1998) *Goodness beyond Virtue: Jacobins during the French Revolution*, Cambridge, Mass.: Harvard University Press.

Hill, C. (1986) *The Collected Essays of Christopher Hill*, volume 3: *People and Ideas in Seventeenth-Century England*, Amherst: University of Massachusetts Press.

Hill, K.A. and J.E. Hughes (1998) *Cyberpolitics: Citizen Activism in the Age of the Internet*, Lanham: Rowman & Littlefield.

Hirst, P. and G.Thompson (2000) *Globalization in Question: The International Economy and the Possibilities of Governance*, Cambridge: Polity.

Hobsbawm, E. (1962) *The Age of Revolution, 1789–1848*, New York: New American Library.

—— (1986) 'Revolutions', in R. Porter and M. Teich (eds) *Revolution in History*, Cambridge: Cambridge University Press, pp. 5–46.

Holm, H.-H. and G. Sørensen (1995) *Whose World Order? Uneven Globalization and the End of the Cold War*, Boulder: Westview Press.

Holsti, K.J. (1992) 'Polyarchy in nineteenth-century Europe', in J. Rosenau and E.-O. Czempiel (eds) *Governing without Governance: Order and Change in World Politics*, Cambridge: Cambridge University Press, pp. 30–57.

Horkheimer, M. and T.W. Adorno (1997) *Dialectic of Enlightenment*, New York: Continuum.

Hunter, S.T. (1986) 'The Gulf economic crisis and its social and political consequences', *Middle East Journal* 40 (4): 593–613.

Huntington, S.P. (1968) *Political Order in Changing Societies*, New Haven: Yale University Press.

Iran Bulletin [London]. Various issues.

Irish-Bramble, K. (2000) 'Predicting revolutions', M.A. thesis, New York University.

Jackson, R. (1990) *Quasi-states: Sovereignty, International Relations and the Third World*, Cambridge: Cambridge University Press.

Johnston, J. (2000) 'Pedagogical guerrillas, armed democrats, and revolutionary counterpublics: examining paradox in the Zapatista uprising in Chiapas Mexico', *Theory and Society* 29 (4): 463–505.

Joseph, G. and D. Nugent (1994) *Everyday Forms of State Formation: Revolution and the Negotiation of Rule in Modern Mexico*, Durham, N.C.: Duke University Press.

Kagan, R. (2000) 'The centrality of the United States', in M. F. Plattner and A. Smolar (eds) *Globalization, Power, and Democracy*, Baltimore: Johns Hopkins

University Press, pp. 97–113.

Kagarlitsky, B. (2000) 'The lessons of Prague', *International Socialism* 89: 49–58.

Kampwirth, K. (2002) *Women and Guerrilla Movements: Nicaragua, El Salvador, Chiapas, Cuba*, University Park: Penn State University Press.

Katz, F. (1981) *The Secret War in Mexico: Europe, the United States, and the Mexican Revolution*, Chicago: University of Chicago Press.

Katz, M.N. (1999) *Reflections on Revolutions*, London: Macmillan.

Katzenberger, E. (ed.) (1995) *First World, Ha Ha Ha! The Zapatista Challenge*, San Francisco: City Lights.

Katzman, K. (2000) 'Congressional Research Service: issues for US policy, 2000', Washington: Congressional Research Service.

Kechichian, J. (2000) 'The throne in the sultanate of Oman', in Joseph Kostiner (ed.) *Middle East Monarchies: The Challenge of Modernity*, Boulder: Lynne Rienner, pp. 187–211.

Keck, M.E. and K. Sikkink (1998) *Activists Beyond Borders: Advocacy Networks in International Politics*, Ithaca: Cornell University Press.

Keddie, N.R. (1995) (ed.) *Debating Revolutions*, New York: New York University Press.

——— (1995a) 'Can revolutions be predicted; can their causes be understood?', in N.R. Keddie (ed.) *Debating Revolutions*, New York: New York University Press, pp. 3–26.

Kellner, D. (1984) *Herbert Marcuse and the Crisis of Marxism*, Berkeley: University of California Press.

——— (1995) 'Intellectuals and new technologies', *Media, Culture and Society* 17: 427–48.

——— (1997) 'Intellectuals, the new public spheres, and technopolitics', *New Political Science* 41–42 (Fall): 169–88.

——— (1998) 'Multiple literacies and critical pedagogy in a multicultural society', *Educational Theory* 48 (1): 103–22.

——— (2000) 'New technologies/new literacies: reconstructing education for the new millennium', *Teaching Education* 11 (3): 245–65.

——— (2001) *Grand Theft 2000*, Lanham: Rowman & Littlefield.

Kimmel, M. (1988) *Absolutism and its Discontents: State and Society in Seventeenth Century France and England*, New York: Transaction Books.

——— (1990) *Revolution: A Sociological Interpretation*, Philadelphia: Temple University Press.

Konrad, G. and I. Szelenyi (1979) *The Intellectuals on the Road to Class Power*, New York: Harcourt Brace Jovanovich.

Kornai, J. (1992) *The Socialist System*, Princeton: Princeton University Press.

Kostiner, J. (ed.) (2000) *Middle East Monarchies: The Challenge of Modernity*, Boulder: Lynne Rienner.

Kuran, T. (1995) 'Why revolutions are better understood than predicted: the essential role of preference falsification', in N.R. Keddie (ed.) *Debating Revolutions*, New York: New York University Press, pp. 27–35.

Laclau, E. (ed.) (1994) *The Making of Political Identities*, London: Verso.

——— (2002) *The Populist Reason*, London: Verso.

Laclau, E. and C. Mouffe (1985) *Hegemony and Socialist Strategy: Towards a Radical Democratic Politics*, London: Verso.

Lagos, M. (1997) 'Actitudes económicas y democracia en Latinoamérica', *Este País* (January): 2–9.

Lake, A. (1993) *From Containment to Enlargement*, Washington: Johns Hopkins University School of Advanced International Studies.

Larbaud, V. (1983) 'Ode', in M. Décaudin (ed.) *Anthologie de la poésie française du XXe. siècle*, Paris: Gallimard, pp. 196–7.

Lasch, S. and J. Urry (1987) *The End of Organized Capitalism*, Madison: University of Wisconsin Press.

Legorreta Díaz, M. (1998) *Religión, Política y Guerrilla en Las Cañadas de la Selva Lacandona*, Mexico City: Cal y Arena.

Lemann, N. (2001) 'The quiet man: Dick Cheney's direct rise to unprecedented power', *New Yorker*, 7 May: 56–71.

Lenin, V.I. (1931) [1917] *The State and Revolution*, Moscow: International Publishers.

——— (1997) [1916] *Imperialism, The Highest Stage of Capitalism: A Popular Outline*, New York: International Publishers.

Liljeström, R., E. Lindskog, N. Van Ang and V. Xuan Tinh (1998) *Profit and Poverty in Rural Vietnam: Winners and Losers of a Dismantled Revolution*, Richmond: Curzon.

Lipset, S. (1960) *Political Man: The Social Bases of Politics*, Garden City: Doubleday.

——— (1996) *American Exceptionalism: A Double-Edged Sword*, New York: Norton.

Lipton, M. (1977) *Why Poor People Stay Poor: A Study of Urban Bias in World Development*, London: Temple Smith.

Lloyd, J, and L. Pérez Rosales. (eds) (1995) *Paisajes Rebeldes: Una larga noche de rebelión indígena*, Mexico City: Universidad Iberoamericano.

Longva, A.N. (1997) *Walls Built on Sand: Migration, Exclusion, and Society in Kuwait*, Boulder: Westview.

López-Maya, M. and L. Lander (2000) 'Refounding the republic: the political project of *Chavismo*', *NACLA Report on the Americas* XXIII (6): 22–8.

Luke, T. W. (1985), 'Dependent development and the OPEC states: state formation in Saudi Arabia and Iran under the international energy regime', *Studies in Comparative International Development* 20 (1): 31–54.

Luxemburg, R. (1968) [1912] *The Accumulation of Capital*, New York: Monthly Review Press.

Macedo-Cintra, M. (1999) 'A dinâmica do novo regime monetário-financeiro americano: una hipótese de interpretação', paper presented at the VIIIth Congress of Latin American and Caribbean Economics, Rio de Janeiro (September).

Maley, W. (ed.) (1998) *Fundamentalism Reborn? Afghanistan and the Taliban*, New York: New York University Press.

Mao Zedong (1967) *Report on an Investigation of the Peasant Movement in Hunan*, Beijing: Foreign Languages Press.

Marcos, Subcomandante (1995) *Shadows of Tender Fury: The Letters and Communiqués of Subcomandante Marcos and the Zapatista Army of National Liberation*, trans. F. Bardacke, L. López and the Watsonville, California, Human Rights Committee, New York: Monthly Review Press.

——— (1995a) 'Historia de Marcos y de los hombres de la noche', interview with C. Castillo and T. Brisac, 24 October 1994, in A. Gilly, Subcomandante Marcos and C. Ginzburg (eds) *Discusión sobre la historia*, Mexico: Taurus, pp. 131–42.

——— (1996) 'The future must be made by and for women: Marcos', in *Libertad*, the publication of the National Commission for Democracy in Mexico, 2 (March): 1–2.

——— (2001) 'Interview by Gabriel García Márquez and Robert Pombo', *New Left Review*, second series, 9 (May/June): 69–79.

Marcos et al. (1995) 'In truth anything can happen', Communiqué from the Clandestine Indigenous Revolutionary Committee High Command of the Zapatista National Liberation Army, 26 February 1994, in S. Marcos, *Shadows of Tender Fury: The Letters and Communiqués of Subcomandante Marcos and the Zapatista Army of National Liberation*, New York: Monthly Review Press, pp. 150–3.

Marsden, P. (1999) *The Taliban: War, Religion and the New World Order in Afghanistan*, London: Zed Books.

Martens, M.H. and S. Mitter (eds) (1994) *Women in Trade Unions: Organizing the Unorganized*, Geneva: ILO.

Martin, J. (1992) 'When the people were strong and united: stories of the past and the transformation of politics in a Mexican community', in C. Nordstrom and J. Martin (eds) *The Paths to Domination, Resistance, and Terror*, Berkeley: University of California, pp. 177–89.

Marx, K. (1972) [1852] 'The eighteenth Brumaire of Louis Bonaparte', in R.C. Tucker (ed.) *The Marx–Engels Reader*, New York: Norton, pp. 436–525.

——— (1978) [1845] 'Theses on Feuerbach', in R. Tucker (ed.) *The Marx–Engels Reader*, second edition, New York: Norton, pp. 145–7.

Marx, K. and F. Engels (1978a) [1848] 'Manifesto of the Communist Party', in R. Tucker (ed.) *The Marx–Engels Reader*, second edition, New York: Norton, pp. 473–500.

Mathews, G. (2000) *Global Culture/Individual Identity: Searching for Home in the Cultural Supermarket*, London: Routledge.

Matinuddin, K. (1999) *The Taliban Phenomenon: Afghanistan 1994–1997*, Karachi: Oxford University Press.

McAdam, D., S. Tarrow and C. Tilly (1997) 'Towards an integrated perspective on social movements and revolution', in M. Lichbach and A. Zuckerman (eds) *Comparative Politics: Rationality, Culture, and Structure*, Cambridge: Cambridge University Press, pp. 142–73.

——— (2001) *Dynamics of Contention*, Cambridge: Cambridge University Press.

McAuley, C. (1997) 'Race and the process of the American revolutions', in J. Foran (ed.) *Theorizing Revolutions*, London: Routledge, pp. 168–202.

McCaughan, E. J. (1997) *Reinventing Revolution: The Renovation of the Left Discourse in Cuba and Mexico*, Boulder: Westview.

McClintock, C. (1998) *Revolutionary Movements in Latin America: El Salvador's FMLN and Peru's Shining Path*, Washington: United States Institute of Peace Press.

McDaniel, T. (1991) *Autocracy, Modernization, and Revolution in Russia and Iran*, Princeton: Princeton University Press.

McKay, G. (1996) *Senseless Acts of Beauty: Cultures of Resistance*, London: Verso.

McMichael, P. (1990) 'Incorporating comparison within a world-historical perspective: an alternative comparative method', *American Sociological Review* 55 (3): 385–97.

——— (2000) *Development and Social Change: A Global Perspective*, second edition, Thousand Oaks, Calif.: Pine Forge.

McWilliams, M. (1995) 'Struggling for peace and justice: reflections on women's activism in Northern Ireland', *Journal of Women's History* 6 (4) and 7 (1) (Winter/Spring): 13–39.

Meintjes, S. (1998) 'Gender, nationalism and transformation: difference and commonality in South Africa's past and present', in R. Wilford and R.L. Miller (eds)

Women, Ethnicity and Nationalism: The Politics of Transition, London: Routledge, pp. 62–86.

Meyer, A. (1965) *The Soviet Political System*, New York: Random House.

Midlarsky, M., and K. Roberts (1986) 'Inequality, the state, and revolution in Central America', in M. Midlarsky (ed.) *Inequality and Contemporary Revolutions*, Denver: University of Colorado Press, pp. 11–33.

Migdal, J. (1988) *Strong States and Weak Societies: State–Society Relations and State Capabilities in the Third World*, Princeton: Princeton University Press.

Milanovic, B. (1999) 'True world income distribution 1988 and 1993: first calculations based on household surveys alone', Washington, D.C.: World Bank.

Mills, C. (1962) *The Marxists*, New York: Dell.

Milward, A. (1992) *The European Rescue of the Nation-State*, London: Routledge.

Mmembe, A. and J. Roitman (1996) 'Figures of the subject in times of crisis', in P. Yaeger (ed.) *The Geography of Identity*, Ann Arbor: University of Michigan Press, pp. 153–86.

Moaddel, M. (1993) *Class, Politics, and Ideology in the Iranian Revolution*, New York: Columbia University Press.

Moghadam, V. M. (1993) *Modernizing Women: Gender and Social Change in the Middle East*, Boulder: Lynne Rienner.

——— (ed.) (1993a) *Democratic Reform and the Position of Women in Transitional Economies*, Oxford: Clarendon Press.

——— (1997) 'Gender and revolutions', in J. Foran (ed.) *Theorizing Revolutions*, New York: Routledge, pp. 137–67.

——— (1999) 'Gender and the global economy', in M. Marx Ferree, J. Lorber and B.B. Hess (eds), *Revisioning Gender*, Thousand Oaks, Calif.: Sage, pp. 128–60.

——— (1999a) 'Revolution, religion, and gender politics: Iran and Afghanistan compared', *Journal of Women's History* 10 (4) (Winter): 172–95.

——— (1999b) 'The student protests and the social movement for reform in Iran', *Journal of Iranian Research and Analysis* 15 (2) (November): 97–105.

——— (2000) 'Transnational feminist networks: collective action in an era of globalization', *International Sociology* 15 (1) (March): 57–85.

——— (2001) 'For gender justice and economic justice: transnational feminism and global inequalities', paper prepared for the meetings of the International Studies Association, Chicago.

——— (2002) 'Patriarchy, the Taleban and the politics of public space in Afghanistan', *Women's Studies International Forum* 25 (1) (Spring): 19–31.

Moghissi, H. (1999) *Feminism and Islamic Fundamentalism: The Limits of Postmodern Analysis*, London: Zed Books.

Møller, B. (1997) *The United States and the 'New World Order': Part of the Problem or Part of the Solution*, COPRI Working Paper 12, Copenhagen: Copenhagen Peace Research Centre.

Moody, K. (1997) *Workers in a Lean World: Unions in the International Economy*, London: Verso.

——— (1998) *An Injury to No One*, London: Verso.

Moore, B. (1978) *Injustice: The Social Basis of Obedience and Revolt*, White Plains: M.E. Sharpe.

Motyl, A. (1991), *Revolutions, Nations, Empires: Conceptual Limits and Theoretical Possibilities*, New York: Columbia University Press.

Munson, H., Jr. (1988) *Islam and Revolution in the Middle* East, New Haven: Yale University Press.

Murphy, C.N. (2001) 'Political consequences of the new inequality', *International Studies Quarterly* 45 (3) (September): 347–56.

Nederveen Pieterse, J. (2000) 'Globalization north and south; representations of uneven development and interaction of modernities', *Theory, Culture and Society* 17 (1): 129–37.

Nelson, J. (1979) *Access to Power: Politics and the Urban Poor in Developing Nations*, Princeton: Princeton University Press.

Nodia, G. (2000) 'The end of revolution?' *Journal of Democracy* 11 (1) (January): 164–71.

O'Brien, R. (1991) *Global Financial Integration: The End of Geography*, London: Pinter.

Offe, K. (1985) *Disorganized Capital: Contemporary Transformations of Work and Politics*, Cambridge, Mass.: MIT Press.

Ohmae, K. (1990) *The Borderless World*, New York: Collins.

Oppenheimer, M. (1971) 'The limitations of socialism: some sociological observations on participatory democracy', in C.G. Benello and D. Roussopoulos (eds) *The Case for Participatory Democracy*, New York: Grossman, pp. 270–82.

Oren, I. (1996) 'The subjectivity of the "democratic" peace: changing U.S. perceptions of imperial Germany', in M. Brown, S. Lynn-Jones and S. Miller (eds) *Debating the Democratic Peace*, Cambridge, Mass.: MIT Press.

Paidar, P. (1995) *Women and the Political Process in Twentieth Century Iran*, Cambridge: Cambridge University Press.

Paige, J.M. (1975) *Agrarian Revolution*, New York: Free Press.

Panitch, L. (2000) 'The new imperial state', *New Left Review*, second series, 2 (March/April): 6–18.

Parker, N. (1999) *Revolutions and History: An Essay in Interpretation*, Cambridge: Polity.

Parsa, M. (1985) 'Economic development and political transformation: a comparative analysis of the United States, Russia, Nicaragua, and Iran', *Theory and Society* 14: 623–75.

——— (1989) *Social Origins of the Iranian Revolution*, New Brunswick: Rutgers University Press.

——— (2000) *States, Ideologies, and Social Revolutions: A Comparative analysis of Iran, Nicaragua, and the Philippines*, Cambridge: Cambridge University Press.

Peil, M. and P.O. Sada (1984) *African Urban Society*, New York: John Wiley.

Pérez, L.A. (1999) *On Becoming Cuban: Identity, Nationality and Culture*, Chapel Hill: University of North Carolina Press.

Perlez, J. (2001) 'Bush's team's counsel is divided on foreign policy', *New York Times*, 27 March.

Petras, J. and M. Morley (1990) *U.S. Hegemony Under Siege: Class, Politics and Development in Latin America*, London: Verso.

Piven, F.F. and R. Cloward (1977) *Poor People's Movements: Why They Succeed, How They Fail*, New York: Vintage.

Plesu, A. (1997) 'Towards a European patriotism: obstacles as seen from the East', *East European Constitutional Review* 6 (2 and 3): 53–6.

Polakoff, E. (1996) 'Gender and the Latin American left', *Z Magazine* (November): 20–3.

Polanyi, K. (1957) [1944] *The Great Transformation: The Political and Economic Origins of Our Time*, Boston: Beacon Press.

Ponce de Leon, J. (ed.) (2001) *Our Word is Our Weapon: Selected Writings of Sub-comandante Insurgente Marcos*, New York: Seven Seas Press.

Portes, A. and J. Walton (1976) *Urban Latin America: The Political Condition From Above and Below*, Austin: University of Texas Press.

Poster, M. (1975) *Existential Marxism in Postwar France: From Sartre to Althusser*, Princeton: Princeton University Press.

———— (1995) 'Cyberdemocracy: Internet and the public sphere', www.hnet. uci.edu/mposter/writings/democ.html.

Poulantzas, N. (1978) *State, Power, Socialism*, trans. P. Camiller, London: Verso.

Poulin, R. and P. Salama (eds) (1998) *L'insoutenable misère du monde. Économie et sociologie de la pauvreté*, Quebec: Editions Vents d'Ouest.

Poya, M. (1999) *Women, Work and Islamism: Ideology and Resistance in Iran*, London: Zed Books.

Przeworski, A. (1991) *Democracy and the Market: Political and Economic Reforms in Eastern Europe and Latin America*, Cambridge: Cambridge University Press.

Rabasa, J. (1997) 'Of Zapatismo: reflections on the folkloric and the impossible in a subaltern insurrection', in L. Lowe and D. Lloyd (eds) *The Politics of Culture in the Shadow of Capital*, Durham, N.C. and London: Duke University Press, pp. 399–431.

Radu, M. (2000) 'The perilous appeasement of guerrillas', *Orbis* 44 (3): 362–79.

Rashid, A. (2000) *Taliban: Militant Islam, Oil, and Fundamentalism in Central Asia*, New Haven: Yale University Press.

Reddy, W. (1986) 'The structure of a cultural crisis: thinking about cloth in France before and after the revolution', in A. Appadurai (ed.) *The Social Life of Things: Commodities in Cultural Perspective*, Cambridge: Cambridge University Press, pp. 261–84.

Reed, J.-P. (2000) 'Revolutionary subjectivity: eventful, cultural, and ideological explanations in the Nicaraguan revolution', Ph.D. dissertation, Department of Sociology, University of California, Santa Barbara.

Riasanovsky, N.V. (1984) *A History of Russia*, New York: Oxford University Press.

Rist, G. (1997) *The History of Development: From Western Origins to Global Faith*, trans. P. Camiller, London: Zed Books.

Roberts, B.R. (1995) *The Making of Citizens: Cities of Peasants Revisited*, London: Arnold.

Robertson, R. (1991) 'Social theory, cultural relativity and the problem of globality', in A.D. King (ed.) *Culture, Globalization and the World-System*, London: Macmillan, pp. 69–90.

———— (1992) *Globalization: Social Theory and Global Culture*, London: Sage.

———— (1995) 'Glocalization: time–space and homogeneity–heterogeneity', in M. Featherstone, S. Lash and R. Robertson (eds) *Global Modernities*, London: Sage, pp. 25–44.

Robinson, W.I. (1996) *Promoting Polyarchy: Globalization, US Intervention, and Hegemony*, Cambridge: Cambridge University Press.

Rodriguez-Reina, J. (1993) 'La "privatización" de la política', *Expansión* 619 ((July): 54–79.

Ronfeldt, D. et al. (1998) *The Zapatista 'Social Netwar' in Mexico*, Santa Monica: Rand.

Roseberry, W. (1994) 'Hegemony and the language of contention', in G. Joseph and D. Nugent (eds) *Everyday Forms of State Formation: Revolution and the*

Negotiation of Rule in Modern Mexico, Durham, N.C.: Duke University Press, pp. 355–66.

Rosenau, J. (1980) 'Pre-theories and theories of foreign policy', in J. Rosenau (ed.) *The Scientific Study of Foreign Policy: Essays on the Analysis of World Politics*, revised edition, New York: Frances Pinter and Nichols, pp. 115–69.

Rosenberg, J. (1994) *The Empire of Civil Society: A Critique of the Realist Theory of International Relations*, London: Verso.

———— (2001) *The Follies of Globalisation Theory*, London: Verso.

Ross, J. (2000) 'Voters reject PRI', *Latinamerica Press*, 10 July: 3.

———— (2000a) 'Are the Zapatistas history?' *Latinamerica Press*, November: 2.

Ross, M.H. (1975) *Grass Roots in an African City: Political Behavior in Nairobi*, Cambridge, Mass.: MIT Press.

Roux, R. (1999) 'Historia y comunidad estatal en México', *Viento del Sur* 15 (July): 47–56.

Roy, O. (1994) *The Failure of Political Islam*, London: Verso.

———— (1999) 'Changing patterns among radical Islamist movements', *Brown Journal of World Affairs* 6 (1) (Winter/Spring): 109–20.

Rueschemeyer, D. and P. Evans (1985) 'The state and economic transformation: toward an analysis of the conditions underlying effective state intervention', in P. Evans, D. Rueschemeyer and T. Skocpol (eds), *Bringing the State Back In*, Cambridge: Cambridge University Press, pp. 44–77.

Ruiz, H. (1980) 'La montaña era como un inmenso crisol donde se forjaban los mejores cuadros', *Nicaráuac* 1: 8–24.

Ruiz, R.E. (1980) *The Great Rebellion: Mexico, 1905–1924*, New York: Norton.

Ryan, H. B. (1998) *The Fall of Che Guevara: A Story of Soldiers, Spies, and Diplomats*, New York: Oxford University Press.

Saghafi, M. (1999) 'The temptation of democracy: a conversation with Morad Saghafi', *Middle East Report* 29 (3): 47–51.

Said, E. (1993) *Culture and Imperialism*, London: Chatto & Windus.

Salvatori, D. (2001) *Dizionario delle Canzone Italiane*, Rome: Elle U Multimedia.

Sanasarian, E. (1983) 'An analysis of Fida'i and Mujahidin positions on women's rights', in G. Neshat (ed.) *Women and Revolution in Iran*, Boulder: Westview, pp. 97–108.

Scherrer, C. (1997) *Central Africa: Conflict Impact Assessment and Policy Options*, COPRI Working Paper 25, Copenhagen: Copenhagen Peace Research Centre.

Schiller, D. (1999) *Digital Capitalism*, Cambridge, Mass.: MIT Press.

Schultz, D. (1997) 'Between a rock and a hard place: The United States, Mexico, and the challenge of national security', *Low Intensity Conflict and Law Enforcement* 6 (3): 1–40.

Schumpeter, J. (1950) *Capitalism, Socialism, and Democracy*, New York: Harper & Row.

Scott, J. C. (1990) *Domination and the Arts of Resistance – Hidden Transcripts*, New Haven: Yale University Press.

———— (1998) *Seeing Like a State: How Certain Schemes to Improve the Human Condition Have Failed*, New Haven: Yale University Press.

Selbin, E. (1997) 'Revolution in the real world: bringing agency back in', in J. Foran (ed.) *Theorizing Revolutions*, New York: Routledge, pp. 123–36.

———— (1997a) 'Magical revolutions: the future of revolution in the land of magical realism', paper presented at the 1997 meetings of the Latin American Studies Association, Guadalajara, Mexico.

—— (1998) 'Same as it ever was: the future of revolution at the end of the century', paper presented at the meetings of the International Studies Association, Minneapolis; a version also appeared in M. Katz (ed.), *Revolution and International Relations: A Reader*, Washington: Congressional Quarterly, 2001.

—— (1999) *Modern Latin American Revolutions*, second revised edition, Boulder: Westview.

Sen, A. (1981) *Poverty and Famines: An Essay on Entitlement and Deprivation*, Oxford: Clarendon Press.

Sen, G. and C. Grown (1987) *Development, Crises and Alternative Visions: Third World Women's Perspectives*, New York: Monthly Review Press.

Sewell, W. (1985) 'Ideologies and social revolutions: reflections on the French case', *Journal of Modern History* 57 (March): 57–85.

Shahidian, H. (1994) 'The Iranian left and the "woman question" in the revolution of 1978–79', *International Journal of Middle East Studies* 26 (2): 223–47.

Shayne, J.D. (2000) '"The revolution question:" feminism in Cuba, Chile, and El Salvador compared (1952–1999)', Ph.D. dissertation, Department of Sociology, University of California, Santa Barbara.

Simkins, J. (2000) 'Investors will need some convincing', Economic Survey of Greece, *Financial Times*, 13 December.

Singer, D. (1999) *Whose Millennium? Theirs or Ours?* New York: Monthly Review Press.

Sklair, L. (1995) *Sociology of the Global System*, second edition, Baltimore: Johns Hopkins University Press.

—— (2001) *The Transnational Capitalist Class*, Oxford: Blackwell.

Skocpol, T. (1979) *States and Social Revolutions: A Comparative Analysis of France, Russia, and China*, Cambridge: Cambridge University Press.

—— (1982) 'Rentier state and Shi'i Islam in the Iranian revolution', *Theory and Society* 11 (3): 265–83.

—— (ed.) (1994) *Social Revolutions in the Modern World*, Cambridge: Cambridge University Press.

Smith, A. (1995) *Nations and Nationalism in a Global Era*, Cambridge: Polity.

Smith, C. A. (ed.) (1990) *Guatemalan Indians and the State, 1540 to 1988*, Austin: University of Texas Press.

Smith, J., C. Chatfield and R. Pagnucco (eds) (1997) *Transnational Social Movements and Global Politics*, Syracuse: Syracuse University Press.

Smith, J.E. (1992) *George Bush's War*, New York: Henry Holt.

Smith, P.J. and E. Smythe (2000) 'Globalization, citizenship and technology: the MAI meets the internet', International Studies Association, Los Angeles (March).

—— (2001) 'Sleepless in Seattle: challenging the WTO in a globalizing world', paper presented to the International Studies Association, Chicago (February).

Snyder, R. (1998) 'Paths out of sultanistic regimes: combining structural and voluntarist perspectives', in H.E. Chehabi and J.J. Linz (eds) *Sultanistic Regimes*, Baltimore: Johns Hopkins University Press, pp. 49–81.

Snyder, R.S. (1999) 'The end of revolution?' *The Review of Politics* 61 (1) (Winter): 5–28.

Speed, S. and J. Collier (2000) 'Limiting indigenous autonomy in Chiapas, Mexico: the state government's use of human rights', *Human Rights Quarterly* 22: 877–905.

Spruyt, H. (1994) *The Sovereign State and Its Competitors: An Analysis of Systems Change*, Princeton: Princeton University Press.

Steinmetz, G. (1992) 'Reflections on the role of social narratives in working-class formation: narrative theory in the social sciences', *Social Science History* 16 (3): 489–515.

Streeten, P. (1997) 'Globalization and competitiveness: implications for development theory and practice', in L. Emmerij (ed.) *Economic and Social Development into the XXI Century*, Washington: Inter-American Development Bank and Johns Hopkins University Press, pp. 107–47.

Tarrow, S. (1994) *Power in Movement: Social Movements, Collective Action and Politics*, Cambridge: Cambridge University Press.

Taussig, M. T. (1980) *The Devil and Commodity Fetishism in South America*, Chapel Hill: University of North Carolina Press.

Taylor, C. (1992) *Multiculturalism and Politics of Recognition*, Princeton: Princeton University Press.

Taylor, P. J. (1996) *The Way the Modern World Works: World Hegemony to World Impasse*, Chichester and New York: John Wiley.

———— (1999) *Modernities: A Geohistorical Interpretation*, Minneapolis: University of Minnesota Press.

Tejera Gaona, H. (1996) 'Las causas del conflicto en Chiapas', in H. De Grammont and H. Tejera Gaona (eds) *La Sociedad Rural Frente Al Nuevo Milenio*, volume IV: *Los Nuevos Actores Sociales y Procesos Políticos en el Campo*, Mexico City: Plaza y Valdés, pp. 299–332.

Tétreault, M.A. (1991) 'Autonomy, necessity, and the small state: ruling Kuwait in the twentieth century', *International Organization* 45 (4) (Autumn): 565–91.

———— (1995) *The Kuwait Petroleum Corporation and the Economics of the New World Order*, Westport: Quorum Books.

———— (1999) 'Sex and violence: social reactions to economic restructuring in Kuwait', *International Feminist Journal of Politics* 1 (2) (September): 237–55.

———— (2000) *Stories of Democracy: Politics and Society in Contemporary Kuwait*, New York: Columbia University Press.

———— (2000a) 'The economics of national autonomy in the UAE', in J.A. Kechichian (ed.) *A Century in Thirty Years: Shaykh Zayed and the United Arab Emirates*, Washington: Middle East Policy Council, pp. 107–48.

———— (2000b) 'International relations', in D.J. Gerner (ed.) *Understanding the Contemporary Middle East*, Boulder: Lynne Rienner, pp. 129–60.

Tétreault, M. A. and H. al-Mughni (1995) 'Gender, citizenship, and nationalism in Kuwait', *British Journal of Middle Eastern Studies* 22 (1–2): 64–80.

Therborn, G. (1989) 'Revolution and reform: reflections on their linkages through the great French Revolution', in J. Böhlin et al., *Samhällsvetenskap, ekonomi, historia*, Göteborg: Daidalus.

———— (2000) 'Reconsidering revolution', *New Left Review*, second series, 2 (March/April): 148–53.

Thompson. E.P. (1966) [1963] *The Making of the English Working Class*, Reading: Addison-Wesley.

———— (1991) *Customs in Common*, London: Merlin Press.

Tilly, C. (1975) 'Reflections on the history of European state-making', in C. Tilly (ed.) *The Formation of National States in Western Europe*, Princeton: Princeton University Press, pp. 3–83.

—— (1985) 'War making and state making as organized crime', in P. Evans, D. Rueschemeyer and T. Skocpol (eds) *Bringing the State Back In*, New York: Cambridge University Press: 169–91.

—— (1990) *Coercion, Capital and European States, AD 990–1992*, Oxford: Blackwell.

—— (1993) *European Revolutions, 1492–1992*, Oxford: Blackwell.

Tilly, C., L. Tilly and R. Tilly (1975) *The Rebellious Century: 1830–1930*, London: Dent.

Tiruneh, A. (1993) *The Ethiopian Revolution 1974–87: A Transformation from an Aristocratic to a Totalitarian Autocracy*, Cambridge: Cambridge University Press.

Tocqueville, A. de (1990) [1840] *Democracy in America*, volume II, New York: Vintage.

Tohidi, N. (1994) 'Modernity, Islamization and women in Iran', in V.M. Moghadam (ed.) *Gender and National Identity: Women and Politics in Muslim Societies*, London: Zed Books, pp. 110–47.

Touraine, A. (1971) *The May Movement; Revolt and Reform: May 1968 – The Student Rebellion and Workers' Strikes – The Birth of a Social Movement*, trans. L.F.X. Mayhew, New York: Random House.

Trotsky, L. (1961) [1932] *The History of the Russian Revolution*, volume III, New York: Monad Press.

Tucker, L. (1994) 'Recovering the conjure woman: texts and contexts in Gloria Naylor's *Mama Day*', *African American Review* 28 (2): 173–83.

Ulam, A. (1973) *Stalin: The Man and His Era*, New York: Viking.

—— (1981) *Russia's Failed Revolutions: From the Decembrists to the Dissidents*, New York: Basic Books.

UNDP [United Nations Development Program] (1996) *Human Development Report 1996*, New York: Oxford University Press.

—— (1997) *Human Development Report 1997*, New York: Oxford University Press.

—— (1999) *Human Development Report 1999*, New York: Oxford University Press.

Vazquez Montalban, M. (2000) *Marcos: el hombre de los espejos*, Mexico City: Aguilar.

Verdery, K. (1996) *What was Socialism, and What Comes Next?* Princeton: Princeton University Press.

Vidal, J. (1997) *McLibel: Burger Culture on Trial*, London: Macmillan.

Vilas, C. (1995) 'Forward back: capitalist restructuring, the state and the working class in Latin America', in B. Magnus and S. Cullenberg (eds) *Whither Marxism? Global Crisis in International Perspective*, New York and London: Routledge, pp. 123–51.

—— (1997) 'Participation, inequality, and the whereabouts of democracy', in D. Chalmers, C. Vilas, K. Hite, and S. Martin (eds) *The New Politics of Inequality in Latin America*, Oxford: Oxford University Press, pp. 2–42.

—— (2000) 'Más allá del "Consenso de Washington"? Un enfoque desde la política de algunas propuestas del Banco Mundial sobre reforma institucional', *Reforma y Democracia. Revista del CLAD* 18: 25–76.

—— (2001) 'La sociología política latinoamericana y el "caso" Chávez: entre la sorpresa y el *dejá vu*', *Revista Venezolana de Economía y Ciencias Sociales* 7 (2): 129–45.

Vincent, J.-M. (2001) *Un autre Marx. Après les marxismes*, Paris: Editions Page Deux.

Viqueira, J. and W. Sonnleitner, coordinators (2000) *Democracia en tierras indígenas: Las elecciones en Los Altos de Chiapas (1991–1998)*, Mexico, D.F.: Centro de Investigaciones y Estudios Superiores en Antropología Social, El Colegio de México, and Instituto Federal Electoral.

von Laue, T. (1987) *The World Revolution of Westernization: The Twentieth Century in Global Perspective*, Oxford: Oxford University Press.

Wade, R. (2001) 'Showdown at the World Bank', *New Left Review*, second series, 7: 124–37.

Wade, R. and F. Veneroso (1998) 'The Asian crisis: the high debt model versus the Wall Street–Treasury–IMF complex', *New Left Review* 228: 3–23.

Waites, B. (1999) *Europe and the Third World: From Colonisation to Decolonisation, c. 1500–1998*, London: Macmillan.

Walker, A. (1997) *Anything We Love Can Be Saved: A Writer's Activism*, New York: Random House.

Wallerstein, I. (1979) *The Capitalist World Economy*, Cambridge: Cambridge University Press.

———— (1984) *The Politics of the World Economy: The States, the Movements and the Civilisations*, Cambridge: Cambridge University Press.

———— (1991) *Geopolitics and Geoculture: Essays on the Changing World System*, Cambridge: Polity.

———— (2000) 'Globalization or the age of transition? A long-term view of the trajectory of the world-system', *International Sociology* 15 (2): 249–65.

Walton, J. (1984) *Reluctant Rebels: Comparative Studies of Revolution and Underdevelopment*. New York: Columbia University Press.

———— and M. Udayagiri (2000) 'From shantytowns to Seattles: globalization and counter movements', paper presented at the Conference on Political Contention in the Developing World, Harvard University (October).

Walzer, M. (1985) *Exodus and Revolution*, New York: Basic Books.

Ward, K. (ed.) (1990) *Women Workers and Global Restructuring*, Ithaca: ILR Press.

Waterman, P. (1990) 'Communicating labor internationalism: a review of relevant literature and resources', *Communications: European Journal of Communications* 15 (1/2): 85–103.

———— (1992) 'International labour communication by computer: the fifth international?' Working Paper Series 129, The Hague: Institute of Social Studies.

Weiner, T. (2000) 'Mexico's new leader swiftly seeks peace in Chiapas', *New York Times*, 4 December.

Weiss, L. (1997) 'Globalization and the myth of the powerless state', *New Left Review* 225: 3–27.

———— (1998) *The Myth of the Powerless State*, Ithaca: Cornell University Press.

Wheeler, D. (2000) 'New media, globalization and Kuwaiti national identity', *Middle East Journal* 54 (3): 432–44.

White, G. (1988) *Developmental States in East Asia*, London: Macmillan.

White, P. (2000) *Primitive Rebels or Revolutionary Modernizers? The Kurdish National Movement in Turkey*, London: Zed Books.

Wolf, E. (1969) *Peasant Wars of the Twentieth Century*, New York: Harper & Row.

———— (1997) *Europe and the People Without History*, Berkeley: University of California Press.

Womack, Jr., J. (1970) *Zapata and the Mexican Revolution*, New York: Vintage.

———— (1999) *Rebellion in Chiapas: An Historical Reader*, New York: New Press.

Wood, E. (2000) *Forging Democracy from Below: Insurgent Transitions in South Africa and El Salvador*, Cambridge: Cambridge University Press.

Wood, G.S. (1993) *The Radicalism of the American Revolution*, New York: Random House–Vintage.

World Bank (1997) *The State in a Changing World: World Development Report 1997*, New York: Oxford University Press.

Wright, E. (1997) *Class Counts: Comparative Studies in Class Analysis*, Cambridge: Cambridge University Press.

Wright, R. (2000) *The Last Great Revolution: Turmoil and Transformation in Iran*, New York: Knopf.

Yeganeh, N. (1982) 'Women's struggles in the Islamic Republic of Iran', in A. Tabari and N. Yeganeh (eds) *In the Shadow of Islam: The Women's Movement in Iran*, London: Zed Books, pp. 26–74.

Zapatistas Collective (1994) *Zapatistas: Documents of the New Mexican Revolution*, New York: Autonomedia.

Zibechi, R. (2000) 'The growth of the Uruguayan left', *NACLA Report on the Americas* XXXIII (4) (January–February): 1.

Zugman, K. (2001) 'Mexican awakening in postcolonial America: Zapatistas in urban spaces in Mexico City', Ph.D. dissertation, Department of Sociology, University of California, Santa Barbara.

Notes on Contributors

Ralph Armbruster-Sandoval is an assistant professor of Chicano studies at the University of California, Santa Barbara. He is a coordinating editor for *Latin American Perspectives* and a board member of Witness for Peace. He has been active in the global justice movement and has just completed a book manuscript entitled 'Globalization and Cross-Border Labor Organizing: The Anti-Sweatshop Movement and the Struggle for Social Justice'.

Kate Bruhn is an associate professor of political science at the University of California, Santa Barbara. She is the author of *Taking on Goliath: The Emergence of a New Left Party and the Struggle for Democracy in Mexico* (Pennsylvania State University, 1997) and co-author with Daniel C. Levy of *Mexico: The Struggle for Democratic Development* (California University Press, 2001). She has written articles and book chapters on the Mexican left, and on the ideological discourse of Mexican guerrilla movements.

George A. Collier is Emeritus Professor of Anthropology at Stanford University. He has studied peasant and indigenous activism in the context of agrarian change in Chiapas, Mexico since the 1960s and in rural Spain. He is the author of *Socialists of Rural Andalusia: Unacknowledged Revolutionaries of the Second Republic* (Stanford University Press, 1987), and *Basta! Land and the Zapatista Rebellion in Chiapas* (Food First Books, 1994, 1999).

Jane F. Collier is Emerita Professor of Anthropology at Stanford University. She is a specialist in anthropological contributions to law and society studies. She is the author of *Law and Social Change in Zinacantan* (Stanford University Press, 1973), and *History and Power in the Study of Law*, co-edited with June Starr (Cornell University Press, 1989), as well as co-editor of *Sanctioned Identities*, a special issue of *Identities* (vol. 2, nos 1–2, 1995). She has conducted research in Chiapas since 1960.

Abdollah Dashti is an independent scholar with a doctorate from the University of Michigan. He has done fieldwork in Nicaragua, Iran and Tajikistan. His research focuses on the interplay of social revolutions and civil wars, on the one hand, and the formation of historical consciousness and national cultural identities, on the other. Within the larger research project on the Iranian revolution he is currently exploring popular theories of secrecy and conspiracy and the ways cultural authority and Islamic identity are being renegotiated. Another project examines competing identities, civil war, and nation building in Tajikistan. His book manuscript entitled 'The Forbidden Revolution: Participatory Democracy and the Cultural Politics of Identity in Nicaragua', is currently under review.

Farideh Farhi is an independent researcher who has taught comparative politics at the University of Colorado at Boulder, the University of Hawaii at Manoa (where she was an associate professor until 1994), Tehran University, and Shahid Beheshti University in Tehran. She is the author of *States and Urban-Based Revolutions: Iran and Nicaragua* (Illinois University Press, 1990), and her comparative reflections on revolutions have appeared in *Comparative Political Studies, Journal of Development Studies, Theory and Society*, the *Iranian Journal of International Affairs*, the *Brown Journal of World Affairs*, and as book chapters. Her current project focuses on Iran's post-revolutionary political dynamics and the way they are reshaping the public space.

John Foran is professor of sociology at the University of California, Santa Barbara, where he also participates in the programs in Latin American and Iberian studies; Islamic and Near Eastern studies; global and international studies; and women, culture and development. He was visiting professor of sociology at Smith College from 2000 to 2002. He is the author of *Fragile Resistance: Social Transformation in Iran from 1500 to the Revolution* (Westview Press, 1993), editor of *A Century of Revolution: Social Movements in Iran* (Minnesota University Press, 1994) and of *Theorizing Revolutions* (Routledge, 1997), and co-editor with Kum-Kum Bhavnani and Priya Kurian of *Feminist Futures: Re-imagining Women, Culture and Development* (Zed Books, 2002). He is presently completing a book on the origins of revolutions.

Adolfo Gilly is a professor at the faculty of political sciences, National University of Mexico (UNAM), and has been a visiting professor at the universities of Chicago, Columbia, Maryland, and Stanford. He was a political prisoner in Mexico between 1966 and 1972. His books include *Inside the Cuban Revolution* (Monthly Review Press, 1964); *The Mexican Revolution* (Verso, 1983); *El cardenismo: una utopía mexican* (Cal y Arena, 1994), and *Chiapas: la razón ardiente* (Era, 1997), which has appeared in English as 'Chiapas and the rebellion of the enchanted world', in Daniel Nugent, ed., *Rural Revolt in Mexico: U.S. Intervention and the Domain of Subaltern Politics* (Duke University Press, 1998).

Jeff Goodwin teaches sociology at New York University. He is the author of a new comparative study of revolutions, *No Other Way Out: States and Revolutionary Movements, 1945–1991* (Cambridge University Press, 2001), and numerous articles on revolutions, social movements and collective action. He is editor, with James M. Jasper and Francesca Polletta, of *Passionate Politics: Emitions and Social Movements* (University of Chicago Press, 2001) and, with James M. Jasper, of *The Social*

Movements Reader: Cases and Concepts (Blackwell, 2003) and *Rethinking Social Movements* (Rowman & Littlefield, 2003).

Fred Halliday is professor of international relations at the London School of Economics and author of numerous works on revolutions, including, most recently *Revolution and World Politics: The Rise and Fall of the Sixth Great Power* (Duke University Press, 1999), as well as *The Ethiopian Revolution* (Verso, 1982), and *Iran: Dictatorship and Development* (Penguin, 1978).

Tim Harding is Professor of History, Emeritus at California State University at Los Angeles and visiting professor of Latin American and Iberian studies at University of California, Santa Barbara. He is a coordinating editor of *Latin American Perspectives*, where he has specialized in social movements in Latin America, recently editing with James Petras special issues of the journal on 'Democratization and Class Struggle' (summer 1998) and 'Radical Left Responses to Global Impoverishment' (September 2000).

Karen Kampwirth is associate professor of political science and chair of the Latin American studies program at Knox College. She has published articles on women's organizing and revolutionary movements in the *Bulletin of Latin American Research, Latin American Perspectives, Political Science Quarterly, Women's Studies International Forum*, and *Social Politics*. She is co-editor with Victoria González of *Radical Women in Latin America: Left and Right* (Penn State University Press, 2001), and author of *Women and Guerrilla movements in Latin America: Nicaragua, El Salvador, Chiapas, Cuba* (Penn State University Press, 2002).

Douglas Kellner is professor of philosophy at UCLA. He is the author or editor of many books, among them *Critical Theory, Marxism, and Modernity* (Johns Hopkins University Press, 1989), and with Ann Cvetkovich, co-eds, *Articulating the Global and the Local: Globalization and Cultural Studies* (Westview, 1987).

Christopher A. McAuley teaches political economy in the department of black studies at the University of California, Santa Barbara. His dissertation dealt with the racial origins of world capitalism. He is the author of 'Race and the Process of the American Revolutions', among other essays, and of *The Mind of Oliver C. Cox* (University of Notre Dame Press, 2003).

Valentine Moghadam is director of the women's studies program and associate professor of sociology at Illinois State University. Born in Iran, she has published widely on revolution in Iran and Afghanistan, and on gender and political economy in the Middle East and North Africa. She is the editor of a number of books, and author of *Modernizing Women: Gender and Social Change in the Middle East* (Lynne Rienner, 1993). Her work on the Iranian revolution has examined the nature of the populist coalition, its breakdown in the post-revolutionary political contestation, the process of Islamization, its tensions with embourgeoisement, and its gender dimension. She has also sought to theorize the gendered nature of revolutions. Her current research interests include globalization, gender, and transnational feminist movements.

Jeffery M. Paige is professor of sociology at the University of Michigan. Revolution has been a central intellectual interest throughout his career. His first book,

Agrarian Revolution (Free Press, 1975), developed a cross-national model of the agrarian base of twentieth-century revolutionary movements in the Third World and applied the model to peasant revolution in Vietnam, Angola and Peru. His most recent book, *Coffee and Power: Revolution and the Rise of Democracy in Central America* (Harvard University Press, 1997), develops a model of democracy as the unintended consequence of failed socialist revolutions in Central America. The book contrasts the revolutionary crisis of the 1980s with those of the 1930s and is based on extensive field research in Costa Rica, Nicaragua and El Salvador in the midst of the revolutionary conflicts of the 1980s. His current work on class, race and gender as facets of capitalist modernity grows out of a critical concern with the failures of traditional Marxism both in sociological theory and in revolutionary practice.

Noel Parker is associate professor of political science at the University of Copenhagen, and author of various studies of revolution and of other modern European patterns of change, notably *Revolutions and History: An Essay in Interpretation* (Polity, 1999), and *Margins in European Integration* (Macmillan, 2000).

Misagh Parsa is professor of sociology at Dartmouth College, and author of *Social Origins of the Iranian Revolution* (Rutgers University Press, 1989) and *States, Ideologies, and Social Revolutions: A Comparative Analysis of Iran, Nicaragua, and the Philippines* (Cambridge University Press, 2000).

Jan Rus has been director of the Maya Publishing Project (INAREMAC), San Cristóbal, Chiapas, since 1985, and is a coordinating editor for *Latin American Perspectives*. His Ph.D. in anthropology is in preparation at the University of California, Riverside. His long-term research interest is the history of the Tzotzil and Tzeltal Mayas of Highland Chiapas since the mid-eighteenth century, and his most recent work concerns the impact on indigenous people of the economic and political crises since the 1970s. Publications include: 'The "Comunidad Revolucionaria Institucional": The Subversion of Native Government in Highland Chiapas, 1936–1968' (1994); 'Local Adaptation to Global Change: The Reordering of Native Society in Highland Chiapas, 1974–1994' (1995); 'The First Two Months of the Zapatistas' (1996); 'Las voces indígenas del mercado de San Cristóbal' (2000). He is co-editor with Rosalva Aída Hernández Castillo and Shannan Mattiace of *The Indigenous People of Chiapas and the State in the Wake of the Zapatista Movement* (forthcoming); and with Diane Rus, Salvador Guzmán and Andrés Aubry *Visión literaria de los Tzotziles* (forthcoming).

Eric Selbin is Brown Distinguished Research Professor and associate professor of political science at Southwestern University, where he also chairs the international studies program. His work to date has focused primarily on the roles of agency and culture in revolutionary processes, with particular attention to the consolidation as opposed to the institutionalization of revolutionary processes and the likelihood of future revolutions. His current work addresses what may be thought of as the prior question to these: how come revolutions happen here and not there, now and not then, with special emphasis on myth, memory and modernity. He is the author of *Modern Latin American Revolutions* (Westview, 1993, 1999), and a number of chapters and articles on these topics.

Mary Ann Tétreault is the Una Chapman Cox Distinguished Professor of International Affairs at Trinity University in San Antonio, Texas. She has written extensively on the international oil industry, particularly its impact on the politics and societies of Arab gulf nations. She is editor of *Women and Revolution in Africa, Asia, and the New World* (South Carolina University Press, 1994), co-editor with Robin L. Teske of *Conscious Acts and the Politics of Social Change* (South Carolina University Press, 2000), and author of *Stories of Democracy: Politics and Society in Contemporary Kuwait* (Columbia University Press, 2000). She has also published numerous articles on women and revolution, and politics, gender and culture in Kuwait and Slovakia, among other topics.

Carlos M. Vilas is a political scientist and political economist, and chair of the Argentine Institute on Economic Development. He is the author of *The Sandinista Revolution: National Liberation and Social Transformation* (Monthly Review Press, 1985), winner of the Casa de las Americas Award, and *Between Earthquakes and Volcanoes: Market, State and the Revolutions in Central America* (Monthly Review Press, 1995), as well as numerous essays on the revolutions of the 1980s in Central America.

John Walton is Professor of Sociology at the University of California, Davis. His books include the award-winning *Western Times and Water Wars: State, Culture, and Rebellion in California* (California University Press, 1992), *Free Markets and Food Riots: The Politics of Global Adjustment* (Oxford University Press, 1994), and *Reluctant Rebels: Comparative Studies of Revolution and Underdevelopment* (Columbia University Press, 1984), as well as a number of articles on social movements and political protest. His new book, *Reclaiming History: Community and Memory in Monterey* is forthcoming with California University Press.

Index